Racine

Racine

From Ancient Myth to Tragic Modernity

Mitchell Greenberg

University of Minnesota Press
Minneapolis
London

Published by the University of Minnesota Press
111 Third Avenue South, Suite 290
Minneapolis, MN 55401-2520
http://www.upress.umn.edu

Library of Congress Cataloging-in-Publication Data

Greenberg, Mitchell
    Racine : from ancient myth to tragic modernity / Mitchell Greenberg.
        p.   cm.
    Includes bibliographical references and index.
    ISBN 978-0-8166-6083-4 (hc : alk. paper) — ISBN 978-0-8166-6084-1
(pbk. : alk. paper)
    1. Racine, Jean, 1639–1699—Criticism and interpretation. 2. French drama (Tragedy)—History and criticism.   I. Title.
    PQ1905.G68   2009
    842'.4—dc22

                                                        2009046589

Printed in the United States of America on acid-free paper

15 14 13 12 11 10   10 9 8 7 6 5 4 3

Para las de siempre
Marie-Claire y Julia
Gracias a la vida

The social bond is a tragic bond.

—*Eugène Enriquez*, De la horde à l'État

Contents

A Note on Text and Translations

The quotations of Racine are from *Racine: Théâtre, poésie*, edited by Georges Forestier (Paris: Gallimard, 1999). For translations of the plays, I used *The Complete Plays of Jean Racine*, translated into English verse with a foreword and notes by Samuel Solomon (New York: Random House, 1967). All other translations, unless otherwise indicated, are my own. I have tried, in all cases, to provide as literal a translation as possible.

Preface

Despite the revolutionary changes in French society during the three hundred years since his death, Racine appears to have spanned the centuries and to have emerged as at once the most familiar and the most alien icon of French culture. In the spirit of a certain polemic, we might even say that Racine stands in the pantheon of French letters as a metaphor for France itself, if by "France" we mean the absolute epitome of an ideal of classical harmony and grace, a poetic equipoise rarely, if ever, matched since its elaboration in the seventeenth century. In his celebrated essay *On Racine*, Roland Barthes begins by telling us that Racine is "the greatest French writer." At the same time that he extols Racine as the supreme writer in the French tradition, Barthes claims that the specificity of Racine's tragic production remains always tantalizingly beyond the reach of any critical idiom that would, by appropriating it, undermine its seduction. What is particularly Racinian escapes any univocal interpretation. Paradoxically, Barthes tells us, Racine is France's matchless dramatist because the Racinian text is "an empty critical cipher," "a blank space, eternally offering itself to interpretation." It is precisely the classical harmony, the seeming transparency of his tragic verse that, ironically, makes of Racine an object open and yet resistant to almost any critical discourse one could apply to him.[1]

It is true that since the explosion of critical works on Racine in the 1950s and 1960s with masterful readings by Mauron, Barthes, Goldmann, and with the heated controversy between the supporters of Barthes and the followers of Picard, one has the impression that at the beginning of the twenty-first century Racinian criticism has settled into a less exciting dynamic: in the last decade or so, we have seen the studies on Racine follow a more sociological and biographical approach, where the author of some of the most erotically charged tragedies in the world canon has been reduced to the role of a social-climbing parvenu, navigating his way through the various cliques and coteries at the court of Louis XIV.[2] At the same time, the work of historical exegesis continues unabated: Racine's relations to the court and Port-Royal, his (supposed) amorous imbroglios tainted with the hint of scandal and poison, and his relations to Boileau, to the elder Corneille, and to his rivals continue to fill the scholarly community with never-ending subjects of dissertations, biographies, and an inexhaustible stream of erudite articles. Simultaneously, his theater, along with that of his contemporary and patron/rival Molière (another subject of endless argument), continues to be staged throughout the world in both traditional and startlingly innovative productions (see the Wooster Group's production of *Phèdre*—"To You, the Birdie...") with ongoing success.

There seems to be, perhaps there always was, a disconnect between the historical personage of Racine—what I would call the "object-Racine," the seventeenth-century figure, fossilized in the amber-hued chrysalis of Versailles, more idealized than real—and a text, the "affective Racine," that continues to touch contemporary audiences who, we can be reasonably sure, know little or nothing of the elaborately Byzantine politics of the court of Louis XIV. It would be safe to say that for contemporary audiences, the heated debates around Jansenism, Port-Royal, and the *Augustinus* that were among the most impassioned issues of the seventeenth century are as distant as the ruins of ancient Egypt. The rites and rituals of absolutist France have been relegated to the arcana of the distant past. And yet, despite the historic distance and the cultural ignorance of the vast majority of contemporary theatergoers, we can say of the Racinian legacy—his tragic theater—*E pur si muove*. Racine, or what I would like to call the "Racine effect," still works. We still go to see that particular theater of beauty and cruelty that is Racinian tragedy, and despite the disparities in time and history, we are caught in its seductive spell.

"Seduction," of course, always brings with it the hint of scandal, for it implies that in some delicate way a coercion of the body has triumphed over the dictates of the mind—the body led astray, led into a place, a position, or a pleasure the mind cannot, in good conscience, admit to. For this reason, the theater, the most physical of the canonical forms of representation, has been the object of profound mistrust by the guardians of public mores from the very beginning—the celebrated attack on the theater by Plato in the *Republic*. The condemnation of the theater's harmful effects, perhaps in direct rapport with its increasing popularity during the reigns of Louis XIII and Louis XIV, was no less heated in the seventeenth century.[3] We only have to look at one of the many antitheatrical tracts, for instance, the Prince de Conti's *Traité de la comédie et des spectacles* (Paris, 1667), to be reminded that despite all the intellectual explanations that could be mustered in arguments against the theater, it was ultimately the sensual—the nonrational, passional dynamics of theatrical representation, its supposedly nefarious effects on the audience, and the stirring up of passions that in a well-ordered state are best left quiescent—that most disturbs the opponents, both lay and clerical, of the theater. Conti tells us that "poets may be masters of the passions that they represent but not of those that they stir up in the audience." Finally, however, despite the intellectual and moral arguments against the theater that Conti has culled from the ancients, with many learned quotations buttressing his antitheatrical tract, this zealous convert to a dour religiosity, who in his youth enjoyed, even patronized, the theater, returns to the central and unnerving fear of bodily excess to seal his arguments and the theater's fate. Appealing to no less an authority than Tertulian, Conti reminds his reader that the theatrical spectacle was, when all was said and done, "a form of voluptuousness."[4]

Of course, this fear of the aroused passions of the body is but one side of the theatrical coin. On the other, the same bodily metaphors were used, and from the most celebrated antiquity, Aristotle's *Poetics*, in defense, precisely, of the theater's role in a well-run state. "Catharsis," that much-debated, never quite defined term, the aim, according to Aristotle, of a perfect tragedy, always remains attached to its earliest etymological references to a bodily cleansing. The discharge of noxious vapors that have been aroused and eliminated by the tragic experience leaves the spectator replenished and able to assume (it was trusted) his proper role in the polis. All the major playwrights of the seventeenth century, as well as those *doctes* (the abbé d'Aubignac, La Mesnardière) who defended the role of the theater in public life, return again and again to the eternally problematic role of mimesis—both its positive and negative effects on any potential audience—to the problem of the passions, to the body caught in an emotional imbroglio whose effects always potentially exceed any intentional control that the playwright could claim to exercise on his texts, and to the theater as a bodily experience in this, paradoxically, the most bodiless of tragic stages. For in the long, often anxious development of what we consider French classicism, the body, or at least all those vulgar references to bodily parts, functions, and the very physicality of the body, had been, by the time Racine emerges on the stage of seventeenth-century dramaturgy, banned as too lowly for so refined a spectacle as tragedy.

The justification most often invoked to explain the absence of any but the most veiled references to the body in its *Kreaturlichkeit* in Racinian tragedy is the concept of *bienséances*, which, when coupled with those other rules of French neoclassical protocols, the "three unities," can be seen as doing to the theatrical body precisely what Foucault suggested the general epistemic shift of the seventeenth century did to those suddenly socially undesirable others—the mad, the heterodox, and the feminine. The body is circumscribed; limits are imposed on it (limits to its visibility). It is objectified as foreign to a certain aesthetic (but also sexual and political) ideal, and then it is banished.[5] The body in French classical drama is expelled from the stage, exiled to another site, to the wings of representation, because its presence proves too disruptive of the absolutist call to order.[6] If we follow Foucault's argument, we can see that the seventeenth century in its diverse discursive practices, of which the *bienséances* must figure, begins to encircle a carnality that in its excessiveness appeared too threatening to the unitary order that was being elaborated. The quiddity of bodies onstage proves, because seductive, to be too potentially dangerous to the political agenda of absolutism.

That the appeal of the body could always seduce the spectator and could undermine, as the Prince de Conti argued, the entire moral/religious order in place[7] is confirmed when we look into the diaries of François Hébert, curate of Versailles. His vaguely troubling discomfort upon viewing the young ladies of Saint-Cyr performing in *Esther* reveals both the enticements and dangers of the body. He writes, "Do you really believe that it is fitting for people of our station to watch a tragedy performed by attractive young ladies, whom one cannot stop oneself from gazing upon for hours? Aren't we exposing ourselves to temptation, and can one do so in good conscious?" In another passage he continues in the same vein, "Some courtiers admitted to me that the sight of these young ladies made a very strong impression on their hearts, and that knowing that they were 'respectable' they were even more moved than they would be by actresses."[8]

To avoid these strong impressions, when staging *Athalie* at the same venue the *demoiselles* are rendered as unappealing as possible. Although they are not removed entirely from the stage, there are no more elaborate costumes, no throngs of courtiers admitted nightly to see the play, no dancing, and no music.[9] What remains is a theater "where there is practically no physical description."[10] In its stead we have, on stage, before our eyes, bodies reduced to talking heads, bodies that are there and yet curiously absent. Or rather, the presence of the body is not in the body but of the body, the body transformed into language. Paradoxically, this language, the marvelously seductive verse of Racine, must be embodied, spoken to an audience whose participation in the passion and tragedy of the Racinian hero returns the body to itself but in a different place. Confronted with a tragic world from which the body is effaced, Racine's audiences respond corporally; they weep.

Writing to Mme de Sévigné, the marquise de Coulanges tells her, "*Mithridate* is a lovely play; it makes one cry; we remain enthralled throughout."[11] In his own preface to *Bérénice*, Racine refers to the tears of his audience, tears that he thinks reflect the pleasure his tragedy has given them: "I can't believe that the audience is ill disposed to me for having given them a play that has been graced with so many tears, and the thirtieth performance of which was as ardently attended as the first."[12] As for *Iphigénie*, in the *Entretien sur les tragédies de ce temps* (March–April 1675) we find the following: "Have you been to *Iphigénie*, he asks? It's a play that has enchanted many people. I found it quite wonderful, responds the other, and I am even not ashamed to say that I couldn't help myself from crying once or twice while watching."[13] The audience weeps, signaling an affective resonance—the sign that the trials of these characters reduced to the status of talking heads become incorporated in those bodies that are at the margins of the represented universe, those bodies that are silently, breathlessly present at the sacrifice that the play unfolds before them.

The body, banished from the realm of dramatic representation by the dictates of classicism (dictates that, we must insist, are as much political as aesthetic), resists and remains present but is displaced to the margins of representation, to the audience. How are we to understand this plangent pleasure that was so suspect because also political, these tears, signs of an affective state that the psychoanalyst Joyce McDougall tells us is situated in an indeterminate locus, floating between psyche and soma. An affect, she writes, is "never a purely psychic phenomenon nor purely a somatic one."[14] So the question remains double—how is theatrical affect a potentially incendiary political apparatus, and, more precisely in this context, what affect(s)? Why did Racine's audiences weep? Why do they continue, at the start of a new millennium, to become emotionally engaged in these seemingly so foreign plays? What have they seen, what have they come to see that induces tears? Or perhaps, more pertinent questions, since we are dealing with Racine, would be What have they heard? What do the remains of the body, traduced into the voice of the actors, tell the audience? And how does this telling move them?

In a sense, and by way of a very preliminary answer, we can propose that these are tears of mourning, the melancholic tears of a body responding to its own effacement, its (self-)immolation on the stage of French classicism. The classical stage represents the ceremony by which and through which the modern, passionate ego is called into being by the sacrifice of what was its grounding in a world that vanished in the tumultuous cauldron of change that seventeenth-century France underwent in its evolution from an outmoded feudal society to the triumph of the absolutist monarchy. I would suggest that it emerges precisely in that indeterminate space separating and joining the Racinian spectacle to its spectators. It is a reticent and melancholy space, the tearful space of tragedy.[15]

Introduction

Spectacle, Myth, Sacrifice: Racinian Tragedy and the Origins of Modernity

Traditionally, the seventeenth century is seen as the apogee of both France's political and aesthetic hegemony in Europe. With the exhaustion and collapse of Spain's military and economic dominance and despite the unparalleled prosperity of the merchant republic of the Netherlands, France, under the leadership first of the Cardinal de Richelieu and then of Louis XIV, becomes the dominant power on the continent. The supremacy of France as a military power is buttressed, as we know, by the harnessing of the creative forces of the nation—the poets, painters, playwrights, architects—into the artistic celebration of the French monarchy. While the political program of absolutism was essentially a centralizing effort whose goal was to make a unified nation out of what was, at the beginning of the century, basically a patchwork of different legal, economic, and cultural practices, the cultural role of the artists enrolled in the program of celebrating the monarchy was to reflect aesthetically the same ideology of order and control the government with greater or lesser success was imposing on the nation. What we have come to know as the dictates of classical aesthetics (whose rules and evolution have been exhaustively discussed by generations of scholars) are based essentially on an ideal of unity—of harmony, of symmetry, of an artistic structure (be it in literature, painting, architecture,

or music)—that has often been seen as reflecting as a poiesis the political principles of the never complete, never entirely realized program of
absolutism.[1] At the same time, as an indispensable corollary, the absolute/
classical ideal must be seen as subtended by a revolutionary philosophical system that served as the necessary—although heatedly debated
underpinnings—of the ideal classical subject. Descartes' inauguration
of a self-sufficient, unitary ego that can observe, reason, and eventually
control the ambient world will become the symbolic equivalent in both
philosophy and psychology of the self-contained, unitary European subject who with the certainty of its self-authorization will be able to go
forth and colonize the world with its own universalizing and self-serving
agenda. Although this new classical subject, the *homo absolutus* of the
seventeenth century, can only metaphorically be attributed to the Carte-
sian method, certainly this method is part of a general epistemic shift
that classicism, with its concomitant economic and political policies,
puts into place.

The above cursory description is meant to be, in part, parodic of a
certain dominant vision of the seventeenth century and its politico/
aesthetic productions. It is a vision of seventeenth-century society as a
static pyramid where change is frowned on, if not impossible, and where
people are fixed in a social ballet rigid in its principles and practices,
and where a marmoreal court legislates all aspects of daily life. This is a
world of suffocating conformity, where innovation is discouraged and
conservative convention dominates the production of not only quotidian existence but artistic production as well. Even a critic as perceptive
as Leo Bersani has described the seventeenth century's most famous
dramatis personae in the following terms:

> Classical French literature is a conservative social force not merely be-
> cause its pessimism about human nature would discourage any hopeful
> view of what might be accomplished by changes in social conditions,
> but also because it helps to reinforce the hierarchical structure of
> seventeenth-century French society. Racinian tragedy is full of chaotic
> passions, but as far as ideologies of the self are concerned, the implied
> existential chaos is perhaps less important than the Racinian image of a
> permanently ordered self. Passion disrupts his characters' lives, but it also
> orders their personalities. Thanks to a dominant enslaving passion, all
> behavior in Racine can be "placed" in relation to a fixed psychological
> center. Words and gestures can always be referred to that passion; they
> can, in other words, be reliably interpreted. The literary myth of a

rigidly ordered self contributes to a pervasive cultural ideology of the
self which serves the established social order.[2]

This type of critique, for all of Bersani's subtlety, essentially reflects a
rather conventional appreciation of both aesthetics and ideology. Fundamentally, what we have here seems to be precisely at odds with what
Bersani would argue for in his analysis of modernity—that desire or a
certain psychic ambivalence seems not to be at play in French classicism. Finally, we are comforted with the affirmation that classicism is
what it pretends to be—essentially conservative, monolithic, and absolute. Certainly these are assessments that the many vocal proponents
of classicism would welcome as their own. It does strike me, however,
that when dealing with the theater, especially Racinian tragedy, things
are never that univocal. The theater is, after all, that most public of all
forms of representation, a form that by its very nature entails a promiscuous exchange with its audience that is, we must remember, an integral part of the theatrical experience, an always present, never merely
passive spectator.[3] In a very real sense, as Jean-Pierre Vernant and Pierre
Vidal-Naquet insist when talking about the tragic drama of ancient
Athens, the theater does not simply create poetic works, objects of consumption for its audience, but rather "through the spectacle, culture,
mimesis and the establishment of a literary tradition, the creation of a
'subject,' of a tragic consciousness, the coming into being of tragic man."[4]
That is to say, in their paraphrasing of Marx, not only does the theater
create objects for its subjects (the theatergoing public) but it creates
subjects for its object: Racinian tragedy, we can propose, constructs
(how will be determined in due course) its own novel subjectivity, the
new subject of classical tragedy.

Periods of great tragic production—the golden periods of the theater—are quite limited: Athens in the fifth century; Spain, England, and
France in a period spanning a little more than one hundred years from
the end of the sixteenth century to the end of the seventeenth century;
Romanticism; and (some would argue) the dramatic production of the
mid-twentieth century. What these very different periods seem to have
in common, what would seem to be the fertile ground for tragedy, is
that each represents a moment of enormous societal change, a period of
uncertainty where old social structures are being replaced by newly emerging, as yet indeterminate alternatives. A general sense of anxiety that

may or may not be articulable in everyday discourse makes itself heard
in the flowering of tragic drama. It would be a mistake, however, to read
tragedy as the mere reflection of social reality. Anne Ubersfeld reminds
us that such an interpretation contains at least two important risks:

> We must be mindful of two dangers: first of all considering the work
> merely in respect to its immediate connections, to its sociopolitical
> conditions, because that would be to subject it to what it isn't, to make
> of it a document rather than a production. Next would be to think
> there is an automatic relation between social structures and works of
> art . . . that would be to imagine that social structures are simple and
> reducible to class relations or economic infrastructures, and it would
> be forgetting the infinite dialectical complexity of society on all its
> different levels.[5]

Rather than a mere reflection of contemporary reality, tragedy questions
that reality.[6] Thus, in a sense, we can say that tragedy is, and this is probably its most seductive appeal, inherently ambivalent, at one and the
same time, as Vernant and Vidal-Naquet claim, "both an order and a
disorder."[7] Tragedy is a both/and rather than an either/or. It is, therefore,
an open question as to why, when dealing with French classicism, most
critics choose to emphasize the order rather than the disorder.

Above all, the theater's inherent ambivalence defines it as a mediating space blurring the boundaries between public and private, between
seeming and being, between exterior reality and inner psychic reality—
thus both the appeal and the anxiety it generates in the more traditional political sphere. In his study of Elizabethan theater, *The Place of
the Stage*, Steven Mullaney has insisted on the actual ambivalent place-
ment of the English theater in Shakespeare's time. Neither within the
corporate boundaries of the city of London nor in the legal structures of
the county beyond the city, the theater was "literally in a no man's
(legal) land," an ambivalence that Mullaney takes to be emblematic of
the role of the theater in general.[8] Of course, in France the theater was
not ex-centric to the seats of power. Situated in the very heart of Paris,
the two main theatrical venues, the Hôtel de Bourgogne and the Théâtre
du Marais, were at the center of Parisian life. When the court eventually settled into life at Versailles, the theater maintained the privileged
status it had enjoyed from the beginning of Louis XIV's personal reign.
This is not to suggest that the metaphorical ambivalence that is so important to Mullaney's argument does not hold true for French theater

as well. Quite the contrary, as perhaps the most important venue of social exchange, seventeenth-century French theater can be considered a place where the anxieties and desires of a society in transformation were continually being essayed and rehearsed. Although it is too easy to view the productions of France's great playwrights—Corneille, Molière, and particularly Racine—as representing, not unproblematically but rather monolithically, the hegemonic discourse of French classicism as a reflection of the absolutism of Richelieu and Louis XIV, we would do well to bear in mind Mullaney's redefinition of the role of dominant ideology in dramatic productions:

> Hegemonic culture is (moreover) a historical dynamic, an ongoing, diachronic negotiation between the old and the new. The dominant culture in any given period cannot hope to include or even account for all human aspirations and energies; present culture is continually limited, challenged or modified by culture past and culture yet to come.[9]

In all the emerging nation-states of the seventeenth century, the theater as a form of spectacle was intimately allied to the mise-en-scène of absolutist ideology. As a privileged form of representation, the theater, along with its sister arts the court ballet and later the opera, served in court society as the most seductive of state apparatuses. In the court life of the seventeenth century, spectacle and royal ceremony went hand in hand. It is interesting, nevertheless, to note that during this period, and particularly during the reign of Louis XIV, traditional court ceremonials that had been used for centuries to mark important moments of individual reigns had been gradually suppressed. In his study *Cérémonial et puissance souveraine*, Ralph Giesey, following the groundbreaking work of Ernst Kantorwicz, *The King's Two Bodies*, has traced the curve of these spectacular moments in the life of the monarchy from their apotheosis in the late fifteenth and early sixteenth centuries to their virtual elimination, by Louis XIV, in the seventeenth century. It is important to remember that these ceremonials—the display of the royal effigy at state funerals, the royal "entrées," the *lits de justice*, and, of course, the *sacre* (coronation)—marked at regular intervals important moments in the history of each reign. The ceremonials were highly spectacular demonstrations of state power. They were some of the most important ideological state apparatuses of the monarchy, for they allowed a visual promiscuity between the body of the state (the immortal body, the procreative body) and the subjects of that body. These ceremonials were hieratic rituals that displayed, on fixed occasions, the royal presence to its admiring and (subjected) subjects.

Several of Giesey's findings become particularly intriguing for interpreting the renewed enthusiasm for and importance of the theater as it becomes one of the most important ideological apparatuses of seventeenth-century French absolutism. First, we learn from Giesey that in comparison with the English court ceremonial of the same time, in France, traditionally, "instead of being juridical and discursive it was almost exclusively dramatic and visual."[10] In other words, the visual aspects of the ceremonial seemed to take precedence over the more discursive practices of the English court. Although the importance of the monarch's munificence, displayed most effectively in court spectacles— by the strategic stagings of his persona—had been a lesson handed down from the princely courts of the Renaissance, it would seem that the visual importance of these spectacles gained increasing importance in the evolution of the French monarchy as is attested by Giesey's descriptions of the more elaborate ceremonials that marked those funeral ceremonies throughout the sixteenth century.

Furthermore, Giesey informs us that perhaps the most intriguing of the ceremonials, the display of the royal funerary effigy—a practice that is perhaps the most striking crystallization of the abstract ideological concept that was key to the French monarchy, "the King never dies"—was abandoned; it was used for the last time at the death and funeral of Henri IV in 1610.[11] The actual representation of the "king's two bodies" disappears: it is, in a sense, swept off the stage of royal ceremonial protocol, never to be seen again. Of course, this raises the intriguing question: Where does the body of the king go? As it is suppressed, repressed from a public viewing, where does it, as all that is repressed does, return to? Finally, we learn that Louis XIV eventually suppresses all the traditional *ceremonials d'état:* "Throughout the entire second half of the reign of Louis XIV...not a single State ceremony took place. The grandiose 'entrance' into Paris in 1660 for the marriage of Louis...was the swan song of royal entrances in French history."[12] Since, as we know, Louis was both the privileged spectator and the greatest spectacle of his time, this suppression of the traditional forms of royal ceremonial must strike us as odd and atypical of a monarch who took every occasion possible to make of himself a living allegory of royal authority. It is only if we understand the suppression of both the royal effigy and the traditional court ceremonials as a displacement, perhaps a propagandistic shift of allegorical space from the ceremonial to the theater, that we can see the theater emerging as a major tool of royal propaganda. It is to the theater that we must look and to tragedy in particular if we wish to understand the translation of the king's two bodies from the old models of court ceremonials to the modern example of the theatrical stage. In a sense, as Giesey suggests, the state ceremonial revealed royal power on infrequent and special occasions, but Louis, by making a spectacle of himself—by organizing court life around his spectacular appearances and orchestrated rituals, by patronizing the theater, the ballet, the opera—rather than simply reducing the display of royal authority and supremacy at incisive, punctual occasions, now "reveals his power . . . at every moment."[13] One might propose that by sacrificing the traditional ceremonials Louis traduces his power and prestige onto ever more omnipresent venues. By so doing, this sacrifice of the royal effigy becomes, in its transformation into theater, the dramatic foundation of a new, tragic subjectivity where the mediating role of the theater reasserts its primitive role of ritualizing and organizing the foundational origins of the nation.

It does strike me, and in this I am in agreement with the French scholar Hélène Merlin-Kajman, that the frequent use of the words "ceremony" and "ceremonial" to describe the tragic theater of Racine both fails to do justice to and is a misreading of the extremely intense, affective response Racinian tragedy conjures up in its audience.[14] "Ceremony" is too static an image for the violence, the cruelty, and the beauty of Racinian tragedy. Certainly, this tragedy, the most perfectly formal creation of French classicism, comes closest than any other theatrical creation of the seventeenth century to evoking a universe of primordial, originary aggression and sexuality, all bathed in scenarios of crime and punishment worthy of some of the greatest works of Greek antiquity. Rather than the courtly notion of ceremony, it would be more appropriate, given the intensely primitive emotions that this tragic theater evokes, to speak more precisely of sacrifice, especially when we consider the deeply convoluted relations between the tragic theater of ancient Greece that

serves as the polestar of Racine's own creation and the sacrificial practices that reverberate throughout his ancient sources and in his own
tragic creation.[15]

The sacrificial ceremony is inherently theatrical: a stage is set on
which the officiating priest and his helpers confront an innocent victim. Around them, around the altar, the members of the community—
the other actors in this spectacle—stand in witness. It is important to
remember that the sacrifice is inherently a communal experience, an
experience for and through which a community defines itself to itself.
The relation between actors and spectators is, therefore, both essential
and reciprocal.[16] Without the testimony of these onlookers, a sacrifice
would prove meaningless. Thus, from its very center, in its spectacular-
ity the ceremony of immolation appears structurally analogous to the
theater. It may even be, as many have argued, that the origins of theater
are to be found in sacrificial rituals. Sacrifice and theater, particularly
tragic drama, seem conjoined at their origins and their end: both have
a particularly telling role in representing to the community the laws of
the sacred and the consequences of their transgressions. In order to exist
as a cohesive unit, society must be constantly reminded of its past, its
origins, its aspirations, and its promised continuity into the future.

Among the different social and religious roles of the sacrificial act,
one stands out. In a situation of social uncertainty, with the threat of
impinging chaos, the immolation helps to reaffirm limits, both temporal
and spatial, of the community. Sacrifice is always seen as an originary
act, an act that establishes a before and an after.[17] Spatial limits tracing
a border between an inside and an outside, in a sense, between an "us"
and a "them," are also constituted. In this fashion the parameters that
serve to define the habitus of a community are justified by this act.[18] By
constituting these limits, both temporal and spatial, a community defines
itself over and against its other(s).[19] In ancient society, the locus of
sacrifice, and in later, more developed polities, the place of the stage,
represent the foundational rituals through which a nation recognizes
itself. It is not simply a felicitous coincidence that the English word
"scaffold" (deriving from the French *échafaud*) in its earliest meanings
referred to the platform on which either an execution was carried out
or a drama was performed.[20] Although the violence of the scaffold was
never far removed from the lived experience of most seventeenth-century

urban life, there was a constant displacement at work during the period by which the violence of the sacrificial act, its bloody reality, was, for courtly society and that portion of the bourgeoisie that defined itself in the image of court life, gradually transposed from the executioner's block to the theatrical stage. I might propose here, with the promise of greater elucidation in a moment, that the theater, especially the passionate tragedy of Racinian drama, in its plots but also in its function as social mediator, continues to enact the ongoing fascination of the sacrificial ritual carried over and transformed in the realm of dramatic sublimation.[21] In both cases we are called on to witness the imposition of the law that for many psychoanalytically informed anthropologists and sociologists would ultimately be the incest-taboo, the moral imperative by which a particular society defines the place of the subject in relation to the difference between the generations and the difference between the sexes. This law exists, in one form or another, in all commonwealths and establishes, it has been argued, the difference between human and nonhuman societies.

There is obviously a difference between the actual sacrificial ritual and its translation into/as representation. As Nicole Loraux reminds us, even in those more primitive times of ancient Greece, while the polis, in its tragedies, offered itself the ambivalent pleasures of those many scenes where young virgins are offered up in sacrifice, it was representing in tragedy what the state would never have dreamed of enacting in reality: "Of course, in real life the city did not sacrifice its young girls, but during a performance it gave its inhabitants the double satisfaction of transgressing in imagination the taboo of *phonos* and about dreaming about virgins' blood."[22] Loraux is underlining here the duplicitous, sadomasochistic dynamic of tragic representation that, as Freud had already implied, is an essential part of the compelling fascination the theater exerts on its audience.[23] As she does, so must we underline the importance of this transgressive satisfaction as imaginary, that is, as a highly convoluted psychic act in which individual fantasies and collective myths are, for a moment, allowed to coalesce and to produce theatrical pleasure. The sacrificial function of theater is an extremely rich area of overlap, where the external social, political, and sexual ideologies that legislate the public life of the citizen (with their corresponding myths) in the polis come inverted into the intrapsychic life of the spectator and, for the time of the spectacle, they cohabit, reflecting each other in the affective response of the spectator to the theatrical illusion.

Perhaps no dramatist of the classical age better understood and manipulated this ambivalent space where outer reality and inner fantasy intermixed than Racine. In all his tragedies the protagonists waver between the demands of the state and the demands of desire, demands that are, in fact, inseparable. These demands come bound so tightly in Racine, as nowhere else on the classical stage, in the convoluted portrayal of the family as the primary locus at once of politics and desire. It is true that the elaboration of the newly emerging subject of classicism, born on the seventeenth-century stage, is a long process of continual reinventions and reworkings. From the first baroque dramas of the beginning of the century through the great creations of Corneille in the 1630s and 1640s, the relation between politics (the state) and eroticism (individual desire) is constantly rescripted in ever more tightly convoluted scenarios as the aesthetic perfection of classical drama evolves in and through the works of playwrights and the critical discussions of the learned community, and as the political realities of absolutism assume ever greater influence over the lives and tastes of the theatergoing public.[24] While the locus of Racinian tragedy is always the family, this familial space has become acute in its narrowness and intensity. Racine has always been seen, especially in comparison with his elder rival Corneille, as able to coordinate perfectly his tragic plots with the dictates of classical aesthetics. This tightly condensed world of his tragic productions condemns the Racinian protagonist to ever greater and more violent attempts to free himself from a fate whose horrifying consequences will, he knows, end by destroying him.

This tightening of the familial scenario allows us to speculate on the main differences that separate the two greatest tragic playwrights of French classicism, Corneille and Racine, and on the type of tragic subjectivity each places on the seventeenth-century stage. This is not meant to be just another in the never-ending series of comparisons between the two, comparisons that have not ceased since the seventeenth century, but a way of elucidating the evolution, across and through the theatrical careers of the two dominant figures of French neoclassical tragedy, of the very real, epistemic changes that these two tragic visions perform for us. In his seminal *Les mots et les choses*, Michel Foucault argued, in the early stages of his critical trajectory, for seeing the seven-

teenth century as a liminal period separating and joining one representation of the configurations of human subjectivity—the analogical—that,
he claims, was the principal episteme up to and through the Renaissance,
to the "transparency of Classical representation," which established its
firm hold on the West in the eighteenth century.[25] The seventeenth
century would figure the moment of passage between these two epistemes,
participating in both, seeing (but not, of course, in any clearly articulable
fashion) the gradual, inexorable disappearance of outmoded discursive
practices and the emergence from within these very practices of new,
radically different ways of thinking/being. At the same time, the seventeenth century seems to function as a seductive fulcrum for Foucault.
In another, contemporaneous study, *Histoire de la folie à l'age classique*,
Foucault analyzes yet another facet of this epistemic shift in his
scrutiny and discussion of the imposition of difference, the separation
out of the other—be it the mad, the infirm, or the feminine—during
what Foucault calls "le moment du grand renfermement" (the period of
the great enclosure). The European self is constituted through the
forced exclusion from within its midst of all that is, from this point in
history forward, defined as *unheimliche*.[26] Curiously, for demographic
historians this same period in the history of Western Europe is marked
by a change in the identity of the family, that complex unit of political,
economic, and sexual forces. They perceive a shift away from an increas-
ingly outmoded definition, which identified the family as an extended
household *(maisonée)*, to that of the more modern concept that sees
the family as essentially limited to those related by blood. Finally, in its
ultimate articulation in the eighteenth century, the family's contrac-
tion will be limited to the nuclear unit of parents and children.[27]

The dramatic productions of the seventeenth century, particularly
the canonical dramas of Corneille and Racine, can be seen to reflect in
their own tragic worlds the very same shifts in epistemes that Foucault
tried to circumscribe in his reading of scientific, philosophical, and theological works from the same period, as evidenced by the way each playwright constructs his tragic scenarios within the convoluted political
structure of the family. Writing at critical moments of the century, we
can follow, *grosso modo*, in the light of Foucault's hypotheses, this same
movement represented across their texts as we move in Corneille's major
plays of the late 1630s and 1640s from a world on the cusp of the epistemic divide, plunging (but with hesitations and resistance) into the

classical medium, to Racine, writing in the late 1660s and 1670s within
a paradigm more definitely ensconced in this brave new world of classical transparency.

In Corneille, for instance, this moment of passage from one side of
the great divide to the other would be marked by the clear separation
of his dramatic world into symmetrically opposed political and sexual
camps. In Corneillean tragedy we are usually presented with the importance of this symmetry, a symmetry that is reflected not only on the
thematic level of his tragedies but in the formal structure of his verse as
well: the sexual separation of the protagonists into masculine and feminine camps where their passion is exacerbated by this very difference at
the same time that this personal imbroglio is projected, as the tragic
conflict, onto a screen of political and social unrest. The Corneillean
political crisis always pits the individual, his or her desire, against the
will, the better interests, or simply the unavoidable *raison d'état* of the
state. Typically, the political crisis that threatens the world in Corneillean
tragedy always telescopes the passionate antagonism of the young protagonists, each a representative of a particular family/clan, onto the
state. Nevertheless, there is always in the great tragedies of Corneille a
separation, even if it is only the separation of the mirror, between the
family and the state: the one reflects and stands in a homologous relation to the other.

In Racine, we have already passed to the other side of the enclosure.
His is a world already firmly ensconced within the parameters of classical representation. This, of course, has several important consequences
for Racinian drama. On the one hand, there is no longer any separation between the family and the state: from a dramatic point of view,
from the very beginning, in *La Thébaïde* the family is the state. There is
no longer any division possible between the political dimensions of the
tragic and the private passionate/sexual world of his protagonists. The
origin of the tragic and the origin of the family are one and the same:
the founding moment of the state is a politico/sexual moment, the
alliance of the throne and the bed:

> Malgré tout son orgueil, ce monarque si fier,
> A son trône, à son lit daigna l'associer...
>
> In spite of all his pride, this splendid Prince
> Deigned to unite her to his throne and bed...
>   (*Bajazet*, 2.1.467–68)

Peut-être on t'a confié la fameuse disgrâce
De l'altière Vasthi, dont j'occupe la place.
Lorsque le roi, contre elle enflammé de dépit,
La chassa de son trône, ainsi que de son lit.

You have perhaps heard tell the loud disgrace
Of haughty Vashti, whom I have succeeded,
And how the king, against her hot with rage,
Drove her both from his throne and from his bed.
(*Esther*, 1.1.33–36)

On the other hand, what this also means for Racinian tragedy is that once reduced to its most tightly wound, intimate dynamics, once this world is presented as entirely enclosed, once there is no longer any possibility of an outside, once we are trapped in the suffocating locus of the family/state, the very precise limits of sexuality that regulated the sociopolitical world of Corneillean tragedy become ambiguous. With the characters of Racinian tragedy and their desires trapped in a closed universe, the contradictions of passion and politics are all turned inward: they become, as guilt and bad faith, part of the inner world of the characters. In Racine, difference, which was still presented in Corneille as imposed from the outside, from the political world, becomes a difference within. And, as Roland Barthes has suggested, this new dynamic has profound consequences for the definition of sexuality in the seventeenth century. According to Barthes, what we see in Racine, as opposed to Corneille, is that sexuality is no longer posited as a biological, natural given.[28] Nature is now shown to be a production, a play of forces in which are opposed the weak to the strong, the victim to the executioner. It is this play of forces that determines sexuality in the Racinian universe. The essential natural (that is, biological) difference between the sexes so firmly enunciated in the Corneillean canon (even if it is also put into question) is no longer operative in Racine's world.

In Corneille, difference (the dramatic conflict) is imposed from without; the hero's dilemma is conventionally an impossible choice between his sexual desire and the right political or social choice that is antithetical to this desire: this dilemma is, however, presented as exterior to desire. In Corneille, the dramatic conflict is born from the opposition between the individual and the social. A sense of self, of an independent subjectivity, develops from this conflict. The "moi" of the Corneillean hero emerges from the conflict by repressing the politically unacceptable object and by suturing the wounds of sacrificed desire in the exultation of this sacrifice's reflection in the eyes of the polis.

For Racine, on the other hand—and this is, perhaps, already a sign of his modernity—difference is always a difference within. His characters suffer as they struggle against an internal division that can never be sutured. Their suffering refuses any compromise with the omnipresent social gaze that envelops them, forever increasing their feelings of guilt. This interior wound, which we could describe schematically as the sense of always being watched, represents a form of both individual and collective paranoia, the feeling of always being observed but also of seeing oneself being observed, which plays a double role in the definition of Racinian subjectivity. This division is at once projected outward into the world in the form of all those doubles that inhabit the Racinian universe and also inward as guilty conscience. This interior conflict condemns the Racinian protagonists to a constantly fleeing prolepsis; they persistently project into the future a harmonization in the world that they cannot find in themselves. On the other hand, this division forces them to return, over and over again, to their past, to an exploration of their genealogy where once again they are confronted with an inherent duality. They are never able to attain to a world without difference, the world of the absolute to which they strive, because wherever they turn they are confronted with duality and difference, in other words, a world of sexuality and the eternal mystery of sex.[29] Thus in the absolutist ideology of French classicism, where all and everything aspires to the world of the One, the Unique, the In-different, the possibility of ever finding a nonguilty, nonconflicted stasis, other than death, always escapes them, always remains beyond their grasp. Because they are, because they bear within them, the sign of their duality, the sign of their division (sex equals sextus equals cut/split), they are marked, unbearably for them, as sexual beings, beings of division, and as such are therefore condemned to be both desirous and guilty.

Paradoxically Racine's heightening and intensification of the tragic locus corresponds to a step backward in representation. Racine leaves the world of history so successfully exploited by Corneille and returns, in his greatest tragedies (*Andromaque, Iphigénie, Phèdre*), to the archaic world of myth. It would seem that moments of ideological crisis—moments such as the one I have, following Foucault, been describing, where the tectonic shifts in human society threaten to overwhelm, with the ensuing menace of chaotic dispersion, the subject caught at the interstice of forces he or she cannot articulate, old myths (and I insist on the importance of the word/phenomenon of "myth")—reemerge as culturally accessible receptacles for new anxieties.[30] As Lévi-Strauss has suggested, "myths are eternal" in the sense that while offering an explanation of the inexplicable—Where do we come from? How does one come from two?—by proposing a sort of compromise formation of logically irreducible phenomena, the myth offers answers to the enigma of origins while remaining itself without origin.[31] At the same time, Lévi-Strauss also argues, myths continually rescript themselves throughout history. No one version of the myth can be privileged as the true one: all versions are integral parts of the myth.[32] More important for our purposes is the fact that myths are phenomena that are neither collective nor individual but, according to Jean-Paul Valabrega, both at once. For this reason, social anxieties can be captured and refashioned by myths in ways that allow them to explain the inexplicable to a receptive audience. By so doing they also transform that audience in their own image.[33] In other words, society has recourse to old (eternal) fables that are used to fashion, in the sense of providing mimetic parameters, novel subjectivities. And what myth could be more receptive to the turbulent changes in familial, social, and sexual configurations of the emerging classical subject than the myth of Oedipus, a myth inextricably, although not exclusively, linked to tragic theater?[34]

All of Racine's plays are, as Phillip Lewis has so amply demonstrated, linked genealogically to the foundational myth of Oedipus, his family, and his progeny, with all the varied consequences of this tragic destiny.[35] Even those historic tragedies *Britannicus* and *Mithridate* or the biblical tragedies *Esther* and *Athalie,* by conjuring up as they do the unconscious terrors of familial sexuality, seem to exceed the picturesque qualities of the historic scenario and to plunge us into the frightening depths of Oedipal fantasies.[36] In the Racinian canon, all the tragedies are linked to a mythic vision that is both familial and terrifying. Can we, therefore, propose the following hypothesis: the entire Racinian endeavor would be the rescription of the Oedipus legend as it becomes intertwined with the ideological dilemma of the nascent absolutist subject?

It has often been proposed that all people (that is, nations) have recourse to mythic narratives to explain the distant, obscure origins of
their present political structures.[37] (However varied the form those particular structures might take, for our purposes I will use the highly
charged shorthand "the state" as a label for them all.) There is, Marcel
Detienne tells us, no "nation [people] whose history does not start with
fables or mythology."[38] We know how important individual mythic
themes or figures as sources and subjects of allegorical representations
were to the artists, artisans, and propagandists at work in the construction of the glorious image of Louis XIV's reign (Apollo, Mars, Charity,
Justice, etc.). On the other hand, equally important was the recourse to
more general, less easily circumscribed mythic paradigms that came to
dominate the ideological structures being elaborated to reaffirm, while
transforming, the imaginary foundational origins of the emerging absolutist state. These more general mythic paradigms were invoked as originary and thus validating narratives of the developing political structures
that were being put, with more or less success, into place during the
long, conflicted seventeenth century.

We might suggest that these originary myths correspond, in their
ideological role of offering an explanation of the inexplicable mystery
of the state's foundation, to the function of originary fantasies in the
construction of individual identity. The role of originary fantasies in
the psychic life of the individual is to function as an ex post facto construction (a sort of personal poiesis) through which the individual subject gives a coherent, if purely imaginary, structure to the mystery of his/
her own origins.[39] Certainly, the legend of Oedipus—the most complete
political myth of Greek mythology with its inextricable interweave of
the political and the sexual—offered an ideal cultural vessel ready to
serve as the hinge between the political edifice of the emerging absolutist state and the individual subjugation to that state of its newly
formed subjects. Guy Rosolato in his several essays on the intersection
of individual and social mythology has suggested that for each of the
four primal (or originary) fantasies ("primal scene," "seduction," "sexual difference," and "return to the womb") there corresponds a cultural
myth nurtured by each of the major monotheistic religions in its own
attempt to explain and thus naturalize the role of the individual
in relation to the sacred. Rosolato writes that each of the four primal
fantasies attempts to answer one of the following elemental questions:

"Where do we come from? What can we do? What do we know? Where are we going?"[40] And it is in the theater, particularly the tragic theater, where, through the mediation inherent in the dramatic spectacle, trans-individual and individual forms of myth, and originary fables of national foundations and primary fantasies, meet in their attempt to give a coherent, if obscure, response to these persistent questions.[41]

It is here, in an almost tautological fashion, that we can begin to perceive the intimate and inextricable relation that binds the birth of the individual as a subject to social laws that preexist his or her being in the complex mysteries of the family, that is, to the state into which as a subject he or she must be born in order to achieve a viable social existence. How, of course, this conjuncture functions represents one of the great appeals of the myth—a narration seemingly come from nowhere but that we all recognize as speaking immediately to us and to which we all pay tribute. How are we to understand the meeting of political and individual myths? Where, that is, can we find the point of suture, where the one becomes conjoined with the other? To begin to answer this question we might do well to turn to Rosolato, who proposes a key to understanding this suturing role of myth:

> The particular antidotal quality represented by the myth comes from a sort of unification, an attraction even, of the differences that each individual discovers in relation to the myth, and which, finally, flow together into a common stream. So that starting from a "singularity," with no future, which might even be thought of as nefarious, the subject can maintain a fascination or identification with a communal endeavor. By this process, the individual subject becomes able to accept without knowing it the social and in particular the moral laws for which his or her (psychic) structure is not suited. We can interpret this identification process as a fetishistic effect of the myth in relation to the drives of the subject.[42]

Using as a point of departure this definition of the fetishistic function of myth, we can begin to understand how the mythic dimension of Racinian theater mediates the impossible and contradictory demands of an absolutist ideology. This ideology would impose, as an ideal, the order of the One—the unitary order of classicism—onto a subject who, always riven, that is, "divided, double, two," cannot but feel itself as guilty, unworthy, and therefore as a subject destined for punishment and death.

On the one hand, I think that it is necessary as a first step to understand that in a very important sense the much-beloved division between

the public and the private has led us to view the separation of the individual from the social in too Manichaean a fashion. In a very obvious
sense, the individual is a social creation.[43] Individual phantasy partakes
of the subject's insertion, from before his/her actual existence, in a network of societal laws and desires into which he or she must come to be
a viable civic subject.[44] All desiring beings are social beings. On the
other hand, it is important to underline the different ideological structures that insist on the major narratives of the dominant culture into
which this individual comes to be. Certainly, in seventeenth-century
France, a society still deeply uneasy about its recent tumultuous past,
the fear of disorder underlies the thoroughgoing centralizing impetus in
all spheres of social life. In a nation shaken by a century of religious turmoil, monarchal assassinations, nobiliary revolts, and the constant
threat of foreign invasions, a pervasive anxiety (of the return to political chaos) seems to underlie Louis XIV's obsessive desire for order. To
the reality of these historical traumas corresponds a much less easily
definable metaphysical sense of angst. As Eugène Enriquez points out,
almost all civilizations can be said to live psychically with the fear of a
return to some primordial chaos. This collective psychic fear is not, he
suggests, "against chaos as it might or might not have really existed
in prehistoric times, but against the phantasms of a primordial chaos,
of a primitive disorder, of a mixture, or a state of indifferentiation, of
originary violence."[45] In times of social unrest, when the fear of impending chaos seems to loom ever closer on the horizon, the desire for
a protective, reassuring presence reveals itself in the turn to and adulation of the charismatic leader/king who incarnates in his spectacular
persona stability, law, and order. In one of those singular historical con-
junctures, seventeenth-century France found in its young king a rare
example of a leader who perceived this anxious need and responded to
it by making of himself a grandiose, public, and (at the beginning of his
reign, at least) protective persona. Louis, with a keen sense of mediation, offered himself to his people and to the world as the embodiment
of radiant majesty. Although it might be difficult for us to understand
(despite the history of the twentieth century's deadly flirtations with
charismatic leaders), it would be hard to overestimate the deep personal attachment the average ancien régime French subject felt for his
king, especially when we consider the overlapping ideological layers
of religion, politics, and paternity that all combine in the image and

imaginary of the reigning monarch.[46] Certainly the role of the king in a Christian monarchy was subtended by both the metaphoric allusions to patriarchy, which established a figurative chain that linked the monarch both to God, the Eternal Father of Christianity, and to the father, god of each individual household. The king was, as tradition had it and as Louis liked to remind his nation, "le père du peuple" (father of his people). As such, Louis took seriously his providential paternal role by governing France as does "un bon père de famille" (good head of the household).[47] It is around the image of this charismatic leader/father/king, the head of the *patrie,* that France begins to constitute itself as a modern nation.[48]

This filial attachment to the king as father, is not, as we have learned from Freud, without a deep charge of psychic ambivalence. If the father/king is the vehicle for such intense affection, the object of so many insatiable desires, he is also, and at the same time, the object of unavowable (unconscious) murderous aggression.[49] The unthinkable of seventeenth-century political theory was, precisely, regicide, which in its horror was always coupled with patricide as the most unnatural of crimes. Despite or perhaps because of France's recent history, which had seen the assassination of two of its kings (Henri III and Henri IV), and despite the presence in Louis XIV's court of the recently widowed wife of the executed Charles I of England, the direct attack on the monarch remained the most reprehensible, the most monstrous of all political crimes. The fantasies of regicide/patricide that are banished from political discourse resurface, nevertheless, in poetic inventions—in the epic, the novel, and, of course, the theater. It is in the theater, particularly the tragic theater of the period, that we can see how this ambivalence, which was not allowed into political reality, was permitted to play itself out in tragedy, particularly as tragedy arrays itself in the attire of Greek mythology. And who better than Oedipus, both the *tyrannos* and the *pharmakos* of the Greek world, to form the unitary link between social and individual fantasy, uniting as he does in his legend the realms of the political and the sexual in the adulation and sacrifice of the father/king?

In one of his earliest references to the Oedipus legend, Freud, in the *Interpretation of Dreams,* asks himself and his reader why it is that this particular myth, in its tragic version, continues to affect modern audiences as much as it did contemporary Greek ones. He goes on to offer the beginnings of an answer:

> If *Oedipus Rex* moves a modern audience no less than it did the con-
> temporary Greek one, the explanation can only be that its effect does
> not lie in the contrast between destiny and human will, but is to be
> looked for in the particular nature of the material on which that con-
> trast is exemplified. There must be something which makes a voice
> within us ready to recognize the compelling force of destiny.[50]

There is, Freud is saying, an affective resonance between the dramatic
narration of Sophocles' tragedy and the effective lived experience of
audiences—regardless of historic differences. As we know, Sophocles'
drama is only one, granted the most influential, version of the myth.[51]
Yet the myth of Oedipus, which is older and more detailed than the
version we have inherited from Sophocles, stands as perhaps the most
significant of the Greek myths and the most fertile for future elaboration
precisely because it provides us with the most complete, in the charac-
terization of Marie Delcourt, political legend in the entire corpus of
Greek mythology. The legend of the most famous of the Labdacids represents, she says, "the most detailed amalgamation in one narration of
the mythic preparations for kingship."[52] In other words, the legend of
Oedipus the king is an anthology of the different moral and physical
struggles necessary to assume the leadership of the polis. At the same
time, as Delcourt goes on to demonstrate, Oedipus's political role, his
position as king, is inextricably tied to his libidinal life, which is from
the beginning predestined to the horrors of uncontrolled, incestuous
sexuality. Oedipus, therefore, as king, the hero who saves the city, cleanses
it but also is the defiler who introduces impurity into the polis. From its
genesis, the myth of Oedipus represents in its ambivalence the impossibility of separating out politics from sexuality: the hero as civil liberator
but also as contaminator and therefore as sacrificial victim: Oedipus
tyrannos but also Oedipus *pharmakos*, ambivalence residing in a single
character who is at one and the same time father, king, and victim—
and whose political role as king and sexual role as incestuous murderer
are one and the same and inseparable from the dynamics and mysteries
of familial sacrifice.

Oedipus legend/Oedipus complex: is it possible to separate the one
from the other? Or do we need to? It would seem that from the beginning the enmeshments of politics and sexuality in one narrative forever

impel us on a hermeneutic quest where the unraveling of the one from the other leads us into never-ending ideological aporia. Is the "complex" simply (although it is never simple) the imagination of a late nineteenth-century Victorian, and therefore it is disreputable because of the universalizing ideology it would impose on a startlingly diversified world, no longer subject to the colonizing gestures of Western intellectual imperialism? Or is it possible that what the Oedipus complex tells us is inextricable from the legend but also its other side? What I am suggesting is that the Oedipus legend is a myth that must be seen as an orthopedic configuration that serves as a prolegomenon for the proper acquisition of political power (kingship) that has dominated Western thinking about power, the state, and its rule from the ancient Greeks through French classicism and down to us. When this legend is reread and replayed on the stage of seventeenth-century France, we might see its dramatic translation as the conscious reflection of the coming into being and at the same time the eventual demise of the subject of absolutism, mirrored in the plot (the diegesis) of the theater.[53] In other words, the Oedipus legend would be, in fact, used to plot out, and in that sense to affirm, the trials and tribulations of *homo absolutus* at the same time that it contains within itself the seeds of his dissolution. It could be seen as one of the main supports—aesthetic and ethical—of the underlying unitary and unifying drive of absolutist ideology as that ideology prepares, unbeknownst to itself, the eventual coming into being of the republican citizen.

On another, simultaneous, level, the legend (as the narration of a political lesson) cannot control—especially in its dramatic version— the affective resonance it carries with it, especially in its convoluted presentation of familial libido. We cannot forget that the theater, particularly the tragic theater of Racine, is the scene of the public and the private, the political and the sexual, plot and fantasy. It is the pull of fantasy, which, as all antitheatrical treatises have reminded, is in fact a form of *voluptas*, that, in its intimate connection to sexuality, is constantly working to undermine any monolithic control our conscious life would impose. There is a never-ending struggle in these dramas between the more rational elements the plot would impose on our identity as social beings and the more obscure, destabilizing forces of aggression and libido that are carried along both by the thematics of desire, incest, and murder and by the more ephemeral, incantatory force of the Racine's verse.[54] What we would have, therefore, in Racine's rescripting of the Oedipus legend/complex is a constantly evolving scenario of the desire for and yet the impossibility of ever achieving the construction of a self-sufficient, absolute subjectivity—that is, the constant undermining of plot (Oedipal legend) by fantasy, the Oedipus complex—which, in a sense, would be the marker of Racine's modernity. Does not this impossible but seductive commingling of plot and fantasy correspond to what we now think of as the split, the difference within, of the modern subject? This new subject is constantly riven and at the same time just as constantly attempting to ignore this split. He strives to present himself as that shining image of integrity and totality that he or she sees in the idol/king, standing always just beyond his grasp.

Oedipus was sacrificed on the altar of his family/polis for a familial crime of which he was ignorant if not innocent. Before Oedipus killed his father (Laius), his father tried to kill him. Laius's guilt is a sexual guilt, or rather he is guilty of sexuality, the unfettered desire that refuses the social enclosure of the libido within strictly defined roles and postures: at a banquet to which he had been invited, Laius rapes his host's son, Chrysippus, who, out of desperation, hangs himself. From the beginning, therefore, the Oedipus legend returns us to the body and the body's desires that, unfettered, wreak havoc on civil life.[55] Homosexuality and incest, by refusing the limits of sexual difference and generational difference, blur the primary distinctions that make political life possible. The children are sacrificed to the sins of the parents, sins that are always beyond their ken but that nevertheless fashion who they are and how they live their lives and meet their death.

Perhaps here we can begin to understand the particular hold of Racine's tragic theater on his contemporaries and on us. In the world of Racinian tragedy, just as in the Oedipal trilogy of Sophocles, we are caught in the suffocating embrace of the family/state. There is no separation possible between the political (public) and the sexual (private); both are inextricably intertwined in the dramatic plots and in the psychology of the characters in Racine's theater. It is precisely the fact that they are caught within the mesh of their own ambivalent natures that makes of these characters dramatis personae. The French psychoanalyst André Green has written persuasively on the particularly strong affective resonance familial tragedy evokes in its audience:

The family, then, is the tragic space par excellence, no doubt because
in the family the knots of love—and therefore of hate—are not
only the earliest, but also the most important ones. The tragic space
is the space of the unveiling, the revelation, of some original kinship
relation.[56]

Racine's tragic theater, garbing the newly emerging, conflicted family
of the seventeenth century in mythic dress, allows, through the imposition of myth on tragedy, for the theater to mediate the inchoate demands
these new structures make on the individual subject who appears at
their ambivalent interstice. The theater's role is proleptically to represent changes in social formations that are still only immanent in society at large. It seems like more than a fortuitous coincidence that the
theater should emerge in the late sixteenth and seventeenth centuries
as the privileged form of representation in a society undergoing such
fundamental realignments of its most essential structures. The stage
mediates between the individual and the collective in an extraordinarily charged moment of dramatic social exchange. Anne Ubersfeld, in a
Marxist-semiotic perspective, tells us that the theater "appears to be a
privileged form of art of capital importance since it demonstrates better
than other forms of art how the individual psyche is invested in a collective relation." Furthermore, she goes on to say that "every theatrical
text is the response to a desire on the part of the audience, and it is in
this relation that the articulation of theatrical discourse with history
and ideology is most easily made."[57] In a similar vein, Green writes:

> Between the two, at the meeting-point of the individual and society,
> between the personal resonance of the work's content and its social
> function, art occupies a transitional position, which qualifies the domain
> of illusion, which permits an inhibited and displaced *jouissance* obtained
> by means of objects that both are and are not what they represent.[58]

Finally, we could also invoke, in a parallel vein, the work of the anthropologist Victor Turner, whose studies on the liminality of cultural performance also point, in another vocabulary, to the ambivalence inherent
in these forms of social theatricality. In *The Anthropology of Performance*,
he writes:

> Liminality... is often the scene and time for the emergence of a
> society's deepest values in the form of sacred dramas and objects—
> sometimes in the re-enactment periodically of cosmogomic narratives

or deeds of saintly, godly, or heroic establishers of morality, basic institutions, or ways of approaching transcendent beings or powers. But it
also may be the venue and occasion for the most radical scepticism—
always relative, of course, to the given culture's repertoire of skeptical
concepts and images—about cherished values and rules. Ambiguity
reigns.[59]

In other words, what these students of the theater, each writing within
the parameters of his or her own particular theoretical approach (semi-
otics, psychoanalysis, anthropology), are telling us is that the theater
functions as a transitional space mediating the shift between the public
and the private, between the inarticulable societal fears and aspirations
of the group and the fears and desires of the individual spectator. It is in
the space of the theater, particularly the highly formalized theater of
absolutist France, that these two forms of desire tend to coalesce in
and around the shared experience of the sacrificial ceremony that the
theater relays.[60] One might say that this ritualized sacrifice functions
because of the simultaneous identifications between the spectating subject with the character/actors on stage, his fellow spectators, and more
subversely with the ever-present gaze of the absent father/monarch who
is also always watching the drama unfold. This complex identification
of the spectating subject with both the spectacle and the imaginary
projections that underlie it should not, however, be interpreted as a purely
sympathetic act. Identification is multiple and fractious. It is also never
merely jubilatory. We should remember that the most primitive form of
identification is incorporation, the desire to make part of oneself the
object of identification, to devour and thus to destroy that object. Our
theatrical identifications, therefore, are to be understood as inherently
ambivalent, relaying the (unconscious) political ambivalence of the
subject toward those ideological parameters, for which the father/king
is the spectacular support, that pleasure and subjugate him.

In a world subjected to the desire for and hatred of the charismatic
father, Racinian tragedy becomes a cruelly sublime experience where
we are called on to participate in fantasies of sexuality and death that
are at the heart of our identity as social and private subjects.[61] We become, in order to achieve (an illusory achievement) the plenitude of
being promised in our subjection to the image, the *imaginaire* of the
corps glorieux of the father/king, that is, we become members of a totality, a unity, that offers protection, love, and the chance to see ourselves

as the reflection of so much power and glory. At the same time, the embrace of the monarch becomes too suffocating, too lethal not to evoke the vengeful image(s) of his death and dismemberment in a sacrificial frenzy—a fantasy that denotes the power of a libido not easily contained by the Law of the Father. It is to this ambivalent fantasy, to this public/private exchange of fear and desire, that the tragedy of Racine invited the audience of classical France and to which it continues to invite the audience of the twenty-first century. We remain as split, ambivalent subjects, subjects of desire and fear, as attuned to the fearful beauty and intensity of Racine's tragic plots and transcendental poetry that continue to resonate in us with a haunting evocations of a world we both recognize and ignore. As the sorry history of the twentieth century bears witness, we remain as attached to the tantalizing images of charismatic leaders as were the subjects of Louis XIV. And perhaps we, even more than they, still need the tragedy of Racine to remind us that this sacrifice of our political reason to the mystifying fantasies of plenitude and power always carries with it, as its inarticulable underside, the horror and fascination of death.

1

La Thébaïde:
Politics and Monstrous Origins

Although we know that Racine toyed with the idea of writing his own version of Sophocles' *Oedipus Tyrannus*, the closest he ever came to any direct refashioning of the myth of the Labdacids was his first, derivative, "unsuccessful" tragedy, *La Thébaïde ou les frères ennemis*.[1] Racine chooses to tackle "le sujet le plus tragique de l'Antiquité" (the most tragic theme of the Ancient)[2] obliquely rather than head-on. The subject of *La Thébaïde*, the impossibility of polity and the impossibility of family—the two are inextricably interwoven—represents an irresolvable crisis of culture left in Oedipus's wake. The father has disappeared (at least in Racine's version), leaving behind the chaos his decision to share the throne between his two sons has created in the polis. This paternal legacy (a curse?) has cast the very survival of Thebes and its ruling family into doubt. At the outset of the drama both the family and the state are set on a downward spiral of blood lust, violence, and death, from which, we soon realize, neither can emerge unscathed.

Tragedy, which always seems to flourish in moments of societal upheaval, defined by Foucault as moments of "epistemic change," would appear to express in its dramatic scenarios the anxieties that these changes generate. Certainly, even if we only look to that other great seventeenth-century dramatist, Corneille, it becomes clear that his celebrated plays all have as their dramatic backdrop moments of political crisis, when one world order is waning and another, still inchoate order is attempting to emerge and to impose its sociopolitical parameters on a society resistant to change. It is this moment of conflict, between old values and customs that still exist in conjunction with newly emerging social/ economic/political structures, that Racine figured in his tragedies. It is the tension between these several structures that the tragic reflects at the same time that, we might speculate, it becomes itself constitutive of a new form of subjectivity (that is, where its own mimesis becomes a poesis). Tragedy, by essaying the different possibilities opened up in these new social circumstances, develops the innovative interweave in the ways the human subject is constituted by these emergent sensitivities to and channeling of socially evolving institutions.

Jean-Pierre Vernant and Pierre Vidal-Naquet, discussing the emergence of Athenian drama in the fifth century, affirm that tragedy is always "le débat avec un passé toujours vivant" (a debate with a still living past).[3] If we apply their claim to tragedy in general, we have to nuance the thesis of Jean-Marie Apostolidès, for whom seventeenth-century French tragedy "se présente comme un rituel qui permet à la collectivité d'accomplir le 'travail de deuil' de ses valeurs anciennes, absolues, féodales" (appears as a ritual that allows the community to accomplish the 'work of mourning' for its ancient, absolute, feudal values).[4] More than a work of mourning for old values that are still very much alive but in conflict with other more original ones, it seems to me that Racinian tragedy plays out, in the dialectics of sacrifice and redemption, the confused origins of a new world. This emerging configuration, because of its own internal conflicts, can only ever represent its forward historical march as a regression to some of Western culture's earliest mythic narratives. It is these myths, inherited from a perennial tradition of cultural metabolization, by which the West has always held onto and readapted those originary narratives of ancient Greece in order to give form to what remains largely immanent, unknowable, and feared in moments of social realignments. In a sense, Racine's entire dramatic production, starting most pointedly with *La Thébaïde,* will garb itself in the guise of myth before venturing into the realm of history so successfully exploited by his elder rival Corneille.

Racine, too, beginning in *La Thébaïde*, always foregrounds the erotically charged imbroglios of his protagonists against a backdrop of political crisis that threatens the world of these dramatis personae. In Racine,
at least in the great tragedies, the political and the erotic are inextricably
bound together in intense libidinal contradictions. The eruption of
desire and of the chaos that is inevitably connected to it in Racine is
focused on/in the family, as that most heated locus of political and sexual antagonism. In fact, we could see (as many have already seen) that
while the family as the central social structure is constantly invoked in
Racine, this invocation is always to some virtual family and thus always
in contradiction with the dramatic reality of the families at hand. In
the plays themselves (in their narrative line) the family exists only as a
dysfunctional, destructive unit, its dysfunction measured and judged in
relation to some ideal family that would not be contaminated by sexuality and aggression (by Oedipus). All the families in Racine are families
cursed. They are the prey of forces that are at once internal and exterior
to them and that threaten them with disintegration, estrangement, and
death. From the beginning of his dramatic career, Racine always posits
the ideal of family at the same time that this very notion is undermined
by the confused, conflicted familial structures in all the tragedies.

La Thébaïde, of course, would figure as the *ur-szene* of the tragedies
to come by situating the origins of all that is monstrous in the Racinian
universe in murder and incest.[5] Starting here and in each of the successive plays, sexuality and aggression mark all the familial scenarios where
the family in its structure is always so entangled as to undo itself in
tragedy. There is always some secret, some machination—always a sexual crime—that condemns the family to its own destruction at the same
time that it constantly tries to conceive of itself as the foundational origin of a coherent political structure.

It is perhaps only from the perspective of hindsight, only once we
have experienced the compelling horror and fascination, the tragic
shiver of Racine's full dramatic trajectory, that we can look back at the
Thébaïde and see it for what it puts in place by its rewriting of a certain
Oedipus legend. With hindsight we can see that despite its derivative-
ness, despite its too obvious debt to Corneille, despite its lack of what
will become the hallmark of the mature Racine—that peculiarly seductive evocation of desire and death—it does establish both the mythic
substructure and the political foundations for the tragedies to come.

And by so doing, we might speculate, its influence and importance can be seen to infiltrate the entire classical edifice of which the Racinian canon is perhaps the most accomplished and imitated example.

While caught up in the particular moment of crisis that threatens the existence of the state torn between the two warring brothers, Etéocle and Polynice (the ostensible dramatic conflict of *La Thébaïde*), we must not forget a more overarching ambivalence this fable both hides and reveals: Thebes exists in legend as the polis, that is, as a universal metaphor for culture in its most political sense as an organized human community that in its social structure opposes itself to the chaos of nature. However, it is striking that Thebes, as the backdrop of the entire Oedipus legend, exists in its mythic context only ever as the state in crisis, as a state of crisis. The political coherence of the state from the very beginning, even before the conception of Oedipus, is presented as always threatened by its own unraveling. From its origin, therefore, we can speculate that there is a prescient anxiety that is coeval with any human community that sets itself off and defines itself against nature. Rather than a stable bulwark, the boundary separating the one from the other is permeable, artificial, and incessantly changing. It is this porosity that constantly threatens to collapse these very same boundaries and send the state back into the chaos from which it emerged. In *La Thébaïde* the state and the (royal) family that incarnates it are continuously shown to be incongruent with each other—the former always the victim of the irrational behavior of the members of its regal household. If it is true, as Marie Delcourt has reminded us, "that the Oedipus legend is the most complete political myth" in the Greek canon, then the crisis figured in the legend, the chaos that threatens to overwhelm and destroy Thebes, must be seen as a metaphor for the underlying fear, the anxious fantasy, that all culture offers only a tenuous protection against destructive forces that coexist within culture itself.[6] These forces are held at bay with only the most strenuous efforts, which the myth tells us are doomed to failure. We might, therefore, begin our exploration of the archaeology of the Racinian universe with the rather banal assertion that on at least one level the underlying fear that this dramatic universe plays out for us, the anxiety that it both hides and reveals, is the dread that "culture" and "civilization," however those terms are defined, are but a fragile construction that can at any moment be undone by more nefarious, uncontrollable forces. In other words, the underlying anxiety structuring the Racinian world is the precariousness of all cultured life, the fear that we are always dancing on the edge of an abyss that can open up and send us and our constructed, protected universe plunging into anarchy.

This fear of chaos would seem to be, if we believe the French political theorist Eugène Enriquez, an underlying dread that inhabits our best as well as our most questionable cultural achievements. We are locked into a constant duel between the desire for stability and the dread of social disruption. Ever since its publication in 1913, *Totem and Taboo*, Freud's poetic and tragic vision of the origins of human culture, has been roundly criticized, if not simply rejected out of hand, by social scientists. Recently however, due to innovative work in several inter-related disciplines—anthropology, sociology, ethnopsychiatry, political theory—there has been a renewal of interest in Freud's cultural studies (*Totem and Taboo, Group Psychology and the Analysis of the Ego, Civilization and Its Discontents, Moses and Monotheism*). Much of this rereading of Freud's texts has been done in France. I am thinking of the work of Georges Devereux and Tobie Nathan in ethnopsychiatry, Pierre Kauffmann in political science, Guy Rosolato and André Green in applied psychoanalysis, and Eugène Enriquez in psychosociology.[7] At the same time new, often startlingly original interpretations of myth and the myth-making process, incorporating psychoanalytic theory with anthropology and sociology, have also emerged in France in recent years.[8]

It is perhaps the work of Enriquez, particularly his *De la horde à l'état: Essai de psychanalyse du lien social*, which is both a compellingly complex analysis of the major sociological texts of Freud on the one hand, and the elaboration of Enriquez's own psychoanalytically inflected theory of the development of human societies on the other, which has the most potential interest for an approach to the political significance of the mythic dimension of Racinian tragedy. Although it would be an injustice to attempt to summarize the complex and richly developed analyses of Enriquez in a few lines, I think that it would not be abusive to say that what Enriquez attempts to describe is the tense dynamic between order and chaos (nature and culture) that lies just below the surface of any human society, creating a persistent anxiety that functions as a constant (unconscious) threat to its apparent stability. Whatever equilibrium culture has established is constantly threatened by forces—both real and imaginary—that are uncontrollable. Freud had written that these forces are, *grosso modo,* three: nature itself, which, indifferent to human life, wreaks havoc on our most treasured creations; the aggressivity of our fellow humans; and the precariousness inherent in our life itself subject to its undermining by its very biological/organic nature. The dread we feel in front of these forces is essentially marked by fantasies of dismemberment, fragmentation, and death on an individual level and, on a communal level, by the fears of societal anarchy—the undoing of the body politic. It is important to remember, as Enriquez reminds us, that this anxiety is powerful not because it recalls an actual, historical fall into disorder but because it is the product of a fantasy of that fall: "All civilization is a struggle against chaos. Not against chaos as it could or could not have actually existed in prehistoric times, but against the phantasies of primordial chaos, of primitive disorder, of inmixture, of indifferentiation, of originary violence."[9] Although phantasmatic, these anxieties are nonetheless powerful because of their particularly strong affective resonance. Affect, especially acute affect such as anxiety, signals a regression to archaic scenarios that give form to our very basic fears and desires relating to castration, sexual differentiation, and therefore our fantasized perception of male and female positionings in primal scenarios where violence and sexuality are conjoined.[10] To defend against these desires/fears we produce dreams, myths, and fairy tales as ambivalent wish fulfillments. Our highest cultural creations represent both the ambivalence and fears that these anxieties produce as well as a protective defense against them. As analytic theory would have it, these creations are convoluted personal and communal responses to some of the most powerful enigmas we face—the enigma of origins, both individual and collective. In fact one might say that the attempted search for origins, for the founding moment that would situate us in a definitive point along a comprehensible continuum, takes the form of personal fantasies for individuals and myths or legends for communities. In these fantasies/legends we can discern the primary importance given to the role(s) of sexuality and of sexed reproduction in any attempt (always elusive) at fixing a founding moment.[11] Since sexual relations are always also social interactions involving constant negotiations of power, it is important to understand them at the same time, in the broadest sense, as political relations.[12] In other words, what Enriquez and other contemporary students of psychoanalysis attempt to theorize is the articulation of the relay from the individual to the communal, from subjective psychic fantasy to sociopolitical myths that form a complex interconnecting network. The one is linked to the other through the elaboration of cultural productions in which the workings of ideology, which for our present purposes are understood in the terms of Althusser's famous definition as the "imaginary relation of individuals to their real conditions of existence," serve as the bulwark against the invasion of anxiety.[13]

Indebted to Freud's analysis of group psychology, Enriquez deftly moves from discussions of individual psychic mechanisms such as projection and transference to the theoretical reinscription of these phenomena in large social groups. It goes without saying that Enriquez is aware of the bias that is often at work both in Freud's writing and in the way his own theories reflect the innate contradictions in the almost universally patriarchal social formations he describes. This means that we must be aware that these analyses that point to a masculinist power structure at work in most of our (not exclusively, but certainly dominantly, Western) social organizations will be seen in Enriquez's analyses to trace how male anxieties regarding female sexuality have produced social structures that contain, limit, and control this (fantasized) threat by naturalizing in a universalizing discourse received knowledge about the inherent difference between the sexes. When this anxiety/threat is transferred from the individual psyche to the social via the medium of such cultural productions as myth, philosophy, or drama, both the fear and suppression of a certain feminization of our Western cultures is continually perpetuated through this cultural dialectic. At the same time, of course, this suppression only exacerbates the tensions of what is repressed, leading to a convoluted and unstoppable cycling of sexuality and aggression played out in ceremonies of guilt and expiation.

Civilization, Freud tells us and Enriquez agrees, is born and sustains itself by a crime committed in common: the murder of its most prominent member who, through his murder, focusing on himself both the love and hate of the masses, succeeds in becoming the mythic symbol of social cohesion—the Father/God of our patriarchal societies. In Freud's mythic scenario of the origin of civilization, the brothers of the primal horde band together to kill the father whom they both hate and love and then, in a totemic meal, incorporate the father and his power in themselves. What this modern myth would seem to reveal is twofold:

(a) that only in death, that is, in absence, does the father become the Father (the Law); and (b) that this founding murder, which affirms the cohesion of the group (society), must be periodically repeated in order to remind the community formed initially by this crime and held together by shared feelings of longing and guilt of the original murder/sacrifice. It is only through the repetition of this primal act that the group can be constantly reminded both of its common past and its future aspirations. This collective participation can either take the form (in more primitive societies) of actual sacrifice or (in more "advanced" cultures) displace sacrifice onto other stages. The theater, for instance, can be seen as one of those sites of displacement where the tragic plot invites the theater-going public (and let us not forget that in ancient Greece it was considered a civic duty to attend the theatrical festivals) to the tremulous pleasure of the represented sacrifice of gods, heroes, and virginal maidens.[14]

From the beginning, in the Oedipus legend (before the fratricidal war that is threatening the existence of the state), plague, sterility, and death, not to mention the very overdetermined figure of the Sphinx posted at the city's gate, seem to exist as a reminder of the very tenuous hold any form of culture (that is, the polis) has over or against those more inchoate, uncontrollable forces that lie just below the surface of civilized life. Havoc seems poised, like the Sphinx, ready to burst forth and destroy the society that has, with so much effort, denied those unseemly powers.[15] On the level of an even more profound regression beyond the mere peculiarities of plot, we should note, in the particular dynamics of the Oedipus legend, that these very forces of destruction—the Sphinx, the sterility that descends on crops and flocks, the ever-present warnings against sexuality as politically dangerous (Laius and Jocaste are explicitly told to abstain from sexual relations in order not to produce a child who will call down destruction on their couple and the polis)—are all coded as essentially feminine, associated as they are in the myth with different female characters—Hera, the Sphinx, Jocaste, and others.

One might suggest that on a convoluted, primitive level, the Oedipus legend, one of the oldest in the Greek canon, participates in a generalized mistrust of the feminine (however varied that concept's definitions might have been to the Greek religious universe) that scholars as varied as Delcourt, Vernant, Loraux, and Slater have identified as an essential component in the elaboration of this fundamentally patriarchal society.[16] When Racine chooses this legend with all its cultural allusions as the subject of his *La Thébaïde*, we must assume that he was listening to echoes that cannot have failed to appeal to other, more contemporary patriarchal obsessions of seventeenth-century France. Not only were the horrific memories of the fratricidal wars of religion still fresh in the minds of all, but the even more recent tumult of the *Frondes* revived the anxious fears that the throne and altar were in danger. The response to this threat, the bulwark against chaos, was the idealized image of a new king/savior, a fortified "Père du Peuple" who would be capable of harnessing social anarchy and subjecting civil disorder to the sole splendor of his (male) "corps glorieux."[17] It is tantalizing to speculate, therefore, with these anxieties in mind, that when we begin to interpret *La Thébaïde* we must see it as the template for that curious Racinian particularity: tragedies that are often feminocentric while demonstrating a certain fear of the feminine that, at times, in the tender sadism of his verse, verges on misogyny. This is the first play of the Racinian canon in which the brunt of tragic suffering is brought to bear with more than a hint of aggression on the feminine (not necessarily female) protagonist—here Jocaste/Antigone, but in the following, more successful tragedies all carrying the resonant names of their heroines—Andromaque, Phèdre, Iphigénie, Bérénice, Esther, Athalie. The tragedies that all these plays represent turn around the suffering and sacrifice of the feminine/feminized *pharmakos*, that ambivalent hero/victim whom society both desires and fears and who must be expelled if social order is to be preserved, if political stability is not to fall prey to the unleashed forces of unbridled sexuality.

Guy Rosolato, the French psychoanalyst and cultural theorist, has suggested that it is in moments of social upheaval, when old structures that have held sway are slowly fading out of prominence and new, barely discernible social configurations are emerging, that sacrificial ceremonies endeavoring to harness society's fears and hopes become most prominent.[18] While actual sacrifice continued in ancient societies to represent and thus reassert the primacy of the group over its fears, it has been convincingly argued that by the time we arrive in more developed polities the sacrifice undergoes a metamorphosis; it is represented in/as theater. In other words, it is during the development of more complicated political structures in ancient Greece, particularly with the emergence of the polis during the sixth and fifth centuries, that the theater becomes the vehicle for transmitting throughout the assembled community the same shiver of sacrificial pleasure/guilt that had heretofore been the role of human rather than animal sacrifice.[19] It will come as no surprise that the seventeenth century—that conflicted transitional period mediating the difficult passage between, in Foucault's terms, two major epistemic models, the analogical model of the Renaissance and the transparency of classical representation of the eighteenth century and thus modernity—would make its most profound mark on the cultural history of the West as one of the two or three greatest periods of theater, particularly tragic theater. From the Elizabethans at the end of the sixteenth century, through the great creations of the Spanish stage, up to the flowering of Racinian drama at the end of the seventeenth century, theater becomes the privileged form of representation of the emerging absolutist state. As we see in Racine, the acme of tragic passion is most successfully portrayed, in France at least, as the suffering of the female protagonist.

When Racine undertakes his own version of the Oedipus legend, Oedipus has disappeared and we are left with the confusion his and his wife/mother's incest has wreaked on the state. The sexual fault of the parents creates political havoc: twinship effaces (for the tragic universe) any primogeniture, any way for a society based on the devolution of power from father to son (from king to king) to establish a precedence that would ensure political stability. Instead of the orderly transmission of power from generation to generation, incest produces a deadly oscillation. Furthermore, and this is even more revelatory of Racine's perhaps unconscious motivations in choosing this version of the Oedipus legend, although the monstrosity that wreaks havoc on Theban society is the result of transgressive parental sexuality, this excessive, unnatural sexuality is—because of the text's insistent focus on the pathetic expiatory rhetoric of the mother, Jocaste, and by echoing the hollow silence, the absence of the father—coded as feminine. In a sense Oedipus, whose presence pervades the entire tragedy, is also evacuated from it. His guilt is transferred onto the only surviving member of the incestuous couple, Jocaste, who is thus situated by the play as the originary model of the dangerous, politically anarchic threat of female sexuality. It is the first and most overdetermined example of a threat that will continue to haunt the entire Racinian world.

Jocaste exists as a constant dolorous presence, the presence of the mother who seemingly wants only for her children to live together, peacefully, as "brothers" all the while knowing that the sullied past that spawned them and any possible future that could contain them are irrevocably foreclosed. In her first speech, while lamenting the crimes for which she and Oedipus are responsible, she nevertheless adroitly signals to the audience that these crimes, this past that forever condemns her offspring to death, is only an avatar of a more remote transgression that fixes the origin of her family's unholy destiny in excessive sexuality—the body gone wild. Calling on the Sun as her witness, she exclaims:

> Mais ces Monstres, hélas! ne t'épouvantent guères,
> Le seul sang de Laïus les a rendus vulgaires;
> Tu peux voir sans frayeur les crimes de mes Fils,
> Après ceux que le Père et la Mère ont commis:
> Tu ne t'étonnes pas si mes Fils sont perfides,
> S'ils sont tous deux méchants, et s'ils sont parricides,
> Tu sais qu'ils sont sortis d'un sang incestueux,
> Et tu t'étonnerais s'ils étaient vertueux.
> Ce sang en leur donnant la lumière céleste,
> Leur donna pour le crime une pente funeste,
> Et leurs coeurs infectés de ce fatal poison,
> S'ouvrirent à la haine avant qu'à la raison.

> But why recoil from infamies so base
> The race of Laius makes them commonplace;
> Thou mayest see my sons' crimes without shame
> After the deeds that band their parent's name.
> Thou'rt not amazed my sons are treacherous.
> That both are wicked and both murderous:
> Thou know'st from an incestuous blood they're raised
> And, were they virtuous, wouldst be amazed.[20]
>   (1.1.27–38)

This plangent invocation of the Sun succinctly introduces us to the thematics that will preside over Racine's entire tragic production. In these few dense verses we have incest, murder, and (homo)sexuality all evoked by one intensely ambivalent signifier, at once both a metaphor and a metonymy without any separation of the one from the other, the most resonant word in Racine's poetic vocabulary—*sang* (blood). The origin of the political strife in Thebes is not to be found, according to Jocaste, simply in the "crime" of Oedipus but like all origins is situated in an even more distant past, in an even more archaic misdeed. According to Jocaste, the original sin of the Labdacids is to be found in the *sang* (lineage) of the father, Laius, and it is a violation of the body, a sexual transgression. The blood of Laius, that is, both his genealogy and his progeny, is tainted because of Laius's rape of Chryssipus, which, as the legend tells us, was both a contravention of Greek laws of hospitality and the introduction into the Hellenic world of "unnatural" (homo)sexuality. Although we are used to thinking of a certain tolerance for/of homosexuality in the classical Greek world, the story of Laius's transgression and punishment does indicate a less charitable attitude. Deeply offended by Laius's sexual aggression, Hera, protectress of marriage and childbirth, curses him and his descendants with an unbridled sexuality that will be their undoing.[21]

Sang, which is the most resonant word in *La Thébaïde*, makes its first appearance here in Jocaste's opening lament, but it will go on to weave a complex tissue of ever-expanding echoes that serve to blur the sexual and political distinctions the narrative attempts to keep at bay.[22] Critics have often called *La Thébaïde* the most Corneillean of Racine's plays precisely because of those distinctions that will later, as Roland Barthes has shown, blur into each other but that here maintain a rhetorical and sexual symmetry that is revelatory not only of the young Racine's still groping efforts to find his unique voice but also perhaps of his more youthful obeisance to certain supposedly natural social distinctions.[23]

The transgression that is carried in Laius's blood and that is here invoked by Jocaste echoes the fearsome outcome of the defiance of socialized sexuality. In even broader terms we might suggest that perhaps the sin is sexuality itself, those desires of the body that ignore the cultural structures that would socialize subjects into the proper political/familial order. The capitalization of *Père*, *Mère*, and *Fils*, despite any claim one would like to make regarding seventeenth-century punctuation (or lack thereof), nevertheless and simultaneously has the universalizing effect of lifting this family constellation out of its particular narrative and placing it in the realm of a universalizing generality—the family of Oedipus become the model for all family, the Oedipal family of seventeenth-century France.

Jocaste's opening lament is a masterly introduction not only to the dilemma that threatens the political stability of the world of *La Thébaïde* but also to the tragic vision of Racine's entire theatrical universe. What we have in this first speech, whose dramatic purpose is to offer a pithy recapitulation of the familial/political history that sets the stage for the present conflict—the murderous rivalry of her two sons for the throne of Thebes—is the story of her family cursed by the gods, a story of murder and incest, of the impossibly confused lineage left in the wake of Oedipus. On another level, however, we can see, if we focus on the affective resonances her calamitous rhetoric carries, that Racine's first tragedy also figures the fitful mise-en-scène of two mutually conflicting, confused, and therefore tragic aporia at the heart of any attempt to fix either personal-familial origins, the origin of the subject, or the socio-political origins of the collectivity/state. How does the social emerge out of the natural, and how and in what way is the subjective the origin or the creation of the communal?

At least since Aristotle, the demands of the feminine, which has been associated with the pull of the visceral, with the body whose desires are posited as the representative of all that is unruly and uncontrollable, have been seen as inherently dangerous to the organizing drive of the polis.[24] The state must ignore the convoluted ties of family. It desires itself sovereign, absolute, existing as it does as a "cosa mentale," a play of power and domination (among men). It is a symbolic rather than a biological ideal. But this desire for the symbolic exists more as a virtual (political) principle than a fully attainable reality. It is this impossible longing for the absolute, for a sovereignty that eludes them, that the warring brothers seek, each in his own way. Their quest is constantly frustrated by the call of the maternal as feminine—Jocaste's presence, her ceaseless beseeching, and her tears, the unavoidable reminders of the body, of the body's seduction, that stand in the way of any possible political victory of the brothers.

In other words, *La Thébaïde* offers two mutually interrelated but conflicted visions of politics. On the most archaic level we have "politics" understood not so much in its classical definition as the means of gaining and maintaining power in an organized social structure—that is, politics in the more usual sense of governmental strategies—but politics on a more primal level where the question would be how a particular society acculturates its members into the law of that society.

How, in other words, does ideology affect the way sexed bodies are inscribed in a culture as subjects of that culture? On this level, while it is
still obviously a question of power, it is also a more basic question of
how and in what ways sexual difference—that most basic difference in
society—is encoded as powerful or powerless, with all the inherent
ambivalences such a coding entails. Here politics serves as a metaphor
for the conflict of (sexed) forces where the plangent presence of the
maternal (female) body exercises a fascinating but, we might suggest
following Freud, inhibiting appeal on the male offspring. By calling on
them to recognize the natural bond of their inescapable common origin,
Jocaste positions herself and her desire as precisely what the brothers,
in order to be free, in order to be sovereign, must reject. Jocaste and her
surrogate, Antigone, by constantly appealing to nature, to the supposed
natural bond that unites the two brothers—to the ties of biology, as if
these ties, despite the very obvious contradictory reality of the brothers'
hatred, overrode any base political desire—could be seen to represent a
rather conservative if not reactionary stance to the forward march of
history. The passion of the mother would be to recall her sons to her (in
a sense, if we follow Freud) to continue with them the incestuous, exclusive love that has already wreaked so much harm on the state. Jocaste's
attempt to reunite the two brothers is, in a way, an effort to seduce her
sons, to quell their violent endeavors toward independence into a sexual
stasis, a self-contained passional monad with the mother from which
all difference and all independence is expelled.[25]

When we think of the extraordinarily rich and complex history of
the central role—that is, Antigone's—in the development of Western
theater and philosophy, it is interesting to consider the effects of Racine's
spotlighting the role of the mother, Jocaste, while downplaying the importance that Antigone as sister has for the political implications of his
tragedy. Antigone, we should remember, invokes the role of sister above
all other familial ties as unique. Wives can always remarry, mothers can
have more children, but the fraternal relation with the disappearance
of the parents can never be reduplicated. It is the fraternal/sororal role
that she claims as inimitable and that allows her, in Sophocles and
then in Hegel, to be seen as establishing a constantly destabilizing relation between family and state, to undermine and yet uphold in a tense
dialectic their unspoken interrelation.[26] Racine shifts the focus away
from the sister and onto the mother. By so doing he opens up perhaps a

more profoundly troubling exploration of the impossible question of origins—of the family, of the state—and proposes an equally but differently complex, it seems to me, meditation on the possibility or perhaps the impossibility of political sovereignty and desire.

Jocaste is constantly trying to impose a "partage de femmes" on the brothers, which, rather than separating them and thus setting them free to strive for an independence of being, is always a proposal to pull them closer together, to reunite them, to re-create the union that was theirs in the womb and from which, although she continues to deny it, their hatred sprang. All her pleas are for a physical proximity that only exacerbates their mutual hatred: "Associez un Frère à cet honneur supreme," she proposes, trying to convince Etéocle to share his throne. But, as she would know if she were a man, that is precisely what cannot be shared, what transcends the blood ties of family, and what enables the emergence of the state. It is a law that Créon, the traditional representative of *raison d'état,* is the first to announce and that is repeated most forcefully by Etéocle:

> Jamais dessus le Trône on ne vit plus d'un Maître,
> Il n'en peut tenir deux quelque grand qu'il puisse être
>
> No throne did ever more than one lord see;
> Two do not fit, however broad it be!
> (4.3.1299–1300)

"Une Mère enfin ne peut pas se trahir" (a Mother cannot betray herself). Jocaste's rebuttal to Créon reverberates ironically in the play with all the unspoken aggression that accompanies her relation to her sons. The closer Jocaste comes to having her wish of seeing her two sons reunited in the palace where they were born, to seeing them returned to the closed circle of family, the more heated their fratricidal passion grows. Jocaste cannot comprehend that the nearer she comes to getting her wish the more precarious the survival of the brothers and therefore of the state becomes:

> Me voici donc tantôt au comble de mes voeux
> Puisque déjà le Ciel vous rassemble tous deux.
> Vous revoyez un Frère, après deux ans d'absence,
> Dans ce meme Palais où vous prîtes naissance,
> Et moi par un bonheur où je n'osais penser

L'un et l'autre à la fois je vous puis embrasser.
Commencez donc, mes Fils, cette union si chère,
Et que chacun de vous reconnaise son Frère,
Tous deux dans votre Frère envisagez vos traits;
Mais pour en mieux juger voyez-les de plus près.
Surtout que le Sang parle et fasse son office
Approchez Etéocle, avancez Polynice.

At last I soon shall reach my heart's desire,
Since heaven has now brought both of you together.
After two years, once more you see your brother,
In the same palace where you both were born;
And I in my undreamt of happiness,
May now embrace the two of you together.
Begin, my sons, this precious unity:
Let each of you his brother recognize;
Both, view your features in your brother's face;
To judge them better, pray observe more closely;
Above all let blood speak and play its part.
Come, Eteocles; Polynices, come . . .
  (4.3.1073–84)

The concentration of tragic irony in this brief passage is so obvious as to underscore either the young Racine's still unrefined rhetorical/ psychological talent or to signal that this use of irony points to a blindness in Jocaste that reveals something more intimate and more pernicious, because both unknown and deadly, in her relation to her sons and to the fate of Thebes. On the one hand, all the references in this passage to a fraternal intimacy more idealized than real, all the references that underscore a fraternity that effaces individual difference, that creates, in fact, an indifference ("même Palais," "union si chère," "Tous deux dans votre Frère envisagez vos traits"), point, unbeknownst to Jocaste, to the twins' entrapment in each other; and beyond their ensnarement in the other, it resituates them once again, as enclosed, in the maternal womb.[27] Racine did not have to wait for Freud and for modern psychoanalysis to understand the ambivalence contained in the evocation of the womb. The ambiguous associations to both life and death, their intimate, impossible immixture that allows us to hear Jocaste's maternal desire on several levels—on the level of the tender and on the repressed level of a murderous desire for the twins return to her—has already been evoked by Etéocle. The connection between

fraternal rivalry, the maternal womb, and death is explicitly acknowledged by him when he explains to Créon the history of his competition
with his brother:

> Nous étions ennemis dès la plus tendre enfance,
> Que dis-je? Nous l'étions avant notre naissance.
> Triste et fatal effet d'un sang incestueux.
> Pendant qu'un même sein nous renfermait tous deux,
> Dans les flancs de ma Mère une guerre intestine
> De nos divisions lui marqua l'origine.
> Elles ont, tu le sais, paru dans le berceau,
> Et nous suivront peut-être encore dans le tombeau.

> From tenderest infancy we stood forth foes,
> Indeed, we were so even before our birth:
> Fatal and tragic brood of incestuous blood!
> While one same womb was still enclosing both,
> In our mother's flesh, intestinal war
> Engraved on her the source of our contentions.
> You know how they burst forth within the cradle,
> And in the grave perhaps will follow us.
>   (4.1.1019–26)

When Jocaste calls on "blood" to work its attraction, she is using the
word metaphorically, forgetting that in regard to her family, this "blood"
(as metonym) is corrupted and corrupts *ab origine* in her own womb
all her offspring. Instead of the harmony she hopes for, Laius's blood,
Oedipus's blood, her own blood, reproducing itself from generation to
generation, can only lead to violence and death. For the sons of Jocaste
the womb and the tomb are, in fact, inseparable.

The desire so ardently expressed by Jocaste as an appeal to nature,
to natural feelings, is actually, as far as the brothers' striving for indi-
viduation is concerned, a lethal desire directed at the two sons, a desire
for their confusion. The closer Jocaste comes to seeing her wish realized—the copresence of her sons—the more repulsed each son is by
his double. It has been often noted that one of the innovations Racine
introduced into the dramatic material he found in Euripides was not
only the visceral hatred the two brothers feel for each other but also
the very idea of their being not only brothers but twins.[28] What has
been less noted is that the one depends very much on the other. Twinship is not only, as I have noted, a sign in primitive societies of nature

gone awry, of monstrosity; it also raises to the most telling degree the mortiferous enigma of the double.[29] What this means, especially as it is first inscribed here by Racine (to become, as we know, one of the key structural elements in all the later tragedies) in a dialectics of (male) difference and (female) indifference, is that the insistence on the brothers' twinship is an exacerbated demonstration of what Freud will later analyze in his essay on the "Uncanny" as a confrontation with the double/other who steals one's individuality, who annihilates difference, and who, in the final analysis, becomes the metaphor for the destruction of the subject, for death.[30] By making the brothers mirror images of each other ("Et que chacun de vous reconnaisse son Frère, / Tous deux dans votre Frère envisagez vos traits" [Let each of you recognize his brother, / Each see in your brother your own likeness]), Racine effectively exacerbates the impossibility of their ever achieving, outside of death, the sovereignty they seek that would identify them as unique, absolute, and therefore as the rightful successor to the throne. In his insistence on Jocaste as the character who most ardently wishes their reunion, he makes of her, the mother, their executioner. Beneath the plangent tears of Jocaste lurks the fearsome fantasy of the phallic mother preying on her own sons: Jocaste, the incestuous mother, the destroyer. In a very real sense Jocaste, in her naturalness, is but one more avatar of the forces of female annihilation who, like the Sphinx, devours, in an erotic embrace, the young warriors of Thebes.[31]

To the seductive but inherently deadly invocations of the mother is opposed the constant striving of the male protagonists to assert a political legitimacy that refuses the ties to the body and that would establish a polity inscribed solely within the dynamics of symbolization—the laws that define the parameters of cultural existence. It is of course the inextricable interweave of these two mutually interconnected forces that creates the dramatic tension of the plot. What we witness as the myth becomes drama, and as the drama lures and ensnares the theatergoing public within the confused meshes of its ambivalent desires, it becomes the working of an ideology that both confronts and comforts us with a poetic evocation of our own secret fears and desires.

On an obviously narrative level of dramatic plot, the play presents us with a more prosaic political discussion echoing contemporary seventeenth-century arguments about which of two types of monarchy is best suited for life in the commonwealth: consensual (that is, for early modern France, parliamentary) monarchy, where the vox populi has currency in determining the governance of the state (even as this populace is the already rarefied assembly of the *parlements*), or the emerging absolutist form of monarchy that has, in seventeenth-century France, gradually imposed itself over and against the consensual during the reigns of Henri IV, Louis XIII, and Louis XIV.[32] Each one of these two forms of polity is defended by one of the two brothers, Etéocle and Polynice.

Each brother champions a vision/version of sovereignty that is his only distinguishing feature. In other words, it is their political rhetoric that is their only hope of establishing a unique difference, of severing them from the physicality that undoes their striving for an independent, masculine existence. And each invokes in the defense of his own view of monarchy that most overdetermined of seventeenth-century political arguments, the ill-defined, constantly shifting debates about exactly what constitutes legitimate monarchy and what constitutes tyranny.[33] It is interesting that the term "tyranny" is tossed about and used as an insult/accusation in the mouth of each brother as each defends his claim to the throne and tries to invalidate his twin's entitlement. It is remarkable because we see here that while distancing themselves from the tearful pull of the mother, they nevertheless, by the same rhetoric they use to flee Jocaste's embrace, are linked irrevocably to the equally conflicted paternal legacy. The father has been reproduced, doubled in their twinship. This double reproduction underlines his mythic/political ambivalence: at once, both Oedipus *tyrannos,* the liberator and military leader of Thebes, and Oedipus *pharmakos,* the sacred victim of Thebes, the perpetrator of murder and incest.[34] When each brother hurls the epithet "tyrant" at his twin, he is performing a ritual gesture of sacrificial exclusion attempting to fix his (br)other within only one aspect of their shared Oedipal legacy. That legacy, however, is always ambivalent, containing within itself both legitimate monarchy and the corruption of this legitimacy by aggression and sexual transgression. We might say this corruption is integral to the role of the father to which each aspires, and any of their attempts at legality turns into a repetition of transgression, catching them in political/sexual contradictions from which they struggle in vain to be free.

Grosso modo, Polynice defends an absolutist version of monarchy, a system whose legitimacy is founded solely, as he says, on "blood."

"Est-ce au Peuple, Madame, à se choisir un Maître? (Is it for the people, Madam, to choose their Master?). The "people" is seen by him (in typical seventeenth-century fashion) as a turbulent unruly mass ruled by passion and fickleness. In other words, echoing the Latin maxim *Turba est foemina*, Racine establishes the equation of the masses with the unruly feminine, with the fear of the mother. It is only by ignoring the capriciousness of the crowd that a legitimate sovereign, dependent only on his birthright, can rule:

> Que le Peuple à son gré nous craigne ou nous chérisse,
> Le sang nous met au Trône, et non pas son caprice;
> Ce que le sang lui donne il le doit accepter
> Et s'il n'aime son Prince il le doit respecter.

> The people may at will fear, cherish us;
> Our blood gives us the throne and not their whims.
> And what blood royal gives, they must accept;
> A prince they cannot love they must respect.
> (2.3.555–58)

On the one hand, Polynice would seem to be repeating here the party line of uncompromising absolutist theory: the king is a gift from God to his subjects. His legitimacy is conferred by blood (the devolution of power from father to son). The subjects are always potentially dangerous: unruly, turbulent, incapable of reason, and too easily stirred by passion. They are, therefore, inherently dangerous to the stability of the state.[35]

Jocaste counters that this attitude will only earn him the enmity of his subjects and the reputation of tyrant: "Vous serez un Tyran haï de vos Provinces" (You'll be a tyrant hated by your people). From the late sixteenth through the mid-seventeenth centuries, the major political theorists—Bodin, Cardin LeBret, Naudé, Bossuet, and others—continually debated the questions of what constituted a legitimate monarchy and conversely what represented the corruption of that legitimacy into tyranny. Racine reproduces those debates in the opposition of Etéocle and Polynice. Behind this debate on the type of monarch most suitable for the state rises, however, the specter of the great unavowable fear of all patriarchal monarchies, the fear that once a monarch has morphed into a tyrant the populace may have the right to remove him, and this usually (as had been recently seen in England with the beheading of Charles I) by putting him to death. The haunting fear of regicide/parricide lurks behind all the political debates in *La Thébaïde* where, lest we forget, the immediate crisis has been precipitated by the father's curse on the sons for their "killing" of him. Oedipus has been denied by his sons, sent out to wander, blind, among the no-man's-land of mythical Greece. Instead of coming to his aid, his sons have banished him from the polis, have denied their filial obligations to him and set him adrift, "a-polis." They have in a sense expelled him from the human community, having made him a scapegoat for all the crimes of Thebes. The sons have, in other words, symbolically renounced their king and killed their father who curses them and their state by imposing an impossible oscillation on the throne. They are guilty of deposing the tyrant, their father, and yet not being able to assume his legitimacy.

Racine reprises the difficult questioning of the concept of tyranny/legitimacy by annealing it to the unspoken predicates of patriarchal ideology where sexed notions of primogeniture are underscored by the particular aberrations of this Oedipal monarchy. Etéocle, the first brother to reign, refuses to relinquish the throne to his rival, claiming that he has the support of the Theban populace. According to him Polynice has become a traitor to Thebes by marrying the princess of Argos, a rival power, and leading the Argeian army against his native city.

> Thèbes....
> Voudrait-elle obéir à ce Prince inhumain
> Qui vient d'armer contre elle et le fer et la faim?
> Qui pour tous les Thébains n'a plus que de la haine,
> Qui s'est au Roi d'Argos indignement soumis,
> Et que l'Hymen attache à nos fiers ennemis.
> ....
> Thèbes m'a couronné pour éviter ses chaînes;
> Elle s'attend par moi de voir finir ses peines...
>
> Thebes...
> Would she obey this sanguinary prince,
> Who has just waged against her ravenous war?
> Would she accept as king, Mycenae's slave,
> Who harbours only hate for every Theban,
> Who is the king of Argos' sorry dupe,
> Whom marriage binds to all our bitterest foes?
> ....
> Thebes has crowned me to circumvent his chains;
> She seeks through me an end to all her pains.
>   (1.3.128–44)

In other words, Etéocle claims for himself the other half of the paternal legacy. He defines his role as the defender and savior of the city. His rule has the support of the populace; "Il est aimé de tous," we are told by Jocaste. This love, however, is only a ruse to maintain his status. It is, according to Polynice, just another form of tyranny:

> C'est un tyran qu'on aime
> Qui par cent lâchetés tâche à se maintenir,
> Au rang où par la force il a su parvenir,
> Et son orgueil le rend par un effet contraire,
> Esclave de son Peuple, et Tyran de son Frère,
> Pour commander tout seul il veut bien obéir,
> Et se fait mépriser pour me faire haïr.

> A most beloved despot!
> Who tries, by a hundred dastard deeds, to keep
> The rank that he has violently seized;
> His people's slave and his own brother's despot.
> To reign alone, he stoops low to obey,
> And makes himself despised to make me hated.
> (2.3.564–70)

Neither one of these two forms of government is vouchsafed by the drama, however, because each is undone by the viscerality of the twins' hatred, by their inability ever to separate from the (mother's) body and from their own monstrous physicality and their conflicted paternal political legacy. They are constantly reminded that they are not free, are not unique, are not absolute, but are inextricably trapped in their duality. The unnaturalness of their doubling, the fact that they are doubles of each other, (re)duplicates the parental transgressions that spawned them and that condemn them to the endless repetition of their scandalous origins.

Their twinness stands as the mark and stain of the original, sexual/ political sin in which they originate and from which they can never be free. We might speculate, therefore, that their conflicted, criminal origin, their murderous, incestuous heritage, placed as it is at the outset of his dramatic career, can be seen as the original sin of Racine's political universe. This sin, the presence of the flesh (and this, despite the body's textual expulsion from Racine's classical lexicon), will continue to mark and condemn all his future protagonists as they struggle, just like these originary twins, to be free of the claims the body has on them, to leave behind the sins of the parents and to find redemption as free, that is, absolute beings—a redemption that is, of course, always denied them. In a strange twist this redemption will take the form in the mature tragedies of a sacrifice, the sacrifice of the love object, that conflicted, contradictory (because both internal and external) object of sadomaso-chistic delectation. It is this object that is not yet present in *La Thébaïde*, and thus, with no sacrifice possible, there can be neither a tragic cathar-sis nor a political resolution that would enable the state to project itself into the future.

On the dramatic level of plot, in this first foray into the tragic, the political and the sexual remain, curiously, separate. In *La Thébaïde*, Racine's first tragedy (which is indebted, as generations of scholars have remarked, to another rivalry, Racine's own rivalry with his elder Corneille), that typically Racinian touch, the perversely conflicted erotic/sadistic love element, is only barely suggested. In *La Thébaïde* the ro-mance between Antigone and Hémon remains strangely passionless. Even Créon's designs on his niece fail to elicit either from her or from the audience any sort of sadomasochistic frisson. Perhaps Racine, too intent on imitating Corneille, could only follow his elder's proscription of love as the chief motivation of tragic conflict. According to Corneille's dictates, politics, not love, must be the center of a tragedy, which, as he rather haughtily proclaimed, needed "quelque grand intérêt d'Etat ou quelque passion plus noble et plus mâle que l'amour" (some important matter of state or a nobler and more virile passion than love).[36] The possible consequences of this for *La Thébaïde* as the originary model for Racinian tragedy are twofold. On the one hand, Racine structures his play on a Corneillean model both thematically and sexually: the major dramatic interest of the play is the political threat the warring brothers pose to the survival of the state. On the other, the play is structured, also like Corneille's (cf. *Horace*), by the clear opposition of defined sexual camps. Men and women still maintain the supposedly natural distinction of their sex: as we have seen, all the major male characters are presented as politically motivated beings in that they are all defined by their uni-lateral desire for power represented by the only clearly expressed pas-sion in the play, the obsession with the throne. "Le Trône fit toujours mes ardeurs les plus chères," Créon tells his confident Attale, a desire that is echoed by Etéocle, "Qu'un trône est plus pénible à quitter que la vie," and by Polynice:

> Je ne me connais plus en ce malheur extreme
> En m'arrachant au Trône on m'arrache à moi-même...

> I don't recognize myself in this deep misfortune
> Tearing myself from the Throne, I tear myself from my very being.[37]
>   (4.3.1159–60)

The women, on the other hand, are confined to their status as plangent representatives of the "Kreaturlichkeit," the ties of the body, of blood, of family. For them politics is an incomprehensible rupture of the most intimate of bonds, the blood ties of family:

> La Couronne pour vous a-t-elle tant de charmes
> Si par un parricide il la fallait gagner?
> Ah! mon Fils à ce prix voudriez-vous régner?

> Ah, does the crown for you hold so much charm?
> It it exacted fratricide to win it,
> Would you, my son, wish at that cost to reign?
>   (1.3.92–94)

Within this rather static opposition, an opposition where biological difference is equated to a metaphysical difference (where male equals masculine and female equals feminine), a difference that always seems to be imposed from without, that is, from the separation between the sexes seen as a natural and clearly defined distinction of essence. As we know, however, following the analyses of Roland Barthes, this is precisely not the distinction operative in the major, mature tragedies of Racine. Barthes tells us that in Racine sexuality is "de-essentialized": it is no longer attached to some presupposed biological reality but rather is a production of political forces: "The division of the Racinian world into strong and weak, into tyrants and captives, covers in a sense the division of the sexes: it is their situation in the relation of force that orchestrates some of the characters as virile and others as feminine, without concern for their biological sex."[38] It is this political production of sexuality that enables Barthes to see how certain of Racine's female protagonists—Agrippine, Roxane, Athalie—can be perceived as masculine in that they are active, aggressive, dominating (and essentially castrating), while several of the male characters—Britannicus, Néron,

Bajazet, Hippolyte—are perceived as feminine. The significance of Barthes's analysis of Racinian sexuality allows us to see how in the mature tragedies sexuality is essentially political: it is a complex play of forces and desires all turning around what may strike us as a Nietzschean will to power. What this also means is that the mechanisms of desire are infinitely more complex in the mature Racine where sexual identities are blurred, multiple, and fractious. In the established Racine, difference is always an internal difference, a difference within, and the tragic conflict is produced not as the result of some constraints imposed from without, from a law/desire exterior to the tragic subject, but as a result of that subject's own constitution as an internally riven subject of that law. When he disassociates desire from biological sexuality, Racine introduces us into a confused, contradictory world and creates the split subject of modernity.

At the same time, however, this modern conflicted subject is defined as "monstrous," signaling the return within the subject itself of the chaotic, destructive drives of the Oedipal dynamic. When in the Racinian universe sexuality is shown divorced from biology, by this very same gesture this sexuality is defined as scandalous. This negative projection represents, however, on yet another level, the ideological imperative, the societal desire, for an adequate, that is, normative equation between biology and (psycho)sexuality. All the characters mentioned above are tragic because they are associated with the monstrous that is seen as an aberration in the natural order of the world. Although, as Barthes says, sexuality in Racine is not (self-evidently) natural, it is precisely because it is not natural that the scenario of Racinian sexuality is perfectly consistent with the Oedipal legend that on another level the plays reproduce.

This, of course, is not yet the case in *La Thébaïde*. Difference in this first foray into the tragic is still an external marker; monstrosity is figured in the unnatural doubling of the warring brothers, and love, at least the passionate love we will come to associate with Racine, is absent. Finally, the tragedy also fails as a political ritual, as the originary mise-en-scène of a new world order. Since there is no passionate, conflicted love, there can be no sacrifice either of the lover or the loved object. No *pharmakos* is identified by the play to carry the mark, the scar, of the tragic victim, and there is no sacrificial scapegoat whose death would mark both the end of an exhausted (political) condition and the beginning of new social order.[39] For the same reasons the play cannot represent the origins of a collective guilt and that guilt's repression in communal ceremonies of remembrance and atonement. When Racine transforms this fragment of the Oedipus legend into theater, its political message remains ultimately complex and pessimistic. The brothers remain enemies to the death: there is no reconciliation in a mutual recognition of love and hate and therefore no symbolic creation of the (dead) father as the law. Without this leap into the symbolic, no form of culture is possible.

The play ends with the extinction of the entire royal family and thus, in a sense, with the destruction of the polis they embody. Carrying to the point of paroxysm Créon's cynical but accurate statement that familial hatred—the ties of kinship—are the most intense and therefore the most destructive, this first tragedy ends without any hope of redemption, any possibility of community:

> Il n'est rien qui puisse réunir,
> Ceux que des noeuds si forts n'ont pas su retenir,
> L'on hait avec excès lorsque l'on hait un Frère.
>
> Nothing can bind again
> Those whom such ties were powerless to restrain;
> One hates a brother with a hate that's dire.
>   (3.6.981–83)

Nevertheless, *La Thébaïde* remains of primary interest for our understanding of the elaboration of the Racinian universe, for the tragic vision of the plays to come. Racine chooses a curious subject, "le sujet le plus tragique" (the most tragic subject), precisely because it portrays the triumph of chaos over culture, the impossibility, because the original sin of sexuality cannot find its *aufhebung* in sacrifice, that stands at the outset of Racine's tragic universe as a pessimistic reminder of the presence of transgression (the body) and the futility of our efforts to transcend it. Racine, in this his own originary tragedy, proposes a certain political history, holds out the tantalizing prospect of community, the hope of the possibility of a life in the polis, that would keep at bay all those forces that threaten social existence, only to confound that possibility before our eyes, leaving us with the final image of the city undone, its heroes dead and its future condemned. There is no redemption possible, only the haunting dread of the power of the body, identified for the first time here with the loving yet murderous and incestuous embrace of the mother, which unravels the ties of politics and sends civilization reeling into chaos. It is this fear that will continue to haunt the Racinian world, his heroes and his monsters, in all the plays to come. It is this primal fantasy that serves as a pessimistic foundation for a world that will embrace all Racine's protagonists as they live in dread of transgressions they ignore while hoping for a salvation that flickers on the distant horizon of a world condemned to the fragmentation they both desire and fear.

2

Andromaque:
Myth and Melancholy

Although the success of *La Thébaïde* was modest and the reception of *Alexandre* tepid at most, such was not the case for *Andromaque*.[1] With the possible exception of Corneille's *Le Cid,* no other play of the seventeenth century was greeted with as much public enthusiasm as *Andromaque.* While *La Thébaïde* remained heavily indebted to the prevailing dominion of Corneillean dramaturgy, *Andromaque* strikes a decidedly innovative note in the orchestration of classical tragedy. Racine knew that his first theatrical triumph introduced onto the French stage a new type of hero ("gallant") and a novel form of tragedy.[2] Despite the difference between *Andromaque* and the Corneillean tradition of which *La Thébaïde* can be considered a part, certain obsessive questions, politico/ sexual questions that were already present in his first tragedy, continue to inform the dynamics of plot and character in *Andromaque,* even as this play charts a new course for seventeenth-century tragedy.

Most recent commentators on Racine point to the absence of the father and/or his representative as the origin of social unrest. In *La Thébaïde,* Oedipus is gone. In his disappearance the "horde of brothers" (reduced to Etéocle and Polynice and their warring armies) is engaged in a furious battle for the father's place. Rather than a fraternity of equals who have renounced their desire to be the father, to take his place, each fights furiously for supremacy. It is a struggle to the death, which, as we are shown, precludes any chance of elaborating a viable polis. *La Thébaïde* in its inability to establish a feasible polity ends in the destruction of any durable political structure: the brothers kill each other, and Thebes descends into anarchy. Créon, having sacrificed his own sons, is incapable of forming any erotic/political alliance that would secure his position as leader and thus, we assume, the perennity of the state.

In *Andromaque* the situation is both analogous and more complex. We are still in a world from which the father has been removed (it should be remembered that "father" does not refer to the actual biological father—who is always ever an incarnated placeholder of the symbolic, that is, dead father). In the case of *Andromaque,* where all the characters exist in the shadow of the heroes of the Trojan War, the father(s) who is (are) absent are both multiple and monumental—Agamemnon ("king of kings"), Achille (the greatest of Greek warrior/kings), and Hector (the most valiant of the Trojans). Let us say that the combined aura of the dead warrior kings of the Trojan conflict presides over the universe of the play as the absent reference point of patriarchal authority. This "King" has been replaced by a fraternity, the alliance of the sons, each head of an independent Greek state. I am, obviously, drawing an analogy between the general structure that presides over the mythological narrative of the Trojan War and the narrative of the primal horde that we find in Freud's anthropological musings in *Totem and Taboo.*

We should remember that the initial Greek fraternity that set sail for Troy was, in ways that seem to fit uncannily into Freud's scheme, originally a sexual/political compromise: all the contenders for Helen's hand swore an alliance among themselves to respect Tyndareus's choice of a husband for Helen and collectively to come to the aid of the winner of her hand in case that union be threatened. So what we have, basically, is a group of sexually predacious young men who have internalized the law of the father (which is essentially the law that says that their desire cannot be satisfied) and who, in order not to descend into mutual destruction, accept "castration" (that is, the no to individual desire) for a political solution: they become allies in a collective endeavor. It is, we must assume, because they have accepted the frustration of their desire (for Helen) that they can collectively go to war against Troy, destroy the city, enslave its women and children, and return enriched with the booty of war. Sublimation, for the brothers, does have its rewards.[3]

As we move from La Thébaïde to Andromaque, the essential political question that foregrounds the events of the drama is precisely how to leave the miasma of this war and its desolation that form the backdrop to this new play, how to overcome the trauma of loss and dislocation, how, in other words, to move forward. What kind of society is possible in the aftermath of a cataclysmic war, a disaster that ended in the utter destruction of one civilization by another? It could be here that we start to situate the melancholic unease that pervades the entire drama, as this play, reduced to a small circle of conflicting passions and jealousies, reflects the much larger, undefined political situation of "what now?" How do we live after the apocalypse? What kind of world, what kind of family, what kind of polis is now possible? What have we lost—what has been sacrificed in the destruction of Troy—and how do we go on from that loss?

As the play opens we soon learn that one of the (new generation of) brothers, intriguingly the son of the most recalcitrant and the most valiant of the original band (Achille), impelled by his desire, has once again broken ranks. Pyrrhus's love/lust for Andromaque, his Trojan captive, turns him against his fraternal cohort in a double refusal: he refuses to hand over to the Greeks Hector's son Astyanax, who is perceived by them to represent a grave political threat to their very survival; then to compound his resistance, he declines to wed Hermione, his bartered bride, whose marriage to him was arranged on the battlefields of Troy by their respective fathers (Menelaos and Achille). Pyrrhus becomes, therefore, in the eyes of the Greeks, a traitor to their world.

Both Mauron and Barthes have pointed to Pyrrhus as the only revolutionary in this collection of sad characters. He appears as the lone protagonist who wishes to free himself of the past—that is, of his infeudation to his father, to himself as his father (the constant comparisons and conflations of him with Achille), and more importantly to the stasis of the fraternity of the new generation of Greeks, a fraternity that has killed the father (Priam—Troy) but also, in the distribution and consumption of the spoils of Troy, metaphorically dismembered and devoured him. By so doing they have established a new regime beholden to and enslaved by the trauma of their own profanation. No new sacred has emerged that would free them, no new law (in Barthes's terminology) that by establishing novel limits and thus new transgressions would allow for a forward movement of history.[4] It is not, however, as if

the Greeks wanted to go forward; they seem to be (perhaps because
they are traumatized) quite comfortable to remain fixated on the past.
It is perhaps for this reason, a sense of generalized societal angst, that
they have sent Oreste to Epirus to ask that Pyrrhus hand over to them
what has become, we might say, their counterphobic object, Astyanax,
on whom they focus all their anxieties and guilt. By immolating Astyanax
they hope to calm their fears of an eventual rebirth of Troy and thus
to eliminate the possibilities of cataclysmic reprisals. The sacrifice of
Astyanax becomes the obsessive drive of the new fraternity of the Greeks
that is having such difficulty establishing itself over and against the past.

Pyrrhus's desire for Andromaque, a desire for the fulfillment of which
he is ready to alienate himself and, more important, the state of which
he is head from his Greek brethren is thus at once a private and a public challenge to the reigning political order of his world. Pyrrhus's refusal to meet the Greeks' demands and to fulfill the marriage promise
made to Hermione is a revolutionary gesture where the libidinal is
inseparable from the political, where both are inextricably intermin-
gled. Pyrrhus's love for Andromaque is in a sense a heterosexual challenge to the more pervasive, politically correct homosexual/homosocial
bond of the Greeks between themselves. What Pyrrhus's passion for
Andromaque threatens is to alter radically this homosocial bond, to
break it and therefore to install a new (a)political order. This is precisely
why he cannot love Hermione and why she rages impotently against
his passion for another. Their union would never be anything more
than a reinforcement of the homosocial Greek political order. She is
the gift that has been exchanged by the two fathers on the battlefield
where they triumphed. She is (although she readily accepts her role)
merely an object of exchange between the fathers, an exchange that
would cement their bond.[5]

Perversely, Hermione desires Pyrrhus for the very same reasons Andromaque claims she cannot—his bloody, savage nature and actions, which
reproduce Pyrrhus, at least in Hermione's fantasy, as the savage leader—
the new primal father. His brutal exploits excite Hermione ("Sais-tu
quel est Pyrrhus? T'es-tu fait raconter / Le nombre des Exploits" (Have
you heard? / Tell all his exploits . . . Who can count them all?), defined,
as we will soon learn, by her own homicidal fury. She is excited by
what in Pyrrhus precisely repels Andromaque. What Hermione wants,
what Andromaque rejects, is Pyrrhus as a brutal warrior, the hero of

bloody exploits who maintains a fascinating sexual hold over all the women (Hermione and Andromaque). For this very reason, Hermione cannot love Oreste, her former suitor who returns time and again seeking her affection. Oreste remains, as the representative of the Greeks, too tame, too familiar. He remains always a brother, never a lover. So from the very outset of this tragedy we are presented with the classic double bind of desire and frustration that presides over the universe of the play: "Oreste loves Hermione who loves Pyrrhus who loves Andromaque who loves Hector who is dead." The desire of Pyrrhus, the "freest character in all Racine," is, we assume, so fervent that he attempts to break this cycle of frustration, but doing so pits him against the gods, his fellow Greeks, and their women—against, that is, his entire world.

This world, as the play begins, has been traumatized by the greatest epic adventure in history: the ten-year siege and destruction of Troy by the Greeks. All the characters in the play have been marked in one way or another by these harrowing events. All are the children of larger-than-life, heroic parents, in comparison to whom, as many have pointed out, their own lives seem pale and inconsequential.[6] They all seem to exist in a state of spiritual anomie. The play presents us with the remnants, or the rather pitiful remains, of the heroic horde, the Greeks who conquered Troy. The children are destined not to heroism but to the merely quotidian. They live with the constant knowledge that they are not heroes but mere mortals destined to a life of mediocrity. They are a band of brothers that has not been able to achieve the status of transcendence—either in life or legend. We might say, to paraphrase Freud, that the shadow of Troy has fallen over their egos, condemning them all to an unbearable, because indefinable, loss and thus to a pervasive, invasive melancholia.

"Melancholia" as both a term and a concept has, as we know, an ancient and rich history antedating Freud. The long Saturnian tradition defined "melancholia" as an excess of black bile, linked as it was to the dominant humoral medical theories of the seventeenth century, said to affect the lonely man of genius—the philosopher, the poet, the innovator. Although the concept was slowly evolving in Racine's day from the idea of the solitary mad creator, à la Tasso, toward the idea of a state of depressive withdrawal that will come to mark the modern description of the melancholic temperament and its more tightly confined clinical diagnosis, in Racine's lexicon it still retains, even as it was changing, its classical heritage.[7] In other words, the very concept of melancholy appears to be one of those transhistorical terms that can encompass various philosophical, artistic, and therapeutic categories simultaneously while marking the gradual ideological slippage of emphasis from one to the other. Certainly, in the context of Racinian dramaturgy, the term, the context, will come more and more to define a particular sense of loss and desperation both as an abstract, brooding sociopolitical ambiance surrounding and conditioning the world inside which his characters confront their own destinies and as the individual's sense of his/ her own worthlessness in that world. In the most acute, that is, tragic, of those destinies, melancholia leads inevitably to self-destruction.

In *Andromaque*, for instance, we can see that the word "melancholic" applies most pointedly, although in different declensions, to at least two of the main characters, Oreste and Andromaque. In a more general sense, however, it can be used to describe the world in which all the play's protagonists find themselves trapped. Despite what we might consider the successful outcome of the war that serves as the backdrop for the actions we now are called on to witness, the Greeks, we are told, rather than resting on their victorious laurels, live in a state of ongoing anxiety. They are traumatized by ten years of constant combat, by their own brutality, and by losses they have endured at the hands of the Trojans, especially of Hector, Troy's greatest warrior:

> Ne vous souvient-il plus, Seigneur, quel fut Hector?
> Nos Peuples affaiblis s'en souviennent encore.
> Son nom seul fait frémir nos Veuves, et nos Filles,
> Et dans toute la Grèce, il n'est point de Familles,
> Qui ne demandent compte à ce malheureux Fils,
> D'un Père, ou d'un Epoux, qu'Hector leur a ravis...
>
> My lord, can you forget what Hector was?
> Our weakened population still remembers.
> Our widows, daughters, shudder at his name;
> And in all Greece there's not a family
> That does not call to account his wretched son
> For husbands, fathers, snatched from them by Hector.
>   (1.2.155–60)

The war from which they have returned scarcely a year before the beginning of the action ("Ah! Si du Fils d'Hector la perte était jurée, / Pourquoi d'un an entier l'avons-nous différée?" [Bah! if the death of

Hector's son was sworn / Why have me put it off for one whole year?])
was devastating for the violent destruction it wreaked on an entire civilization and, we must assume, for how it affected the perpetrators of this
violence. All the characters in the drama, in one way or the other, are
the products of this shattering clash of civilizations. They all live with
the harrowing consequences of Troy's destruction and with the shadow
that this devastation has cast over their families, their bodies, and their
psyches. In one way or the other, they remain the walking wounded, the
traumatized survivors of a war that has left them bereft of any grounding
in family and history and that has set them adrift, alienated from their
past and incapable of anything other than a vain attempt to find some
solid anchoring in a maddening attempt to reproduce a heroism that is
always and only defined, when they try to describe it, as a harrowing
muddle of slaying, rape, and arson. Although constantly living in the
shadow of this "heroism" and mouthing the incantatory ideological doxa
that transforms killing into great deeds of valor, they are doomed to a mis-
guided repetition that can lead them nowhere but to their own demise.

Although the Trojan War serves as the backdrop that is a constant
presence in the lives and self-perception of the characters, and although
this war is constantly referred to as a war that opposed two nations, two
peoples, the Hellenes and the Trojans, what is constantly overlooked in
this political confrontation is not so much the continually reinforced
rhetorical differentiation of the one camp from the other but rather
their essential commonality. In reality, there is no difference, other
than a political separation of the Greeks on the one hand and the Trojans
on the other. They are for all intents and purposes interchangeable.
They share the same language, the same gods, and the same social organizations. Very much as in Corneille's *Horace*, where nothing really
distinguishes the warring Albans and Romans ("Nous ne sommes qu'un
sang et qu'un peuple en deux villes" [We are but one people and one
blood in two cities], 1.3.291), what we have here is simply a case of what
Freud called the "narcissism of small differences," that is, the conflict
caused by an exacerbation of created difference on an indistinguishable
unity, an invention that is all the more aggravated by the inability to
establish a real difference and that can and does lead to the most acute
and violent of hostilities.[8] At the same time, ideologically speaking,
the Trojan War can be seen as one of the earliest expressions of a conflict
between what will become the opposition of the West to the East—an

opposition that Racine will continue to decline in different modes (particularly as this first dichotomy is translated into a sexual one, masculine/feminine, where the first term becomes equated to the Western/ Greek civilization and the second to the Orient) throughout his career (for example, *Mithridate, Bérénice, Bajazet*). In a sense, we have here transferred onto the stage of international politics the same deadly fraternal clash—the hatred of the same—of the brother/other that in a more directly familial avatar presided over the fratricidal conflict of *Les frères ennemis*. It left that play, too, plunged into the abyss of melancholic autodestruction.

Into this world defined by loss, by dislocation, by an unmetabolizable trauma, perhaps historically (that is, mythologically speaking) the greatest trauma of the ancient world, Oreste arrives, bringing with him his own very personal melancholy, which has, as Pylade informs him and us, buried his soul. By his incisive use of the word *ensevelie* to rime with *mélancolie*, Racine immediately establishes, as Freud would do two hundred years later, the intimate relation of melancholia and death. Oreste enters the scene of the play and sails into the port of Epirus as the incarnation of a death drive that will make of him both its unwilling executor and its victim, and all this under the guise of unrequited love. He arrives on the seventeenth-century stage, Georges Forestier tells us, having been reconfigured, by the long tradition of romance narratives, with "une maladie d'amour" (lovesickness).[9] This is surely a correct historical description of the Oreste we first encounter as the curtain goes up on the play. Oreste sails into Epirus as the ambassador of the Greek confederation that has successfully triumphed over Troy. Now, however, that confederation feels ever-growing anxiety because it turns out that Astyanax, whom they believed dead, is actually alive and living with his mother Andromaque at the court of Pyrrhus. Oreste is sent to bring the child from Epirus so that he may be once and for all immolated, thus assuring, it is assumed, the security of the Greek world. In truth, however, as Oreste quickly confides to Pylade, he has really come to try once again to win over the woman for whom he has pined in vain (love prevailing over politics, thus the gallantry of Racine's rhetoric of passion), the princess Hermione, daughter of Menelaos and Helen and, genealogically speaking, twice his first cousin: both his parents and hers are brothers/sisters.

I mention this convoluted familial structure to remind us of several interesting details that a merely historical reading of Racine's characters leaves aside. More than fifty years ago Georges May pointed out something that I believe bears repeating. "Racine," he wrote, "dans *Andromaque* fait franchement appel aux connaissance homériques de son public" (Racine . . . in *Andromaque* quite frankly calls upon his audience's knowledge of the Homeric canon).[10] I think it would not be a misreading of May's critical insight to suggest that for "connaissance homérique" (knowledge of Homer) he could just as well have said "connaissance mythologique" (knowledge of mythology). And with this slight change a rather huge field of interpretation opens up in front of us. For surely the audience of Racine's play, much more attuned to classical reference than the public of our own time, could not overlook several glaringly important mythological themes that attach themselves indelibly to the name and fate of Oreste. The first, most obvious and most notorious, is, of course, his matricide. Returning to Mycenae after a long absence, Oreste, egged on by his sister Electra, avenges his father's murder by slaying Clytemnestra, his mother. Now, Forestier and all the other scholars who have dealt with Racine's Oreste are of course correct to point out that nowhere in the text of *Andromaque* is any mention made of this most famous and most shocking of crimes attached to the Oreste legend. This does not prevent the knowledge of his crime (and we do not know in Racine if the crime has already been committed or if it is still in the future in relation to the play's narrative), like the Erinyes who follow him everywhere, from being inextricably attached to his persona. Oreste enters the play, whether acknowledged or not, with all the weight and the opprobrium of his matricide. Further, this same crime brings into the court of Epirus and onto the stage of seventeenth-century French classicism the presence of the only other mythological family, the Atreides, that can stand next to the family of Oedipus as the very origin and definition of the "tragic."[11] His presence imports onto the scene of seventeenth-century tragedy not simply a legendary example of friendship (the couple Oreste forms with Pylade) but an entire family doomed to infanticide (Iphigenia), patricide (Agamemnon), matricide (Clytemnestra), and political turmoil. It is the curse of the Atreides that accompanies Oreste as he disembarks with his strange melancholy at Epirus.

The first lines of the drama tell us that Oreste is melancholic ("Surtout je redoutais cette Mélancolie / Où j'ai vu si longemps votre Âme ensevelie"). In his expository conversation with Pylade he describes himself as despondent, aimlessly drifting around the Greek world. In these same opening remarks, he is the first in this drama to utter the word *funeste* (fatal), which will continue in multiple registers to echo throughout the play in ever louder crescendos accentuating the mounting tension, the underlying force of death, that will culminate in the murder of Pyrrhus and the suicide of Hermione.[12] Oreste's melancholia, he tells first Pylade and then, more (melo)dramatically, Hermione, turned suicidal. But his fate is such that even his attempts to end his life and his suffering proved futile:

> J'ai mendié la Mort, chez des Peuples cruels
> Qui n'apaisaient leurs Dieux que du sang des Mortels:
> Ils m'ont fermé leur Temple, et ces Peuples barbares
> De mon sang prodigué sont devenus avares.
>
> I've begged for death in strange and cruel lands,
> Where only human blood appeased their Gods:
> Their temple barred to me, these barbarous fold
> Fastidiously distained my lavish blood.
>   (2.2491–94)

Oreste is given to self-demeaning outbursts to express his passion for the woman who constantly rejects him:

> ... un Malheureux, qui perd tout ce qu'il aime
> Que tout le monde hait et qui se hait lui-même.
>
> ... a wretch who loses all he loves,
> Whom every man must hate, who hates himself.
>   (3.1.801–2)

And of course, to the sadomasochistic delectation of the punishment he continues to desire and suffer at her hands: "Poursuivez. Il est beau de m'insulter ainsi. Cruelle" (Go on; how sweet of you to taunt me thus / heartless girl).

It would seem, therefore, that in his portrayal of Oreste, Racine has given us a portrait of virtually clinical precision that corresponds almost point by point to Freud's description of the melancholic personality:

The distinguishing mental features of melancholia are a profoundly painful dejection, cessation of interest in the outside world, loss of the capacity to love, inhibition of all activity and a lowering of the self-regarding feelings to a degree that finds utterance in self-reproaches and self-revilings and culminates in a delusional expectation of punishment.[13]

On the other hand, and in contradistinction to Oreste, Andromaque's melancholy appears to us more normal, or at least more comprehensible. Andromaque, who has lost her family, who has seen her hero/husband slain, who has witnessed the city/state over which she was destined to rule reduced to ashes, and who herself has been sent into slavery, shipped off as part of the spoils of war to serve a foreign master in a foreign land, has more than enough real reasons to feel stunned, shocked, depressed ("Captive, toujours triste, importune à moi-même" [Sad captive that I am, weary of living]). On a more profound level, however, when we look closely at her relation to both her dead husband and to her absent hostage of a son, what first appears as a profound, unresolved mourning—in her obstinate refusal to separate herself from the lost object and to face reality (Hector is dead) and in her perseverance in remaining faithful to this lost object by replacing the dead husband with the living (if equally absent) son—begins to seem a bit more perverse.[14] Andromaque appears on stage as the very incarnation of the medieval "dame méréncolyie." Suffering from an inability or a refusal to work through her mourning, she seems stymied in a melancholy that is, effectively, a dislocation from reality so radical that it threatens the very person she claims to want to save. For her most intimate confidant, Cléone, Andromaque appears to have passed the limits of what to the world (that is, to the nontragic characters in the world of the drama, according to Lucien Goldmann) is acceptable: "normal" mourning has become a permanent state of dejection that verges not only on the self-destructive but, because of the threat that it represents for her son's life, on the criminal:

> Madame, à votre Époux c'est être assez fidèle
> Trop de vertu pourrait vous rendre criminelle.

> My lady, you've been loyal to your husband.
> Too great a virtue might prove criminal.
> (3.8.985–86)

Andromaque is dejected, harried, despondent, and, for Pyrrhus at least, extremely desirable.

It is at this juncture where Pyrrhus's passion crosses Andromaque's melancholia that Racine's sadistic genius takes hold: Racine gives her as her only solace in her harrowing state, a son:

> Le seul bien qui me reste, et d'Hector et de Troie
>
> The only treasure Troy and Hector left me.
>   (1.4.262)

> Mais il me reste un Fils. Vous saurez quelque jour,
> Madame, pour un Fils jusqu'où va notre amour.
> . . . .
> Lorsque de tant de biens, qui pouvaient nous flatter,
> C'est le seul qui nous reste. . . .
>
> But I still have a son. You'll know some day
> How strong upon a mother's heart his sway;
> . . . .
> When of so many blessing we might taste
> He is the sole remaining. . . .
>   (3.4.871–77)

And the son becomes the innocent pawn in the cat and mouse game that Pyrrhus sets in motion to tear Andromaque away from her past and into his present. Astyanax is what remains. He is what remains of her marriage, her history, her people. Taken from his mother's embrace, he becomes the hostage in a sexual/political imbroglio that engages all the characters in the play in a dangerous roundelay from which none can escape unscathed.

This opening salvo of Oreste as he first addresses Pyrrhus in his role of ambassador representing the Greek states demonstrates by its compact economy the entire underlying system of familial filiation that has been traumatized, rent by the events of the war, and reduced to a weakened and chaotic dispersion. It is in order to reconstitute what has been sundered that, perversely, the Greeks need to reassure themselves not only of their future safety but of the stability and perennity of their traumatized world; thus they are fixated on Astyanax's immolation. They need the apotropaic function of the sacrifice to reestablish a continuity in their world/lives. It is especially in times of social crisis, of doubt, that a community has recourse to sacrifice in order to reaffirm its sense of self, to reconnect with its (mythic) origins, its values, and its (threatened) worldview.[15] We should pay particular attention, therefore, to the role of sacrifice in *Andromaque*, especially to the way the role of the sacrificial victim is made to shift from the son to the father, from Astyanax to Pyrrhus as the dramatic scenario builds to a political crisis.

An entire society was traumatized by its losses but also, we must assume, by the brutality of its own troops, for whom in the heat of battle nothing nor anyone, neither the elderly nor the women nor the children, was sacred:

> Du vieux Père d'Hector la valeur abattue
> Aux pieds de sa Famille expirante à sa vue,
> Tandis que dans son sein votre bras enfoncé
> Cherche un reste de sang que l'âge avait glacé;
> Dans des ruisseaux de sang Troie ardente plongée
> De votre proper main Polyxène égorgée . . .

> Hector's old father with dejected heart
> Lamenting loud the death of all his sons,
> The while your savage arm deep in his breast
> Scoops out his feeble blood congealed by age?
> All Troy plunged burning in her streams of blood;
> Polyxena, your very hand had slaughtered.
>   (4.5.1341–46)

As long as the characters remain attached to their trauma, to their subservience to the impossible model/life of their parents (and here, of course, one could talk more fully about how precisely Racine underlines the inextricable connection of social-political history to the intimate dynamics of the family—where the one is coeval with the other), they are condemned to the melancholy of that trauma and that loss.

Although, on the surface at least, understanding the pervasive melancholic pall that hangs over the world of *Andromaque* as both the individual and collective response to the loss/death of so many beloved relations appears quite reasonable, this is not an entirely satisfactory answer to the conundrum of melancholia, for as Freud tells us, melancholia results not so much from having lost the much-loved person but rather from having lost something in that person of which we are unaware but which weighs heavily on our psychic life.[16] What Freud is suggesting, by inference, is that we are incapable of recognizing the cause of our melancholia because we are equally powerless to define our love. We may think

we know whom we love but it would be equally difficult for us to point
to exactly what it is in that person that causes us to love him/her. In
other words, once we begin to explore the enigma of melancholia in
Andromaque, we are brought up against the even more mysterious in-
scrutability of love itself. Why, for instance, does Pyrrhus love Andromaque, or Oreste love Hermione, Hermione love Pyrrhus, or even, for
that matter, Andromaque love Hector? While we may think we understand the pervasive atmosphere of melancholy that hangs over the world
of the play given the destruction, loss, and death that all the characters
(in varying degrees) have in common, when we try to understand the
passions of the present, each individual obsession is cloaked in even
greater ambiguity.

In order to begin to understand the impossible dynamics of love that
creates the dramatic tension in the play, perhaps we must turn again to
Freud's discussion of melancholia—that is, the return of the wounded
past, in order to grasp the conflicted present. In *Mourning and Melancholia* Freud argues for understanding melancholia as borrowing, as he
puts it, "some of its features from mourning and others from the process
of regression from narcissistic object choice to narcissism."[17] In other
words, in order to understand perhaps both the love and the loathing of
Racine's characters, we might do well to explore how although on one
level *Andromaque* plunges us into the mythological universe of Oedipus,
the Atreides, and the Trojan War, on another, perhaps more ambiguous
psychic level, the universe of the play conjures up the more pervasive
myth of Narcissus, as that myth reflects the impossibility of a desire
that would be anything other than autoerotic, self-contained, and deadly.
It is with this double myth operating in the play that we can begin to
understand the underlying ideological substructure that the unfolding
drama both upholds and questions.

The narcissistic foundation of *Andromaque* is both thematic and
rhetorical, the two levels reflecting and reinforcing each other, forming
a closed network inside of which the characters and their passion are
trapped. What seems to define the curious mating game in *Andromaque?*
Each of the three main amorous predators, Pyrrhus, Hermione, and
Oreste, desires above all to see him/herself reflected in the eyes of his/
her beloved. This desire is, like all narcissism, essentially totalitarian: it
is the desire for total subjection of the other to the self. The narcissistic
lover wants the absolute possession of the object of his desire: s/he to

have him/her for himself. The Racinian lover needs to enslave his lover/ other in order to protect his own (fragile) sense of self from fragmenting. In this sense we can see still one more tangible connection between the totalizing drive of Racine's protagonists with the dominant political drive of absolutism, which, as Louis Marin reminded us, is wholly entangled in its own narcissistic web and thus with the death drive in its striving for total control and possession.[18]

Each of Racine's protagonists wants to be loved and each, of course, chooses precisely the one person who cannot love (that is, see) him or her, whose gaze is always directed at another, the object of his/her own obsessive desire.

HERMIONE: Ah! Ne souhaitez pas le destin de Pyrrhus,
Je vous haïrais trop.

ORESTE: Vous m'en aimeriez plus
Ah! Que vous me verriez d'un regard bien contraire!
Vous me voulez aimer, et je ne puis vous plaire....

HERMIONE: Do not desire the destiny of Pyrrhus:
I'd hate you too much.

ORESTE: You'd love me more.
With what a different eye you'd look on me!
You wish to love me and I cannot please you....
(2.2.538–41)

PYRRHUS: Mais parmi ces périls, où je cours pour vous plaire,
Me refuserez-vous un regard moins sévère?

But mid these dangers, that I risk for you,
Will you refuse to look on me less coldly?
(1.4.289–90)

ORESTE: ...Un regard m'eût tout fait oublier.

One look would have thrown all aside.
(2.5.640)

PYRRHUS: Mais, Madame, du moins tournez vers moi les yeux.
Voyez si mes regards sont d'un Juge sévère....

But please, dear lady, let me see your eyes:
Just see if mine are those of a strict judge....
(3.7.952–53)

HERMIONE: Mais, Seigneur, s'il le faut, si le Ciel en colère
Réserve à d'autres yeux la gloire de vous plaire,
Achevez votre hymen, j'y consens. Mais du moins

> Ne forcez pas mes yeux d'en être les témoins.
> Pour la dernière fois je vous parle peut-être,
> Vous ne répondez point
> . . . .
> Ton coeur impatient de revoir sa Troyenne,
> Ne souffre qu'à regret qu'un autre t'entretienne,
> Tu lui parles du coeur, tu la cherches des yeux.
>
> But if you must, my lord, if Heaven in anger
> Has given other eyes magnetic power,
> Well marry her, I say, but then at least
> Do not compel my eyes to witness it.
> For the last time perhaps I speak to you;
> . . . .
> Impatient to return to your loved Trojan
> You cannot bear another's company.
> For her your heart cries out, your eyes seek her.
> (4.5.1369–379)

Each of the lovers seeks the eyes of his beloved to confirm his own passion, in effect, his very existence. Without seeing themselves reflected
in the eyes of the love object, they are effectively thrown out of the
world. Denied the firm grounding in their lover's eyes, they drift aimlessly ("j'ai couru partout" [I ran everywhere]) in a world that appears
fragmented and offers no safe harbor. Without the reciprocity in the
eyes of the other, they are reduced to emptiness, to isolation, and therefore to their exclusion from any viable human community. In their frustrated rage they become political outcasts, "a-polis": "Je renonce à la
Grèce, à Sparte, à son Empire, / À toute ma famille" (I renounce Greece,
Sparta, its Empire / My entire family), Hermione cries after learning
that her homicidal plan has been successful. Cut off from any familial/
political community, death is the only harbor left her.

In a simple sense, each of these unrequited passions is narcissistic in
its essence. Each "loves" the (impossible) other in order to find in that
other something that soothes a wound, a loss, in his soul. Hermione
loves Pyrrhus because of his "glorious deeds." His glory, reflected on
her, would at last make her the equal to her mother, Hélène, whose
beauty sent two nations to war ("Ma Mère en sa faveur arma la Grèce
entière" [My mother armed all of Greece for her sake]). Pyrrhus, we can
assume, is enthralled by Andromaque in order to expiate precisely
these same heroic feats that feed Hermione's erotic attachment to him

("Madame, je sais trop, à quel excès de rage / L'ardeur de vous venger emporta mon courage. / Je puis me plaindre à vous du sang que j'ai versé [I know too well to what excessive rage / Revenge for Helen's sake seduced my heart. / To you I may make grievance of the blood I've had to shed]). In his beautiful, if painfully hyperbolic, outburst, Pyrrhus expresses the intense intermingling of desire and guilt:

> Mais que vos yeux sur moi se sont bien exercés!
> Qu'ils m'ont vendu bien cher les pleurs qu'ils ont versés!
> Je souffre tous les maux que j'ai faits devant Troie.
> Vaincu, chargé de fers, de regrets consumé,
> Brûlé de plus de feux que je n'en allumai,
> Tant de soins, tant de pleurs, tant d'ardeurs inquiètes.…
> Hélas! fus-je jamais si cruel que vous l'êtes?
>
> But how your eyes have taken toll of me!
> How dear they've sold to me the tears they've shed!
> Of what remorse have they not made me toy!
> I suffer all the pains I caused to Troy.
> Vanquished and fettered, penitent I sit
> Seared by a greater flame than e'er I lit,
> My restless tears and all my passion true.…
> Ah! was I ever so unkind as you?
> (1.4.315–22)

In an obvious sense his passion, inflamed by Andromaque's indifference, constantly oscillates between the poles of sadistic cruelty and masochistic self-castigation.

Finally, of course, Oreste needs Hermione, "la furie," "l'inhumaine," her sadistic gaze, precisely to assuage his (never mentioned) matricidal guilt, to put him in the place of the victim he had come to immolate: "Ainsi donc il ne me reste rien, / Qu'à venir prendre ici la place du Troyen" (Thus the only thing left for me / Is to take the place of the Trojan). Oreste needs Hermione to punish him either by loving or by rejecting him. Either way he dwells in that punishment with masochistic relish.

The suffocating world of *Andromaque* is very much of a Sartrean *huis clos avant la lettre*. Each of the protagonists needs the narcissistic satisfaction of seeing his/her desire reflected in the only eyes that can save him/her but that, clearly, are always looking elsewhere. What they need most is what they never get. The eyes of the lover are always turned toward another. Andromaque can only look inward in her attempt to

recapture her past, to see Hector and Troy, or away, to the obscene loca-
tion where Pyrrhus holds her son captive. It is precisely the impossibility of being loved by the only person they desire that underlines the frus-
tratingly narcissistic quality of that desire and that makes it so deadly.[19]
Looking for love in all the wrong places leaves each of the protagonists
desperate, bereft, and lethal.

The narcissistic quality of each of the protagonists' doomed love is
supported and relayed by an elaborate lexical network of visual references.
Almost all contemporary scholars writing on Racine have called our attention to the importance of the eyes in his claustrophobic universe.
Roland Barthes has gone so far as to claim for Racine "un fétichisme
des yeux" (a fetishism of the eyes).[20] In a theatrical universe from which
any "Kreaturlichkeit" reference to the body, to bodily functions, has
been banned from the lexicon, the eyes remain in Racine's theater an
overdetermined reference point responsible for expressing an almost
limitless variety of emotions and actions. It is as if from this most ambivalent of bodily references (see Starobinski) that an entire semantic
universe of seeing and being seen, a world of visions, dreams, and illusions, and by metonymical displacement, of tears, weaves a dense textual
network where desire is trapped in its own illusory misprision and where,
once again, the intimate connection between death and Narcissus is
confirmed as the underlying structure of Racinian tragedy.

One might describe the Racinian universe as being a world of "omni-
voyance," where one is always both looking and caught in an ever-
present external gaze. Christine Buci-Glucksmann has described this
omni-voyance as one of the salient features of a baroque universe where
any unilateral truth, any single linguistic interpretation is made impossible because of constant, unstoppable diffraction. Precisely since this
vision/"schaulust" is in essence (like the eye) always open to ambivalent interpretations, it effectively undoes any univocal meaning, political or sexual, that the text would purport to establish. This generalized
appetitive look effectively demonstrates, according to Buci-Glucksmann,
the surreptitious working of the death drive and thus would appear to
function, in the case of Racinian tragedy, as the key to the unconscious
textual network that connects character to plot, melancholia to narcissism, leading inevitably to the tragic finale.[21] In other words, the "mis-
visions" in *Andromaque*, which in the narrative of the play are instantly
translated into all the constant turning of the character's rhetoric into

its opposite—for example, the constant shifting of Pyrrhus as he refuses then assents to hand over Astyanax, and the concurrent shifts in
Andromaque's despair and Hermione's joy—are shattering because they
are created by and create a constant diffraction of desire that has a profound and lethal effect on each of the characters' sense of themselves,
their identity not only as Greek and Trojan but as objects of desire or
nothing.

If *Andromaque* marks, according to Mauron, the "beginning of the
real Racine," because it is in this play that the "Trojan War is transformed into a familial drama, where the conflict becomes internalized,"
then it is also where the metaphors of vision, spectacle, and hallucinations (dreams) become the dominant lexical network in the Racinian
universe.[22] Almost every momentous dramatic passage in the play is
attached to a vision, and as we know, following Jacqueline Rose and
Buci-Glucksmann, "visions are seldom what they seem": they are a lure
for the spectating subject, trapping him/her in the contradictions of
his/her own desire.

Abruptly, cutting short his political conversation with his confidant
Phoenix, a conversation about the potential risks he and his state face
by his refusal to hand over Astyanax to the Greeks, Pyrrhus is struck by
the sight of Andromaque entering his (and our) field of vision: it is a sight
that renders political discourse mute and turns the king into a speechless lover captured by a image. Andromaque enters the stage as a vision,
an apparition: "Une autre fois je t'ouvrirai mon Âme, / Andromaque
paraît" (Another time I'll tell you all / Andromache's here). For Pyrrhus,
Andromaque exists in a strangely ambivalent relation to the real: she is
a vision, inextricably tied to the past that is both a nightmare of blood
and lust and to the future of his own projection that would efface history
by reconstituting it and him no longer as an enemy but as a husband/
father. The problem with this vision is that it is constantly shattered by
present reality, by Andromaque's stubborn resistance to him and to any
compromise. Her fidelity remains fixated on her own vision of the past
because it is there that she can retain a semblance of unalienated identity.[23] Both she and even more so the Greeks refuse to inhabit Pyrrhus's
dream of a new world.

When Pyrrhus's vision is invaded by reality—when, for instance,
Andromaque constantly parries his attempt to blackmail her into submission to his vision of their future—the intensity of his passion turns

(as to be expected) from amorous cajoling to overt aggression, expressed
again in visual terms:

> J'abandonne son Fils. Que de pleurs vont couler!
> De quel nom sa douleur me va-t-elle appeler?
> Quel spectacle pour elle aujourd'hui se dispose!
> Elle en mourra, Phoenix, et j'en serai la cause.
> C'est lui mettre moi-même un poignard dans le sein.
>
> I'll yield her son. How many tears will rain!
> What dire name will she call me in her pain!
> What dreadful scenes—to see him in death's jaws!
> Phoenix, she'll die, and I shall be the cause.
> I should myself be butchering her heart.
>   (2.5.695–99)

In other words, when frustrated, Pyrrhus's fantasy of the future repeats
the trauma of the past, his rage returns to his bloody deeds in Troy
("De votre propre main Polyxène égorgée" [By your own hand Polyxena
butchered]), folding the one into the other, thus confirming what Derrida has so acutely defined as the apophetic quality of traumatic events:
that they are always proleptic, that they occur in the future.

> The trauma remains traumatizing and incurable because it comes from
> the future.... Trauma takes place when one is wounded by a wound
> that has not yet taken place, in an effective fashion, in a way other
> than by the sign of its announcement.[24]

Whether he intends it or not, Pyrrhus enfolds Andromaque in a visual
sphere where she is constantly the object of a passion he cannot satisfy
and a rage he cannot extirpate ("il était violent de son naturel" [He was
violent by nature]). His is a vision that despite its erotic drive, or perhaps
because of it, can only enclose Andromaque in her own nightmare, reinforcing its hold on her and further alienating her from him.

Pyrrhus is undone by his vision. Although he might be the most
radically free character in all of Racine's theater, as Barthes claims (and
certainly in this drama he is the one character who articulates most
forcefully the desire for change, a veritable revolution in the orchestration of the prevailing sexual/political dynamics that preside over the
universe of the play), it is nevertheless precisely this desire, that is, his
lust for Andromaque, informed entirely by what we might call the psychic
play of vision and illusion, that drives him blindly forward and destroys

him.[25] His passion blinds him to anything other than the object of his desire: "il ne voit rien" (he sees nothing), Cléone answers Hermione, describing Pyrrhus as he walks to the wedding altar. Entirely focusing his vision on Andromaque and on his fantasmatic possession of her ("Et d'un oeil qui déjà dévorait son espoir, / S'enivrer, en marchant, du plasir de la voir" [With eyes all sparkling, full of joy and hope, / Intoxicated with her sight he strode]), he fails to see the danger that surrounds him. If Pyrrhus's desire impels the most radical attempts to undo an entire political system, to betray the reigning order of the band of Greek brothers, to turn against the fealty that the patriarchal exchange of women (Hermione) implicitly reaffirms, at the same time, this amorous capture, the rapture of his fantasized possession of Andromaque, emasculates him: he loses, precisely, the rational, tactical skills that have made him a successful warrior, the true son of his father. Lost in his vision, propelled by desire, he becomes oblivious to the (murderous) reality of his surroundings, to the anger of the Greeks massing about him as he makes his way to the altar. Rather than the erotic pleasure of Andromaque's possession, Pryrrhus, lost to his fantasy vision, falls victim to the outrage of the Greeks, thus offering us the tragic proof that if love is blind, this blindness is also deadly.

Of course, Hermione, whom we might define as the active incarnation of death in this play (as opposed to passive Andromaque)—she who pushed the Greeks to reclaim and immolate Astyanax, who wants to do away with Andromaque ("J'ai déjà sur le Fils attiré leur colère. / Je veux qu'on vienne encore lui demander la Mère" [So far I've urged them but the son pursue; / I'll make them now demand the mother too]), who sets Oreste up to kill Pyrrhus, and who eventually undoes Oreste himself—is most appropriately defined by the mortiferous power of her eyes. They inflict wounds: "Je sais que vos regards vont rouvrir mes blessures" (I know your eyes will open all my wounds), Oreste tells her during their first meeting. With all the ambivalence inherent in his gallant rhetoric, Oreste describes her seductive eyes as potent weapons:

ORESTE: Ouvrez les yeux. Songez qu'Oreste est devant vous,
         Oreste si longtemps l'objet de leur courroux.
HERMIONE: Oui, c'est vous dont l'amour naissant avec leurs charmes,
         Leur apprit le premier le pouvoir de leurs armes.

ORESTE: Open your eyes: Oreste stand before you,
         Oreste, so long object of their scorn.

HERMIONE: Yes, you whose love, engendered by their spell,
          First taught them the full meaning of their power.
          (2.2.531–34)

Hermione's eyes both attract and repel:

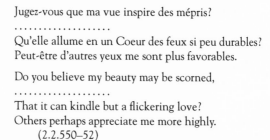

> Jugez-vous que ma vue inspire des mépris?
> ....
> Qu'elle allume en un Coeur des feux si peu durables?
> Peut-être d'autres yeux me sont plus favorables.

> Do you believe my beauty may be scorned,
> ....
> That it can kindle but a flickering love?
> Others perhaps appreciate me more highly.
>   (2.2.550–52)

Underlining her association to the Erinyes, which is established from the very outset of the drama where Hermione, once again enfolded in Racine's gallant rhetoric, is described as "la Furie," prefiguring Oreste's hallucinatory vision of her at the tragedy's close, we should recall that one of the outstanding mythological attributes of the Furies is their eyes that shed tears of blood. Hermione's eyes foreshadow the destruction of all those upon whom her jealous gaze falls. She seems incapable of a tender glance but feeds off the sight of her victims' torment:

> A... Où fuyez-vous, Madame?
> N'est-ce point à vos yeux, un spectacle assez doux
> Que la Veuve d'Hector pleurante à vos genoux?

> ... Where are you fleeing,
> My lady, How you must be gratified,
> With Hector's widow weeping at your feet!
>   (3.4.858–61)

Andromaque seems powerless to parry Hermione's imperious gaze even though she is told that her own eyes have the power, should she focus them on Pyrrhus, to undo those who conspire against her: "Un regard confondrait Hermione et la Grèce" (One look would undo Hermione and Greece). Her vision, however, is always turned inward, where she sees violence, destruction, and death. Pyrrhus uses his vision of Andromaque with its concomitant projection into the future to create a new world freed from the past, while Andromaque, on the contrary, seems locked into that past by the constantly recurring image of the destruction of Troy. Andromaque is haunted by a memory/vision to which she clings and that she projects out into the world as a nightmare. The passage from her own internal trauma to its projection on stage passes through the hallucinatory invocation of the play's primal scene, a scene summoned into representation by the incantatory repetition "Songe, songe Céphise" that carries us into the realm of Andromaque's recurring traumatic vision:

> Songe, songe, Céphise, à cette Nuit cruelle,
> Qui fut pour tout un Peuple une Nuit éternelle,
> Figure-toi Pyrrhus les yeux étincelants,
> Entrant à la lueur de nos Palais brulants:
> Sur tous mes Frères morts se faisant un passage,
> Et de sang tout couvert échauffant le carnage.
> Songe aux cris des Vainqueurs, songe aux cris des Mourants,
> Dans la flamme étouffés, sous le fer expirants.
> Peins-toi dans ces horreurs Andromaque éperdue.
> Voilà comme Pyrrhus vint s'offrir à ma vue....

> Recall, recall, Cephise, that cruel night,
> Which doomed a nation to eternal night.
> Imagine Pyrrhus, with his glittering eyes,
> Entering in the glare of our blazing mansions,
> Kicking aside my brothers' mangled corpses,
> And slaked in blood inciting to fresh slaughter.
> Do you hear the victor's shouts, the wounded's groans,
> Choked by the flames or dying by the sword?
> Do you see Andromache distraught with horror?
> Such is the way I first set eyes on Pyrrhus....
>   (4.3.997–1006)

The evocation of the destruction of Troy, of Pyrrhus's savagery, and of Andromaque's loss is one of the most powerful examples of Racinian hypotyposis (*songe, figure-toi, peins-toi*), and it is made even more suggestive by the seductive sensuality of Racine's verse. The mesmerizing incantation draws the audience not only into the tragic world of Andromaque's trauma but even further down into a more primitive chaos where desire and destruction, love and annihilation are shown to be one and the same.[26]

What we have, therefore, is a roundelay of unrequited love, of the impossibility of love that, narcissistic in its very drive, is relayed both thematically and lexically by an entire network of a crosscutting visual interplay. The passionate and deadly dynamics of this, Racine's first mature tragedy, is conveyed through the web of visual images that creates both the reflecting and deflecting relation of all the characters to each other. Trapped as they are in a world that never sends them back the vision of their passion, or only returns it warped and distorted, the characters are ensnared in an exacerbation of desire, fueled by the false vision of the hated other(s). This exacerbation of desire/hatred becomes focused first on Astyanax and then on Pyrrhus. How this focus gets blurred, how the sacrificial victim of the play slips from the son to the father, is perhaps the crux of Racinian drama, and in *Andromaque* the function of the ensuing tragic sacrifice both attacks the ideological underpinnings of the monarchal state and reaffirms them, too.

In a rather perverse gesture Racine succeeds in focusing the attention of all the protagonists in his play, and that of his audience as well, on the one character who is never there, Astyanax. From the very start of the play Astyanax is presented as the tantalizing object of universal desire: Andromaque needs him as a surrogate for an entire world lost to death; for Pyrrhus he is the lynchpin in his lustful blackmail of Andromaque; for Oreste he is the ostensible object of his embassy that allows him to ply, once again, his troth to Hermione; finally, Hermione needs to use him as a pawn in her attempt to get rid of Andromaque and win back Pyrrhus. On the public political stage, Astyanax is, for the Greeks, Hector (the other absent object of the play), that is, Troy *redivivus*, and thus a strangely ambivalent object of attraction/repulsion, an object of fear, guilt, and fascination that must be eliminated for them to feel at last secure. Finally, for the Trojans, or for what remains of them, he is, as Andromaque constantly reminds us, the incarnation of all they have lost: their history, their past glory, their future king.

> Si tu vivais pour moi, vis pour le Fils d'Hector.
> De l'espoir des Troyens seule dépositaire
> Songe, à combien de Rois tu deviens nécessaire.
>
> If you once lived for me, live now for him.
> Sole guardian of the final hope of Troy,
> Think, how so many monarchs need your aid.
>   (4.1.1104–6)

Around this overdetermined void swirls the passionate universe of the play, and as it does, a rather dramatic metamorphosis takes place. How are we to understand the move from the projected immolation of Astyanax that dominates the entire drama to the actual assassination of Pyrrhus, the move from infanticide to regicide? To begin to answer this question we would do well to look first at the complex identifications Racine establishes between all the male characters and then to inquire how these identifications are inscribed in an overarching system that ensures the perpetuation of the patriarchal political structure that the play puts into question.

On a first and very simple level, Racine adopts from the very start of the dramatic action a neo-Greek affectation of using paternal epithets to identify his male characters. In their initial conversation, Oreste expresses his pride and honor at meeting Pyrrhus, whom he apostrophizes as "le Fils d'Achille, et le Vainqueur de Troie" (the son of Achille and the conqueror of Troy). In his response, Pyrrhus in turn refers to him and to his illustrious lineage by circumlocution: "Qui croirait en effet, qu'une telle enterprise / Du fils d'Agamemnon méritât l'entremise" (Who would have imagined that such a task would have needed the intervention of the son of Agamemnon?). Finally, and still in this very first interview, in order to underscore the danger that Astyanax represents for the Greeks, after the description of the pain Hector had inflicted on them that remains vivid in their collective memory, he, too, refers to Astyanax as "le seul Fils d'Hector" (Hector's only son):

> Seigneur, vous savez trop, avec quel artifice
> Un faux Astyanax fut offert au Supplice
> Où le seul Fils d'Hector devait être conduit.
> Ce n'est pas les Troyens, c'est Hector qu'on poursuit.
> Oui, les Grecs sur le Fils persécutent le Père.

> My lord, your know full well how cunningly
> A false Asytanax went to the death
> That was reserved for Hector's son alone.
> It is not Troy but Hector who is hunted.
> Upon the son, the Greeks pursue the sire.
>   (1.2.221–25)

The use of "son of" establishes (in a society lacking in patronyms) a filiation that inscribes the young male in a lineage, a genealogy, that allows both an individual and a collective identity.[27] At the same time, the individual identity becomes inseparable from and in a sense folded into a structure that constantly reminds the son of a debt to the father.

The father continues to inhabit the son who can become independent precisely because the father is no longer present; he is dead. This death, therefore, allows the son to live, but it is an ambivalent gift: confounding the son with both a sense of freedom and of guilt, his autonomy is won only by the disappearance of the father, a disappearance that has been both ardently desired (during the Oedipal crisis) but has also been, because of the affection felt by the son, just as passionately denied. It is this exacerbation of the ambivalence, love and guilt, that will always seek its appeasement in its projection outward onto an other who in his person will be required to pay the debt that the son cannot. It is through the sacrifice of this other that the son hopes to cancel his debt and comfort his guilt, only, of course, to have both return aggrandized in a cycle of debt and retribution.[28] When this individual debt becomes, as it does in *Andromaque*, a societal one, there is the interesting and mortiferous collusion of the private with the public where the one relays and represents the other, where the private passions of the individual are brought forth in the public arena, where they reflect the underlying societal tensions that the bicephalous figure of the father/son represent for the society at large.[29]

Racine first establishes a contiguous (metonymic) relation between fathers and sons and then clearly states that the father is punished through the sacrifice of the son: contiguity drifts into amalgamation; the relation father/son takes on a fusional quality where the father is the son and vice versa. In *Andromaque*, however, Racine complicates this genealogical scenario even further. Not only is there a confusion between the generations (fathers and sons), but there is an uncanny merger of all the male protagonists: Pyrrhus becomes the "father" of Astyanax ("Je voue à votre Fils une amitié de Père" [I pledge your son a paternal affection]); Oreste starts out by claiming Astyanax as the intended victim of the Greeks who through his immolation hope to avenge their fear of the father (Hector)—"Oui, les Grecs sur le Fils persécutent le Père" (Yes, the Greeks on persecuting the Father in the Son)—but then claims that he, not Astyanax, is the sacrificial object, taking the place of Astynax: "Ainsi donc il ne me reste rien / Qu'à venir prendre ici la place du troyen" (Thus, the only thing left for me / Is to come and take the place of the Trojan). Yet his actual victim will be Pyrrhus, who, usurping the sacrificial place of Astyanax, becomes, in a sense, Astyanax: "Laissez-moi vers l'Autel conduire ma Victime" (Let me lead my victim to the altar), Oreste tells Hermione, referring to Pyrrhus. The victim, who at first was the child, is now the king (Pyrrhus).

Finally (but the slippage cannot be stopped) and perhaps even more perversely, we have the strangely erotic confusion that Andromaque adds to this already complex indifferentiation. First, she tells us that the son is the father: "C'est Hector... voilà ses yeux, sa bouche, et déjà son audace / C'est lui-même, c'est toi, cher Époux, que j'embrasse." ("He's Hector," she would say embracing him; / "I see his eyes, his mouth, his budding courage; / Ah! It is you, dear, husband, I embrace.") Then we are told that Astyanax replaces both her husband and her father: "Il m'aurait tenu lieu d'un Père, et d'un Époux" (He would have replaced both a Father and a Husband). As Astyanax drifts between these various roles, we have a final metamorphosis of the male: Pyrrhus, having assumed the role of father ("Je vous rends votre Fils et je lui sers de Père" [I give your son back to you and I will be his Father]), now becomes Hector: "Pyrrhus de mon Hector semble avoir pris la place" (Pyrrhus seems to have taken my Hector's place). Of course, having taken the place of Hector, Pyrrhus's final transformation, his bloody death at the altar ("Tout sanglant... à l'Autel il est allé tomber" [All bloodied... he fell at the foot of the Altar]), closes the play by associating one more metonymic displacement: Pyrrhus, as he is killed, is recast in the image of the original dead Father, Priam ("Dois-je oublier son Père à mes pieds renversé / Ensanglant l'Autel qu'il tenait embrassé?" [Should I forget his Father fallen at my feet / Bloodying the Altar he embraced?]). What reverberates throughout the play is, therefore, the original crime—the slaying of the father—that the play tells us can never be redressed: it can only be repeated, ad infinitum, as every new generation of men attempts a change that would radically alter this immolation of men on the altar, the site of the sacred, that joins all the men together in their last avatar, their final sacrifice to the god/father for whom the only adequate repayment of their debt to him is death.

What are we to make of the amalgamation in *Andromaque* of all the male protagonists who, while they retain their individual identity on the level of dramatic diegesis, on a more profound level are reduced to an essential masculine being, at once son, husband, and father (the Holy Trinity of classicism?), a reduction that confuses both the separation of generations and of, if not the sexes, at least sexuality, as it is intimately connected to the separation of the generations? On the surface at least, this play owes more to the tradition of the Oresteia, whose mythological genealogy would seem to be allied much more closely with the tragic destiny of the Atreides, which now seems to be invaded not by the direct Oedipus myth itself but by the very confusion that the Oedipus complex seems destined to sort out. How has Racine configured his play to make this confusion appear irresolvable? And what does this confusion tell us about the central dramatic tension in the play, the sacrifice of the child/father?

It should come as no surprise that the Oedipal dilemma, reduced to its most essential dynamics—murder (aggression against the father) and incest—is never very far from the Racinian scenario. While the former seems to be quite apparent, the latter is perhaps, at first glance, not as obvious. When we focus more closely at Andromaque's mortiferous desire, however, with her adamant refusal to look away from the past, her rejection of any compromise with the present, her rejection of any connection with the world other than her relation to her son, with whom, if left to her own devices, she would live alone on some deserted island, separated from the world in a self-sufficient autarchy, this strikes us as a dangerously incestuous desire:

> . . . C'est un Exil que mes pleurs vous demandent.
> Souffrez que loin des Grecs, et même loin de vous
> J'aille cacher mon Fils, et pleurer mon Époux.

> My tears ask only you should exile me.
> Permit me far from Greece, far even from you,
> To hide my son and to lament my husband.
> (1.4.338–40)

> Laissez-moi le cacher en quelque Île déserte.
> Sur les soins de sa Mère on peut s'en assurer,
> Et mon Fils avec moi n'apprendra qu'à pleurer.

> Let me conceal him on some desert isle.
> His mother's lessons spell tranquility
> And he will only learn to weep with me.
> (3.4.878–80)

Andromaque's obstinate stance refuses any being in the world.[30] Throughout the play, Andromaque vacillates between two options: either she accepts Astyanax's surrender to and murder by the Greeks, or she keeps him with her on some deserted island, bound to her grief, reduced to a life of lamentation. In either case the result is lethal. As loving a mother as Andromaque may seem, she, too, in her lachrymose way is another incarnation of the Sphinx that embodies the primitive phallic mother whose presence presided and occulted at the entrance to Racine's tragic world. Andromaque and Hermione are not as different as at first it would appear. To Hermione's active, libidinally infused homicidal rage responds Andromaque's passive but equally deadly stasis. The Sphinx, as we know, preys on those young men who cross her path. She uses adolescent males for her sexual pleasure before destroying them. Thus, the dangerous pull, the incestuous pull ("c'est toi, cher Époux, que j'embrasse" [It's you, dear husband, I kiss]) of Andromaque's retentive love for her son. This retentiveness, perhaps Andromaque's only response to a situation of utter loss, must nevertheless be resisted if there is to be "a future for Astyanax."[31] The question that looms in the background of Racine's melancholic play becomes, therefore, who is more dangerous for the future represented by the child: the Greeks who would slaughter him or his mother who would love him?

Roland Barthes, perhaps first and most cynically, has tried to topple Andromaque from her throne as the *mater dolorosa* of classical theater. "Andromaque," he says, "n'est pas une mère, mais une amante" (Andromache . . . is not a mother but a lover). Reducing her maternity to being merely an attempt to hold on to Hector, to see and to have Hector reincarnated in her son, Barthes reads Andromaque as less of a tragic figure. It is because she is both mother and lover, because she is incapable of distinguishing her son from her husband, that Andromaque is a tragic heroine, in the maternal sense, but this confusion of maternity and sexuality—that is, her obsessive attachment to her dead husband—also makes of her an intriguing presence in the underlying political scenario that the tragedy *Andromaque* performs for us.

Andromaque loves Astyanax because, as an "image" of Hector ("Quoi? Céphise, j'irai voir expirer encore / Ce fils, ma seule joie, et l'image d'Hector"), he can be said to represent Hector to Andromaque; he stands in for the missing husband/lover. As Hector's image not only does he stand in for Hector; he also represents the sign of her subservience to her husband. In the world of patriarchy, the universe of the father, the image of the child/father signals the reproduction of male prerogative: it is the male who, according to the reproductive logic of the ancient Greeks, imposes form on shapeless matter (the maternal contribution), bringing order out of chaos. Astyanax represents what Andromaque desires and what is denied to her (by reality, but also more pervasively by law). In a sense we might say that Astyanax as son/husband is Andromaque's fetish. He signals Andromaque's lack as a woman (in patriarchy) and also her denial of this lack, her refusal to leave the lost object, to leave her desire, and to be placed once again in circulation, that is, into the circuit of another's desire (Pyrrhus). It is because Astyanax exists and constantly reflects Andromaque's desire to her that she is so utterly fused to him. This maternal fusion proves to be frustrating for Pyrrhus, potentially lethal for Astyanax, and more generally speaking inimical for any attempt at radical political change and progression in the stymied universe of the play.

The narrative arc of the drama starts with the threat of immolation that hangs like the sword of Damocles over the head of Astyanax and ends with the assassination of Pyrrhus at the hands of Oreste's Greek retinue. Pyrrhus is killed at the foot of the altar that he had ordered prepared to serve either for the celebration of his marriage to Andromaque or, in the case of her refusal, the immolation of Astyanax:

> Songez-y, je vous laisse, et je viendrai vous prendre,
> Pour vous mener au Temple, où ce Fils doit m'attendre.
> Et là vous me verrez soumis, ou furieux
> Vous couronner, Madame, ou le perdre à vos yeux.
>
> Think well: I leave you. I will come to take you,
> To lead you to the temple, with your son:
> And there you'll see me, with no further sighs,
> Crown you, or slaughter him before your eyes.
>   (3.7.973–76)

Those who study the history of the theater tell us that one of the innovations Racine brings to classical tragedy is the presence of a child on stage. In his last tragedy, *Athalie*, Racine makes real what was only a virtual possibility in *Andromaque*. Joas, the hidden young king of the Israelites, is an integral character in *Athalie* while Astyanax remains off stage, referred to but never seen. Nevertheless, what is striking in Racine's use of the child in his drama is not so much the fact that he is the first to bring that child out onto the stage but that the child is brought out to be sacrificed. It is this haunting problematic of the child that must be killed that is at the center of Racine's tragic production.

In her study of the Oedipus legend, Marie Delcourt reminds us that for the Greeks, infanticide was the least significant of familial crimes; only parricide was unforgivable.[32] By the time we come to the seventeenth century, parricide embraced in its meaning the killing of not only the father but, by extension, any close relative, mother, son or daughter, or person of high rank. Almost two hundred years of European political theorists had established a metaphorical chain that declined the figure of the patriarch from God the Father to the king, father of his people, to the father, head of each individual household. The metonymic displacement of the signifiers of paternity assured a self-enclosed network of patriarchal governance. Any attack on the father, therefore, was at one and the same time an assault on the king and a violence toward God (and vice versa). The role of the father was sacred and any parricide (which by association was assimilated to regicide) was an attack on the very order and stability of the state. For our purposes, what is important to remember is that the role of the father is a symbolic one and that the above-mentioned fathers (God, king, father) are merely placeholders for a transcendent symbolic function that institutes the laws governing the social/political/sexual distribution of roles in any given society. It is from the sexualized imposition of "masculinity" on this abstract function, however, that we can detect the functioning of an ideology of power that, not only in the Greek world that Racine reinvents for his tragedy but also for the world of his seventeenth-century audience and for ours as well, continues to hold sway over its public and to dictate the parameters separating chaos from order, nature from culture, and masculine from feminine. It is for this reason that the role of the father (either in his absence or his presence) is so essential to the political mythology of Racinian tragedy as it maps out for us the limits, the taboos, so to speak, that cannot be transgressed—either by males or females—without tragic consequences for the society at large.

When Oreste claims as representative of the Greeks that Astyanax, adult, will be the avenger of his father/Troy, what he is expressing, one might argue, under this fantasy of political revenge, is simply the Oedipal fear of (all) fathers of being displaced (castrated) by the son. He is expressing through the rhetoric of politics the anxiety of masculinity that this rhetoric and this politics has metabolized and elided: the unspoken fear of the inevitable decline of the father who will be overtaken and replaced/displaced by the son. By so doing he articulates, precisely, the impossible imbrication of politics and eroticism, that is, the underlying sexual attraction/fear that becomes part and parcel of a patriarchal ordering of the world. This fear is focused most acutely on the two social groups that present the greatest threat to patriarchal order: children (in this case, Astyanax) and women.

Without wishing to be too reductive of the enormous complexity of Racinian tragedy or to ignore the equally intricate involution of Racine's personal history in the social problems of his period, I think that we can, for hypothetical reasons, reduce the conflict of Racinian tragedy to a battle for integrity in a subject whose very existence is not integral, that is, not one but two. At the same time, and by the same token, this duality, a duplicity that must be removed, repressed, or extirpated, which forms the impediment propelling tragic action and informing the very being of the tragic hero, is at the heart of myth as it constantly attempts to replay and to refashion the journey of the subject away from forces of duality and contradiction toward an attempted (but always unsuccessful) compromise with societal laws.

It is perhaps here that Racinian tragedy as a form of representation is most intimately reflective of its sociological context, of the context not so much of French society of the seventeenth century as of an absolutist ideology that refuses heterogeneity and strives for (reflecting its inherently narcissistic drive) the order of the One, whose most iconic representative is the glorious (entirely self-enclosed) body of the sun/king. At the opposite, negative end of the absolutist spectrum are all those heterogeneous, monstrous bodies, effluent bodies, and female bodies that would seem to collect all the political anxieties of unbounded states open to invasion on themselves. From the most remote antiquity, and in physical and metaphysical traditions that the seventeenth century inherited from the ancients and in its own way perpetuated, the female has been equated with matter, uncontrollable sexual desire, profligacy, and sin. In order for society to function, this "weaker vessel" must be contained by the masculine, just as the masculine must exert enormous energy to repress, to extirpate, and to deny the presence in itself of what it most fears—the feminine.

If women, therefore, are always the object of male fantasy and fear, so too children—the very symbol of duality (one born from two), of a hybridity that can take on the metaphorization of the monstrous, as we see in Racine (Néron, Phèdre), monstrous first and foremost because of their heterogeneous lineage—are the most troubling of social beings. As long as they remain on the near side of the Oedipal crisis, as long as they remain recalcitrant to the law of castration and death that makes of them socially acceptable masculine or feminine subjects, subjects having renounced their dichotomy and taken their places under the law of the father, they remain a continuous threat to the father and to the society that lives under his law.

In this patriarchal call to order, the weak links in the construction of the patriarchal chain are precisely those intractable subjects, the women and the children, who are the most suspect because they are never entirely subjected to the father. And therefore we can see this fear as the underlying dialectic that presides over the entire Racinian corpus—its *corpus politicum*, so to speak—the never-ending mistrust on the part of the father or his representative that can often lead to the violent elimination of these recalcitrant others. On the other hand, we must also be aware of the desire on the part of these monstrous beings to kill the father, a desire that is tempered at the same time by the fear/love/need for the father that fixes the uneasy stability of the polis. We should not forget that before Oedipus killed his father, Laius, Laius first attempted to eliminate him. We seem, therefore, to be presented, in Racine, with a primitive, unconscious dialectic in which the ambivalence of the relation father/son plays the central role, both in the private sexual dynamics that are at work in his plays but also on the public political stage where this same dynamic introduces the underlying ideology of absolutism that it both espouses and endangers at the same time.[33]

Anchoring his explorations in the fundamental discoveries of Freud in both the clinical and metapsychological works, the French psychoanalyst Guy Rosolato has attempted to examine the irreducible importance of the role of child sacrifice in all three of the major Western monotheisms. Starting with the ancient Hebrews, the (interrupted) sacrifice of his Isaac by Abraham seals the alliance between God and his chosen people. In Christianity, this immolation is carried out in the putting to death of God himself, in the person of the son, and redeemed in the myth of resurrection. Islam, too, resorts to the ritual sacrifice of the son (Ali) to mark a major moment in the foundation of one of its most important sects.[34] While in Greek mythology infanticide appeared to be, as we have seen, the least important of all familial crimes, with the advent of the major monotheisms—all religions of the father—infanticide becomes the central most heavily invested act, the incomprehensible, originary act of that religion's mediating relation between God and the world.[35]

In patriarchal societies, such as those in which monotheism as a religion of the father was born and as it was being reaffirmed in seventeenth-century France, the unthinkable, the blind spot of ideology, is any direct attack on the father in any of his legal, theological, or merely familial avatars.[36] This does not mean that the intense, ambivalent feelings social organizations carry with them do not exist. Rather, the more intense the attachments, the more intense the love that is demanded, the more intense are the feelings of aggressivity and of guilt that must be repressed or sublimated into acceptable outlets. In a curiously paradoxical analysis Rosolato hypothesized that what is actually at stake in all the myths of child sacrifice so essential to the West is the actual murderous drives against—the attack on—the father.[37] In other words, underlying the scenario of child sacrifice is an equally forceful attack not only on the father but on patriarchy, because quite simply, without the child's recognition of the father as father, that role and function do not exist.

This psychoanalytic scenario attempts to explain, on the one hand, how fathers and children, within a hierarchically disposed system of male devolution, are locked into a struggle engaging our most powerful emotions and desires for power, for sovereignty. The son seeks to take the place of the father; the father tries to retain his preeminence by eliminating the son. This is exactly the fear expressed by the Greeks: Astyanax will become Hector; he will kill us all and destroy our world. Nevertheless, what we must also realize, and what this explicit scenario obfuscates, is the mutual imbrication of father and son, in social terms, in a power structure that is there to receive them and their ambivalence in such a way that this ambivalence is socially mediated so as to protect patriarchy against its own dissolution. Racine's theater, especially in its occultation of the conflict between the father and his children in the passion of the heroine, can be seen as one form of mediation where the constant reciprocity of violence and desire is played out for the spectators as a projection of their own potentially dangerous ambivalence toward the parental structure into which they come and which they must, through a sacrifice of their own inherent duality, reproduce.

It is only once we understand infanticide as merely a mirror reflection of patricide that we can begin to understand why the Greeks' desire to recover Astyanax, to immolate him, becomes the tragic center of *Andromaque* and how it aspirates the other elements of the plot into its vortex, remaining the most troubling of the identificatory potentials of Racinian dramaturgy.

For Barthes, too, this potentially muderous confict between father and son is the very crux of Racinian tragedy.[38] Despite his insistence on their alternation, Barthes nevertheless weighs in more heavily on the threat to the father. In this, perhaps, he is demonstrating his familiarity with seventeenth-century political discourse, which never failed to equate parricide with regicide. What Barthes does not mention is that for dramatic purposes we can oppose infanticide to parricide and vice versa but on a more archaic level, on the level of those unconscious drives that are part of the dominant ideology of absolutism, this opposition is interesting not for what it reveals but for what it conceals. On the level of the political unconscious of the Racinian universe, infanticide and parricide are inextricably coeval: a sacrifice of the child (infanticide) is also and at the same time an immolation of the father (parricide). When the play strikes out at the child it also threatens the entire universe of patriarchy, the foundation of which depends on the devolution of power from father to son, ad infinitum. So the real questions are (as Barthes hints): Can one ever get away from the father/law? Is revolution possible? And if so, does the revolution not simply lead back to the instauration of a new father, a new law? What would the difference be? And in *Andromaque*, where would the revolution come from?

Pyrrhus's own death at the altar mirrors, in an irony peculiar to Racine (and to which I have already alluded), his killing (both a parricide and a regicide) of Priam, the Trojan king. The horror of the slaughter of the Ur-Vater of Troy is recounted twice, curiously by the two female protagonists, once by Andromaque:

> Dois-je oublier son Père à mes pieds renversé,
> Ensanglantant l'Autel qu'il tenait embrassé?

> Forget his father cast down at my feet,
> His bleeding body clutching at the altar?
> (3.8.995–96)

and then by Hermione:

> Du vieux Père d'Hector la valeur abattue
> Aux pieds de sa Famille expirante à sa vue,
> Tandis que dans son sein votre bras enfoncé
> Cherche un reste de sang que l'âge avait glacé....
>
> Hector's old father with dejected heart
> Lamenting loud the death of all his sons,
> The while your savage arm deep in his breast
> Scoops out his feeble blood congealed by age?
> (4.5.1341–44)

I say "curiously" because of the differing erotic resonance this murder has for each of them. While for Andromaque this slaying of the father forever situates Pyrrhus in the realm of the taboo, the familial blood he has shed makes him repellent to her (although we must not forget the unconscious, unavowable attraction that this repulsion also reveals). It is this same brutality that most excites Hermione: "Sais-tu quel est Pyrrhus? T'es-tu fait raconter / Le nombre des Exploits" (Can you appraise his greatness? Have you heard / Tell all his exploits... Who can count them all?). Chief among these exploits is the final sack of Troy and the murder of the "vieux Père." We might say, therefore, that the dramatic tension of the play moves from infanticide to parricide with sexual desire (Pyrrhus for Andromaque, Hermione for Pyrrhus, and Oreste for Hermione) as the tragic knot through which the first sacrifice is metamorphosed into the second. It is the passion of the heroine, be she an active incarnation of the phallic mother (Hermione) or her passive-aggressive counterpart (Andromaque), that most adequately fixes this challenge to the father's rule as it is both threatened (in the son) and accomplished (in the king) and that nevertheless leaves the polis in the throes of chaos and madness that only another sacrifice can hope to appease.

3

Britannicus:
Power, Perversion, and Paranoia

The whirlwind of madness that envelops Oreste in the final scene of *Andromaque* is the last depiction of insanity on the classical stage. Oreste's hallucinations, his visions of Pyrrhus, Hermione, and the bloodthirsty Furies pursuing him, are met with his thrashing attempts to ward them off. Pylade and his companions rush him off the stage, ending the tragedy and leaving the audience with this final image of the defeat of reason: a hero undone by his passion. After this hallucinatory finale where delirium seems the only adequate response to so great a political and amorous loss, madness will no longer have its own, contained moment of triumph in Racinian dramaturgy. Instead, Racine's next tragedy, *Britannicus*, presents us with a world that is itself mad, if by "mad" we mean a society completely given over to a dysfunctional dynamics where family and politics, sexuality and "arcana imperii" form so tight a weave that the difference between reality and illusion becomes tragically blurred, a matter for perplexed interrogations. For the characters trapped in this world, where one of the more lucid claims, "Combien tout ce qu'on dit est loin de ce qu'on pense! / Que la bouche et le Coeur sont peu d'intelligence! / Avec combien de joie on y trahit sa foi" (How far is what one says from what one thinks! / Between the mouth and heart how few the links! / With what alacrity one breaks one's word), the separation

between personal desire and communal interests is so rhetorically entangled that it becomes impossible for the individuals ensnared in this
confused web to differentiate reality from pretense. Distinguishing "l'être
du paraître" (being from seeming) becomes the most important interpretative act in this drama. It is not only fraught with incertitude; it is
often a question of life or death. In this universe that is the Roman
court, political intrigue is so tightly implicated in familial trauma and
frustrated desire that politics becomes just one more tool in a deadly
game of power and perversion.

Can there be a better example of the imaginary pull of absolutism
than the seductive and terrifying fantasy of the Roman court as it has
been successively reconfigured in the Western mind for over two thousand years? As readers of Tacitus and Suetonius know well, the history
of this court with its excesses of power, cruelty, and sexual debauchery
shocked, titillated, and inspired historians, political theorists, theologians,
and philosophers as they grappled to explain both the unattainable political triumphs and the depraved morality that coexisted in the shining
image of Roman glory. Over the centuries innumerable scholars penned
reams in their attempts to analyze Rome's labyrinthine genealogies and
successive regimes. In their efforts to fix a model for contemporary aspirations, they perpetuated the scandal and fascination of a historical
phenomenon that took on mythic status. Rome remains a fabled entity,
a lost paradise of Empire, the mythic model that all of Europe's new
emperors from Charlemagne to Mussolini strove to resurrect.[1]

This confusion between history and myth in Racinian dramaturgy,
which Jean-Marie Apostolidès has so appropriately termed "mythistoire,"
is already present in Racine's aggressive preface to *Britannicus*.[2] Seemingly exasperated at the criticism his play has received, Racine responds
to his learned censors with what becomes his usual tactic when confronting his critics: he will, by a display of his erudite references to the
Ancients, confound his detractors with their own methods. He is accused of having been unfaithful to history when he extended the life of
Britannicus (and Narcisse) longer than they actually lived;[3] when he
used as a model for Junie, his innocent, virginal heroine, a historical Junia
who was in reality a scandalous hedonist;[4] and when he distorted the
personalities of several of his other characters. Grounding himself in
Tacitus and other less-well-known chroniclers of Rome, Racine answers
the different objections to his play with counterexamples drawn from

these original historians of Rome. To all these charges Racine responds, citing texts and theory (Aristotle) to defend both his own erudition and, more important, the license he allows himself as a poet. The first two pages of the preface to the play are a defense of the different liberties he took with historical detail/facts. In effect, his justification is interesting because we see that as he proceeds to answer his critics with a string of references that contradict them and often each other, he actually succeeds, by the force of example and counterexample, in undermining the claims of a univocal historical reality, and thus in a sense of history, in favor of the greater dramatic coherence and integrity of the play's *poeisis*. One could maintain that in his defense of his play and of his method, Racine is demonstrating the subjective, rhetorically complex construction of history, a construction that undermines any claim to objectivity. By so doing Racine situates his drama on the side of poetic truth rather than that of historical reality. In Racine's self-defense, history slips into fiction while fiction, in this case the re-creation of an intensely over-determined familial scenario of murder and incest, drifts over into the veiled realm of myth.

Racinian drama inhabits a tragic locus novel in its intensity and its narrowness of focus. However grandiose its exterior trappings (imperial Rome, majestic early Greece, ancient biblical royalty, the princely seraglio of Istanbul), the tightly organized tragic arena in Racine always points away from the stately decor of majesty and returns us to the restricted confines of the family. André Green suggests that this constrained familial space most adequately represents the earliest and deepest ties—ties of love and of hate, binding children to parents—and thus also has the greatest potential for engendering tragic emotions.[5] Michel Foucault, in a decidedly less psychoanalytic vein, has also pointed out that it was precisely during the course of the seventeenth century that the family as the nexus in which the private (the sexual) and the public (the social) are inextricably intermeshed came to assume an even more heated role as the mediator between societal (juridical) injunctions and (subjective) sexuality. The family becomes, according to Foucault, "the interchange of sexuality and alliance: it conveys the law and the juridical dimension in the deployment of sexuality; and it conveys the economy of pleasure and the intensity of sensations in the regime of alliance."[6] Racine's tragedy, as the tragedy of familial passions, reflects the intensity of this mediation at the same time that it rescripts for us, within the decor(s) of variable regal settings, the foundational story of conflicted origins, the legend of Oedipus and of his and his family's fate.

While, therefore, the setting of *Britannicus* is in Rome, at the imperial court, and while the characters he puts on that stage are familiar, as Mauron reminds us, to all the educated members of his audience, the intensity of tragic affect that Racine generates by reducing Rome to the narrow confines of the imperial family, with its torturous, twisted genealogies of power, corruption, and sexuality successfully blurs distinctions between ancient history and mythology, creating an indeterminate tragic locus that oscillates from one to the other.[7] One could argue further that the very protagonists that Racine chose for his tragedy—Néron and Agrippina—exist in the public domain not so much as actual, historical entities (although they are that, too) but rather as "figura," allegorical representations of shocking perversions, both sexual and political. Separately each can be seen to represent unbound aggression and ruthless betrayal of family and friends, not to mention assassination and incest:

> Mais ce lien du sang qui nous joignait tous deux
> Ecartait Claudius d'un lit incestueux.
> Il n'osait épouser la fille de son frère.
> Le Senat fut séduit. Une loi monis sévère
> Mit Claude dans mon lit, et Rome à mes genoux.
>
> But this consanguine tie which joined us both
> Forbade to Claudius an incestuous bed.
> He did not dare to wed his brother's daughter.
> The Senate was seduced: a laxer law
> Put Claudius in my bed, Rome at my feet.
> (4.2.1133–36)

Together, they become, *avant la letter,* a textbook Sadean couple where sexual perversion and political paranoia are conjoined in a horrifying yet fascinating example of an aborted attempt at sovereignty (in the Bataillean sense) and of the breaking of all ties, both cultural and natural, in an attempt to live in the realm of the absolute.

Very quickly, however, it becomes apparent that there exists a profound contradiction between the drive for the absolute, which, as we know, is the realm of an exacerbated narcissism, and the constitution of Racine's perverse couple. In *Britannicus* the desire for political power and sexual liberty that asserts with ever greater urgency its demands on the young emperor Néron is directly frustrated not so much by his "trois ans de vertu" (three virtuous years) but rather by the fascinating and terrifying hold that his mother, Agrippine, has on him.[8] It is his attempts to break this hold, attempts that deny his own complicity in the couple he forms with his mother, that inform the dramatic and finally tragic motor of the tragedy. As with all the perverse couples in literature, when the perverse contract is broken, the aggression that it helped contain turns against the now hated partner with fatal results.

Just as it is impossible to abstract the characters of *La Thébaïde* or *Andromaque* from the long cultural tradition of which they are a part, just as Oreste cannot step onto a stage without immediately summoning forth the Erinyes (even if these castigating creatures of the night now exist only as the reflection in the eyes of the audience), so too Néron cannot be mentioned without immediately conjuring up fantasies of tyranny, sexual perversion, matricide, and the fiery destruction of Rome.[9] Racine tells us, however, that his new tragedy does not deal with the tyrant that Néron became and with those actions that ensure his infamous reputation in Western culture. ("Il n'a pas encore mis le feu à Rome. Il n'a pas tué sa Mère, sa Femme, ses Gouverneurs." [He has not yet set fire to Rome. He has not killed his mother, his wife, his tutors.]) Rather this is not, Racine insists, primarily a political drama; it is a familial story ("Néron est ici dans son particulier et dans sa famille" [Nero is here depicted as an individual and in the bosom of his family], 372). Although Racine will protect the refined sensibilities of his contemporaries from anything that might shock them, we also know that they were perfectly well aware, through other sources, of the sexual and political scandals that are attached to Néron's name: his sexual debauchery, his homosexual relations with his "brother" Britannicus, and, of course, the persistent rumors relayed by Tacitus and Suetonius of incest with Agrippina, his mother (incest that, according to the sources in question, was variously attributed to the desires of either the mother or the son). All this is both known and ignored. In its place we are given not so much a political tragedy à la Corneille but a play where there is no separation possible between the familial and the political, between what will become known as the public and private spheres, even as these intermingling spaces become the site of an ever present and never avowed conflation of passion and death.[10]

In the preface to his 1675 edition of his play, Racine reminds us that "ma Tragédie n'est pas moins la disgrâce d'Agrippine que la mort de Britannicus" (my tragedy is not less the fall of Agrippina than the death of Britannicus).[11] In other words, once again we have a familial tragedy, as in *La Thébaïde*, a fratricidal rivalry (here both political and sexual) and a monstrous mother who, if not destroyed like the Sphinx, is sufficiently undermined so that her end (both hidden and known to all) is foretold. It would seem that there has been a shift of emphasis in this tragedy. Although Britannicus lends his name to the title, he strikes us as perhaps the least interesting and the least tragic of the characters in the play. Perhaps it is simply that monsters are more interesting than victims or that Britannicus seems to us too bland and certainly too incredulous to be the tragic center of this drama. His inability to see what is going on around him might be excused by his youth. It is in stark contrast, however, with Junie's quick and correct evaluation of court life. Junie, who has spent her life away from this court, realizes quite soon after her forced entrance into it that it is a world of hypocrisy, subterfuge, and danger. Britannicus, who has been raised at court his entire life and has seen his father abandon him and his inheritance stripped from him, who has seen his friends desert him and now his betrothed stolen from him, never seems, in the end, to change, to have any understanding of the clouded illegibility of his world and of his place in it. His only answer to his fate is to seek solace in the embrace of a woman whose fortune has been as unlucky as his own. In a sense he strikes us more as a straw man, a plot device that Racine needs (fraternal rivalry) to set his play in motion, while at the same time distracting us with a sentimental love story from the murderous aggression and sexual predation that is the true tragic center of the play, that is, the perverse Oedipal struggle between Néron and Agrippine.

Racine is unique among the great tragic authors of the West in focusing his drama almost exclusively on the conflicting desires of an antagonistic couple. He constructs his tragic scenario around the opposition of two protagonists whose antagonism situates them on opposite sides of both a sexual and political (power) divide.[12] This struggle always involves an unequal division of power; the desirous partner has unlimited authority over the object of his/her passion. That this heated mix of sexuality and power has been analyzed as essentially sadomasochistic (both in the colloquial and clinical acceptation of the term) only underlines the very deep fault lines that join the politics of empire with individual desire, creating at their intersection social turmoil and tragic fatality. Of all the couples in Racinian tragedy, couples who decline in ever more refined scenarios the dialectics of desire and death, none strikes us as more shockingly perverse than Néron and Agrippine, not least of all because this Racinian couple is not, as we know (ostensibly at least), lovers or potential lovers but mother and child. This perverse nexus will spawn a whole series of dysfunctional couplings—Néron/Junie, Néron/Narcisse, Narcisse/Britannicus, Néron/Britannicus, Agrippine/Burrhus—that form a tragic roundelay where desire and power fuel each couples' ambitions and their ruses.

The semantic field of the word "perversion" is vast, and even in clinical psychoanalytic vocabularies the term covers an area too large to be explored in any detail here. I would like, nevertheless, to speak briefly about my use (quite partial and particular) of the term in the context of my discussion of *Britannicus*. Following the definition given by Jean Laplanche and Jean Baptiste Pontalis in their *Vocabulaire de la psychanalyse*, we could begin with the hypothesis that, interpreted most broadly, human sexuality is always a perversion (that is, in its etymological sense, a turning away) if we recognize that sexual pleasure (in whatever form it takes) is already redirected (perverted) from the satisfaction of an original organic need.[13] The most famous and foundational example of this is, of course, Freud's description, in *Three Essays on the Theory of Sexuality*, of the smiling, rosy-cheeked infant falling asleep in his mother's arms after an extended period of sucking on the breast. In this case, Freud tells us, we can already see that the pleasure of sucking has taken precedence over the instinctual need for nourishment.[14]

While in general parlance we can speak of moral perversion, political perversion, and the like, for psychoanalysis, perversion is always associated with sexuality.[15] For Freud and his followers, perversion comes to mean more specifically the obtaining of sexual pleasure (to orgasmic release) through other than (and even this can be nuanced) standard heterosexual genital intercourse. Thus, for Freud, "perversions" would include homosexuality, oral or anal sex, incest, sadomasochism, transvestism, and on and on. Finally, another large area of the semantic field of perversion is allied with the equally not inconsiderable and diffuse notion of fetishism. It is more in this direction that I would like to turn our attention because the etiology of fetishism, even more than the other sexual perversions, bears the indelible mark of the mother/child relation in which both sexuality and power are most acutely at stake.

In his article "Fetishism" (1927) Freud explored what is seen as an almost exclusively masculine perversion: certain men can attain sexual fulfillment only through the use of a fetish—an object, a piece of clothing, a particular body part, a tone of voice (almost anything can be a fetish)—that dominates and determines their sexual life. Freud came to understand the fetish as a substitute formation that at one and the same time allowed the male child, traumatized by the sight/knowledge of the mother's castration (that is, that the mother, contrary to generalized infantile belief that all people, regardless of sex, had a penis, doesn't). The discovery that the mother does not have a penis, that she has lost it or has been deprived of it (castration), has, Freud postulated, so distressing an effect on some young boys that in order to control their anxiety that they too might lose so precious and pleasurable a body part, in order to save themselves from the same fate (castration), they create a compromise formation, a fetish, that at one and the same time both admits reality (the mother does not have a penis) and denies it (she does have a penis). This compromise, that is, the fetish, according to Freud, allows the boy to accept the "castrated" woman as a sexual object, thus avoiding a turn toward homosexuality. The possibility of holding two contradictory beliefs without one eliminating the other is the result of a splitting of the ego, a process that Freud will demonstrate to be a major characteristic of unconscious life.

Recent theorists have expanded Freud's initial description of the etiology of fetishism. While retaining the importance of the main elements—castration anxiety, denial, and compromise formation—Jean Clavreul, for example, has proposed to extend Freud's initial description of the construction of fetishism by insisting more particularly on the important role of the scopic drive, the *schaulust* (of both the son and the mother), as a principal component in the fetishistic scenario. The question for Clavreul becomes, what motivates the boy, at the precise moment that he notices the traumatic evidence that the mother has/does not have a penis, to see? The desire to see is here equated with the desire to know, so that Clavreul, thanks to French homophony, can make the seductive connection between *voir* and *savoir*. This homology has interesting consequences for Clavreul's discussion of the "perverse couple," which originates, he intimates, in the mother's collusion in the

child's epistemological (visual) quest.[16] The mother, he suggests, is complicitous, because she knows that the child is seeing something for which
reason has not prepared him. In turn her reciprocal, if ambiguous, look
("de quel oeil la mère voit-elle son enfant qui la regarde?" [how exactly
does the mother see her child looking at her?"—with a play of words
on "de quel oeil"—with what eye]) becomes an important foundational
moment in what will become the "perverse contract" connecting the
two.[17] Clavreul claims that this initial ambiguity, filled with questioning, anxiety, and desire, will be the model for all future contracts between the fetishist and his partner(s). It is a contract that requires both
the acquiescence to and the (unconscious) ignorance of the unvarying
practices engaged in by the two partners under the gaze of an absent
Other, the father, who is, Clavreul reminds us, although absent at the
foundational moment, also present in the mother's desire.[18]

It is therefore important to bear in mind two major points in analyzing
the perverse couple. The first is that the contract (unspoken, of course)
linking them together is a secret one. This secret cannot be revealed to
a third party (the world) lest it unleash unbounded aggression. Second,
we must remember that the choice of the partner is never an indifferent one. The partner must always appear, at least in the eyes of the "pervert," innocent; she or he is, nevertheless, always complicitous in the
perverse contract. (We might here see the relation between the partner
in a fetishistic ritual as analogous to the victim of sacrificial ceremonies;
more on this later.) Finally, Clavreul goes on to underline the fact that
"there is always in every perverse act something similar to rape, in that
it is important that the other be led despite himself into an experience
the validity of which is disputed by its entire context."[19] In other words,
Clavreul's elaboration on Freud's initial interrogation of perversion, which
I have only skimmed here, allows us to see how sexuality leeches into
epistemology and how both are inextricably connected (certainly by
their sadomasochistic performances) to a dialectics of power. Without
being too reductive we might propose, extrapolating from Freud, that
this intimate scenario of desire and power can be seen as an originary
model of politics in the broadest sense and more specifically of absolutism
when we remember the particular importance for absolutism of the
deployment of an entire panoply of illusion and sexual prowess as a
reflection of the spectacular hold the persona of the monarch exercises
over a desirous, fascinated, and receptive populace.[20] At the same time

it returns us to the mother/child dyad as the origin of an expanding nebula of sexuality, perversion, and power that is at the very center of Racinian tragedy.

As usual for Racine, the tragic scenario of *Britannicus* is confined to the most tightly restricted circle at the very apex of Empire. It is here in this lethal empyrean where family and state form an indivisible unity that the locus of tragedy and the space of family are conflated.[21] And it is here in this ambiguous space of politics and desire that the absolutist fantasy is presented in its most acute form as a scenario of perversion and paranoia that retains, nonetheless, its almost orgasmic hold on those who are in its thrall. The aphrodisia of power works its most nefarious effects on those who are about to lose it, most prominently Agrippine. Bewailing her impending disgrace, Agrippine reveals, unbeknownst to herself, the convoluted web of sexuality and power she thought she manipulated but wherein she now finds herself trapped:

> Quoi tu ne vois donc pas jusqu'où l'on me ravale,
> Albine? C'est à moi qu'on donne une Rivale.
> Bientôt si je ne romps ce funeste lien,
> Ma place est occupée, et je ne suis plus rien.
> Jusqu'ici d'un vain titre Octavie honorée
> Inutile à la Cour, en était ignorée.
> Les grâces, les honneurs par moi seule versés
> M'attiraient des mortels les voeux intéressés.
> Une autre de César a surpris la tendresse,
> Elle aura le pouvoir d'Epouse et de Maîtresse...

> Can you not see how far I am abased,
> Albina? Upon me he foists a rival.
> If I do not soon snap this fatal bond,
> My place is filled and I become a cipher.
> Till now Octavia, with her empty title,
> Powerless at Court, could be ignored by it.
> Rewards and honors, showered as I saw fit,
> Drew to me all the selfish prayers of men.
> Another woman captures Caesar's love:
> She'll wield the influence both of wife and mistress.
>   (3.4.879–888)

Up until this moment, Agrippine was convinced that she controlled the reins of power ("J'étais de ce grand Corps l'Âme toute-puissante" [The almighty spirit of that mighty body]) by manipulating all aspects of her son's political and sexual life. Through a series of complex intrigues Agrippine was able to place the son she had with Oenobarbus more firmly in line for the imperial throne. She inveigled to have him adopted by her new husband, the emperor Claudius, who renamed him Néron. Having accomplished this, she proceeded to mystify a sick and perhaps senile Claudius into preferring her child to his own: Claudius appoints Néron his successor, supplanting his son Britannicus. To concentrate and ensure her stranglehold on power, Agrippine arranges the marriage of Néron to Octavie, Britannicus's sister, a direct descendant of Augustus. Through this marriage Agrippine hopes to join two different branches of the imperial family into one solid political entity impervious to attack from other rival factions with a claim to the throne.

As the play begins, however, all her scheming is about to unravel because of one element, the loose cannon that she has ignored and that refuses to be contained in her political scenario: her son's desire. And while at first glance this desire appears to be Néron's fixation on his cousin Junie, we soon realize that in reality this desire, as usual, is more complicated, more multifaceted than he or those around him assume: while, as Serge Doubrovsky has argued, Junie appears as the actual object of Néron's love/lust, one can detect a more ambivalent object behind her. Néron is both fascinated and repelled by his mother Agrippine from whose suffocating embrace he struggles to free himself.[22]

The verses quoted above are interesting not only for what they reveal about Agrippine's anxiety but also how this anxiety is presented rhetorically as a conflation of a political and sexual crisis. The political emergency is immediately sexualized as a fantasmatic scenario of incest. Agrippine sees Junie as her (sexual) rival in that she, unlike Octavie, Néron's legal but ineffectual and barren wife, is able to do what Octavie never could, displace Agrippine. Agrippine arranged the marriage between Néron and Octavie for dynastic security but also, we must assume, because she needed a bride who exerted no erotic pull and, therefore, no political influence on her son. That influence remained hers. Now, however, with Néron's passion aroused, Agrippine realizes that her own authority is jeopardized. Once Néron's lust turns toward another woman capable of conjoining in her person the dynastic legacy of a legitimate wife with the erotic enticements of a mistress ("Elle aura le pouvoir d'Epouse et de Maîtresse" [She'll wield the influence of both wife and mistress]), Agrippine's role, indeed her life, unravels. Agrippine has, she fears, met her match—not so much the innocent, virginal Junie, "seul reste du débris d'une illustre Famille (the last remains of the ruined and illustrious family), but her son's passion.

The entire tragic arc of the play will follow the deflections of Néron's desire from his mother onto a more normative path that envelops the innocent (but are they really innocent, politically speaking?) couple of young lovers, the disinherited descendants of another Rome, Britannicus and Junie.[23] Along its erratic course what originates in a conflicted, ambivalent manipulation of sexuality will quickly, as is usually the case, widen its sphere of influence to contaminate and coerce not only the familial sphere but the entire political future of the Roman Empire. In a sense, as clever and manipulative as she is, Agrippine, who always needs a complacent male mediator to represent her, has made a fundamental error in confusing what the French anthropologist Maurice Godelier has defined as two separate but interconnected realms of human sexuality, "sexualité-désir" and "sexualité-reproduction," when she believes she has fixed her son in his role as her surrogate.[24] In Godelier's analyses of how the individual and the social are made to function as an interconnected and constructive social process, he hypothesizes that for the social to exist and to reproduce itself, desire ("sexualité-désir") must be, in some way, brought under the control of the reigning societal laws (as diverse as they may be given the infinite modes of human socialization). The important point (similar to both Freud and Lévi-Strauss) is that whatever the familial structure of a given society (matrilinear, patrilinear, and so on), it is on the children that the double social imperative to "subordinate desire to the social order and to place reproduction under social control" must be most forcefully applied.[25] Finally, and more apropos of our discussion, Godelier demonstrates that whatever the different ways that societies ensure their smooth functioning and reproduction, it is principally through the family, constituted as the primary interdicting instance, that sexuality becomes the nexus in which not only the family is reproduced but also those other forces—political, religious, economic, even aesthetic—are also and at the same time replicated.[26] In other words, Godelier demonstrates how the most intangible systems (economy, politics, religion) that together form the weave of any given society are necessarily reproduced through the way society sexes bodies and then attempts to control them.[27]

In her efforts to maintain herself and her hold on imperium, Agrippine can only resort to what by her own admission is her dysfunctional
familial history where the sins of her ancestors, very much like in the
mythic narrative of Oedipus, weigh heavily on the fate of her descendants. Agrippine has made her way to power through murder and incest
("Mais ce lien du sang qui nous joignait tous deux / Ecartait Claudius
d'un lit incestueux [But this consanguine tie which joined us both /
Forbade to Claudius an incestuous bed]). She is, in essence, an asocial
being and can, therefore, only reproduce herself as such. At the same
time, Agrippine has ignored the force of libidinal desire in others because her own has been so evidently subsumed under a more imperious
libido dominandi. Thus she finds herself, as the play begins, the victim of
her own willingness not to know or recognize a being (her son) and a
desire (his) other than her own. To do so would be tantamount to her
recognition of Néron as an independent entity, not just an extension of
her own will to power. In the patriarchal world of Rome, however, power
can only be wielded by a man. This primary law of imperial Rome com-
pels Agrippine to disguise her power and her influence, to work, as she
says, veiled, literally out of sight of the Roman senate but metaphorically and more dangerously draped in her role as Mother of the emperor.
It is the constant oscillation between these two roles in which Néron
feels trapped that blinds Agrippine to her own political miscalculations
and that creates a pervasive atmosphere of suspicion and paranoia among
all the members of the court's inner circle.

It is curious that of all Racine's major tragedies *Britannicus* is unique
in that it begins with a question: "Quoi?" (What?). At first glance this
might seem simply a rhetorical technique that the playwright adopts to
plunge his audience immediately in medias res, to create in that public
the illusion of participating in an ongoing yet enigmatic action. The
impression of doubt becomes more charged as we soon realize that interrogation is the primary discursive mode throughout the play. More than
any other of Racine's plays, *Britannicus* is dominated by the question
mark. The number of interrogatory verses confers on this play an aura
of indeterminacy and universal anxiety that reflects the Machiavellian
plots and counterplots of Agrippine and the various members of the court.
All of the characters, during the course of the drama, are confused; they
are constantly questioning each other, asking not so much for an answer

but for an ontological assurance that would corroborate their very right
to exist in this world where, to quote from another, contemporary court
drama, things are never what they seem: "Si vous jugez sur les apparences
en ce lieu-ci . . . vous serez souvent trompée: ce qui paraît n'est presque jamais la verité (If you judge by appearances in this place . . . you will be
often mistaken: what appears is almost never true).[28]

Anxiety seems to have gotten the better of Agrippine. The first scene
finds her wandering, to the amazement of her confidante, unattended
about the palace. The events of the night have left Agrippine in a height-
ened state of foreboding:

> (Albine)
> Quoi? Tandis que Néron s'abandonne au sommeil
> Faut-il que vous veniez attendre son réveil?
> Qu'errant dans le Palais sans suite et sans escorte
> La mère de Cesar veille seule à sa porte?
> (Agrippine)
> . . . .
> De quel nom cependant pouvons-nous appeler
> L'attentat que le jour vient de nous révéler?
> Il sait, car leur amour ne peut être ignoré,
> Que de Britannicus Junie est adorée.
> Et ce même Néron que la vertu conduit,
> Fait enlever Junie au milieu de la nuit.
> Que veut-il? Est-ce haine, est-ce amour qui l'inspire?
> Cherche-t-il seulement le plaisir de leur nuire?
> Ou plutôt n'est-ce point que sa malignité
> Punit sur eux l'appui que je leur ai prêté?
>
> (Albine)
> What, Madam, does this mean? While Nero sleeps,
> Must you stand waiting here for him to wake?
> And wandering through the palace, unattended,
> Must Caesar's mother watch beside his door?
> (Agrippine)
> . . . .
> And yet, in what terms may we designate
> The violence the dawn has just unveiled?
> He knows, all the world's aware of it,
> Britannicus has lost his heat to Junia,
> And this same Nero, bent on doing right,
> Drags Junia here, arrested at midnight.
> What does he want? What drives him? Hate or love?

Or does he but delight to do them harm?
Or rather is it not perhaps his spite
To punish them, because I lend them aid?
    (1.1.1–58)

Although Agrippine is at a loss to understand exactly what has motivated Néron's abduction of Junie from her home and her detention in
the imperial palace, the anxiety it causes quickly reveals a restless paranoia. She immediately assumes that this new turn of events, like all of
Néron's actions, has as its goal her humiliation. Despite (or more probably because of) the fact that he owes everything to her ("Il me le doit,
Albine. / Tout, s'il est généreux lui prescrit cette loi" [Indeed, he owes
it to me: If he be noble everything prescribes it]), she lives in constant
fear of his ingratitude ("Mais tout, s'il est ingrat, lui parle contre moi"
[But if he's base, all speaks to him against me]), which would signal her
fall from power into nothingness. It becomes quickly apparent that the
use of questions fulfills more than a merely ornamental rhetorical purpose. On the one hand, as I've said, the questions serve to establish a
general atmosphere of doubt and confusion, of a world of plots and
counterplots. On the other hand, it strikes me that their insistence (What
does Néron really want? Why is he doing this? What does it mean for
me?) reveals an even deeper collusion between desire and power, a highly
charged *libido sciendi,* a drive to know that, as we have seen, is originally
directed, in its voyeuristic urge, at discovering the secrets of sexuality
in the fetishistic scenario where the difference between male and female,
being and seeming, creates an intolerable tension in both the individual
subject and in the world that envelops him.

Agrippine's anxiety signals, of course, the return of her transgressions:
the aporia that she has created for her son and herself. Rome cannot
tolerate the hubris of a woman who sees herself the equal to men and
who uses her son as a mere surrogate for her own veiled power. All the
while claiming that she has acted only for his benefit, she has successfully undermined the independence of the emperor and has, metaphorically, castrated the empire. Néron tells her he is not a dupe to her real
motives: he knows that while pretending to work for him she cares
only about herself: "Vous n'aviez sous mon nom travaillé que pour vous"
(You previously.../ Have only worked, in my name, for yourself). He
goes on to reiterate for her, as if she didn't know, the patriarchal imperative that is the bedrock of Roman society: "Rome veut un Maître, et

non une Maîtresse" (But Rome demands a master, not a mistress). Despite her illustrious genealogy, despite the fact that she is the daughter of Germanicus, a revered warrior/emperor, she cannot escape the constraints of her sex in Roman society.

Agrippine would figure as just another in the long line of emasculating phallic women that haunt the Racinian universe. They are, as Mauron pointed out more than fifty years ago, always coupled and contrasted with the other side of Racine's unconscious fantasy of women, those innocent, virginal, and victimized young women (Junie). In Racine, this clash between the devouring, aggressive mother figure and the overwhelmed son remains a constant until the last act of his final play where the son (helped by a bevy of paternal figures, not least of whom is God) finally triumphs over the monster/mother. Although Mauron's analysis of Racine's unconscious fantasies is certainly convincing within the frame of his theory of artistic creation, it is also instructive to associate these fantasies and their place in Racine's theater with an archaic and analogous narrative in Greek mythology.

In her comprehensive study of the Oedipus legend, Marie Delcourt gives a detailed description of the different versions of various Greek myths that share with the Oedipus legend what she calls its political function: the pedagogical narrative of how a young man achieves the right to rule ("l'habilitation à la royauté"). In the tales of all these heroes (Perseus, Jason, Bellorophon, Oedipus) the champion must confront and overcome various life-threatening obstacles in order to win the hand of a princess and thus accede to the throne. Of these different trials perhaps the most important, surely the most telling about the patriarchal fears concerning women in the ancient Greek world, is the confrontation with and the slaying of a female monster (the Sphinx, Gorgon, and others).[29] This triumph over the female monster is at once a defeat of a female sexuality that is fantasized as emasculating (we should remember that in the legend of the Sphinx, for instance, before she destroyed the young men who could not solve her enigmatic puzzle, she raped them) and a victory for masculinity as intelligence (in the case of Oedipus) as well as the institution, according to Hegel, of the rational over the material and thus the beginning of the masculinist hegemony in Western philosophy.[30] In a very concrete way the slaying of monsters and the containing of the monster that is female sexuality is an essential attribute of the Greek hero.[31] It is in this sense that we can interpret the historical tragedy of *Britannicus* as, on the one hand, a projection of Racine's unconscious, as Mauron would have it, and, on the other, as a continuation (with a twist) in neoclassical drama of these archaic myths that conjoin at their center both the political and sexual narrative of male supremacy that this drama restages for the edification of the emerging modern subject.

In her climb to power Agrippine has transgressed the primordial separation of the sexes and the generations (in other words, she plays too freely with the law of the Oepidal scenario as it structures Roman society). Her gender-crossing hubris has already alienated the army, the ultimate source of her legitimacy:

> Vous avez vu cent fois nos Soldats en courroux
> Porter en murmurant leurs Aigles devant vous,
> Honteux de rabaisser par cet indigne usage
> Les Héros, dont encore elles portent l'image.
> Toute autre se serait rendue à leurs discours,
> Mais si vous ne régnez, vous vous plaignez toujours.

> You've often seen our disaffected soldiers
> Bearing before you their unwilling eagles;
> Ashamed, by this unworthy use, to sully
> The heroes whose great mage they yet bear.
> All others would have yielded to their pain;
> But if you do not reign you still complain.
> (4.2.1245–50)

And it has alienated, of course, Néron, whose sexual life and thus his identity as a man and as emperor has been indentured to her. Complaining to Narcisse about Agrippine's hold over him, Néron tellingly accuses his mother, certainly in a metaphor the echoes of which a seventeenth-century audience would not fail to hear, of bewitching him. His marriage that he describes metaphorically as "un noeud qu'elle (Agrippine) a formé," (a knot tied by her [Agrippine]), is both passionless and barren. In other words, if we extend the metaphor to its larger semantic field, we can hear in Néron's blame his real complaint: Agrippine has, in that untranslatable expression, "noué l'aiguillette" of her son.[32] And it is precisely here, in the conflict caused by Agrippine's blocking his libido (by containing, that is, "castrating" it/him) that the battle with the monster takes place. In this case, however, the hero is not destined to greatness but to depravity, and the monster in question is an ambivalent, we might say a bicephalous, beast, a mother/son dyad where the monstrosity is precisely their mutual involution, where each is inextricably coupled to the other and where precisely the attempt to separate the one from the other leads to tragedy.

Racine famously announces in the preface to *Britannicus* that although he has always considered Néron to be monstrous, in his new play he is only representing the birth of a monster ("Je l'ai toujours regardé comme un monstre. Mais c'est ici un monstre naissant" [I have always thought of him as a monster. But here he is a budding monster]). The preface enumerates those acts that Néron will commit, thus proleptically defining his being by those yet-to-be-accomplished actions. Here, however, in his new play, Racine insists that Néron is only a nascent monster (the coupling of these two words is, it seems to me, heavy with meaning). How are we to understand the resonance of the different semantic and ideological echoes that the word "monster" has for Racine's audience if not by placing it in the context of the master discourse of seventeenth-century absolutism? There, the dominant paradigm for the absolute was the figure of the Unique, the One, incorruptible because indivisible. As a state system, absolutism is perhaps the first modern avatar of a totalitarian government, which Georges Balandier defines in a way I find particularly telling for understanding the metaphoric charge of Racine's use of "monstre" in *Britannicus* as well as in his other tragedies, inscribed as they all are in an ongoing dialogue between individual desire and political imperatives. For Balandier, totalitarianism is a form of government that desires "the submission of all and everything to the State," where "the unifying function of power is carried to its highest degree. The myth of unity becomes the scenario directing the political *mise-en-scène*."[33] Balandier insists on unity as integrity of being, and he opposes it to the (fear of) societal fragmentation. In order for the integral to exist as a social imperative and for that imperative to be embodied in the state, an entire symbolic, economic, and political order must coalesce around the unifying figure, the monarch, a representation that already exists within the cultural/political confines of European civilization but that, at this key moment of transition (the seventeenth century), will be newly invested with the power and prestige, but also with the danger, of the sacred. The state, as it evolves into an ever more centralized bureaucratic structure, takes on the attributes of unity and integrity in the person/persona of the king. In its flight away from heterogeneity— that which is hybrid, a mixture, not integral, thus monstrous—toward the order of the One in what Foucault has called the great confine- ment, the seventeenth century reinforced the image of the father/king at the same time as it began (again following Foucault's hypothesis) through its religious and economic practices to encircle a sexuality that in its excessive drive proved too threatening to the unitary order.[34] It falls to the theater, the most popular form of representation of the pe- riod, to stage this desire for the protection and comfort offered by the monarch (and by contrast, its fear and opposition to the corruption of this kingly figure—the tyrant) in its various productions both comic and tragic that serve to reflect this most intense of political reveries.

It is important to bear in mind, as Franco Moretti reminds us, that the theater is not a realistic reproduction of social institutions (which in reality are obviously not homogeneous but made up of several com- peting, contradictory, and often conflicting social discourses) but of their mythic (that is, ideological) relation to culture:

> If the general culture of absolutism qualified the sovereign power it
> conferred upon the king with countless hesitations and uncertainties...
> tragedy surrenders such power to him wholly and without the slightest
> reserve. In the world of tragedy, the monarch is truly absolute....
> Tragedy then stages not the institutions of absolutism, but its culture,
> its values, its ideology.[35]

In the figure of Néron, Racine is obviously, on the one hand, creating the negative, perverse image of the ideal king, the tyrant, and on the other, his tyranny in its nascent appearance is closely allied to sado- masochism as a form of sexual perversion. In order to understand the etiology of Néron's perversion, to understand why, in other words, he is a monster, who better than his mother to tell us?

> Il commence, il est vrai, par où finit Auguste;
> Mais crains que, l'avenir détruisant le passé,
> Il ne finisse ainsi qu'Auguste a commencé.
> Il se déguise en vain: je lis sur son visage
> Des fiers Domitius l'humeur triste et sauvage;

Il mêle avec l'orgueil qu'il a pris dans leur sang
La fierté des Nérons qu'il puisa dans mon flanc.

True, he begins where great Augustus ended;
But fear, lest, future blotting out the past,
He ends just how Augustus has begun.
In vain he shams: I read upon his face
The dark, wild humours of his savage sires *(the Domitii)*,
Uniting with their fierce and stubborn blood
The pride of all the Neros born of me.
          (1.1.32–38)

Agrippine situates Néron's monstrosity in his duality, which she insists
has its origin in her body (echoes of Jocaste). He is a mixture because
of his double origin in two of the most fabled and cursed Roman clans,
the Domitii and the Julio-Claudians. Like the bull from the sea, the
most famous monster in Racine, Néron is here described as a heterogeneous being: he is the combination of two blood lines, two families,
two parents, two sexes, and as such he is, in the world of the absolute,
condemned to a never-ending battle for a sovereignty, for the elimination
of the difference within that eludes him. This difference is maddening because he can't be free of it or Agrippine. Néron and Agrippine
form a perverse couple where each is trapped in the other. What is
particularly striking in their perversion is the way each, in the battle for
sovereignty in which they are engaged, represents an inverted relation
to both power and sexuality as they are normally defined in prescriptive
accounts of the natural division of the sexes. As we have seen in Barthes's
reading of it, the sexuality of the Racinian hero is a product not of biology but of a Nietzschean will to power. Sexuality, in Racine, is a political
construct: the domination of one character over another determines a
character's being placed in the camp of virility or femininity.[36] Agrippine, as Barthes would say, is masculine insofar as Néron (and a great
part of the Roman public) is concerned because she wields power (albeit
hidden) over Rome and over him. She has, in Lacanian terms, the phallus (which, as we know, can only work veiled). Néron, on the other
hand, is relegated to being her phallus; that is, his desire to have what
he fantasizes is his mother's power places him in a feminine position,
which, as Doubrovsky has argued, is the cause of his murderous resentment.[37] This is, of course, a radical perversion of the normal (if dys-

functional) sexual positions as Lacan defined them. In Lacan's account of sexuality, of sexual positioning, the man *has* the phallus for the woman who *is* the phallus for the man.[38] The perversion so clearly articulated in *Britannicus* of the sexual and therefore the political roles represented by the monstrosity of the central heterosexual couple of the play, the primary confusion of having and being, has repercussions that recur, in metaphor, in the major psychic structures (sadism/masochism, exhibitionism/voyeurism) that are elaborated as the play constructs its deadly trap into which Britannicus and Agrippine will eventually fall.

As we have already noticed and as innumerable critics have mentioned, in Racine where words can kill, where gesture is reduced to a minimum, and where reigns, as here in *Britannicus*, an overall sense of paranoia and mistrust, the eyes become the most important if ambivalent revelator of the hidden intentions and passions of the various protagonists. It is also the eyes that give the different characters their only (mis)perceptions of those inscrutable others who populate their world and control their fate.[39] In *Britannicus* the importance of seeing, or rather spying on, others is particularly perverse as it is also principally indicative of the play of power and sexuality that link and oppose first Néron and Agrippine and then, of course, Néron and his prey. In a very real sense Agrippine's eye, her piercing, imperious gaze, is the fetishistic object of Néron's anxiety and desire. Her eyes are for Néron (by a typical displacement from lower to higher) the metaphor for her power over him, for the phallus Néron fears and desires. It is the terrifying image of his mother's fiery eye(s) that Néron invokes when he tries to explain what thwarts his lust for Junie:

> Et ne connais-tu pas l'implacable Agrippine?
> Mon amour inquiet déjà se l'imagine,
> Qui m'amène Octavie, et d'un oeil enflammé
> Atteste les saints droits d'un noeud qu'elle a formé,
> Et portant à mon Coeur des atteintes plus rudes,
> Me fait un long récit de mes ingratitudes.
> De quel front soutenir ce fâcheux entretien?

> Do you not know the angry Agrippina?
> My anxious love already pictures her
> Leading Octavia to me and attesting,
> With flaming eyes, her sacred marriage rights;
> And, striking shaper bows upon my soul,

> Telling long tales of my ungrateful role
> How could I listen to this tedious moan?
>   (2.2.483–89)

Néron cannot tolerate his mother's Medusa-like gaze.[40] He is rendered speechless, inarticulate, impotent. He can, he says, only be himself, Emperor, when he frees himself of those eyes, which constantly remind him of his debt (lack) to her ("Eloigné de ses yeux j'ordonne, je menace" [Safe from her eyes, I threaten, I command]). This obligation that he sees/reads in Agrippine's eyes propels Néron's malice as it is a constant reminder of his "castration":

> Sitôt que mon malheur me ramène à sa vue,
> Soit que je n'ose encore démentir le pouvoir
> De ses yeux, où j'ai lu si longtemps mon devoir,
> . . . .
> Mais enfin mes efforts ne me servent de rien,
> Mon Génie etonné tremble devant le sien.

> But,
> As soon as, by ill-luck I'm in her sight
> Whether I dare not yet deny the power of
> Those eyes, where I have so long read my duty;
> . . . .
> My strength against her I in vain assemble:
> My startled Genius before hers must tremble.
>   (2.2.496–506)

Néron's passivity before his mother's gaze turns into aggression when he imitates her visual control over the political life of Rome in his attempts to undermine Junie's love for Britannicus. Hiding to spy on their meeting, he is in the analogous position to Agrippine watching the workings of the Roman senate. We might say that Néron here identifies with his mother, but at the same time acknowledges that this identification only compounds his sense of frustration and thus his sadism:

> Caché près de ces lieux je vous verrai, Madame.
> Renfermez votre amour dans le fond de votre âme.
> Vous n'aurez point pour moi de langages secrets.
> J'entendrai des regards que vous croirez muets.
> Et sa perte sera l'infaillible salaire
> D'un geste, ou d'un soupir échappé pour lui plaire.

Concealed nearby, I'll watch you from the start,
Entomb your love deep down within your heart.
You'll have no language secret for my ear;
The glances you think dumb I'll overhear;
And, without fail. His doom shall be the fees
Of any sign or gesture meant to please.
    (2.4.679–84)

Madame, en le voyant, songez que je vous vois.

Remember, when you see him, I too see.
    (2.4.690)

Here, the gaze turns murderous, as Néron identifies with the power and the perversion he imagines in his mother's eyes. It is only in that perverse identification, which is always a fragmentary, fracturing relation both to the visual and to the sexual, that he is able to pleasure.[41] "Je me fais de sa peine une image charmante" (I keep a charming picture of his smart), he says to Narcisse, contemplating the suffering of Britannicus, and his own (temporary) triumph over his rival. It is, of course, but a pyrrhic victory as he realizes that he is able to reign only over a couple of innocent, powerless lovers, while his mother controlled the Roman Empire.

When, in her confrontation with Burrhus, the stern military leader she had personally chosen as one of her son's two tutors and whom she perceives as attempting to limit her access to him, Agrippine declines her imperial genealogy—"Moi, fille, femme, soeur, et mère de vos Maîtres" (I, daughter, wife, sister and mother of your Lords)—she underscores both how close and how far she is from real power. Agrippine has just totalized in one verse all the female positions—mother, sister, daughter, wife—that she joins in her person. She occupies the very pinnacle of feminine proximity to empire, but by this very same genealogy she has also demonstrated how infinitely separated she is from it. Agrippine's political transgressions are the same as all of Racine's phallic women. They transgress the limits imposed on the sexes by society and by so doing bring down on themselves divine (or merely societal) retribution. While at the end of his career Racine will have his last, most terrifying female protagonist, Athalie, stride into the temple and place herself "dans un parvis aux hommes réservé" (in a court reserved for men) in a clear and final defiance of male prerogative, Agrippine is not so openly bold (perhaps she is more politically savvy): she remains, as we know, veiled, out of sight:

> Non, non, le temps n'est plus que Néron jeune encore
> Me renvoyait les voeux d'une Cour, qui l'adore,
> Lorsqu'il se reposait sur moi de tout l'Etat
> Que mon ordre au Palais assemblait le Sénat,
> Et que derrière un voile, invisible, et présente
> J'étais de ce grand Corps l'Ame toute-puissante

> No, no, gone is the time when Nero, young,
> Sent me the prayers of an adoring Court;
> When he left all affairs of State to me.
> When at my word the Senate would assemble
> Within the palace, where, behind a veil.
> Invisible and present, I became
> The almighty spirit of that mighty body.
>   (1.1.91–96)

Nevertheless, on more ceremonial occasions she has made a spectacle of herself, focusing all eyes on her as she shares the throne with Néron. The first sign that her political power is on the wane comes as Néron skillfully displaces her:

> Sur son Trône avec lui j'allais prendre ma place.
> J'ignore quel conseil prépara ma disgrâce.
> Quoi qu'il en soit, Néron d'aussi loin qu'il me vit,
> Laissa sur son visage éclater son dépit.
> Mon Coeur même en conçut un malheureux augure.
> L'Ingrat d'un faux respect colorant son injure,
> Se leva par avance, et courant m'embrasser
> Il m'écarta du Trône ou je m'allais placer.
> Depuis ce coup fatal, le pouvoir d'Agrippine
> Vers sa chute, à grands pas, chaque jour s'achemine.

> I was about to mount the throne with him.
> I do not know what hint urged my disgrace;
> But Nero, from the moment he beheld me,
> Showed his displeasure plainly on his face.
> Deep in my heart I felt the dreaded omen.
> Gilding his insult with a false respect,
> The wretch stood up and, with swift embrace,
> Barred me the throne I was about to mount.
> And, ever since that fatal blow, my power
> Slides each day, avalanching to its doom.
>   (1.1.103–12)

Agrippine, by overstepping the boundaries of her sex, has transgressed what Racine had already announced as the essential principle of absolutism, that sovereignty is indivisible: "Jamais dessus le Trône on ne vit plus d'un Maître / Il n'en peut tenir deux quelque grand qu'il puisse être." (No throne did ever more than one lord see; / Two do not fit, however broad it be.) The throne is the symbol of male sovereignty. As a woman Agrippine has no (political) place.

In both his public ceremonial functions as emperor and his intimate relations as son and lover/husband, Néron strives to liberate himself from the omnipresence of the mother and thus seems to be just one more example of those weak males who populate the Racinian universe and are the prey of an aggressive, retentive, devouring femininity from which they must separate if the social order of their world is not to return to undifferentiated chaos. As we have seen in both *La Thébaïde* and *Andromaque* and as we are now seeing in *Britannicus*, the political (absolutist) order of the Racinian world would seem to follow, with greater urgency and difficulty, one direct imperative: the (male) child must leave the embrace of the mother, be she loving and/or devouring, in order for society to perpetuate itself and not to fall into a fatal stasis.[42]

Anthropologists tell us that this separation of the child from the mother, of the young male from the world of women, is accomplished by all societies, from the most primitive to the most advanced, through institutionalized rites of passage. During these rituals, the young boy is symbolically torn from the world of women, undergoes a symbolic passage through death, and is "reborn," often through the help of male "midwives," into his new life as a man. Certainly we can perceive a perverted version of these rites in the conflicted relationship between Agrippine and Néron's tutors/surrogate fathers, Burrhus and (the absent) Seneca. Running throughout the play is a tug of war between the retentive efforts of Agrippine to keep Néron (and thus her power) attached to her and the equally strong attempts of the tutors to form the young emperor into an independent monarch. He has been removed (at least physically) from the proximity of his mother and entrusted to these older men whose charge it is to make him an able warrior and a philosopher king. They are constantly thwarted in their efforts by the encroaching presence of the mother and by Néron's own inability to live independently of her. Unable to remain within the orbit of these two masculine ideals (strength and wisdom—separated from the feminine pull of the body), Néron becomes the easy prey of the effeminate freedman Narcisse who occupies an interesting position of middleman.

Néron has been vacillating between the two contradictory sides of his nature. Will he give into his lust and become a monstrous tyrant, or will the benevolent monarch, the savior of Rome, win out? He has had Narcisse prepare a poison that he plans to administer to Britannicus, thus finally ridding himself of an amorous and political rival. But he is still caught between two imperious demands. On the one hand there is the world of his masculine tutors, a world of virtue and honor, a world of ideality where if he follows his tutor's precepts he is sure to receive the rewards of a just ruler who will be remembered by history as the benefactor of Rome. On the other, there is the world of material lust, the world of the body and its pleasures, which, as we also know, is ultimately for Racine the sinful world of the mother. Hesitating between these two paths, Néron allows himself, at first, to be swayed by the exhortations of Burrhus who tries one last time to "birth" Néron into the world of Roman masculinity. Invoking the disincarnated voice of judgment, of the ambiguous One that Barthes has defined as the "anonymity of the world,"[43] Burrhus attempts to give Néron the "phallus" (the immaterial sign of Roman virtue), to finally draw him away from his corrupted maternal inheritance, and to place him squarely on the path of the righteous Roman *pater patriae:* "Le chemin est tracé, rien ne vous retient plus. / Vous n'avez qu'à marcher de vertus en vertus" (The path is marked, there's nothing more to stop you). Virtue, that highest of Roman values and the most masculine (where, of course, resounds the masculine ring of the Latin *vir*), rewarded by the love of his people and the paeans of history, is the glorious image that Burrhus holds up to his young charge. And for a moment its fascination is almost strong enough to make Néron forget his body—almost, that is, until Narcisse turns Néron's gaze away from the anonymous Roman populace and fixes it once again on his mother.

Narcisse shuttles treacherously from the gullible Britannicus to the hesitant Néron and confounds in his ambivalent persona/position any attempts at establishing a clearly defined gendered, that is, political, stance. Narcisse is, as we know and as is repeated throughout the play, a freedman. As such he can never fully cast off the opprobrium of the slave he was, nor can he be free of the feminization that is ascribed to slaves in the ancient world. In this way, he too is a hybrid character, a mixed

being, like those other evil counselors—eunuchs or deviant priests—
who populate the Racinian world and who, because they participate as
ambivalent beings in the world of both sexes, are able to corrupt their
all too willing superiors with their perversely seductive rhetoric. In this
Narcisse, true to his name, functions as a perverting mirror, reflecting
back to Néron the image he would like to have of himself. He serves as
a reflection of Néron's desire for what Néron cannot as yet articulate
on his own: Narcisse, better than Burrhus, serves as the midwife to the
new Néron, egging him on with images that are at once seductive and
perverse. Through insinuation that finds a fertile terrain in Néron's own
paranoid jealousy of Britannicus and in his furious frustration at his
own virility's being held hostage to his mother, Narcisse's ministrations
succeed in bringing forth Néron's new monstrous self. Just at the moment
when Néron seems to have opted for virtue, for the path of ideality,
and has rejected the corrupting influence of the body, just as he decides
to renounce his murderous project and to reconcile for the sake of
Rome's political stability and his own desire not to be remembered as a
parricide, he vacillates:

> Mais de tout l'Univers quel sera le langage?
> Sur les pas des Tyrans veux-tu que je m'engage,
> Et que Rome effaçant tant de titres d'honneur
> Me laisse pour tous noms celui d'empoisonneur?
> Ils mettront ma vengeance au rang des parricides.

> But then, how will the babbling world regard it?
> Do you insist I choose the tyrant's path
> That Rome, erasing all marks of esteem,
> Should leave me but the name of poisoner?
> My vengeance they will brand as fratricide.
> (4.4.1427–31)

Narcisse brandishes before him the images of his mother, Agrippine,
gloating over her triumph, and of his tutors, who direct his every move.
Narcisse reflects back to Néron the image that haunts him and that he
rails against, the image of an ineffectual puppet controlled by his mother
and his tutors and mocked behind his back by the Roman populace:

> Néron . . . n'est point né pour l'Empire.
> Il ne dit, il ne fait, que ce qu'on lui prescrit,
> Burrhus conduit son Coeur, Sénèque son esprit.
> Pour toute ambition, pour vertu singulière,

Il excelle à conduire un char dans la carrière,
A disputer des prix indignes de ses mains,
A se donner lui-même en spectacle aux Romains. . . .

"Nero," they hint, "was not born to the Throne;
He only says and does what he is told.
His mind controlled by Seneca, his heart
By Burrhus. His highest aim, his noblest part
Is to excel as Rome's first charioteer,
To strive for prizes that may raise a cheer
But are unworthy of Caesar. . . .
        (4.4.1468–74)

From the beginning, Néron has been the prey of images: of the weep-
ing, frightened Junie ravished by the brawny soldiers who bring her to
his palace, of the love of Junie and Britannicus, of his mother's "fiery
eyes," of the virtuous emperor he is exhorted to become, and finally of his
own histrionic self.[44] It is, of course, in the play of these images, in the
intersection of sadism and masochism, voyeurism and exhibitionism, that
these images conflate and perpetuate and Néron and the world of which
he is the aberrant center are undone. By his uncanny ability to distort
and reflect these images back to Néron, Narcisse succeeds in undermining
any possibility of Néron's salvation. Néron's relation to and dependence
on Narcisse marks his entrapment in the nether world, neither male
nor female, of this reprobate former slave and thus his inability, despite
his aggressive rhetoric, to be free of the world of his mother. She remains, relayed by Narcisse's pandering to his desires, present in/as his
body. The only avenue left open to Néron is the monstrous: he will become a parricide, the impassive assassin of his brother, his mother, his
wife, and his tutors, and responsible for the destruction of Rome.

Even in his monstrousness Néron cannot be free from his origins,
cannot be free from Agrippine. To the end they are locked in a perverse embrace where, although she thinks she is the instrument of the
brothers' reconciliation, it turns out that she is but the messenger of
death. Britannicus, to the end, remains blissfully unaware of the dangers surrounding him. Convinced once again that Agrippine has labored
on his behalf, he is anxious to join the young revelers at the banquet
that is to seal his refound fraternity. He is convinced that Néron has
abandoned Junie to him and that their future happiness is now assured.
Junie, more prescient, is much less sure. She has, in her brief time at

this court, learned to distrust even the most candid assurances of the
emperor and Agrippine:

> Seigneur, ne jugez pas de son Coeur par le vôtre.
> Sur des pas différents vous marchez l'un et l'autre.
> Je ne connais Néron et la Cour que d'un jour.
> Mais, (si je l'ose dire) hélas! dans cette Cour
> Combien tout ce qu'on dit est loin de ce qu'on pense!
> Que la bouche et le Coeur sont peu d'intelligence!
> Avec combien de joie on y trahit sa foi!
> Quel séjour étranger et pour vous et pour moi!

> Ah! do not judge his heart, my lord, by yours:
> You walk on different paths the two of you.
> I know the Court and Nero but one day;
> But in this Court alas! I dare to say
> How far is what one says from what one thinks!
> Between the mouth and heart how few the links!
> With what alacrity one breaks one's word!
> A strange abode for you and me, my lord!
>
> (5.1.1519–26)

Junie tries to keep Britannicus with her. She asks him not to hurry off
to the banquet, to wait until he is summoned. Her last words to him
are, "Mais du moins attendez qu'on vous vienne avertir" (But wait at
least until they tell you so). And, of course, the summons follows directly
on her plea, and it comes from Agrippine. Rushing onto the stage, Agrippine, flushed with what she thinks is her victory over her son's resistance and confident in her newly enhanced status at court, is eager to
see the reconciliation that she has orchestrated, confirmed by the fraternal embrace that she tells Britannicus awaits him in the banquet
hall. It is Agrippine who sends Britannicus to his death:

> Prince, que tardez-vous? Partez en diligence.
> Néron impatient se plaint de votre absence.
> La joie et le plaisir de tous les Conviés
> Attend pour éclater que vous vous embrassiez.

> Why are you dallying, Prince? Be off, at once:
> The impatient Nero murmurs at your absence.
> The joy and pleasure of the company
> To reach their climax wait for your embrace.
>
> (5.2.1571–74)

As we have already seen in *La Thébaïde*, however, when two brothers are pushed together by a demanding mother, the expected fraternal
embrace turns deadly. In a sense we might say that the end of *Britannicus*—and of Britannicus—shows us once more the unequal battle between those two facets of femininity that preside over Racine's tragic
universe: on the one side, the woman as comforter and soul mate, loving but ineffectual, and on the other, the woman as aggression and
death, the reborn Sphinx who feeds off those young men too naive, or
simply not smart enough, to respond adequately to her enigma. Britannicus, caught in a world of illusion and perversion that he cannot master, dies. We might see him as simply just one more victim of Agrippine's climb to power. Or we might just as easily see him as the first
victim of the son, Néron, who, although fiendish, although responsible
for the destruction of his family and of Rome, may signal not just the
birth of a monster but the beginnings of the end of an ideological struggle that only the triumph of an absolutism that is merely glimpsed at in
this tragedy can hope to impose on a fearful world.

4

Bérénice, Bajazet, Mithridate:
Oriental Oedipus

After *Britannicus* Racine writes three tragedies that, however different each is from the others, however dissimilar in time, cultural settings, and geographic locations, are all related, it seems to me, by what appears to be a common politico/ideological drive: each in its own (tragic) way traces through the sexualization of its political plot the tenuous but necessary triumph of an idealized Western (Christian) monarchy over an Oriental (barbarian/Muslim) despotism. It is perhaps in this new turn that Racinian tragedy, seemingly having strayed from its anchoring in Greek mythology, reconfigures the social prejudices of Hellenic patriarchy in new scenarios where Oedipus and his legacy are rescripted in more acutely political dramas. Let us not forget that at least since Hegel the Oedipus legend has been interpreted not only as a cautionary tale of incest and parricide but also and at the same time as the originary narrative of the birth of Western philosophy: Oedipus the philosopher, as Jean-Joseph Goux has written.[1] This philosophy, as consciousness of self, however, has also been shown to embody the same sociosexual prejudices that are seductively integral to the corpus of Greek mythology. In an influential article published more than twenty years ago, Stephen Heath demonstrates that while Hegel's reading of Oedipus presents the legend as the triumph of Western philosophy as a philosophy of self-reflection, it remains a philosophy in which "self" means to both recognize and exclude what is other. It is over and against this other that it can define, and thus delimit, itself as thinking subject. In other words, a form of self-sufficient ideality excludes the material, here represented by the Sphinx, the oriental, female other. Heath returns to the founding moment of Western self-reflexivity, to this determining moment when, in the space of a syllable, Oedipus constitutes himself as the measure of all things and emphasizes what, in the scene of his confrontation with the Sphinx, is ideologically (sexually) overdetermined:

> For Hegel, the Sphinx stands at the beginning of the history of consciousness. Or rather, that beginning comes with its defeat: Oedipus solves the riddle, flings the Sphinx over the rock, gets rid of the monstrous; philosophy, consciousness in its movement to attain true knowledge, starts from there, from that solution, the passage to the Greek world. Which means that what is put aside as Oedipus answers "man" and Hegel repeats him is the otherness—as it then becomes—to that Western term: the cultural difference of the Sphinx-Orient immobile to history, before the stirring of consciousness... the sexual difference of the Sphinx-Woman troubling identity in her representation, as riddling presence at the city gates, the hybrid to which man's "man" replies, ending the trouble by erasure.[2]

The politics that the Oedipus myth represents in this interpretation, the politics that is condensed in and on the figure of the riddle-solving perpetrator of parricide and incest, is also the originary moment of Western masculine hegemony. It is an absolutist politics that the very answer "man" sends the Sphinx—oriental, female, monster—to her suicide. It is this verbal gesture of inclusion/exclusion that will mark the coming into being of Western consciousness as both consciousness of self and therefore of the idea of a self that necessarily excludes its other. The Sphinx and all that her monstrousness represents—the body as difference, as voracious sexuality, as death—is cast beyond the pale, while Oedipus, having triumphed over this final obstacle on his road to the absolute, is rewarded with both a wife and a kingdom.

In his new role as king he is, as we know, destined first for glory and then for terror. After the revelation of his incest and parricide, after (in Sophocles' version) Jocaste's suicide, Oedipus puts out his eyes, those eyes that have gazed on his own transgressions. Blinded, he leaves Thebes to wander aimlessly in the Greek hinterland. Oedipus, the *pharmakos*, is expelled from the city he ruled, leaving his wife/mother and their monstrous progeny behind. Wandering sightless across the deserts that separate the space of nature and the limits of civilization (the *poleis*), Oedipus is doomed to the fate of the unruly body that betrayed him. Only at the end of his wanderings, at the moment of his death, which predates the tragic conflict that Racine stages for us in *La Thébaïde*, does his wandering end at the gates of Athens. There and only there can his sacrifice be fully valorized as an acceptance of a divine knowledge that is simultaneously the terror of a self-knowledge that blinds and a divine insight into the secrets of sovereignty. Welcomed by Theseus, and at last afforded the hospitality of the polis, Oedipus becomes Athens's "holy terror."[3] As he disappears into the grove of the Eumenides, Oedipus regains a semblance of majesty. At the very moment that he is divested of his sacred suffering, the sovereignty of his fate is transferred to Theseus, that slayer of monsters and seducer of women, the hero who most forcefully represents by these dual feats the civilizing, masculine virtues of Greek society. In return for Athens's hospitality, for Athens's accepting him as a citizen and providing him with a sepulcher (*Oedipus at Colonnus*), Oedipus's hallowed secret of majesty remains with the kings of that city. It is a secret that is passed from king to king, forming a chain, an Oedipal legacy of sovereignty. The Oedipal desire for the rule of the One, the masculine imperative of/for hegemony, passes from Thebes to Athens, and from Athens it goes on to colonize the entire Western world.[4]

I have sketched out, very briefly, what strikes me as two of the most important, different but interrelated aspects of the Oedipus legend that are perhaps not quite as familiar as the more spectacular and admittedly more essential facets (incest and parricide) whose notoriety is universally recognized. I do so, however, only to insist on how these aspects of the legend simply expand on the central core—the core that most intensely deals with aggression and sexuality in their familial context— in order to show that already the political play of power and desire is at work there and that this work radiates out into all the other aspects of the legend so that although one might choose to emphasize the more directly familial (the private) or the more specifically political (public) ramifications of the legend, in fact we are dealing, as Racine was, with all the aspects, public and private, at once. While his first tragedies dealt more intimately with the enmeshment of familial desires in the public sphere of the polis, we now are confronted with a series of plays where passion, if just as blistering, appears to be at the (dis)service of not so much a particular political situation (although it is that, too) but at the service of a much more diffuse ideological conflict. In the next plays that Racine produces in quick succession, we can detect that those elements that were already present in his previous dramas take on a novel intensity as they come to represent not so much a mythological underpinning rooted in the Greek world but an intensified refraction of that world's mistrust of the other, an other always identified with the sexual excesses of the flesh that have been declined in a metaphoric chain that extends from the ancient Greeks' suspicion of women and "barbaroi" to the misogynistic musings of the Christian West where the barbaroi are now firmly ensconced within: they are the seductive, sinful daughters of Eve.

Racine's shift in focus onto these sexualized barbarians (the Oriental protagonists of *Bérénice, Bajazet,* and *Mithridate*) at this point in his writing and political career might signal us to look more allegorically than we have up to this point at what the new ideological subtext of these tragedies reflects as they follow the meanderings of the Oedipus legend tracing the contours of a particularly Western economy of sexual politics as it defines itself over and against the most prominent example of difference, its feared and seductive Oriental other. It is interesting to note, as Lucette Valensi has reminded us, that although the latest avatar of the Eastern other, the Ottoman Empire, had, at least since the fall of Constantinople in 1453, been a subject of alarm and respect in the West, and although its social, political, and sexual mores had been detailed and studied during the fifteenth and sixteenth centuries, the particular form of government of the Ottoman state was not described as "despotic" with the dark overtones that word was to acquire in Montesquieu.[5] Neither Machiavelli nor Bodin, those two essential theorists of absolutism, describe the empire of the Turk as a despotic regime. During the seventeenth century, however, through the reports of embassies, missionaries, savants, and merchants, the perception of the East shifts (in a centuries-old atavism), going from respectful admiration for a powerful but rightful monarchical state to the description of an "unnatural" despotism. "Despotic," in fact, as Valensi notes, makes its appearance in European vocabulary during the first decades of the seventeenth century.[6]

In its most powerful, that is, culturally charged, definition, a despotic state is a monarchy that "is ruled by the passions and by (self)-interest."[7] In the Western imaging of the Orient and the Oriental despot, there is a strong dose of sadomasochistic projection in which sexuality, a cruel, absolute desire, and an unquenchable, unyielding pursuit of pleasure become the image and definition of the Oriental other. Alain Grosrichard has suggested that the chief character of the Oriental, the despot, is situated in the involution of the political and the sexual; unlimited sexual pleasure becomes, tautologically, the definition of despotism as a tyrannical, that is, political, structure. Paradoxically, this supreme right to *jouissance*, Grosrichard tells us, leads to an effective absence of sovereign power at the very center of the political structure. The Oriental despot condemned to pleasure, condemned to a total unrelenting attention to his body as site of pleasure, to the body's imperious and incessant demands, cannot exercise any real political power in the state.[8]

What we have in these images of the Oriental monarch is essentially a taxonomy of difference between an Eastern body and a Western (European/Christian) mind, between body (pleasure) and reason (reality principle), between, eventually, effeminacy (thus the feminine) and martial vigor (thus masculinity). If we were to contrast the Oriental despot to the absolute sovereign as we see the concept developed in the mid- to late sixteenth century, we could reduce schematically the opposition the West establishes between itself and its other as one between a body that refuses the law of castration, the law that would be anything other than the demands of its own pleasure and the body subjugated to castration, to the "no" of the law, the principle of negation and thus sublimation.

Even among those writers in the French tradition who are the theorists of absolutism (and here Bodin will serve as an exemplary figure), although it was admitted that the prince was *legibus solutus* in respect to civil law, he was *legibus alligatus* in respect to natural law.[9] What this meant, essentially, was that while the sovereignty of the state resided in the prince, who was above civil law, he was not, could not be, above natural law. He could not act contrary to the basic laws of the realm (in France, the Salic law, for instance) nor could he infringe on the property rights of his subjects by expropriating their private domain or levying new taxes on them. Although sovereign, he was (in/by theory) limited. The king, in other words, in the theory of Western monarchy, cannot be a slave to his earthly body, in which case he would be merely a tyrant and thus (although this was hotly debated) removable. He is sovereign precisely because he accepts "castration," the loss of his private body for the good of the polis. Subjected to the law of "no," the law that eliminates the other (body) that inheres in him, he sacrifices this body private in the immolation of his privates: (in theory) he becomes sovereign—one, absolute. It is, however, as yet another version of sacrifice (and perhaps redemption) that this large, evolving, sociosexual scenario enters onto the stage of Racine's tragic productions in Oriental garb.

Bérénice

In Racine's impressively rapid succession of tragedies, *Bérénice* (1670) follows *Britannicus* and precedes *Bajazet*. This new play, sandwiched between two of the most artfully perverse and bloody dramas in the Racinian repertory, has from the beginning been a challenge to critics who have struggled with its exceptionalism. *Bérénice* does not seem to fit neatly into any of the interpretative schemas that have been offered for understanding the overarching construction of Racine's tragic universe. In his recent Pléiade edition of Racine's theater, George Forestier, the latest of Racine's French exegetes, insists once again on the uniqueness of the play: "Cas unique en son temps, elle repose sur un sujet dans lequel l'amour constitue l'enjeu politique de la tragédie" (a unique case for its time, the drama is based on a story where love forms the political stakes of the tragedy, 1443); "*Bérénice* présente le cas unique dans la production racinienne depuis *Andromaque* jusqu'à *Phèdre*, la synthèse entre pureté et passion" (*Bérénice* offers a unique case in Racine's output from *Andromaque* to *Phèdre*, the synthesis of purity and passion, 1444). More radical in his judgment, Voltaire famously announced that *Bérénice* was not a tragedy at all. Rather it was, he said, merely an extended elegy. In this he was simply repeating one of the first reactions to the play, the judgment of the Abbé de Villars, who in 1671 in *La critique de Bérénice* had declared that the play was "une pièce de Théâtre, qui depuis le commencement jusqu'à la fin, n'est qu'un tissu gallant de Madrigaux et d'Elégies" (a play that from the beginning to the end is but a gallant tapestry of Madrigals and Elegies).[10]

Bérénice seems, at first, to be the odd play out in Racine's oeuvre, not really a tragedy but an elegy, a mournful dirge, a judgment that nevertheless had been strenuously rebutted by Racine, who took pains to tell us in his preface to the play why this play where no blood is spilled, where no one dies, is in fact a tragedy:

> Ce n'est point une nécessité qu'il y ait du sang et des morts dans une Tragédie; il suffit que l'Action en soit grande, que les Acteurs en soient héroïques, que les Passions y soient excitées, et que tout s'y ressente de cette tristesse majestueuse qui fait tout le plaisir de la Tragédie.

> Neither the spilling of blood nor deaths are a necessity in a tragedy; it is enough that the plot be grandiose and the actors heroic, that the passions be stirred up and that everything be touched by that majestic melancholy that produces the real pleasure of Tragedy.[11]

Tears rather than blood is the confirmation, for Racine, of his play's tragic affect, the plentiful tears shed by the audience: "Je ne puis croire que le Public me sache mauvais gré de lui avoir donné une Tragédie qui a été honorée de tant de larmes" (I cannot believe that the audience is annoyed with me for having given it a Tragedy that received the homage of so many tears).[12]

What we have, therefore, according to Racine, is a melancholic tragedy of loss, constructed, as he disarmingly claims, "out of nothing." It is a tragedy of tears rather than of blood, but if death has been expelled from it, there nevertheless remains, by Racine's artful comparisons in his preface to the play, the trace of another, similar story whose tragic ending casts its pall over *Bérénice*. Racine reaches back through history to literary mythology, to the *Aeneid*, in order to conjure up "en sourdine," as a model for his own pair of ill-fated lovers, the doomed passion of Dido and Aeneas with, as we know, a difference.[13] In Racine's rewriting of history as tragedy and in order to save appearances and not cast aspersions on the character of his latest heroine, Racine tells us that, unlike Dido, Bérénice "n'ayant pas ici avec Titus les derniers engagements que Didon avait avec Enée, elle n'est pas obligée comme elle de renoncer à la vie" (not having here with Titus the most intimate of relations that Dido had with Aeneas, she is not forced like the latter to end her life).[14]

Racine's invocation of the myth of Dido and Aeneas in conjunction with his own tragedy, the sources for which were mainly provided by his reading of Suetonius and Flavius Josephus, has the interesting effect of both bringing sexuality and death into play in order immediately to banish them to the periphery of his tragedy, both present by implication and by literary, mythological contamination but also both absent in order to avoid any unseemly physicality on the part of his incorporeal protagonists. It is but another miracle of artistic creation that Racine was able to take the two middle-aged voluptuaries he found in Suetonius and turn them into paragons of the most rarefied ideals of abnegation and courtly love. Racine's first radical move in composing *Bérénice* was to eliminate (metaphorically) the body. In Racine's dramatization of history, where there is no sex, there is, tautologically, no death. Having done away with sexuality and death, the play presents us with purely ethereal heroes who are condemned to carry with them a pervasive melancholia, the ambivalent marker of their tragic sacrifice.

When the tragedy begins, Bérénice and Titus have been happily in love for the last five years. Titus, having been sent to the Orient to quell the uprising of the rebellious Hebrews, met and fell in love with Bérénice, who returned his affection. They returned together to Rome where, due to her influence on him, Titus abandoned his debauched ways learned at Nero's court. From a dissolute aristocrat he became a model of imperial wisdom and largesse:

> Tu ne l'ignores pas, toujours la Renommée
> Avec le même éclat n'a pas semé mon nom.
> Ma jeunesse nourrie à la Cour de Néron
> S'égarait, cher Paulin, par l'exemple abusée,
> Et suivait du plaisir la pente trop aisée.
> Bérénice me plut. Que ne fait point un Coeur
> Pour plaire à ce qu'il aime, et gagner son Vainqueur!
> . . . .
> J'entrepris le bonheur de mille Malheureux.
> Ma main avec plaisir apprit à se répandre;
> Heureux! et plus heureux que tu ne peux comprendre
> Quand je pouvais paraître à ses yeux satisfaits
> Chargé de mille coeurs conquis par mes bienfaits.

> You know it well. This shining fame was not
> From the beginning broidered with my name:
> Raised at the Court of Nero in my youth,
> By bad example I was led astray
> And still pursued the slippery slope of pleasure.
> I fell in love with Bérénice. To impress her
> And gain her love, I did my very best.
> . . . .

> I strove to make a thousand wretches glad,
> And my beneficence spread all around.
> Happy! And happier far than you imagine
> When I could come before her beaming eyes,
> Bearing a thousand hearts won by my boons!
> (2.2.504–18)

Behind Titus's military prowess and magnanimity stands the image of Bérénice. She leads him away from the easy road of sensual pleasure, away from the monstrous sexuality that reigned at Nero's court and down the thorny path of moral rectitude. She certainly appears to occupy a maternal rather than passionate role in Titus's description of her. This maternal, in the sense of nonsexual, and wise pedagogue leads the child-man still captive of his senses out of the prison of his body's pleasure and into the light of mature, that is, sublimated, humanitarianism. At the same time she is presented as the embodiment of a conventional allegorical representation of the Orient: Bérénice is here garbed as Sophia, a traditional figure of Oriental wisdom whose historic abode was in the East (in Egypt).

It is precisely because of this doubling, of this combination of the love-object as maternal and Oriental, that Bérénice is doomed. Once Titus accedes to the imperial throne, what was an idyllic love affair becomes an "affaire d'Etat": Roman tradition refuses any return of a hated monarchal legacy. Although Bérénice would like to believe that she can live her love as a utopian idyll, the play never lets us forget that the idyll is threatened by the invisible presence of the Roman people who are nevertheless omnipresent. This social injunction, this drive that refuses the pleasure of individual desire, will move the protagonists into positions that society defines for them and that are inimical to any compromise that would allow a foreign "queen" a place in Roman society.

When Titus asks his confidant, Paulin, what rumors he hears about Bérénice and himself, Paulin responds:

> J'entends de tous côtés
> Publier vos vertus, Seigneur, et ses beautés.

> I hear everywhere,
> My lord, your virtues and her beauty praised.
> (2.2.345–46)

Through its obvious echoes, "vertus" establishes an entire chain of sexual/political allusions that are coded as male and Roman. "Beautés," functioning as a metonymy for Bérénice, establishes another chain in hierarchical opposition to the first and declines an economy of otherness: beauty, female, Oriental. Paulin continues to give voice to the traditions of Rome that the marriage of Titus and Bérénice would transgress and at the same time underscores the ideological (racial) prejudices that tradition embodies:

> N'en doutz point, Seigneur. Soit raison ou caprice,
> Rome ne l'attend point pour son Impératrice.
> On sait qu'elle est charmante. Et de si belles mains
> Semblent vous demander l'Empire des Humains.
> Elle a même, dit-on le Coeur d'une Romaine.
> Elle a mille vertus. Mais, Seigneur, elle est Reine.
> Rome par une Loi, qui ne se peut changer,
> N'admet avec son sang aucun sang étranger,
> Et ne reconnaît point les fruits illégitimes
> Qui naissent d'un Hymen contraire à ses maximes.

> You may be sure of it: be it right or wrong,
> Rome does not wish to see her as her Empress.
> They know her spell; and such exquisite hands
> Seem made to hold dominion over men.
> She even has, they say, a Roman heart;
> She has a thousand virtues, but is Queen.
> Rome, by an ancient law, that brooks no change,
> To her blood will admit no foreign blood,
> Will recognize no lawless progeny
> Sprung from a marriage counter to her code.
>   (2.2.371–80)

It would not be too far-fetched to propose that this vox populi that comes from everywhere and nowhere, that is immaterial and originless, this voice that enunciates Roman law and that speaks through Paulin, is the voice of the gods, the voice of the law, that has, in the funeral rites that have just ended, deified Titus's dead father, Vespasian:[15]

> Vous fûtes spectateur de cette nuit dernière,
> Lorsque, pour seconder ses soins religieux,
> Le sénat a placé son père entre les dieux.

> You saw, yourself, the spectacle last night,
> When, setting seal on his religious rites,
> The Senate raised his father to the gods.
>   (1.4.164–66)

Deifying the dead father, placing him in a space beyond death, suc-cessfully makes Vespasian one with a certain ideal that Titus, if he wishes to correspond to the image that Bérénice reflects to him, the universal-izing image of emperor, will have to attain. It is a place that we know Titus desires ("J'ai même souhaité la place de mon père" [I've even wished to fill my father's place]). He wishes to become one with his image, with his father; and the dictates of the voice of this father, confounded in/as the generalized voice of the people, articulate to Titus the sacrifi-cial gesture by which he may finally achieve his desire.

In order to make the sacrifice palatable, or at least communally acceptable, the sacrificial victim must be turned by the tragedy's rheto-ric into a scapegoat. It will seem that I am stating the obvious to insist that in a highly patriarchal society the relation between sovereignty in both its political forms (monarchy) and its metaphysical imperatives (the relation between God and the world) turns, as Freud suggests, equally on the elevation and sublimation of the figure of the father and his destruction.[16] No divine-right monarchy is possible without the integral backing of a theological view of the universe that unites God, kingship, and paternity along the same metaphoric axis, establishing a universe in which the devolution of power from male to male is medi-ated through the sacrifice of patriarchy's other, the representation of the other, woman, of the feminine, that must be eliminated.

In the case of *Bérénice*, the conflation functions sexually, politically, and racially. On a first level, Paulin announces Bérénice's unacceptability to the Romans on the ground of her royal status: she is a queen. From this first enunciation of the historical/mythical *obstat*, the speech passes from the idea of Bérénice as generic queen to allusions to a specifically overinvested (for Romans) queen—Cleopatra. Here to the rather bland political connotations are added the more sulfurously enticing attrib-utes of sexuality, luxury, and Orientalism. *Bérénice* incorporates into its very center the most overdetermined signifier of sexual excess, of the Oriental femme fatale who, by seducing both Julius Caesar and Mark Antony almost caused the entire history of the world to deviate from its predestined (Roman) course. Cleopatra's monstrosity, the foreignness so necessary to authorize her (and her "sisters'") sacrifice, is introduced rhetorically by a negative comparison with those political monsters Caligula and Nero, whose misdeeds, however egregious, stopped short of the ultimate horror of a foreign marriage:

> Depuis ce temps, Seigneur, Caligula, Néron,
> Monstres, dont à regret je cite ici le nom
> Et qui ne conservant que la figure d'Homme,
> Foulèrent à leurs pieds toutes les Lois de Rome,
> Ont craint cette Loi seule, et n'ont point à nos yeux
> Allumé le Flambeau d'un Hymen odieux.

> Since then, my lord, Caligula and Nero,
> Monsters, whose names I mention with regret,
> And who, retaining but a man's appearance.
> Trampled on all the sacred laws of Rome,
> Feared this one law and did not dare to light
> A nuptial torch abhorrent in our eyes.
>   (2.2.397–402)

This fear that stopped emperors did not stop the brother of a base free-man, Pallas, from passing, quite surprisingly, from the prisons of Claudius Felix to the marriage bed of not one but two Oriental queens:

> De l'affranchi Pallas nous avons vu le Frère
> Des fers de Claudius Felix encore flétri
> De deux Reines, Seigneur, devenir le Mari.

> We've seen the brother of the freedman Pallas,
> Felix, still bearing marks of Claudius' chains
> Become, my lord the husband of two queens.
>   (2.2.404–6)

And as the coup de grâce, the speech ends in a crescendo of rhetorical violence by embracing all the previously mentioned allusions to sexu-ality, femininity, and Orientalism with the clincher:

> Et s'il faut jusqu'au bout que je vous obéisse,
> Ces deux Reines étaient du sang de Bérénice.

> And if I must obey you to the end,
> These two queens were of Bérénice's blood.
>   (2.2.407–8)

"Blood"—that extraordinarily overdetermined signifier for all systems of nobiliary aristocracy—is brought in at the end of the speech to underline the contaminating possibilities that the words "fruits illégitimes" and "hymen odieux" had already suggested.[17] The fear of the other that the speech has adumbrated is finally summarized in the ultimate rhetorical chiasmus where the theme of the inherent abjection of Bérénice, her guilt by association of gender and of race, is expulsed from the realm of Roman possibility:

> Et vous pourriez, Seigneur, sans blesser nos regards,
> Faire entrer une Reine au Lit de nos Césars,
> Tandis que l'Orient dans le Lit de ses Reines
> Voit passer un Esclave au sortir de nos chaînes?

> And yet you think you may, without offence,
> Conduct a queen into our Caesar's bed,
> While the Orient sees its queenly beds defiled
> By slaves, but lately freed from Roman chains?
> (2.2.409–10)

Paulin's speech enunciates the law of Romanness, which is a law of exclusion and, of course, death. In order to empower this law from the space of enunciation, that place is never relativized. Rather, what is at work is simply the arrogance of power staking out its own limits by defining itself over and against its weaker other. Bérénice is victimized, rendered abject by a sliding series of naturalized (for Rome) oppositions that are all implicitly or explicitly validated in and through this exclusion. Ideas of fatherland, history, and racial difference are articulated by stating what they are not: feminine, sexual, Oriental. At the same time, this image of Bérénice as unwitting sacrificial other, her sacrificeability, is rendered all the more poignant by the love she inspires in Titus. This love, the maternal love as it has been described by Titus, is contrasted to that abject other to which the law/speech has reduced her.

In Paulin's depiction, therefore, we have the inverted portrait of the picture suggested by Titus. To the passive, demur, and maternal Bérénice of Titus's description is opposed the sultry, aggressive, inherently dangerous Cleopatra. That these two contrasting images of women haunt the dramatic universe of Racine comes as no surprise to modern students reading in the wake of Freud.[18] On a simple level what we have in these antithetical images of Bérénice is the classic dichotomy of the woman as mother/whore that Freud discussed in his essay "A Special Type of Object Choice Made by Men." In that essay, Freud wrote that "a thing which in consciousness makes its appearance as two contraries is often in the unconscious a united whole."[19] It would seem, however, that what we have in *Bérénice* is what is so often presented as separate characters in the bloodier tragedies of Racine—on the one hand, the aggressive threatening phallic woman and, on the other, the submissive, virginal, passive female. It is this amalgamation, this coincidence of antithetical qualities, both conscious and unconscious, the ambivalence that inheres in her, that makes Bérénice particularly appealing and ultimately the most melancholic character in Racine. As we've seen, the central question asked of melancholia is not so much *who* is the particular person (or ideal) one has lost but *what* in that person has been sacrificed. It might appear at first sight that all the characters in *Bérénice* are losers because they all have lost the love that was their only chance of happiness. By losing this love, they have lost everything, and they are condemned each in his/her own way to a life empty of all joy, to the internal desert they now carry with them irrigated only by their tears. It is also obvious that in the sexual/political dynamics of the play there are those who have not lost everything.

Titus, for instance, will suffer, will flagellate himself, will shed tears of frustration and loss and even threaten to kill himself, but the die is cast (as it has been since the very beginning of the play): Bérénice will be sent back to "l'orient desert," there to serve as a glorious example of self-sacrifice, held up to the admiration of the "Universe." In a sense, we might say that Titus succeeds where Néron failed. He has, with a heavy dose of bad faith, been able to enter into the world of Roman virility ("Contemplez mon devoir dans toute sa rigueur" [Regard my duty in its awful strictness]), the world of men, by separating himself from his too possessive mother/lover, from the totalizing ("Beauté, Gloire, Vertu, je trouve tout en elle" [Fame, virtue, beauty, all I find in her]) maternal body whose embrace denies the call of the empire, the call of the law.[20] But this sacrifice of his love, of his other/body, is the first step on his way toward deification, to becoming not only the perfect Roman emperor but "les délices du genre humain." Through the sacrifice of his lover/mother, Titus achieves a greater narcissistic pleasure that more than compensates for the loss of Bérénice. Free of his Oriental queen,

Titus can now go on to become part of history, to join his father in the pantheon of Roman emperor/gods who will continue to serve as models of divinely inspired kingship through the centuries. At the same time he also serves as the greatest model of the rightful Christian monarch: eschewing the passion of the body, Titus appears as the exemplary, dutiful, and righteous Western leader, virile in his refusal of the feminine, imbued with the double halo of duty and virtue. As such he stands as the perfect symbol of probity, the desexualized father of his people(s) whose sacrifice stands in marked contrast to the despotic rulers of the East and who awaits his reincarnation centuries after his death in the new model of the perfect Christian king, Louis XIV.[21]

While there has been the persistent (if incorrect) rumor in the annals of "la petite histoire" that Racine's tragedy (as well as Corneille's *Tite et Bérénice*) was inspired by the doomed love of the young Louis and Marie Mancini, niece of cardinal Mazarin, it seems more pertinent to recall not so much this particular romantic interlude in the life of the king but rather the creation of Louis' royal persona by the bevy of salaried propagandists who recast the image of their monarch in the different molds of Apollo, Mars, and of course Titus.[22] While the legend of Louis' youthful escapades was used to highlight the virility of the young monarch and thus the vigor of the new reign, at the same time we cannot ignore his overarching mistrust of the nefarious influence women were bound to exercise in the affairs of state if given the opportunity to influence a reigning prince. Writing to the dauphin in his *Mémoires*, Louis warns his son never to let sexual passion get in the way of *raison d'état*:

> Dès lors que vous donnez la liberté à une femme de vous parler des choses importantes, il est impossible qu'elle ne nous fassent faillir. La tendresse que nous avons pour elles, nous faisant goûter leurs plus mauvaises raisons, nous fait tomber insensiblement du côté où elles penchent; et la faiblesse qu'elles ont naturellement, leur faisant souvent préférer des intérêt de bagatelles aux plus solides considérations, leur fait presque toujours prendre le mauvais parti. Elle sont éloquentes dans leurs expressions, pressantes dans leurs prières, opiniâtres dans leurs sentiments.

> As soon as you allow a woman to speak to you about important matters, it is impossible that she not lead you into error. The tender feelings we have for them which makes us enjoy their worst ideas makes us lean in the same direction to which they incline; and their natural weakness which makes them often prefer trifling matters over more weighty

concerns, almost always makes them choose the wrong side. They are eloquent in their pleas, pestering in their demands, and stubborn in their inclinations.[23]

It would seem that it is in following Louis' advice (concern, fears) rather than his love life that Racine writes his first Oriental tragedy, where the sacrifice of love/pleasure is transformed into a melancholic elegy for that part of oneself that we all have to immolate on the altar of the law if the state is to be spared the disastrous consequences of acquiescing to the lure of the feminine.[24]

Bajazet

Bajazet, which followed *Bérénice* on the Parisian stage in 1672, would seem to exist as the contemporary, dramatic proof of Louis' misogynistic warning to the dauphin following *Bérénice*. The least traditionally violent of Racine's plays, *Bajazet* is the most murderous: the play ends in a veritable bloodbath with the slaughter/suicide of the three principal characters. It is also, perversely, the most obscene. As we have already noted, all the recent critics who have renewed our understanding of the Racinian corpus have commented, one way or the other, on the importance in this corpus of the eye(s), of seeing and of being seen in the elaboration of Racine's tragic universe. Barthes, Mauron, and Starobinski have led us to understand the importance of this textual/lexical presence that informs Racine's tragic vision. Racine has been admired for his ability (especially in the inevitable comparison with Corneille) to work with apparent effortlessness and elegance within the restraints placed on seventeenth-century playwrights by the "règles de bienséance." These rules forbade any too overt mention of the body and its organs in their *Kreaturlichkeit*. The eye(s), however, because of their almost ephemeral quality—they are the physical organ of sight but also, metaphorically, the conduit of understanding, of knowledge, and of passion—seem to lend themselves by a certain sleight of hand to the transformation of materiality into ideality: the eye becomes one with a vision, a gaze, a glance, that floating free from any anchoring in the physical attains the realm of the purely immaterial, of the ideal.

The fact that this organ exerts such a strong pressure inside the Racinian text, appearing as a series of verbs ("voir," "regarder," "apercevoir") or as nominatives ("oeil," "yeux," "regards"), reveals, of course, the presence of an even stronger impulse, which Freud was the first to identify as an independent psychic drive—a powerful *schaulust* that, in Racine, joins sexuality, through the sadomasochistic emphasis Racine gives it (and in this he was presciently Freudian, *avant la lettre*), to the tragic and political force of his theater. This drive to see, to understand, to penetrate, to know, and thus to control is intimately linked in Racine to a strategy of power. As we move through the tragedies, the force of this visual drive has progressively gained more prominence. Of course the essential question remains: what drives the drive? What, exactly, does one want to "see"? What is the object of this *shaulust* reduced to its most elementary level?

Traditionally, the response to this question is given within the gender-biased ideology that informs the very phrasing of it. The gaze has been equated with a supposedly inherent desire of the male to "see" the difference of female sexuality, a sight that is both horrifying and exciting to him.[25] Although I believe that this response is appropriate to Racine, it is only a partial answer. I think that a broader definition, one that would place a more ambivalent twist on the standard male gaze response, would offer a larger exploratory terrain on which to understand the underlying psychic tensions in Racine's production. It would be perhaps better for us to answer the question with a less gender-specific response and say that what one wants to see is simply the unknowable difference, the point at which difference becomes, if not ascertainable—that is, fixed into a comfortable dual sexual model—nevertheless perceptible, but only tremulously so. As Starobinski put it more eloquently in his "Racine et la poétique du regard," "Chez Racine derrière ce qu l'on voit, il y ce que l'on entrevoit, et plus loin, ce dont on ne peut que pressentir la réalité sans en rien voir" (In Racine, behind what we see, there is what we can barely distinguish, and further still, a reality that we can barely make out without seeing anything at all).[26] And it is this mirage of difference, floating tantalizingly just out of sight, that impels the characters, trapped as they are in the illusions of knowledge and power that this seeing provides, to look further, to push ahead, in an attempt to focus this absent object of their vision in order to guarantee both its and their "reality." The image, of course, always an illusion, escapes such capture and drifts free of any hold that by fixing it would annihilate it.

Naturally, this analysis applies first and foremost to the intradiegetic spectators in Racine's textual world, lost as they are in a universe that denies them any empirical grounding that would allow them to situate and understand themselves in the imbroglio of desire in which they find themselves. I would like to complicate the matter a bit by extending this world of vision(s) to the extradiegetic universe, in other words, to underline the voyeurism inherent in the theatrical spectacle that captivates the audience. This is, I believe, the perverse gesture of *Bajazet* where, more self-consciously than in his other plays, Racine makes voyeurs of his audience, seducing them into a universe that is first and foremost defined as not for their eyes, a universe where looking, gazing on the unseeable, is effectively a death sentence. At the same time this hidden world becomes the tantalizing object of a strange desire—a sexual/cultural desire—the desire to see, to know the other, the other woman, the other Oriental, an object that, crystallized in one word—"seraglio"—contains countless cultural fantasies of the exotic, erotic Orient.[27]

The entire tragedy unfolds within the hidden/exposed confines of the seraglio—a veiled, secret place, off limits to male eyes, a truly obscene space—the space of the feminine, of feminine desire, and, of course, the most highly invested, fantasmatic space of Western projections about Oriental sexuality. This is a world prohibited to men, and yet Racine exposes it to the eyes of the theatergoing public.[28] By way of Racine's verse we are transported into a locus that is inaccessible, the space of the other, and what we see here, in this space of exacerbated sexual desire, is death. From the beginning (and we are warned of this from the very first lines) there is the equation of femininity with death. The seraglio reconfigures the alluring displacement of the "dark continent" of female sexuality with the accoutrements of Western fantasies of the luxurious, secret, enclosed world of the Orient. The specter of the Sphinx, waiting to pounce on young men, has returned to her Oriental origins and haunts the play from the very start:

> Et depuis quand, Seigneur, entre-t-on en ces Lieux,
> Dont l'accès était même interdit à nos yeux?
> Jadis une mort prompte eût suivi cette audace
>
> Since when, Sir, dare we set foot in this place
> Where access even to our eyes was banned?
> Such boldness would have once brought speedy death.
> (1.1.3–5)

The fact that Racine chose to situate his new play in the suffocating locus of the Oriental harem might lead us to think that he had abandoned the Greco-Roman terrain that had up until this point proved so fertile a ground for his tragic imagination. It was in the myths and histories so familiar to his contemporaries that he had achieved his rapid ascension into the highest, most exclusive firmament of contemporary playwrights. His choice, therefore, of Constantinople, and more particularly of "le Sérail du Grand Seigneur," might signal an equally important change in his tragic scenario. We know that this is not the case. Rather than a radical shift in tragic perspective, *Bajazet* inhabits the same tragic space as his other plays but with an Oriental twist. We realize now that we must take with more than a small grain of salt Racine's own explanation of his choice of a subject for his new play. He writes that he was told the story of Bajazet's assassination, which had occurred barely thirty years earlier, from the chevalier de Nantouillet, who urged him to use it for the subject of his new tragedy.[29] This proximity in time, which normally would preclude its suitability for tragic transposition, is nevertheless not really an obstacle since, Racine tells us, distance in space is conflated with remoteness in time:

> L'éloignement des pays répare en quelque sorte la trop grande proximité des temps. Car le peuple ne met guère de différence entre ce qui est, si j'ose ainsi parler, à mille ans de lui, et ce qui en est à mille lieues.... Nous avons si peu de commerce avec les Princes et les autres Personnes qui vivent dans le Sérail, que nous les considérons, pour ainsi dire, comme des gens qui vivent dans un autre siècle que le nôtre.

> The remoteness of the countries makes up for, in a sense, the too great proximity in time. For people hardly see any difference between what is, I dare say, a thousand years in the past and what is at thousand miles distant from them.... We have so little dealings with the Princes and other persons who live in the Seraglio, that we think of them, so to speak, as people who live in another century than our own.[30]

In other words, the contemporary Ottomans are as real and as unreal as the heroes of Greek myth and Roman history. To complicate matters further, according to the literary historians who have exhaustively studied the genesis of *Bajazet*, the play's plot actually owes more to Segrais's *Floridon ou l'amour imprudent* (1657), which in turn is indebted to Heliodorus's popular *Theagenes and Chariclea* (better known as *Aethiopica*), than to historical reality. So despite its Oriental garb, it would seem that the inspiration for the play comes as much from the Greek tradition as from the murderous rivalries within the Ottoman court.[31] What does seem important, however, is how Racine uses his Oriental setting to rescript once again the recurrent myth—both Greek and biblical—of warring brothers, and how this myth, inserted as it is within the confines of the sexually charged fantasy of the seraglio, becomes inscribed in a more universalizing scenario that carries the sexual/political confusion for which the myth is merely the vehicle out of a Eurocentric context and imposes it on the geopolitical map where the emerging nation-states of the West are engaged in a battle not only for sovereignty but more importantly for legitimacy as well.

As in *Bérénice*, which exists in a strange chiasmus with his new play, the question of legitimacy works through the ideological projection of a fantasmatic scenario in which questions of subjective and cultural identity are shown to be vulnerable to the same degree that the tragic scenario is affective. Both plays reproduce, with infinitely more violence in *Bajazet*, a fraternal rivalry that is compounded by the presence of a troubling, passionate woman whose desire poses a potentially revolutionary threat to the established sociopolitical order.[32] Both plays can be said to be apposite exempla of good and bad governance: *Bérénice*, with its emphasis on Roman virtue and respect for religion and for self-sacrifice, would represent the ideal of a just, Western, absolute monarchy, while *Bajazet*, in its Oriental splendor, represents the nefarious results of placing (almost) absolute power in the hands of a woman. In its excess, in its inversion of sexual roles and positions, where passion rules in the place of reason, *Bajazet* epitomizes the opposite of a well-ordered, patriarchal monarchy. Women and despotism, women as despots, *Bajazet* seems to be telling us, send the state reeling into bloody ruin.

However different the main female protagonists of these two plays are from each other—Bérénice is cast as a rather passive mother/lover in her relation to Titus, while Roxane stands as one of the greatest examples of the frightening phallic Mother, aggressive, devouring, murderous—both represent, by their insistence on marriage, the same threat to the society into which they have been brought. Let us not forget that for all their disparities they are both foreigners brought from the margins into the heart of the empire. And it is from this central, secret core that they launch (Medea-like) an assault on the very foundations of society by asking for marriage.

It may at first strike us as odd that marriage should be so overdetermined a metaphor in the construction of Racine's universe. Traditionally marriage—the joining of two families in an economic union whose purpose it is to ensure both the reproduction and the perpetuation of the social "same" and thus the assurance ad infinitum of a certain social status quo—has always been seen as the most elemental building block of the social edifice. Why, therefore, is so essential an institution so overwrought in Racine? It comes as no surprise that while the question of marriage reaches its incandescent, tragic apogee in *Bajazet*, the problem of marriage is the crucial impetus to tragic action in all of Racine (*Andromaque, Britannicus, Bérénice, Mithridate, Iphigénie*, and perversely in *Phèdre*) because it is through the conflation of passion and politics that the Racininan marriage is able to cathect all the other Oedipal conflicts that the dramatic plot embraces (fraternal rivalry, paternal jealousy, the mortiferous combat between the primal father and the phallic mother, and so on) and project them as a geopolitical scenario of social chaos and death.

In traditional societies marriage is always an economic contract. In the marriage of persons of princely rank, which is a highly elaborate dynastic negotiation, the question of personal preference (love) is never allowed to interfere with political realities. Racine complicates and thus subverts this contract by introducing passion into what is supposed to represent a rational administration of property and genealogy. In other words, Racine's introduction of desire as tragedy reveals a strategic turning point in a millennial organization of society, a turning point that remains ambiguous because projected as inherently tragic. Nevertheless, it is precisely this dramatic ambivalence that dominates the Racinian stage, symbolized, as has often been remarked, by the silent, emblematic presence of the altar in all of Racine's tragedies. The omnipresent altar, a synecdoche for the God(s), denotes the enigmatic authority presiding over the fate of Racine's protagonists. The altar is a conflicted space where one never knows if a marriage is to be celebrated or a sacrifice performed. And of course this dichotomy avoids the even more uncomfortable conflation that the ambivalence of the altar both veils and reveals: marriage is also, at the same time, a sacrifice.

Racine was not alone in placing the problem of marriage at the center of his dramatic production. His two most illustrious contemporaries,
Corneille and Molière, also use marriage as the most obvious plot device to advance the narrative action of their plays. Racine, however,
seems particularly perverse in his use of marriage, perhaps because of
his already having undermined the natural disposition of the sexes and
sexuality in the construction of his characters. By disassociating sexuality
from its biological grounding, nuptials in Racine take on a more perversely subversive role in the political sphere. The traditional comparison with Corneille might, for once, prove illuminating in focusing on
the modernity of Racine's use of marriage in the elaboration of a tragic
vision of both sexual positioning and social organization.

To state the case briefly: in Corneille, too, marriage is the central
dramatic knot complicating the tragic scenario of his four great plays
(*Le Cid, Horace, Cinna,* and *Polyeucte*). In these plays—and this strikes
me as crucial—we have a world defined by essentially sexual difference.
That is, Corneille's tragedies posit a clear division of the world into two
camps, the male and the female. To each of these camps (biological in
origin) are attributed qualities (metaphors) of masculinity (strength,
martial courage, "vertu," inflexibility, reason) and femininity (tears,
ambivalence, division, confusion). While these attributes may vary and
waver, in the end masculinity prevails as the highest, most prized ethical
value. This is not to say that the Corneillean world is without tensions,
sacrifices, and crises, brought on precisely by the attempt of fixing sexuality into gendered roles, but in the end these roles are posited in their
nature, and society is structured around this "natural" fixation of sexuality. Of course, the greatest sacrifice in Corneille is the appropriation of
the feminine by the masculine through marriage. It is marriage that
supposedly fixes the recalcitrance of feminine ambiguity within the
tight confines of the patriarchal family. Perhaps nowhere more explicitly than in *Horace* is this social imperative expressed in the conflicting
roles of the two main female protagonists, Camille and Sabine. In their
anguished plight the two women confront their different familial, moral,
and passional obligations. Sabine (an Alban married to a Roman) claims
that her marriage has made her more an object of pity than Camille (who
is only betrothed to a man in the enemy camp). In rebuffing Sabine's
contention that she rather than Camille is actually more pitiful, Camille

tells her that, on the contrary, marriage resolves the problem of a woman's dual loyalty by placing her squarely in the family of her husband:

> L'hymen qui nous attache en une autre famille
> Nous détache de celle où l'on a vécu fille.

> The marriage that attaches us to another family
> Detaches us from the one where as maidens we lived.[33]
>   (3.4.883–84)

But as the rhetoric of her statement reveals, this appropriation is never a totally untainted transferal. We can see that while here Camille is talking about the political consequences of marriage ("l'hymen" as a metaphor for marriage), her use of words reveals consequences that are far more important for the tragedy. If we take "hymen" in its metonymic rather than in its metaphoric sense, the word functions as a signifier for the woman herself. If we understand Camille's statement purely as a metaphor we are following a (masculine) slippage that reflects the political significance of marriage and elides the violent gesture that this appropriation implies. Camille tells us, however, that marriage serves a dual function; it "attache" and "détache" the women. It seems clear that the affirmation/denial at work in the prefixes ("at" and "dé") really suppresses another reading that defies their either/or rhetoric. Marriage, that is, the hymen's appropriation by the male, his piercing of it, is paid for in blood. The hymen both "at-tache'" and "dé-tache," but what it seems most significantly to do is "tâcher" (that is, "to stain"). The man and the social construction he represents are tainted by his appropriation of the female, by his placing of the female inside his structures of representation. This act can never be contained. It provokes, at the very instant that the hymen is celebrated/breached, a new violence, the flowing of blood, the blood of sacrifice.[34] We might conclude that in the Corneillean world this "sacrifice" is always necessary to eliminate any space of indifference, that is, any space that would reveal the repression necessary to maintain the political division of the world into two clearly defined (but unequal) sexes. Nevertheless, this repression continues to haunt the characters and their world as it resurfaces as the tragic resistance that confounds the destiny of Corneille's protagonists.[35]

In Racine sexuality is considerably more confused, thus the political organization required to circumscribe it is perhaps both more repressive and more precarious. As Barthes pointed out in his reading of Racine, and as I have mentioned, Racinian sexuality is not natural.[36] There is no longer an essential link between biology and metaphysics. Rather, in Racine, sexuality is already political in the sense that it is always defined by the play of power and passion, a play that is in essence sado-masochistic. Certainly the relation between Roxane and Bajazet is one of the most emblematic of Racine's redefinitions of the muddled lines separating/joining sex and gender in the classical period. While Barthes speaks of an inversion of roles wherein Roxane is cast as the predator and Bajazet her prey who is slowly but surely reduced to being but a powerless object of the sultana's desire, we can also recast this formula into those mythic terms that have served us until now: Roxane as the new avatar of the Sphinx and Bajazet as the young prince who is sac-rificed because he is unable to answer her riddle. He is, in other words, a failed Oedipus.[37]

Roxane's riddle is both sexual and dangerously political. We should remember that Roxane has been left behind in Constantinople invested with the sultan's absolute power. Amurat is a strangely hybrid figure in the Racinian canon. His is a doubly inscribed Oedipal role—both father and brother. On the one hand, he is presented as the absent father of the primal horde, omnipotent, lustful (all the women of the harem are his), and punishing. On the other hand, he is also and at the same time the rivalrous brother of Bajazet. Not having as yet sired an heir to the throne, Amurat cannot, for political reasons, have Bajazet eliminated ("le cruel Amurat / Avant qu'un Fils naissant eût rassuré l'Etat / N'osait sacrifier ce Frère à sa vengeance" [the cruel Murat / Dared not, in jeal-ousy, destroy his brother, / Before a son was born to save succession]). To complicate matters further, at the beginning of the play, there are rumors that the sultan who is absent from Byzance has been killed in battle ("Peut-être te souvient qu'un récit peu fidèle / De la mort d'Amurat fit courir la nouvelle" [Perhaps you now recall the baseless tale / That whispered news of Sultan Murat's death]). In his role as father, Amurat is in an uncomfortably analogous position to those other absent fathers who populate the Racinian world (Oedipus, Hector, Vespasian) except that he is (as will be Mithridate and Thésée) both dead and alive. It is this ambiguity that makes of him a particularly feared, despotic presence. Although absent from his capital and feared/wished dead, Amurat's specter is omnipresent, hovering over the seraglio. In his absence the sultan is more fearfully present to all the characters in the play, trapped as they are within his all-seeing but invisible gaze.

Amurat had gone off on a campaign against the Persians in an attempt to conquer Babylon. This war is crucial for him because although he is presented as absolute there are nevertheless, as Osmin his emissary informs Acomat at the beginning of the play, murmurings of discontent among his Janissaries. His sovereignty is both absolute and yet not invulnerable:

> Le succès du combat réglera leur conduite.
> Il faut voir du Sultan la victoire ou la fuite.
> Quoique à regret, Seigneur, ils marchent sous ses lois,
> Ils ne trahiront point l'honneur de tant d'années.
> Mais enfin le succès dépend des destinées.
> Si l'heureux Amurat secondant leur grand Coeur
> Aux champs de Babylone est déclaré vainqueur,
> Vous les verrez soumis rapporter dans Byzance
> L'exemple d'une aveugle et basse obéissance.
> Mais si dans ce combat le Destin plus puissant
> Marque de quelque affront son Empire naissant;
> S'il fuit; ne doutez point que fiers de sa disgrâce
> A la haine bientôt ils ne joignent l'audace.

> The outcome of the fight will rule their conduct:
> The Sultan either triumphs or must flee.
> They must maintain the fame of their exploits.
> And never will besmirch their ancient honour.
> But Victory or defeat depends on fate.
> If happy, Murat, partner of their prowess,
> Is hailed as victor on the battlefield,
> They will return to Istanbul, submissive,
> Trailing a blind and base obedience.
> But if a harsher destiny deals blows,
> In course of battle, on his budding empire,
> If he must flee, emboldened by his fall,
> They soon will add sedition to their hate.
> (1.1.53–65)

It is this chink in the armor of sovereignty that seduces the characters left behind in Constantinople into imagining another life: Acomat, jaded by his long experience of the court, goads Bajazet to rebellion in an attempt to assure his own power; Roxane imagines a new role for herself, no longer a favorite but the legitimate partner of the new sultan;

Bajazet and Atalide envisage the possibility of a life together. They are all seduced by a tantalizing illusion that the primitive, vengeful, despotic "father" can be done away with and that once he has been vanquished they will be free. This illusion of freedom is, however, just that, a fantasy, a self-deception, because, as they will all learn, the father cannot be so easily eliminated; his ruthlessness is not an arbitrary attribute but part and parcel of their own desire, of their own political machinations.

When Roxane imposes as a condition for freeing Bajazet from the confines of the seraglio that he marry her, she not only threatens the love of Atalide and Bajazet but, more important, the traditional political structures of the Ottoman Empire:

> Oui, je sais que depuis qu'un de vos Empereurs,
> Bajazet d'un Barbare éprouvant les fureurs,
> Vit au Char du Vainqueur son Epouse enchaînée,
> Et par toute l'Asie à sa suite trainée;
> De l'honneur Ottoman ses Successeurs jaloux
> Ont daigné rarement prendre le nom d'Epoux.

> I know since Emperor Bajazet, your namesake,
> Subjected to the rage of a barbarian,
> Beheld his consort chained to the victor's chariot,
> And in his wake dragged through the whole of Asia,
> His scions, jealous of the Imperial honour,
> Have rarely deigned to take the name of husband.
>   (2.2.455–60)

Despite Bajazet's attempt at reasoning with her, that is, explaining all the political reasons why he cannot/should not marry her, Roxane in her response listens only to her passion. What we have, therefore is a (hypocritical) recourse to reason, to the upholding of a certain, noble tradition, to the young prince as defender of the customary laws of the realm contrasted to a rhetoric of desire that reveals passion's murderous intensity. To all of Bajazet's hypothetical reasons for rejecting her ultimatum in the name of Ottoman law, Roxane counters with her own passionate rationale couched in not very veiled threats:

> Mais avez-vous prévu, si vous ne m'épousez
> Les périls plus certains où vous vous exposez?
> Songez-vous que sans moi tout vous devient contraire,
> Que c'est à moi surtout qu'il importe de plaire?
> Songez-vous que je tiens les portes du Palais,

Que je puis vous l'ouvrir, ou fermer pour jamais,
Que j'ai sur votre vie un empire suprême
Que vous ne respirez qu'autant que je vous aime?
Et sans ce même amour, qu'offensent vos refus,
Songez-vous dès longtemps que vous ne seriez plus?

But if we do not wed, have you foreseen
The greater perils you must surely face?
Do you not know you're lost except for me?
That I, above all, am the one to please?
Do you not know I hold the place gates,
That I may open or forever shut them,
That I have sovereign power upon your life,
That you may only breathe as long as I love you.
And that but for this love your frowns offend,
Do you not know, you would long since be dead?
        (2.1.502–12)

In a strange chiasmus, Roxane, having been entrusted by Amurat with "un pouvoir absolu," assumes the posture of the punishing, murderous primal father. The image she projects is that of a devouring, sexually aggressive, primitive force that can at any moment turn on the child/ prince and destroy him:

> ...Amurat desarmé
> Laissa dans le Serail Bajazet enfermé.
> Il partit, et voulut que fidèle à sa haine,
> Et des jours de son Frère arbitre souveraine,
> Roxane au moindre bruit, et sans autres raisons,
> Le fit sacrifier à ses moindres soupçons.

> Thus Murat held his hand a little while,
> With Bajazet imprisoned in the palace.
> On his departure, he assigned Roxane
> Supreme control over his brother's life.
> Directing, loyal to his hate, she should,
> At the least rumble, without other cause.
> Put him to death upon the least suspicion.
>   (1.1.127–33)

Mistress of the seraglio, Roxane can have Bajazet killed at any moment. If we may be permitted to indulge in a bit of Kleinian language, we would describe the impact of the fearsome image Roxane projects as a "monster." A hybrid being (like the Sphinx), she is, in a very real sense, the image of the infernal parental couple: behind the phallic mother appears the outline of the primal father.[38] This image, like the iconic image of the Sphinx, stands in a very primitive relation to the Oedipal hero. By his triumph over the Sphinx/women, the young prince would mark his passage to both sexual and political maturity. Unfortunately, Bajazet, although we are told that he is quite capable of bloody deeds (he has, we know, tasted "tout sanglant le plaisir et la gloire" [all bloodied the pleasure and glory of battle]), is here incapable of confronting the monster and slaying her.

The cards are, it must be said, stacked against him. If in his skirmishes with Roxane Bajazet appears outflanked, he is also vulnerable to the attacks of the other murderous woman in the play, the young, timorous, but passively aggressive Atalide. Atalide is one more replica of the young virgins who constitute the supposedly positive (that is, unthreatening) aspect of Racine's schizophrenic image of woman (the "sororal" love interest, in Mauron's terms). In *Bajazet*, however, this supposedly benevolent presence has been corrupted by jealousy to the point of undermining the security of the prince she is allegedly protecting. Atalide, like Roxane, is a complicated hybrid character. Just as Roxane combines in her negativity the threat of the primitive parental couple, Atalide is a combination of the protective (but retentive) mother and the adoring sister.[39] Just as Roxane has been invested with and becomes the surrogate of the father's power ("Maîtresse du Sérail, Arbitre de ta vie, / Et même de l'Etat qu'Amurat me confie" [Mistress of the Seraglio, of your life / And even of the State Murat entrusts me]), Atalide twice asserts the legitimacy of her claim to Bajazet by appealing to the primacy of a maternal endorsement:

> Dès nos plus jeunes ans, tu t'en souviens assez,
> L'amour serra les noeuds par le sang commencés;
> Elevée avec lui dans le sein de sa Mère,
> . . . .
> Elle-même avec joie unit nos volontés.

> Why, from our childhood days, as you well know,
> Love further bound the knots by blood begun.
> Brought up with him upon his mother's lap,
> . . . .
> And she herself united us with joy.
> (1.4.359–63)

Je l'aimais dès l'enfance. Et dès ce temps, Madame,
J'avais par mille soins su prévenir son âme.
La Sultane sa Mère ignorant l'avenir,
Hélas, pour son Malheur! se plut à nous unir.

I loved him from our childhood; ever since,
I'd won his heart by numberless attentions.
His royal mother, who could not foresee
The future, chose to unite us, to his ruin.
    (5.6.1581–84)

It is an endorsement that signals the transference of the feminine possession of the son from the mother to the sister, lover ("Elevée avec lui
dans le sein de sa Mère" [Brought up with him upon his mother's lap])
while keeping him firmly ensconced within the familial enclosure ("le
sein"—lap/bosom). Whichever way he turns, whether toward Roxane
or toward Atalide, Bajazet is trapped, either literally imprisoned in the
seraglio or emotionally imprisoned in the equally suffocating bind of
the (m)other.[40] The personal and the political are here presented as
one and the same: the physically torturous, dark, secretive, and dangerous twists and turns of the seraglio are also just a metaphor for the suffocating, retentive love of the mother. Bajazet's attempts to free himself
from one or the other of his confinements are doomed as they reflect and
relay each other. As he turns from one woman to the other, he is adrift
in a play of power and passion in which, whichever side he chooses, he
loses. Atalide, despite her melodramatic protests to the contrary, is as
relentless in her passion as Roxane. Atalide's solution to their plight is
as absolute as Roxane's ultimatum: death, either hers or Bajazet's. Neither
is willing to sacrifice her retentive passion; each wants to retain Bajazet
within the confines of her own desire.

    Bajazet cannot save himself, cannot free himself, from this suffocating
embrace. Caught in the conflicting swirl, torn between these two women,
Bajazet is effectively rendered speechless ("O Ciel! Que ne puis-je parler!" [Oh, If only I could speak!]). He cannot speak his desire—this is
what first arouses suspicion in Roxane—he cannot give voice to the love
that has been spoken for him ("Pour quoi faut-il au moins que pour me
consoler / L'Ingrat ne parle pas comme on le fait parler?" [Why does the
wretch, at least to comfort me, / Not speak to me as you give out he
speaks?]). Without wishing to appear too strained in my analysis, I would

nevertheless, like to point out that Bajazet is presented as the most autistic of Racine's male characters. His inability to speak, to articulate his desire, keeps him (analytically speaking) excluded from the register of the symbolic (the register of the father and his law). Speechless, Bajazet remains a prisoner of the imaginary, the realm fantasmatically represented by his capture in the deadly embrace of Roxane/Atalide.

Just as Néron is unable to liberate himself from what Racine has presented as the murderous hold of the maternal, so too Bajazet is the victim of his inability to leave the world of the mother(s). If we recall not so much the psychoanalytic categories we have been using to explore the Racine's desirous universe as the anthropological, we would seem to be confronted once again in *Bajazet* with the fundamental problem of male differentiation that we have already met *en sourdine* in the previous plays: how to separate the young male from the world of women in which he has been raised and to "rebirth" him into the world of men (essentially a "fratrie," that is, a world of idealized fraternity, which in Racine is presented as an unattainable ideal) as an independent (masculine) man. We know that in most societies the rituals involved in this process of separation are often marked by scenarios of regression (to the womb), labor, and rebirth during which the older men (often fathers, or father surrogates such as uncles and grandfathers) inflict harrowing trials on the young initiates. Most often these rituals involve a frightening passage through "death," an initiation marked by bodily mutilation and scarring. These scars are the permanent reminder of what has been both lost by leaving the world of the mother and gained by entering the universe of men; the scarring (often a form of circumcision) is the inscription of male law on the body that now, having gone through death, exists as the embodiment of this law (and its privileges).

In Racine this passage is more often than not a failed one where death is not so much a ritual illusion but real. In general the passage into the world of men is disastrous because the male guides chosen (or imposed) as the models and help for the adolescent boy are ineffectual in front of the overpowering force of female desire. Here, in *Bajazet*, the only male able to come to Bajazet's aid is Acomat. But Acomat is unequal to this role. He is unable to separate Bajazet from the world of the females and lead him into the circle of men because he himself is tainted as asexual (if not actually castrated); his role places him uneasily close to the eunuchs, the only other males allowed entrance into the seraglio.[41] Acomat's warrior status is a distant memory. He has been barred from the army by Aumuat. Old and asexual, his interest in Atalide is, as he himself admits, purely political:

> Voudrais-tu qu'à mon âge?
> Je fisse de l'amour le vil apprentissage?
> Qu'un Coeur qu'ont endurci la fatigue et les ans,
> Suivit d'un vain plaisir les conseils imprudents?
> C'est par d'autres attraits qu'elle plaît à ma vue.
> J'aime en elle le sang dont elle est descendue.
> Par elle Bajazet, en m'approchant de lui,
> Me va contre lui-même assurer un appui.
> Un Vizir aux Sultans fait toujours quelque ombrage.
> A peine ils l'ont choisi, qu'ils craignent leur ouvrage.
> Sa dépouille est un bien, qu'ils veulent recueillir;
> Et jamais leurs chagrins ne nous laissent vieillir.

> Do you fancy at my age
> I should become the sorry slave of love?
> Should heed the foolish promptings of vain pleasure?
> It is by other magnets she attracts.
> I love in her the blood from which she springs:
> And drawing me through her to him, Bajazet,
> Himself ensures to me a prop against him.
> Vizirs are ever irksome to their Sultans.
> Hardly has one been chose when they fear him.
> Their hands forever itch topsoil his wealth,
> And in their spleen, we never may grow old.
> (1.1.177–88)

Acomat fails in his attempts to lead Bajazet out of the seraglio and into the world of men. His lack of sexual interest, its sublimation into purely political motives, signals his inherent infeudation to the only commanding male authority in the tragedy, Amurat. But, as has been mentioned, Amurat is a purely negative presence, a presence of fear, punishment, and death, who hovers, out of sight, over the scene of the tragedy only to materialize at its end in the figure of the obscene Orcan, the black eunuch sent by Amurat to dispatch both his young brother and unfaithful mistress. Bajazet is trapped within the seraglio, whose labyrinthian structure is an all too obvious metaphor for the deadly passion of the two women who vie for his possession. Caught between two highly charged, fantasmatic projections of feminine desire, hounded by the implacable condemnation of his brother/father, persecuted by the father, pursued by the mother(s), Bajazet appears as the most plaintive sacrificial victim in the Racinian canon. The only way out of the seraglio is death. The end of *Bajazet* is, as I have said, the bloodiest finale in all of Racine; all the major characters are destroyed. In a sense the bloody denouement can be seen as simply the logical, political lesson that the play teaches us: despotism feeds on itself until, satiated, it destroys the body politic. This, of course, was a reflection of conventional Western self-fashioning. Louis XIV had warned the dauphin that the influence of women in the running of the state was nefarious. Worse, he warned that the prince who gives in to his passion, who ignores the difficulties of sublimation, who refuses the sacrifice masculine "vertu" demands, condemns his state to cataclysmic devastation:

> Je vous avouerai bien qu'un prince dont le Coeur est fortement touché par l'amour, étant aussi toujours prévenu d'une forte estime pour ce qu'il aime, a peine de goûter toutes ces précautions. Mais c'est dans les choses difficiles que nous faisons paraître notre vertu. Et, d'ailleurs, il est certain qu'elles sont d'une nécessité absolue et c'est faute de les avoir observées que nous voyons dans l'histoire tant de funestes exemples des maisons éteintes, des trônes renversés, des provinces ruinées, des empires détruits.[42]

> I will admit to you that a prince whose heart is strongly inclined to love, and who is always enraptured by what he loves, will have difficulty appreciating these warnings. But it is in difficult choices that our virtue shines brightest. Besides, it is a fact that these warnings are absolutely necessary and it is because they have not been heeded that we see in history so many fatal examples of great houses wiped out, thrones toppled, entire provinces brought to ruin, and empires destroyed.

Bajazet ends on a note of civic turmoil. Panic has taken hold of the seraglio ("je ne vois que des troupes craintives, / D'Esclaves effrayés, de Femmes fugitives" [I see only timorous troops / Of trembling slaves and fleeing womenfolk]). Might I suggest that in *Bajazet* (as in *La Thébaïde, Andromaque,* and *Britannicus*) the tragic sacrifice of the hero(es), the punishment of the son, precipitates social chaos? This seems to be the conflicted message of Racine's tragic theater: the struggle between the father and the son, mediated through the aggressive sexuality of the (m)other, can only lead to the death of the young prince and to the fragmentation of polity. There can be no hope for a society where the son is sacrificed on the altar of patriarchy for the simple reason that this sacrifice, while appeasing the anger/jealousy of the father, also effectively undoes the entire patriarchal social structure: without a son there can be no hope for patriarchy, because its future has been sacrificed to this immolation.[43] By eliminating the son(s) the father effectively does away with the possibility of fraternity, with any hope of a dissemination of the restrictive bonds that would channel divisive aggression and sexuality into productive social ties. Up until this point in Racine's career (if we choose to view the arc of his tragic creation diachronically as well as synchronically), there has been a never-ending battle between the lustful, all powerful (absent/dead) father and the young sons who are caught in a web of desire and aggression that makes them no match in their struggle with him. At the same time, these sons have been incapable of freeing themselves from the haunting image of female sexuality, represented either by the aggressions of older, powerful women or by the retentiveness of the young virginal sister/lovers. Of course, in their striving to take the father's place, the young princes must best the father by becoming like him, that is, they must confront the "monster" of female sexuality, the Sphinx, that bars their way to masculinity, and confound her.

Oedipus killed his father, albeit unknowingly. We must remember, however, that this father, Laius, cursed by the gods for his own original sin, had, quite knowingly, tried to kill him first. Sexuality and aggression from the beginning condemn Laius and his progeny to a constant repetition of uncontrolled sexuality and aggression that condemns them all to death. At the same time, the state over which they rule is destined for plague, infertility, and dissolution. When Racine shifts the locus of his tragedies to the Orient, he transports into these new scenarios the entire weight of the Oedipus legend but imbues it with an acutely novel cultural focus—the cause of the princes' downfall is now the despotism of the East figured by the excessive demands of the Oriental woman—either Bérénice or Roxane/Atalide. Despotism, and therefore the impossibility of polity (at least as it is conceived of in the developing Western monarchies and their republican avatars), is impossible as long as free rein is given to women who stand as surrogates for the implacable law of the father and whose excess always serves, one way or another, to undermine fraternity. The possible (if improbable) escape from the

hothouse atmosphere of the seraglio or from the equally suffocating embrace of the mother's retentive hold on her child only begins to surface,
in a constant play of *fort-da*, in Racine's next Oriental tragedy, *Mithridate*.

Mithridate

Mithridate appears at first to be the least claustrophobic of Racine's
tragedies. Perhaps that is because the scene is set, as Racine so baroquely
describes it, at Nymphea, "port de Mer dans le Bosphore Cimmérien,
autrement dit la Taurique Chersonès" (a seaport on the Cimmerian
Bosphorus in the Tauric Chersonesus), where the expanse of the sea
with its constant promise of open horizons leads us to believe that we
have left far behind the stifling confines of the seraglio. Or perhaps this
initial feeling of expansiveness is due to the rather frenetic displacements,
the military campaigns both real and imagined, that mark Mithridate's
life. Here, more than in any other of his plays, we are allowed to wander
over the length and breadth of the ancient world. Compared to the tight
confines of the harem, Racine's new play opens out onto the world.

   At the same time, the outsized persona of Mithridate, with a reputation as the sole defense of the Orient ("Moi seul je leur résiste" [I alone
resist them]) against the hegemonic thrust of Rome, is magnified by the
manic rhetoric of his fantasized march on and destruction of Rome.
Mithridate's self-fashioning projects the image of a larger than life
father/king whose presence seems to fill the entire world. Very much like
the fantasy construction of Néron, Mithridate the historical figure exists as a strangely ambiguous rhetorical construct. His is a historic figure
that drifts off into mythic allegory. As the symbol of a grandiose resistance to Roman hegemony, Mithridate enters on the scene of tragedy as
a parable of pride and also of its opposite, hubris. Having spent his life
defending not only his empire but battling for a non-Roman world, Mithridate, represents, we are told, a greater menace to Rome than either
Hannibal or Spartacus. His military feats have made him a legendary
figure of domineering imperiousness, whose word is law and whose law
more often than not means death to anyone, most particularly anyone in
his family, who contravenes it/him. In a sense this barbarian hero is the
last avatar of a millennial line of Oriental threats to Western hegemony.
Mithridate establishes this anti-Western genealogy when he pointedly
calls attention to his ancestry. He is, he tells his sons, a direct descen-

dent of Cyrus ("un Roi longtemps victorieux, / Qui voit jusqu'à Cyrus re-
monter ses Aïeux" [a brilliant king, / Whose ancestors from Cyrus
spring]) and thus from that even greater warrior/statesman Darius, historically two of the most powerful threats to Western (that is, Greek)
independence.

Mithridate garbs itself in the most spectacular of rhetorical displays,
where politics and desire, arrogance and cruelty, and narcissism and
megalomania create the image of this last wounded but still dangerous
and magnificent "father" whose defeat represents not only his own ruin
but the inevitable obliteration of an entire world order. Mithridate will
be defeated, the Orient will fall under the sway of Rome, and the course
of world history will be changed. Racine's new Oriental tragedy portrays
the death throes of not only a defeated warrior but an entire world, a
world that has resisted Roman tyranny and that here, in its last stand,
is about to be engulfed. A man, an empire, and a man who is an empire
are about to be wiped off the map of the world, and in their stead, we
are led to believe, Rome will finally establish her dominion over the last
vestiges of those Eastern barbarians who have resisted and threatened
the onward march of (Western) civilization. Mithridate's defeat will at
last pave the way for the ultimate triumph of Greco-Roman civilization, a culture of "light and reason," ultimately a "Christian" polity,
that can hold Eastern barbarism at bay.[44]

As usual in Racine, the impression of openness is an illusion. Against
the background of the fall of an empire, Racine focuses his tragedy on
murderous familial dissension. In this most clearly Oedipal drama, Racine
reduces the overriding political stakes that his tragedy encompasses to
dramatic themes with which we are now familiar: two warring brothers
who lust after the same woman, a woman who happens to be and not
be the wife of their father, and a father whose depiction lifts him out of
the realm of history and places him squarely in the territory of myth/
legend. Long before Freud's description of the primal father in *Totem
and Taboo*, Racine gives us Mithridate, a terrifying image of this all-
consuming, lustful, and murderous despot:

> Mithridate revient, peut-être inexorable,
> Plus il est malheureux, plus il est redoubtable.
> Le péril est pressant plus que vous ne pensez.
> Nous sommes criminels, et vous le connaissez.
> Rarement l'amitié désarme sa colère.

Ses propres Fils n'ont point de Juge plus sévère.
Et nous l'avons vu même à ses cruels soupçons
Sacrifier deux Fils pour de moindres raisons.
Craignons pour vous, pour moi, pour la Reine elle-même.
Je la plains, d'autant plus que Mithridate l'aime.
Amant avec transport, mais jaloux sans retour
Sa haine va toujours plus loin que son amour.

Mithridate's back, perhaps implacable;
He's savager the more his fortune sags
We stand in greater danger than you deem.
We are both guilty as you know full well.
His anger rarely yields to tenderness;
His own sons cannot have a sterner judge;
And we have seen him, moved by harsh suspicions,
For the least reasons put to death two sons.
Fear for yourself, for me and for the Queen:
I pity her the more our father loves.
A passionate lover, jealous to the core,
The more his love, his hate is even more!
          (1.5.343–54)

The constricting circle of this family-become-tragedy closes in on the protagonists whose world is finally reduced to the point of a sword that, putting an end to Mithridate's life, leaves his errant sons and their kingdom(s) prey to dissension, treachery, and social upheaval. But before we come to this end, that is, the demise of the father, we must start at the beginning, where the concupiscence of the sons has been aroused because, as we learn, the father is already dead:

Rome en effet triomphe, et Mithridate est mort.
Les Romains vers l'Euphrate ont attaqué mon Père,
Et trompé dans la nuit sa prudence ordinaire...

Rome triumphs now with Mithridate dead.
The Romans struck, my sire near the Euphrates,
Surprising in the night his wonted caution...
          (1.1.2–4)

From the very first lines, Racine announces the father's death. This news has profound reverberations for the erotico-political ambitions of his sons that instantly situate them at opposite poles of an antithetical ethical dilemma: Xipharès, the good (anti-Roman, faithful) but tainted son, is placed in amorous rivalry with his elder brother, Pharnace, who not only has turned against the familial political tradition (he is pro-Roman), manifesting thus a filial rebellion against the father, but, to complicate matters even further, is now attempting to compel his father's bride to marry him. In other words, Racine introduces the dynamics of filial guilt, which, as Mauron has written, is the unconscious dynamic that, reflecting the two major factors of the Oedipus complex incest and aggression, will inform the entire tragic narrative of *Mithridate*.[45]

The two brothers love the same (taboo) woman, Monime. This amorous rivalry immediately precludes any hope of polity. Once their father is thought dead, the brothers cannot unite in a common goal. Instead of incorporating the father, which in this instance we may assume would take the form of their adopting his life's goal of resisting Rome and thus of avenging his death, the brothers are incapable of fraternity:

> Ainsi ce Roi, qui seul a durant quarante ans
> Lassé tout ce que Rome eut de Chefs importants,
> Et qui dans l'Orient balançant la Fortune
> Vengeait de tous les Rois la querelle commune,
> Meurt, et laisse après lui pour venger son trépas,
> Deux Fils infortunés qui ne s'accordent pas.

> And thus this king, who through full forty years
> Wearied alone the whole leadership of Rome,
> Who in the East held Fortune's scales in balance,
> Avenging the common cause of every king,
> Dies, leaving as avengers of his death,
> Two most unhappy sons who quarrel still.
>   (1.1.9–14)

We might say that the equation Racine establishes at the outset of his drama is one between being and having. The brothers, motivated (primarily, but not entirely) by lust, desire the same woman as their father. In other words, they desire to "be" the father, perpetuating, on one level at least, a legacy of patriarchal autocracy. This desire is exclusive. The father (as his avatar, the throne) is singular; there cannot be two fathers. Were they to renounce the taboo woman and unite in a common goal, they would be, in a sense, accepting the dead father by internalizing his law ("castration") and thus, at least according to the Freudian schema I am here following, by having (internalized) him, be able to construct a culture of exchange: the exchange of love (sublimated as fraternity and exogamy) and thus eventually the construction, through renunciation and the recognition of mutual dependency, of community. But this, of course, is a Freudian and not a Racinian scenario. Instead, Racine offers us another choice that does not efface the Oedipal scheme but proportions it differently. Although sexual desire ignites the rivalry between the brothers (and eventually between the brothers and the father), it is really employed to underline an ethical conflict between filial loyalty and treason, which of course is merely the other side of the Oedipal coin, since in Racine's world disloyalty to the father is, in this case, tantamount to patricide, which in turn is the end of any law, any coherent polity.[46]

For Barthes, the relation between fathers and children in Racine is always one of cruelty and guilt. Despite the malevolence of the father, the child nevertheless wants, Barthes writes, to remain his child.[47] To do this the child must take as his own the father's guilt. The question, however, of what they are guilty of and why they feel this constant guilt remains an essential enigma unless we consider the Oedipal scenario as an anthropological working-through of an impossible political scenario: the scenario of all patriarchal genealogies whereby male prerogative is transferred (along with guilt) from father to son through the exchange of women. In *Mithridate* this scheme appears as strangely twisted first by the doubling of the brothers and their split into good and bad sons and then by Xipharès, whose guilt stems not only from his transgressive love for his father's wife, a love he has been able to repress, but from the narcissistic wound he experiences by his mother's betrayal. The two, of course, are not as unrelated as would first appear. In fact, rhetorically, one follows the other:

> Juge de mes douleurs, quand des bruits trop certains
> M'annoncèrent du Roi l'amour et les desseins,
> Quand je sus qu'à son lit Monime réservée
> Avait pris avec toi le chemin de Nymphée.
> Hélas! j'appris encore dans ce temps odieux,
> Qu'aux offers des Romains ma Mère ouvrit les yeux,
> Ou pour venger sa foi par cet hymen trompée
> Ou ménageant pour moi la faveur de Pompée,
> Elle trahit mon Père, et rendit aux Romains
> La Place et les Trésors confiés en ses mains.

> Imagine then my grief, when sure report
> Confirmed to me the King's love and his plan;
> When I discovered Monima, now pledged

To him, had left with you for Nymphaeum!
Alas! This was still in those hateful days,
When my own mother stooped to Roman offers'
Whether in vengeance for this latest marriage,
Or to solicit for me Pompey's favour,
She duped my sire, surrendering to Rome
The town and treasures vested in her care.
    (1.1.57–66)

It is as if the crimes of the mother efface, in a striking example of bad faith, Xipharès' own (undeclared) transgression. One might speculate on the damage his mother's betrayal (an act, he intimates, that was the product of her jealousy of being replaced in Mithridate's affection by Monime, but also perhaps her attempt to curry favor for him from the Romans) has wrought in the already undermined relation between the son and the father. This example, however, is a clear rejection of the mother, a first in the Racinian corpus. Xipharès seems to have crossed over into the world of men, to have separated himself from the world of women to which his mother's betrayal condemns him, only to find himself alone in this world, facing the very real threat of his father's jealous wrath.

Whether Xipharès is doomed by his mother's betrayal or by his own desire, it seems clear that in either case the cause of the son's guilt toward his father is always, in the final analysis for Racine, the fault of a woman. In this particular case, the women, the lover and the mother, are made responsible for the double transgression (incest and murder) of the son. More profoundly, in the patriarchal schema that Racine adopts for his mythico-historical tragedies, the son and the father are involved in an endless roundelay of aggression and guilt because, in a very primitive sense, in the ideology of patriarchy that the plays apparently espouse, the father is the son, and vice versa, and both are always inherently guilty. Both participate in the same underlying dynamic: the father wishes to destroy the son, symbol of his own inevitable decline; the son wishes to kill the father in order to take his place and his woman.[48]

When Mithridate resorts to a ruse in order to entrap Monime into admitting her love for Xipharès and, more important for him, Xipharès' love for her, he begins by admitting that after all he is old. He is no longer the brilliant, conquering warrior but a defeated, aged man:

Jusqu'ici la Fortune, et la Victoire mêmes
Cachaient mes cheveux blancs sous trente Diadèmes.
Mais ce temps-là n'est plus. Je régnais, et je fuis.
Mes ans se sont accrues. Mes honneurs sont détruits.
Et mon front dépouillé d'un si noble avantage
Du Temps, qui l'a flétri, laisse voir tout l'outrage.

Till now my chance and victories succeeded
In hiding my grey hairs with thirty crowns.
That time is past. I reigned then, now I flee.
My years have piled up and my honours paled;
And, stripped of all its finery, my brow
Exposes all the scars of withering time.
            (3.5.1039–44)

Mithridate's stratagem for entrapment reveals a truth that he both knows and wishes to ignore. At the same time, continuing his feint, he proposes a solution; he will give Monime to his double/son Xipharès:

... C'est un autre moi-même
Un Fils victorieux, qui me chérit, que j'aime
L'ennemi des Romains, l'Héritier, et l'appui
D'un Empire, et d'un Nom qui va renaître en lui.

... He is my other I,
A son victorious, loving and beloved,
The Roman's foe, the heir and the support
Of an Empire and a name, reborn in him.
            (3.5.1067–69)

It is this promise of renaissance, the perpetually renewed image of himself as fixed in a moment of eternal, youthful virility, that seduces Mithridate and that he hopes/schemes will seduce Monime. When he discovers that his fantasy is, in fact, reality, that Monime does love Xipharès ("Vous l'aimez?" [You love him?]) and in turn is loved by him ("Nous nous aimions" [We loved each other]), a more primitive, destructive impulse ("Seigneur, vous changez de visage!" [You grow pale, my Lord]) destroys the harmony of the projected narcissistic illusion and calls up, in its stead, the archaic rage of the (not yet entirely) beaten old man who decides on a slaughter of the innocents to appease his wrath and, he claims, the gods:

Ma colère revient, et je me reconnais.
Immolons en partant trois Ingrats à la fois.

Je vais à Rome, et c'est par de tels sacrifices
Qu'il me faut à ma fureur rendre les Dieux propices.

My wrath returns. Once more I'm Mithridate.
Let us, departing, strike three traitors down.
I go to Rome; and by such sacrifice
I must persuade the Gods to bless my mania.
(4.5.1385–87)

Although, in Mithridate's plan to march on Rome, a set piece of Racinian oratory, the violence of his megalomania is carefully mastered by the seductive alexandrines, his affective aggression is unbound. His brutal slaying of his children and of his wives/mistresses ("Vous dépendez ici d'une main violente, / Que le sang le plus cher rarement épouvante" [Your fate depends on one of violent mood, / Who seldom shrinks to shed his dearest blood]) defines him as the father of the primal horde and at the same time (and this is particularly important for the underlying politics of this tragedy) as a nontranscendent figure of the law and community.[49] Mithridate, like all supreme narcissists, cannot abide the ties of love, either to his children or to his wives, because those ties are restrictive. They impose limits on a desire that wishes to encompass the universe. This is a libidinal force that is too powerful to be able to find satisfaction as a mere mortal.[50] Those very defining characteristics of the primal father that make Mithridate both admirable and fearsome create a pointedly political, that is, ideological, dilemma. As long as the Mithridate remains in the position of the raging, lustful, brutal warrior, he remains, rather than the incarnation of the law that would found polity and community, merely its parody (thus the unspoken contrast established between the righteous king, father of his people, bound by and representative of the law, and the Oriental despot, symbol of unbound desire who annihilates his children). Simply put, the limitless fury that would immolate the son(s) also destroys the father because without the son to recognize the paternal role, the father and the entire system (religious, political, social) that he incarnates and perpetuates are undone.

The French psychoanalyst Guy Rosolato has written convincingly about the role of sacrifice in the Western tradition, particularly in the three great monotheisms: Judaism, Christianity, and Islam. For Rosolato the murder of the child (in reality or in fantasy) is always a disguised attack on the father.[51] On the one hand, this attack on the father is the

product of ambivalent Oedipal fantasies of jealousy and impotence but
also of love on the part of (all) children. On the other, on the level of
political theory as it was reformulated in the sixteenth and seventeenth
centuries, primarily from a reinterpretation (Bossuet) of the Bible, any
attack on the father is tantamount to the destruction of the law and of
the social structures erected around that law. The analogy of parricide
to regicide elaborated by those theorists of political economy from Bodin
on is one of the major tenets of Western monarchy. Nevertheless, the
ambivalence of the role of the father and of the child's desire for him,
an ambivalence that we see schematized in the fraternal doubling and
opposition of Xipharès to Pharnace, remains for the most part the inarticulable threat to patriarchal rule. It is, in its ambivalence, too threatening to be allowed into political ideology in any way other than disguised, turned into its obverse: rather than the attack on the father, the
sacrifice of the child.[52] When Mithridate plans the triple murder of his
sons and Monime, he is confirming not only his identification with the
mythic primal father but, precisely, the impossibility of this father's
existence as a political being.[53] He also, of course, represents the worst
fantasies of the Oriental despot who, despite his unbending resistance
to Rome, which he perceives as a threat to all kings, actually shows the
Orient's inability to guarantee any form of polity that is not in the service of lust and blood.

It is this underlying, irresolvable paradox of patriarchy that *Mithridate* plays out. As long as Mithridate remains alive there is no chance
of love or of polity. But, as Racine pointedly tell us, the subject of his
tragedy is not the life but the death of Mithridate ("sa Mort, qui est
l'action de ma Tragédie" [his death, which is the action of my tragedy]),
and this death is the transformative moment whereby the tyrant becomes
a king. Mithridate dies twice in this play. At the beginning his death is a
hoax, perpetrated by Mithridate himself to mislead his Roman enemies;
at the end, surrounded and outnumbered by these same enemies, Mithridate commits suicide in that most Roman of fashions—he falls on (or
rather stabs himself with) the sword that had served him so well in his
past battles—his ultimate attempt at resisting Roman imperialism:

> J'ai vengé l'Univers autant que je l'ai pu.
> La Mort dans ce projet m'a seule interrompu.
> Ennemi des Romans, et de la Tyrannie
> Je n'ai point de leur joug subi l'ignominie.

> I have avenged the world as far as I could
> And death alone has stayed my noble plans.
> Inveterate foe of tyranny and Rome.
>   (5, scène dernière, 1653–55)

Before this final act of defiance, Mithridate had condemned his wife and his son(s). Just before the battle that will be his last stand he sends a poisoned cup to Monime with orders for her to drink it. At the same time he rushes forth to defeat the attacking Romans and his two treacherous sons. In the confusion surrounding the secret landing of the Romans in Nymphée, Mithridate believes that Xipharès has joined the rebellion and is thought to be fighting alongside Pharnace against him.

He is, of course, wrong. Rather than side with the enemy, Xipharès, loyal to the end, routs the Romans. It is at this critical moment, after considerable peripeteia, that Mithridate realizes his error, orders the cup of poison dashed from Monime's hand just as she is about to down it, and stabs himself in order not to be captured alive by his enemies. In a final scene, reminiscent of Corneille, all the main characters (except Pharnace, who has fled with the Romans) appear on stage with the dying Mithridate and proclaim their love for him.[54] *Mithridate* has long been considered the most Corneillean of Racine's tragedies. Certainly the finale does make us think of Corneille, particularly of the very perverse, politically speaking, ending of *Cinna*.[55] At the sight of the dying king, the long persecuted Monime—who has twice been foiled in her attempt to free herself of Mithridate's lustful tyranny by suicide (she tries to hang herself with the royal "bandeau" first and then accepts joyfully the poisoned cup sent to her, "Ah quelle comble de joie!" [Ah! what ecstasy!])—cries out:

> Vivez, Seigneur, vivez, pour nous voir l'un et l'autre
> Sacrifier toujours notre bonheur au vôtre.
> Vivez, pour triompher d'un Ennemi vaincu,
> Pour venger...
>
> Live, my lord, live, for the weal of the world
> And for her freedom, that depends on you;
> Live to triumph over a beaten foe,
> To avenge...
>   (5, scène dernière, 1675–78)

To which Mithridate, responds, oracularly, "C'en est fait, Madame, et j'ai vécu" (The sands are out, my lady, I have lived).

This is a strange moment of apotheosis, of mutation, during which the dying, almost dead Mithridate, the last Oriental tyrant, successfully triumphs in his most difficult battle. He has, like Corneille's Auguste, succeeded in winning over the hearts of those who most had reason to be repulsed by him. He triumphs by dying, by becoming one with the tutelary gods (shades of Vespasian in *Bérénice*). Death transforms Mithridate from despot to king and from king to transcendent father. His death inscribes the law (as the law of castration) of privation onto the hearts of the two children his lust and aggression had tormented. The play can end with this significant metamorphosis of the primal father who now presides more powerfully than he ever could in life over the fate of the children he leaves behind and whose task it will be to try to reconstruct themselves and their world in his image.

Despite, or perhaps because of, its epic sweep, *Mithridate* remains the least affective of Racine's plays for modern audiences.[56] This has not always been the case. For its contemporaries the tragedy proved to be an emotionally cathartic experience. It even won over, perhaps because of its perceived Corneillean echoes, those who had been most dismissive of Racine. Mme de Coulanges, for instance, writing to one of Corneille's great admirers, Mme de Sévigné, tells her: "*Mithridate* est une pièce charmante; on y pleure; on y est dans une continuelle admiration; on la voit trente fois, on la trouve plus belle la trentième que la première" (*Mithridate* is an enchanting play, one cries, one is in a state of perpetual admiration; one can see it thirty times, (and) one finds it as beautiful the thirtieth time as the first).[57] For reasons that are perhaps not at first apparent, *Mithridate* seems to have been one of Louis XIV's favorite tragedies.[58] Of course, literary historians will tell us that Louis, who prided himself on his military prowess, probably found the epic quality of Racine's new subject to his liking. At the same time, it strikes me as interesting that this play, which many commentators have pointed out marks the return of the father in Racine's tragic universe and thus signals a turning point in the rhetorical articulation, the *poiesis* of Racinian tragedy, is not quite that. It is true that in this tragedy, compared to those that came before, the father reappears, but—and this strikes me as even more important—he once again disappears. And with this disappearance, unique in all of Racine's tragedies, he leaves in his wake some semblance of social/political hope. By this I mean that with his death and internalization (the love of the young couple who remain) there is at least the promise of a future (however illusory or theatrical that promise is for those who know history, where the actual characters have both already been killed without ever having inhabited the same space—but that is another story). In other words, *Mithridate* is the only one of Racine's tragedies that ends with a positive transformation: the Orient has been defeated and the Oriental despot transformed, by his death, into a model of a good king. This is, we might suggest, a double triumph for absolutism. On the one hand, this transformation, this death by transfiguration, has a profoundly Christian aura to it. On the other, Louis can (and this is perhaps why we can't) see this play as a narcissistic mirror reflecting back to him his own desired image. As he told the dauphin, the king is first and foremost a "good Father to his people/ children."[59] It is this good father who is responsible for the prosperity and well-being of his family. And *Mithridate* alone of Racine's tragedies probably spoke this message to Louis, a message he wanted to believe about his own rule and that he wanted his subjects to believe as well.

5

Iphigénie:
Sacrifice and Sovereignty

The story of Iphigenia's sacrifice is, Racine tells us, the most renowned of all the ancient myths. Nothing is "plus célèbre dans les Poètes que le Sacrifice d'Iphigénie" (more famous in the Bards than the sacrifice of Iphigenia).[1] Rising thus to the challenge of competing not only with the great ancients but more specifically with the most tragic of Greek playwrights, Euripides, Racine's version of the legend—adapted from Euripides' *Iphigenia in Aulis* and produced for the first time at Versailles during the festivities marking Louis XIV's return from the triumphant Dutch campaign in 1674—can be said almost to attain the very pinnacle of seventeenth-century tragedy: almost, but not quite. Certainly, if we are to believe Louis Racine's account of the reception of this new tragedy in the study he pens of his father's life and career, *Iphigénie* created a particularly intense affective reaction (tears) in his audience: "Jamais pièce, dans sa naissance, ne resta plus longtemps sur le théâtre, et ne fit couler tant de pleurs" (Never had a play from its first performance remained so long in the theater, nor caused so great an outpouring of tears).[2] Modern commentators concur that the play's emotional appeal was almost unprecedented.[3]

The tragic theme of a father called on by his civic duty to sacrifice his child for the well-being of the state resonates, with conflicted and shocking echoes, from ancient Athens to seventeenth-century France and from the stately corridors of Versailles down to us.[4] This theme of child sacrifice, however, which must have appeared if not commonplace at least conventional in the mythico-religious world within which the citizens of ancient Athens placed their tragedies, was differently disturbing to the Christian audience of seventeenth-century France. Although the question of infanticide, of the child who must be killed and on whose fate turns the entire tragic dilemma of the drama, is present in all of Racine's tragedies in one form or another, *Iphigénie* is the first play that directly invokes the necessity of a propitiatory immolation of a child in a formally ritualized sacrifice.[5] Adapting both an ancient myth and Euripides' retelling of it for the stage, Racine transforms what was immanent in his previous tragedies into a compelling tragic spectacle and succeeds in conjuring up in his audience the ambivalent affects of guilt and pleasure, horror and relief, as they wait for Iphigenia's immolation.

The legend of Iphigenia, daughter of Clytemnestra and Agamemnon, sister of Electra and Oreste, presented Racine with the conundrum of successfully adapting one of the ur-myths of the Greek world for the more refined sensibilities of absolutist France. Although Racine tells us that "mes Spectateurs ont été émus des mêmes choses qui ont mis autrefois en larmes le plus savant peuple de la Grèce" (my audience was moved by the same things that long ago brought tears to the most sophisticated people of Greece) and that this was proof enough that "le goût de Paris s'est trouvé conforme à celui d'Athènes" (the taste of Paris is found to agree with the taste of Athens), his contemporaries were not really ready to accept the same theatrical conventions as their Athenian counterparts. Racine could not, he tells us, end his play with the sacrifice of Iphigenia, nor could he resort to the use of supernatural phenomena (the deus ex machina of the Greco-Roman world), because these two possible endings would be unacceptable to contemporary audiences.[6] Instead he must come up with a modern ending. But before doing so and in order to make that ending dramatically plausible, he invites us on a rather curious excursion into the myth's complex ramifications in order to establish his own dramatic bona fides.

In the preface to the play, Racine, as is his habit, declines for his readers a long list of his sources. Curiously, however, as we read through the preface we realize that Racine is pointing to the discrepancies between the various versions of the Iphigenia myth, their discordances.

First we are told that, according to Aeschylus, Sophocles, and Horace, Iphigenia was sacrificed at Aulis so that the curse that had becalmed the Greek fleet there assembled could at last be lifted and the ships allowed to sail for Troy. Others, however (Euripides and Ovid, for instance), talk about Iphigenia's rescue/rapture by Artemis: instead of her immolation, Iphigenia is in extremis whisked away by the goddess and in her place, on the sacrificial altar, Artemis substitutes a stag. Still others (Pausaunias) talk of another Iphigenia, a daughter of Helen and Theseus. In order to permit Helen's new marriage to Menelaus, these first nuptials were kept secret and the daughter born of them hidden away in Egypt. Her parents would not admit to her existence. Finally, Racine invokes the prestige of Homer, who doesn't mention a sacrifice at all. Rather, his account in the *Iliad* simply has Iphigenia betrothed to Achille.

Instead of simply a vain display of classical erudition, I think that what Racine is underlining in the preface to this play is precisely the lability of myth, a lability that precludes the positing of any univocal meaning or origin. The possible origins of the myth are as contradictory as they are revelatory. Racine only corroborates what we have come to expect of mythic narratives. What, in fact, is the role of all myth (reduced to its essential) if not to offer itself as an explanation of the inexplicable? The most difficult explanation possible would be the answer to the enigmatic question, where do I come from? (the question directly asked in the play by Eriphile/Iphigénie), but which only serves as the portal to the more general dilemma—how does one mark a beginning, and where is the point, the fixed origin, the solid rock of the thing itself, on which the vast edifice of human civilization can be made to stand? Finally, without this rock, the more disturbing question would be, can community prevail at all over chaos? The question(ing) of Iphigenia's sacrifice, the sacrifice that is at the origin of the Greek expedition's setting forth and destroying Troy, is in this play already an enigma. It is made mysterious by Racine's deracinating the myth from any textual grounding. On this mystery's resolution, that is, the tragic denouement, depend, nevertheless, not just the fate of a particular child or her family but the fate of nations and entire civilizations. When we consider the consequences of Iphigenia's sacrifice, we realize that on its successful completion hangs the triumph or the defeat of one of the two major antagonistic views of the world, either (once again) the Western Greek or the Eastern Trojan (Asiatic). In other words, the immolation of this child in Racine's rewriting the familial conflict endemic to the House of Atreus is also and at the same time recast as the *ur-szene* of the triumph of the sociopolitical ethos that underlies contemporary French culture (contemporary both to Racine's context and to ours). The sacrifice conceals a political-sexual imbroglio wherein gendered differences are cast into opposing ethical camps, camps that will oppose the rights of the individual to the exigencies of the state and that, therefore, represent in dramatic form the proleptic fate of the civilized French nation as it is made to confront its own mysterious origins in Racine's new tragedy.

On the one hand, Racine's return to the world of myth for his new tragedy can be seen as just a continuing exploration of the same sexual/political concerns that he had probed, in different registers, throughout his meteoric career. On the other, his choice of the legend of Iphigenia and thus, by implication, of the convoluted myth of the accursed House of Atreus does mark a particularly acute turn in his dramatic trajectory. For while we have already been placed, peripherally, in the orbit of the Atreides (Oreste's in *Andromaque,* who represents the postapocalyptic world of the Trojan War), this new tragedy plunges us into the traumatic center of the fable. Without wishing to belabor the obvious, I want to review the central importance of these mythic characters not only for Racine's play but more broadly for our understanding of the enduring hold they have on the Western literary and philosophical tradition.

In fact, in this tradition, we might suggest that there are only two families that exert, equally, their hold of horror and fascination on us: the Labdacids (the family of Oedipus) and the Atreides.[7] That these two families, or rather their legends, are interconnected goes without saying, the one completing the other in their constantly shifting elaborations of conflicting scenarios of sexual politics.[8] In *Iphigénie* we have for the first time in Racine's theater, as Barthes pointed out, an entire family assembled on stage: father, mother, daughter, and fiancé.[9] It is from inside this nuclear family (which we are constantly being reminded is an invention of the modern, industrial age) that the violence of this tragedy will reach its paroxysm. It is the ever escalating threat of the imminent immolation of Iphigénie that heightens the dramatic tension among the different family members, exposing their conflicted relations to each other and to the community of which they are (the most elevated) part.

André Green reminds us that the family is the "tragic locus" par excellence, because, as he says, it is in the family that the ties of love and
thus of hate are the most primitive and the most compelling.[10] What
Green is emphasizing is both the intensity of those first early ties that
bind the members of a family together and also their ambivalence. It is
essential to remember the fundamental role that ambivalence plays in
most of our unconscious life, an importance that was repeatedly underscored by Freud. While most often the negative side of our ambivalent
feelings concerning those to whom we are closest is effectively sublimated, in situations of extreme affective tension ambivalence reemerges,
often in a life-or-death struggle, as the threatened ego attempts to save
its (illusory) integrity. At the same time, as Mauron remarked more than
fifty years ago, in this life and death struggle, which informs the central
tragic imbroglio in Racine, his depiction of these extreme passions leads
to an emotional regression to primitive psychic states.[11] In other words,
when trying to understand the intensely cathartic effect produced in
the audience by the recasting of this particular family's traumatic encounter with the real (the immolation of a child as the unshakeable
law/desire of the community), that is, with a political imperative that
creates a whirlwind of contradictory, ambivalent tension, we will have
to be attentive to the very primitive emotions that the play sets in motion
while at the same time realizing the difficulty of representing, in other
than more or less classic dichotomies (male/female, active/passive,
sadism/masochism, etc.), the ambivalence that these emotions evoke.
To do this we must try constantly to balance, as an interpretive exercise, characters who dramatically represent stable entities (mother, father,
daughter, suitor, and so on) and the recognition that these personifica-
tions embody powerful psychic forces of indeterminate ambivalence.

Nowhere else in Racine's tragic production is the family so unilater-
ally opposed to the state than here in *Iphigénie*. And nowhere else is so
much pressure exerted to open a breach between, on the one hand, the
masculine imperative to sublimation as politics (the often invoked *raison
d'état*) and the equally adamant feminine appeal to the priority of the
bonds of blood and family. While Agamemnon, despite his anguish and
wavering, agrees to offer his daughter up in a propitiatory sacrifice in
order to obey the dictates of the god(s) and to free the becalmed Greek
fleet, Clytemnestra rails against what can only strike her as a blasphe-
mous perversion of the most sacred of human ties. The sacrifice that the

oracle asserts is the only way out of history's being held hostage in the harbor of Aulis is, therefore, the black hole of the tragedy, drawing first all the various members of Agamemnon's family and then the entire Greek camp into its promise of death and release. It is, of course, an ambiguous promise, as ambiguous and as opaque as the oracle that claims to reveal the will of the gods.

In her study of ancient Greek tragedy, *Façons tragiques de tuer une femme*, especially insofar as it concerns the ways in which the heroines of this tragedy meet their end, Nicole Loraux has proposed a number of paradigms that prove helpful in understanding how certain ambiguities in Racine's *Iphigénie* are actually carefully worked out responses to the dramatic imperatives he inherited from Euripides and yet had to transform in order to make his sacrifice palatable to his contemporaries. The major distinction Loraux makes is sexual: men and women (and Loraux is careful to distinguish between the married woman and the young virgin as well) die differently on the ancient stage. In general, a virile death is death by the sword. Males, in order to confirm precisely a well-anchored notion of masculinity as activity, resort to suicide by the blade. Married women hang themselves out of sight, usually in the most intimate space of the household, the bedroom, or what passed for such in ancient Greece, while young virgins are offered up to the knife as sacrificial victims, killed to appease the wrath of the gods. Loraux insists on the gendered valence of these different types of death in the context of the world that Greek tragedy reflects to its audience.[12] At the same time that she asserts the importance of the sexual division of death, she also, more perversely perhaps, suggests that this sexual difference is one of the main (unconscious) ideological components of the pleasure and even of the catharsis produced by the tragedy in the members of the audience.[13] Although Loraux tells us that state would never in real life sacrifice its young women, for the time of the dramatic spectacle, she says, the polis "offre aux citoyens la double satisfaction de trangresser imaginarement l'interdit du *phonos* et de rêver sur le sang des vierges" (offers its citizens the double satisfaction of transgressing in imagination the taboo of *phonos* and of dreaming about virgin blood, 63).

Following Loraux's lead, we might ask ourselves, when it comes to Racine, what therefore is at stake, sexually and politically, in *Iphigénie*, where Racine, too, bases the tragic frisson of his play precisely on the sacrifice of this young, innocent, and attractive girl. What is the role of sacrifice that Racine conjures up, for the first time explicitly, in this new tragedy, and how does the threat of this impending ritual immolation affect not only the characters of the drama but the spectators in the audience? What, in other words, does this myth transformed into tragedy tell us about our own relation both conscious and unconscious to the ritual murder of children?

Sacrifice has, of course, been the subject of inquiry for a vast array of scholars. Anthropologists, sociologists, ethnographers, and psychoanalysts have produced an immense corpus on the different rites, rituals, and meanings attributed to sacrifice by ancient, primitive, and religious societies throughout history and around the globe.[14] While taking into account their major intuitions, I will, for the purposes that concern me here—the relation between tragedy, sacrifice, and catharsis, a relation that Loraux herself intimated is in essence unconscious (her "imaginaire-ment")—refer to the work of the French psychoanalyst and critic Guy Rosolato, whose *Le sacrifice: Repères psychanalytiques* offers a suggestive theoretical entry into this most mysterious of relations. I do so with one caveat: Rosolato seems almost exclusively fixated on the sacrificial ceremony only insofar as it concerns a male victim (given that his interest focuses on the sacrificial tradition in the three Western monotheistic traditions where it is the son who is the usual sacrificial victim). The role of the female victim will, therefore, have to be analyzed in ways that both confirm and contradict some of Rosolato's most interesting hypotheses.

According to Rosolato, the main role of sacrifice is to regulate both guilt and aggression within society. Guilt and the violence that often accompanies it are, however, difficult to control. Guilt is not only the by-product of some external, objectifiable misdeed (that in principle could be dealt with through different social systems that are in place in all societies, law, religion, expiation rites, and so on) but rather and more perversely of unconscious wishes or desires, most often sexual and most frequently related to Oedipal ambivalence; classically, the young boy wishes to kill his father and to possess his mother.[15] Since the father is an object of not only aggressive impulses but also of loving ones, the conflict raised by such violent fantasies leads to the emergence of feelings of guilt vis-à-vis the father. We must remember, too, that these aggressive feelings and the guilt that accompanies them are not the exclusive purview of the child (both male and female) but that the parents also harbor retaliatory violent emotions against their offspring:

before Oedipus killed his father, that father attempted to murder him. Freud suggested that these same guilt-inducing fantasies that are so prevalent in young childrên continue into our adult lives where the guilt and violence are often displaced onto other figures of authority or even onto such abstract concepts as the state, in whose abstraction can be found the transformation of the father/king into a corporate entity.[16] These fantasies, even as they are never acted on in reality, are nevertheless powerful enough to create overwhelming feelings of guilt in individuals who, incapable of metabolizing them, turn them instead, infused as they are with a strong current of libido, into aggression.[17] The question remains whether this hypothesis of personal guilt is transposable from the individual to the social.

Freud and his followers suggest that it is. In *Totem and Taboo* and, perhaps more relevant to our discussion here, in *Moses and Monotheism* and in *Group Psychology and the Analysis of the Ego,* Freud suggested that individuals, once formed into social groups, renounce part of their own narcissism, which they project onto an idealized charismatic leader, who seems able to contain both their wishes and fears.[18] It is their mutual idealization of the leader that joins individuals together in a libidinally bound group. This complicated process of idealization, is, however, potentially dangerous: the stronger the libidinal ties to the leader, the more powerful the aggression of which he becomes the object when he fails to satisfy the enormous erotic investments (with their toll of renunciation) that his people have placed in him.[19] It would seem that these very mechanisms are incorporated by Racine in the plot of *Iphigénie*. I want to suggest that they serve to create the political backdrop against which and in relation to which the intimate familial drama will be played out.

A leitmotif pertaining to almost all the protagonists, whatever their role or sex, runs through the play: Troy must be destroyed and her riches brought back as booty to Greece. From the very beginning and throughout the play we hear the same refrain: We are going to burn Troy ("Achille . . . veut dans Troie embrasée allumer le flambeau" [Achille . . . wishes in blazing Troy to light the torch]); kill her soldiers ("Puis-je ne point chérir l'heureuse occasion / D'aller du sang Troyen sceller notre union, / Et de laisser bientôt sous Troie ensevelie" [May I not grasp with joy the happy chance / Of going to seal our bond in Trojan blood, / And leaving soon beneath the ash of Troy]); enslave her women and bring back her treasures ("Helas! avec plaisir je me faisais conter / Tous les noms des Pays que vous allez dompter, / Et déjà d'Illion présageant la conquête" [Ah! with what joy I loved to hear relate / The names of every land you'd dominate; / Already presaging the fall of Troy]). Iphigénie herself, the victim demanded in sacrifice so that all this carnage can come to pass, is perhaps the most eloquently ardent in expressing this bloodlust:

> Songez, Seigneur, songez à ces moissons de gloire
> Qu'à vos vaillantes mains présente la Victoire.
> Ce champ si glorieux, où vous aspirez tous,
> Si mon sang ne l'arrose, est stérile pour vous.
> Telle est la loi des Dieux à mon Père dictée.
> En vain sourd à Calchas il l'avait rejetée.
> Par la bouche des Grecs contre moi conjurés
> Leurs orders éternels se sont trop déclarés.
> Partez, A vos honneurs j'apporte trop d'obstacles.
> Vous-même dégagez la foi de vos Oracles.
> Signalez ce Héros à la Grèce promis,
> Tournez votre douleur contre ses Ennemis.
> Déjà Priam pâlit. Déjà Troie en alarmes,
> Redoute mon bûcher, et frémit de vos larmes.
> Allez, et dans ses murs vides de Citoyens,
> Faites pleurer ma mort aux Veuves des Troyens.

> Let all your thoughts to that famed harvest wing,
> That victory to your valiant hands shall bring.
> The field of glory you all wish to see
> Unwatered by my blood would desert be.
> Thus to my father the high Gods ordain.
> To Calchas deaf, he disobeyed in vain:
> Through the shouting crowds of Greeks, against me pressed,
> Their eternal orders were made manifest:
> Depart: I am a hindrance to your fame.
> Plunge on the path your oracles proclaim.
> Blaze forth as hero, promised to the Greeks.
> Already Priam pales; Troy, torn with fears,
> Gasps at my pyre and shudders at your tears.
> Go: and ensure upon their desert wall
> The Trojan widow mourn my mortal call.
>   (5.2.151–52)

What I wish to highlight here is how Racine reminds us that the unity of the Greeks is constructed around the shared violent wish to destroy

Troy.[20] We have, in other words, a community united in a common goal and around a common leader, Agamemnon, whose sole purpose is the destruction of the Trojan other.[21] At the same time we must not forget that this colossal communal undertaking ("ces mille vaisseaux" [these thousand ships]), this world-shaking expedition, has at its origin a rather insignificant anecdote of sexual infidelity: a woman (Helen) left her husband (Menelaus) and ran off with her lover (Paris). But of course in terms of guilt and the violence it generates, the myth is not insignificant at all but a rather interesting variation on how the social management of sexual rivalry can be turned into a fraternal community. What does the myth of Helen tell us? As the most beautiful woman in the world she was desired by all the heroes of Greece. In order not to create permanent enmity among these hero/brothers, her father, Tyndareus, at the suggestion of Odysseus, had all the suitors swear an oath to come to the aid of whoever became Helen's husband in case the latter should suffer an offense. In other words, each renounced his desire for Helen and, accepting frustration ("castration"), they were able to forge a community of mutual aid.[22] It takes, therefore, the sexual satisfaction of another man, Paris, in his possession of Helen, to rekindle the aggression that their libidinal renunciation had repressed. Once released, this aggression turns outward: the Greeks, united in a community of "brothers," seek in a universal cataclysm the satisfaction for having renounced their own sexual pleasure. Should the object of their aggression be denied them, the risk is great for the cohesion of society: this same violence would, in that case, turn inward, annihilating the community, Greece itself.[23] And this is where the play begins, with the winds becalmed, the Greeks trapped in Aulis, their prize out of reach. In such a situation of crisis, with chaos looming near, society cries out for a sacrifice, a sacrifice that will appease the god(s), release nature, and maintain social cohesion by fixing the growing violence on an innocent victim and, through her, on Troy.[24] By the immolation of the sacrificial victim aggression is turned away from the social group in question while guilt is both assuaged and redirected in a collective endeavor that defines the ethos of the community.[25]

While Rosolato talks about the necessity for the sacrificial victim to be innocent, he doesn't seem to wish to deal with the different valences, sexual and social, that this innocence implies.[26] For Loraux, on the other hand, there is a decidedly, if unconscious, sexual aspect to the sacrifice of young virgins. She strongly alludes to the fact (an allusion that is echoed by Marcel Detienne) that the immolation is intimately related to the marriage ceremony and that both are, indeed, two faces of sacrifice.[27]

I do not want to suggest that the analogy between sacrifice and sexuality is missing from Rosolato's more male-focused discussion. Obviously, the relation between the father and the sacrificial son, which forms the center of Rosolato's hypothesis, is also, by its very Oedipal nature, sexualized. Using as his primary example the sacrifice of Isaac by Abraham, Rosolato points out the "virilizing fecundity" that is the result of Abraham's gesture, reminding us that the substituted ram is an obvious sexual symbol that promises the multiplication through the generations of Abraham's progeny.[28] Although the (aborted) sacrifice of Isaac has often been coupled with Iphigenia's sacrifice by Agamemnon, as if to show an analogous and sexually symmetrical relation between the two most famous examples of child sacrifice in the Western tradition, the different valences given to male and female children in patriarchy do not make them analogous, just as the relations between the parents of the victims and their god(s) are likewise not analogous.[29] What is similar, however, is the conflicted relation Racine's adult protagonists have with their male offspring, a relation that is marked by sexual jealousy and that usually ends in the destruction of the young prince. In a sense what we have in the relation between Agamemnon and his daughter is one view of a perverted Oedipal relation where sexuality and violence are coupled in a dangerously explosive moment of societal trauma and where, therefore, drives that are normally channeled into productive social structures reemerge with unbridled force threatening those very same structures.

Confronted with a dramatic situation where violence, sexuality, sacrifice, and prevailing social norms did not allow for him to resort to the tragic solution chosen by Euripides, Racine had to find his own way out. In order for Racine to take up the challenge of both representing this elemental conflict of social and sexual forces and of making this representation palatable to an audience likely to react with dismay to the killing of a young, sympathetic girl, Racine, delving back to find a rather obscure version of the myth (Pausanias's), resorts to a doubling of his heroine, to a splitting of the victim into two, a dramatic tactic that he had heretofore reserved for his young male protagonists. Rather than the theme of rival brothers, Racine sexually flips this traditional rivalry and gives us instead a good princess and her evil stepsister.

Although the split Iphigénie/Eriphile is the most obvious of doublings in the play, I contend that other doubles or, perhaps better, contrasting characters are made to embody an ambivalence too great to be borne by a single character. Racine divides his characters, having each personify in his/her own way one side of the dramatic conundrum. He refashions the givens both of the myth and of the Euripidean tragedy by providing a double for each character so that the inherent ambivalence of any one character's unconscious motivations is projected out onto opposing actors in this drama, oppositions that are not unilateral but multiple and changing (Agamemnon/Calchas, Iphigénie/Eriphile, Achille/Agamemnon, and so on). This doubling also has the effect of heightening the tension between the characters by exacerbating the deleterious effects of the narcissism that each of the characters, in his/her own way and given their social positions and libidinal investments, displays.[30] The double always stands in a negatively refracted specular relation to the good character (she or he who embodies the ideals of the community). Placed in negative reflection, the spectral double deflects the hostility of the crowd away from the good object and onto him/herself. The double always threatens the unicity of the ego, and because of this the threat must be eliminated. In a strange fashion, the narcissist encourages imitation (doubling) but then rejects it violently.[31]

The creation of this doubling is a manifestation of the narcissistic impulse that plays so great a role in all of Racine's tragedies, allowing for an aggrandizement of the persona of his protagonists but also always pointing to the destructive, mortiferous link that joins narcissism to melancholia.[32] When we remember how important the thematics of melancholia is in Racine's dramatic production, we can begin to understand the importance of the invention of Eriphile. As one of Racine's great melancholics, her unrepentant resentment will make her an ideal social scapegoat, a perfect victim for the sacrifice that must take place in order for the Trojan War to begin.

That narcissism as both a libidinal and political investment should play so important a role in Racinian theater should come as no revelation when we consider how important a function the creation and projection of self-aggrandizing images had in the political elaboration of the monarch's persona throughout the seventeenth century. The projection of this persona into the different artistic, architectural, linguistic, and political constructions served as the ideological underpinnings of the absolutist state as this state was conceived as standing in a mirrorlike reflection of the monarch (and vice versa).[33] Of all the psychic phenomena theorized by Freud, surely narcissism remains both the most general, the most elusive, and yet the most seductive for any attempt at analyzing the interrelation between the private and public valences of political leaders. If we accept that the underlying drive of narcissism is, as André Green has theorized, "the desire for the One," that it represents a "unitary utopia, an ideal totalization," we can establish a rapport between the internal structures of narcissism and the political drives of absolutism.[34] Both narcissism and absolutism are totalizing impulses where the desire for a unity of being must necessarily ignore and repress what precisely would sunder that being, its own desire:

> Portrait of Narcissus, all powerful in his body and in his mind, which becomes embodied in his speech, independent and autonomous when he wishes to be so, but upon whom others depend without his feeling in any way needy of them. Residing among his own, the members of his family, his clan, his race, chosen by the obvious indications of a divinity, created in his own likeness. He exists at their head, master of the universe, of death, totally involved in his silent dialogue with the solitary deity who bestows all his blessing upon him-up until the moment of his fall through which he becomes the chosen object of his own sacrifice—an intercessor between God and mortals living in the brilliant isolation of his splendor. This shadow of God traces a figure of the same of what is unchanging, intangible, immortal, and intemporal.[35]

Green's description of Narcissus, of the narcissistic personality, is eerily consonant with the image of self-enclosure and power to which Agamemnon aspires. At the very beginning of the play, it is, we might say, an image that others have of him, which he covets but which nevertheless remains always at an asymptotic distance from him. The very first image of Agamemnon's servant Arcas offers us is that of a perfect man:

> Comblé de tant d'honneurs, par quel secret outrage
> Les Dieux à vos désirs toujours si complaisants,
> Vous font-ils méconnaître, et haïr leurs présents?
> Roi, Père, Epoux heureux, Fils du puissant Atrée
> Vous possédez des Grecs la plus riche Contrée.
> Du sang de Jupiter issu de tous côtés,
> L'hymen vous lie encore aux Dieux dont vous sortez.

> Beneath your load of honours, have the Gods,
> Always so gracious towards you, dealt to you
> Some secret hurt to make you hate their gifts?
> King, father, happy husband, Atreus' son,
> You rule the richest region in all Greece.
> On all sides sprung from Jupiter's own blood,
> Marriage will once more knit you to the gods.
> (1.1.14–20)

If we were to suspend the tragic arc of the play at this moment, Agamemnon would coincide with Green's depiction of Narcissus. In Green's presentation, Narcissus is a political leader: he exists in society as its charismatic chief, among the people but above them. He is presented as radically nondesirous; no lack opens him up to the world. This indifference makes others desire him, attaches them to him, and makes them envious of him. Narcissus in his self-sufficient totality is the perfect representation of a desire for closure, for unity, and ultimately for death.[36] Agamemnon, king of kings, leader of the assembled Greek nation(s) under whose rule they are about to change the course of history, would appear to be a Narcissus in the making. There is, however, a condition for this absolute status. Narcissistic unity can be obtained only through the erection and elimination of a difference, an other. This repression of difference seductively allies narcissism with political totalitarianism. "Narcissism maintains a profound complicity with power," writes Mickel Borch-Jacobsen. "Let us be clear about this—tyrannical power, or political madness. . . . Narcissistic desire is by definition, desire for power: the assimilation and thus the subservience of the other to his Majesty the Self."[37] When the other turns out to be his own child, Agamemnon is rent by doubt and desire. The unity of the leader, who has expelled difference from his very being, is undone by the return of the difference (might we suggest the feminine difference), that this perfect male ("Roi, père, époux heureux" [King, father, happy husband]) has denied in himself, because such denial was easy as it fit perfectly into the social role Greek society demanded of its warrior/king. Now, however, that denial has come back to haunt him, to destabilize through doubt and paternal love the place he occupies in his world. In this tragedy, Narcissus is vulnerable and his vulnerability throws the entire Greek undertaking into doubt and irresolution: at one point Agamemnon even tries to convince his followers to abandon the entire endeavor:

> Qu'il faut Princes, qu'il faut que chacun se retire,
> Que d'un crédule espoir trop longtemps abusés
> Nous attendons les vents, qui nous sont refusés.
> Le ciel protège Troie. Et par trop de présages
> Son courroux nous défend d'en chercher les passages.

> Thus we must all, my lords, must all withdraw;
> Too long deluded by a credulous hope,
> We wait on winds that are refused to us.
> Heaven favours Troy and by too many signs
> Heaven in its wrath forbids us passage there.
>   (1.2.214–18)

Agamemnon is unable to sustain the level of renunciation, of sublimation, that would effectively make of him the supreme leader of the Greeks. He has become, in keeping with the ideology of masculinity that is his and that of his world, a compromised, lacking male. Having allowed his emotional attachments to seduce him and make him doubt his political commitment, Agamemnon realizes his own weakness. He recognizes—and this is perhaps what would make him a tragic character— how his familial ties have made him (and thus all of Greece) vulnerable. The Greeks, in the person of Ulysses, also know and fear Agamemnon's wavering. Ulysses' role is to bring him back into the male camp by constantly reminding him of his duty to his fellow warriors. Agamemnon is torn between Ulysses, who along with the ever present but never seen high priest Calchas pulls Agamemnon toward renunciation and duty, and, on the other side, his formidable spouse, Clytemnestra. Clytemnestra stands as the most vocal advocate of family and the ties of blood, which are in direct conflict with the politics of conquest. It is Clytemnestra who speaks of the very real, unsublimated call of the body, of the visceral attachment of parents and children that Agamemnon must flee ("Voilà, voilà les cris que je craignais d'entendre" [Those were the very cries I feared to hear]) if he is not to succumb to his own doubts and fears.

Clytemnestra is, with the possible exception of Agrippine, the most cynically articulate female character in Racine. As Agamemnon's female counterpart, his double, she is his most redoubtable adversary in the ethical/political battle for Iphigénie's life. Clytemnestra is also a strangely ambivalent creation. Although she is one of the most formidable female figures in Greek mythology, when Clytemnestra first appears on stage in *Iphigénie* this most imposing of Greek queens arrives as a petite-bourgeoise bustling about with an air of self-satisfaction at having arranged a good marriage for her daughter ("the son of a goddess!"). It is only once she learns of the subterfuge her husband has employed to lure her and her daughter to the camp and of his intentions of offering up her daughter in sacrifice so that the Greeks may get to Troy that her character divests itself of the superficial trappings of a seventeenth-century bourgeoise. In her withering denunciation of her husband, the Greek army, and its priest, she attains the truly monumental stature that allows us to prefigure the terrifying avenger we know she will become.

The confrontation of Agamemnon and Clytemnestra is the rhetorical climax in *Iphigénie*. It is a duel that opposes not only the maternal to the paternal but, in this fierce opposition, the demands of state to the demands of family. It also serves to underscore the hypocrisy of a polis that feeds on its own citizens by invoking a *raison d'état*, that undoes by its very invocation the basis of the society it is supposedly defending. In this scene, where we have the family united and alone onstage, Clytemnestra, unable to endure what she perceives to be the hypocrisy and chicanery of Agamemnon's self-defense, launches into her attack on him by first invoking—and thus bringing forth from the background where they have been lurking onto the (fantasmatic) stage of the present—his murderous (male) antecedents: "Vous ne démentez pas une Race funeste" (You are a true son of your fatal race). She tells him, "Oui, vous êtes le sang d'Atrée et de Thyeste" (Yes, the blood of Atreus and Thyestes). This salvo immediately transforms the already embroiled present situation into a scene of murder, incest, infanticide, and cannibalism by conjuring up a familial history, familiar to all but up until this point hidden from direct view. The images of the past instantly reinforce the terror of the present, which is only increased by her scathing claim that Agamemnon has done nothing to save his daughter:

> Bourreau de votre Fille, il ne vous reste enfin
> Que d'en faire à sa Mère un horrible festin.
> . . . .
> Où sont-ils ces combats que vous avez rendus?
> Quels flots de sang pour elle avez-vous répandus?
> Quel débris parle ici de votre résistance?
> Quel champ couvert de morts me condamne au silence?
> Voilà par quels témoins il fallait me prouver,
> Cruel, que votre amour a voulu la sauver.

> Your daughter's butcher, it but now remains
> For you to serve her up in a banquet to her mother.
> . . . .
> Tell me where is your eloquent resistance?
> What streams of blood have you made gush for her?
> What heaps of ruins here proclaim your fights?
> What corpse-strewn field condemn me to hold my tongue?
> Such are the witnesses you need to prove
> To me your love has tried to save her, brute!
> (4.4.1251–64)

First, Clytemnestra resituates Agamemnon in a monstrous lineage and then she unmans him by claiming he has been incapable of defending his own child, thus proving himself to be unworthy of the title "father" that both he and Iphigénie had rather conspicuously used in the preceding speeches. By revealing his inadequacies as a father she simultaneously uncovers his shortcoming as a political leader (in Greece as well as in seventeenth-century France, paternity and monarchy were of course linked, metaphorically as well as actually). It is because of this covert shame, his knowledge of his own inability to be the king, that she claims to be the real reason he has agreed to the sacrifice. It is, she says, neither the oracle, which she reminds Agamemnon never really means what people think it does, nor the obligation to revenge a tainted familial honor by recouping Helen for her cuckolded husband. Rather, she says, it is his vanity, his damaged narcissism that seeks absolute imperium in order to mend itself:

> Cette soif de régner, que rien ne peut éteindre,
> L'orgueil de voir vingt Rois vous servir et vous craindre,
> Tous les droits de l'Empire en vos mains confiés,
> Cruel, c'est à ces Dieux que vous sacrifiez.

> This thirst to reign, that nothing can assuage
> The boast of twenty kings dancing attendance;
> All the empire's rights entrusted to your hands,
> These are the Gods to whom you sacrifice.
> (4.4.1289–92)

Her speech intensifies in anger and vitriol, reaching a crescendo of violence in the very brutality of the image, extremely rare in Racine, of her daughter's breast being ripped open by the sacrificial blade, revealing Iphigénie's beating heart:[38]

> Un Prêtre environné d'une foule cruelle,
> Portera sur ma Fille une main criminelle?
> Déchirera son sein? Et d'un oeil curieux
> Dans son Coeur palpitant consultera les Dieux?

> A priest surrounded by a cruel crowd,
> Will raise his criminal hand upon my daughter,
> Tear out her breast and with a curious eye
> Read in her fluttering heart the gods decree!
> (4.4.1301–4)

Her diatribe closes by completely reversing the positive valence given Agamemnon at the very start of the play. There he was a "père heureux"; now he has become a "barbare Epoux" and an "impitoyable Père." This cruel spouse is told he will have first to kill his wife if he attempts to offer his daughter to the Greeks:

> Non, je ne l'aurai point amenée au supplice,
> Ou vous ferez aux Grecs un double sacrifice.
> Ni crainte, ni respect ne m'en peut détacher.
> De mes bras tout sanglants il faudra l'arracher.

> No, no I will not lead her to her death,
> Else you must make a double sacrifice.
> Neither respect nor fear can loose me from her.
> You'll have to tear her from my bleeding arms.
> (4.4.1309–12)

What is important about Clytemnestra's invective is not just that it can be seen to reproduce yet again an example of one more Racinian Fury, a role more realistically occupied in this play by Eriphile, nor because this Fury would seem to fit into the genealogy of the Sphinx, whose presence haunts Racine's theater. In *Iphigénie,* rather than a Fury, Clytemnestra seems to echo another fictional creation of the Greeks, but this time, given the obvious ethical dilemma she confronts, it is in philosophy rather than mythology that we will find her model. Uninvited to the marriage of her daughter, an intruder into this male feast, Clytemnestra figures a new Diotima, come to speak her truth and to teach the assembled males the truth of their pact and their violent desires. One could say that Clytemnestra represents the antihistorical, antiprogressive femininity that refuses the abstract reasoning of (masculine) politics. Hers is a protective, possessive role: she wishes to preserve her offspring, against one and all, within the confines of the feminine sphere (marriage

and *oikos*). But here, her retentive, defensive desire cannot be separated from the truth she speaks, a truth that reveals the hypocrisy of a
society entirely subjected to a masculinist ideology of repression, to a
homosociality (which, of course, is just an attenuated form of homosexuality) that joins the brothers together in their love of the (ideal)
father, to a community that (as Agamemnon's family history reveals) is
born in sexual perversion and violence and that can only survive by new
acts of violence (sacrifice). Finally, by revealing the sexual violence
that is the repressed basis of that society, Clytemnestra teaches them
the truth that has been covered over by their hypocritical political reasoning.[39] But this truth, of course, cannot be heard. Clytemnestra will
be restrained and Iphigénie will be led to the sacrifice because society,
particularly the martial society of the Greek camp fired up as it is by
lust and greed, does not want to hear the truth, preferring, as most societies do, more comforting illusions.

The constantly invoked necessity of abiding by a triumphant *raison
d'état* is not, despite all the reasons invoked, rational but passional.[40]
As Freud pointed out in his *Group Psychology and the Analysis of the
Ego*, "Groups have never thirsted after truth. They demand illusions,
and cannot do without them."[41] Agamemnon turns away from what he
always knew but didn't want to acknowledge. Ulysses and Calchas are
interested in achieving their political goals by any means, which, in
this case, includes the slaying of an innocent child. Iphigénie embraces
the illusion of her own noble sacrifice in order to participate in the
logic of masculine glory, to be, until the end, her father's daughter. Only
one character, Eriphile, really wants to know the truth, which is, of
course, in her case the truth of her origins (Who am I? Where do I come
from?), but, as in all quests for the origin, her questions reveal the imperious, more dangerous drive to know the secrets of sexual and generational difference, an Oedipal quest fraught with unexpected and often
deadly detours. From the beginning Eriphile knows what everyone else
wishes to ignore: the truth, while it might set her free, will also kill her
("Un Oracle effrayant m'attache à mon erreur, / Et quand je veux
chercher le sang qui m'a fait naître, / Me dit, que sans périr, je ne puis
me connaître" [My ignorance is sealed by an oracle; / And, when I wish
to know the race who gave me breath / It warns, I cannot know this
without death]).

The truth that Clytemnestra reveals and that Eriphile desires is simply the truth that resides at the very heart of tragedy; it is the truth that makes tragedy tragic, the reality of death. It is the omnipresence of death, a death that lurks in the Greek camp, that has been repressed, transformed into a political mission, and directed outward at Troy that is the hidden vortex aspirating Agamemnon's family, the Greeks, and, of course, us, the audience. Clytemnestra tells Agamemnon and the Greeks that murder is the hidden center of the political community that unites them into a nation. Even more shocking, death is also the silent, secret link that joins the three young protagonists together in their passionate roundelay. Here death's surrogates, narcissism and melancholia, become the inseparable elements around which swirl the questions of marriage, sacrifice, and suicide and which parade in this dramatic universe as tragic passion.

Appropriately, the only truly tragic passion in the play (if we exclude, for the time being, the maternal/paternal passion of her parents for Iphigénie) is born amid the flames of war. Eriphile first encounters love as she is carried off, captive and unconscious, onto a ship sailing away from her destroyed homeland. Despite the fact that her city has been reduced to ashes, her protector slain, and herself (well, what really did happen to her?) reduced to slavery, when she first opens her eyes and gazes on her bloodied captor, she is, truly, ravished:

> Dans les cruelles mains, par qui je fus ravie
> Je demeurai longtemps sans lumière et sans vie.
> Enfin mes faibles yeux cherchèrent la clarté.
> Et me voyant presser d'un bras ensanglanté,
> Je frémissais, Doris, et d'un vainqueur sauvage
> Craignais de rencontrer l'effroyable visage.
> J'entrai dans son Vaisseau, détestant sa fureur,
> Et toujours détournant ma vue avec horreur.
> Je le vis. Son aspect n'avait rien de farouche.
> Je sentis le reproche expirer dans ma bouche.
> Je sentis contre moi mon Coeur se déclarer,
> J'oubliai ma colère, et ne sus que pleurer.
> Je me laissai conduire à cet aimable guide.
> Je l'aimais à Lesbos, et je l'aime en Aulide.

> In the cruel hands of him who ravished me
> Eyes shut, I long remained in jeopardy.

> At last my sad eyes opened to the light;
> And seeing a bloody arm still hold me tight,
> I shuddered, Doris, dreading still to see
> The fearful face of him who conquered me.
> I set foot on his ship with hatred burning,
> My eyes away with horror ever turning.
> I sudden saw him. He was not uncouth;
> I felt my fury wither in my mouth;
> I felt my heart against me wildly leap;
> My wrath forgetting, I could only weep.
> In his dear footsteps everywhere I'd rove.
> I loved in Lesbos and in Aulis love.
>   (2.1.489–502)

Prefiguring the fate that awaits Troy, the destruction of Lesbos by Achille has far different consequences for his captive. Instead of retreating into the passive melancholia we witnessed in Andromaque, Eriphile, en-raged by jealousy when she contemplates the marriage of Achille to Iphigénie, actively attempts to destroy their promise of happiness by hastening Iphigénie's sacrifice. Revealing Iphigénie's flight out of the camp seals her fate, but also, of course, it hastens the downfall of Troy. Eriphile's passion is intense, primitive, and totally anarchic. She pays no attention to the possible consequences of her betrayal. The only thing that counts is sating her desire for revenge. The question remains, for what is she actually seeking revenge? Not obviously for the crimes that Achille is guilty of having committed. These are not so much crimes as erotic foreplay for her. Eriphile has lived her entire life in the shadow of others' happiness, a happiness that only heightens her own sense of loss. It is, of course, the very idea of happiness that she wishes to attack, reducing the world around her to reflect the inner barrenness she has had to bear since her birth.

Although Eriphile is certainly more active than Andromaque, who is reduced, as we've seen, to a stance of passive aggression, she is not, for that, less of a melancholic. Death has attached itself to her from her birth. It is the absence of her parents, their lack in her life, that forms the black hole of emptiness and envy that she constantly seeks to fill:

> Je vois Iphigénie entre les bras d'un Père.
> Elle fait tout l'orgueil d'une superbe Mère.
> Et moi, toujours en butte à de nouveaux dangers,
> Remise dès l'enfance en des bras étrangers,

Je reçus, et je vois le jour que je respire,
Sans que Mère ni Père ait daigné me sourire.
J'ignore qui je suis...

I see the princess in a father's arms,
She is the sole pride of a haughty mother;
While I, still buffeted by further dangers,
Consigned from infancy to alien arms,
Have breathed from birth until this very day,
Denied a father's or a mother's smile.
I know not who I am...
(2.1.421–27)

Eriphile's whole existence has been a search for a love that she never received, that she sees all around her, that she envies in Iphigénie, and that reflects a wounded narcissism so great that it can never be effectively sutured.[42] Instead, constant envy and resentment are the pure, murderous product of her melancholic rage. This rage is exacerbated by the sight of what she perceives that others have and that she lacks. Her only response is destruction, which, like her passion for Achille, is born in the violence of rape; it is tinged with a perverse erotic charge:

Ah, Doris, quelle joie!
Que d'encens brûlerait dans les Temples de Troie!
Si troublant tous les Grecs et vengeant ma prison
Je pouvais contre Achille armer Agamemnon,
Si leur haine, de Troie oubliant la querelle
Tourner contre eux le fer qu'ils aiguisent contre elle.

Doris, what joy!
Incense would burn in all the shrines of Troy,
If I, plaguing the Greeks, to pay their debt,
Achille against Agamemnon set;
If both their hates—forgetting Troy, instead
With sharpened sword ensured each other bled.
(4.1.1133–38)

Eriphile, the destructive Fury of this play, perfectly understands the political mechanism of sacrifice. She knows that if she is able to displace the violence the sacrifice intends to direct against Troy back onto the Greeks, she can have the satisfaction (in total contradiction to the disregard she has previously shown for the fate of Troy) and the narcissistic glory of having saved her people. Eriphile's constant contradictions, her confusion of her personal sexual jealousy and the political fate of nations, are just one more sign of a powerful affective regression. It is a state of confusion in which the unconscious refuses any distinctions, between self and other, male and female, or life and death. In this passionate break with any contingent reality, Eriphile is perhaps the most enraged of Racine's Furies and the most tragic. Unfortunately for her and despite her prescience, not only is she not needed to turn Agamemnon against Achille (their narcissism is sufficient onto itself to accomplish that goal) but the recognition she so aches for will at last be accorded her at the sacrifice, where she rather than an instrumental participant will become the victim of her own rage.

Iphigénie and Eriphile are two sides of the same coin, on one side the destructive, murderous Fury, a tragic sister of Hermione, Agrippine, and Roxane, and on the other, the young, innocent virgin, the clone of Antigone, Junie, Monime, and Atalide.[43] This division, the splitting of the female protagonist into different versions of the male fantasy of the mother and the whore and their mutual face-off works better in theory than in drama. Although in a very obvious sense Iphigénie and Eriphile represent two distinct dramatis personae, the very confusion of their beings where the one is bound to the other has been marked throughout the drama by a sly play of desire that inflects both the asocial passion of the one and the normative love of the other. Although we do not know how Eriphile came to share in Iphigénie's life, we do know that there has been, in a very brief time, a sisterly intimacy established between the two:

> Maintenant tout vous rit. L'aimable Iphigénie
> D'une amitié sincère avec vous est unie.
> Elle vous plaint, vous voit avec des yeux de Soeur,
> Et vous seriez dans Troie avec moins de douceur.

> Now fortune smiles: and sweet Iphigenia
> Is knit to you in a firm bond of friendship.
> Compassionate, she treats you as her sister,
> And Troy itself could hardly treat you better.
> (2.1.409–12)

It seems that Iphigénie's affection for this Trojan captive grows with each new telling of her story, that is, of her "rape" by Achille. One can only wonder, as Iphigénie herself finally realizes, how, with such rapt attention paid to each detail of the tale, she failed to recognize the desire that all those lurid details both hid and revealed. Only the obvious process of identification that shuttles between the two halves of Iphigénie/ Eriphile, where one quivers at the sexualized trauma of the other, allows this understanding:

> Oui, vous l'aimez, Perfide.
> Et ces mêmes fureurs que vous me dépeignez,
> Ses bras que dans le sang vous avez vus baignés,
> Ces morts, cette Lesbos, ces cendres, cette flamme,
> Sont les traits dont l'amour l'a gravé dans votre âme.
> Et loin d'en détester le cruel souvenir,
> Vous vous plaisez encore à m'en entretenir.
> Déjà plus d'une fois dans vos plaintes forcées
> J'ai dû voir, et j'ai vu le fond de vos pensées.
> Mais toujours sur mes yeux ma facile bonté
> A remis le bandeau que j'avais écarté.

> Yes, you love him, traitress.
> And all these ragings that you paint to me,
> These arms, all bathed in blood, you ever see,
> These ashes, torches, Lesbos' murdered toll,
> Are strokes with which love prints him in your soul;
> And far from cursing his past cruelty,
> You take delight once more to tell it me.
> Already more than once, in your feigned sighs,
> I ought to have and did your heart surprise;
> But ever on my eyes, my natural kindness
> Replaced the blinkers to restore my blindness.
> (2.5.679–88)

We know from experience (Monime) that in Racine the *bandeau* is an ambivalent signifier, both deadly and ineffectual. Even here, where the *bandeau* is invoked as metaphor in order to explain Iphigénie's failure to acknowledge the passion that is evident in Eriphile's narrative, she also uses it to peek at scenes that her upbringing and social position tell her she should never see. This curiosity, a form of blindness and insight into the violence of sexuality that is normally hidden by the *galanterie* of her fiancé, both attracts and repels Iphigénie. The sheltered young innocent, titillated by the images of violence and sexuality, reacts by rejecting the suitor she claims to love as soon as her obedience to her father is at stake, that is, as soon as she risks leaving her father's house for the unknown pleasures of marriage. Rejecting her lover's impetuous

dismissal of her father's claims on her, rejecting, in a sense, him, she retreats from the freedom of marriage into a virginal submission to paternal law:

> C'est mon Père, Seigneur, je vous le dis encore.
> Mais un Père que j'aime, un Père que j'adore,
> Qui me chérit lui-même, et dont jusqu'à ce jour
> Je n'ai jamais reçu que des marques d'amour.
> Mon Coeur dans ce respect élevé dès l'enfance,
> Ne peut que s'affliger de tout ce qui l'offense.

> He is my father and, I say once more,
> A father whom I cherish and adore,
> Who loves me in return and till this hour
> Has shown me only tokens of his love.
> My heart, from childhood raised in his esteem,
> And far from daring now, by a quick change
> To approve the fury that's consuming you.
>   (3.6.1001–6)

Achille's vehemence, his total disregard for the protocols of social
life, his dismissal of the political as mere pretense (his disdain for the
claims of paternity, for the order of the priests, for oracles, and even for
the gods), comes up against a protective wall of filial love. His outburst
proves too threatening for Iphigénie's sense of self. The liberty that
Achille offers her represents precisely the sexual violence (she calls
Achille "un Amant furieux" [a raging Lover]) she both desires and
fears, which makes her retreat into a position of adamant paternalism, a
position that espouses the political side of the father, a renunciation of
the body and its threatening excess. Steeling herself against the claims of
blood and sex, represented by both Clytemnestra and Achille, Iphigénie
opts for the submission to the social imperative, assuming the role of
sacrificial victim and, therefore, heroine of the Greek nation, over and
against the claims of individual happiness. In a sense she seeks the same
immortal fame that is promised to Achille but that is given only at the
price of losing one's life. Her death becomes the promise of eternal glory,
her renunciation the symbol of sublimation's triumph. To her father she
offers her submission to his law:

> Mon Père,
> Cessez de vous troubler, vous n'êtes point trahi.
> Quand vous commanderez, vous serez obéi.

Ma vie est votre bien. Vous voulez le reprendre,
Vos orders sans détour pouvaient se faire entendre.
D'un oeil aussi content, d'un Coeur aussi soumis
Que j'acceptais l'Epoux que vous m'aviez promis,
Je saurai, s'il le faut, Victime obéissante,
Tendre au fer de Calchas une tête innocente,
Et respectant le coup par vous-même ordonné,
Vous rendre tout le sang que vous m'avez donné.

Father,
Do not be troubled, you are not betrayed.
When you command me you shall be obeyed.
You gave me life, you want it back again;
Your orders could be given without strain.
As happily and as submissively
As I took the husband whom you promised me,
I shall, obedient victim, on your word,
Offer my innocent head to Calchas' sword,
And saluting the blow that you decree,
Return you all the blood you've given me.
　　　(4.4.1175–84)

And to her betrothed, she offers herself, already transformed into a Nike, an untouched virgin, a symbol of the Greek victory to come:[44]

Allez, et dans ses murs vides de Citoyens,
Faites pleurer ma mort aux Veuves des Troyens.
Je meurs dans cet espoir satisfaite, et tranquille.
Si je n'ai pas vécu la Compagne d'Achille,
J'espère que du moins un heureux Avenir
A vos faits immortels joindra mon souvenir,
Et qu'un jour mon trépas, source de votre gloire,
Ouvrira le récit d'une si belle Histoire.

Go: and ensure upon their desert wall
The Trojan widows mourn my mortal call.
In this hope I shall die content and free.
If I could not Achille's consort be
I hope at least a happy future greets
My memory, linked with your immortal feats;
And that one day my death, source of your glory.
Will be the first page of a splendid story.
　　　(5.2.1555–62)

Iphigénie positions herself between her father and her lover; she becomes the necessary object, the object of desire for both men. It is through her and her alone that each can achieve the heroic status beyond death to which he aspires. She becomes, in other words, the universal object of desire without which neither man can realize his destiny. As such she can remain, by renunciation, in the position of the untouched, unpolluted innocence that bestows on her a greater glory in death than she could ever achieve in life. And yet in this perverse position, as the object of desire of these two men, Iphigénie reveals a sexual and political animosity that threatens the cohesion of the Greeks and endangers the triumph of Greek civilization over its Oriental other before it even has the opportunity of asserting its hegemony.[45] She successfully turns Achille against Agamemnon and exacerbates Agamemnon's mistrust of Achille.

Achille seems to be the odd man out in the Greek cohort. He is, he reminds us, the only Greek leader who was not a suitor for Helen's hand. He took no part in the collective oath and thus, he claims, owes allegiance to no one but to himself and to his love:

> Jamais Vaisseaux partis des Rives du Scamandre
> Aux champs Thessaliens osèrent-il descendre?
> Et jamais dans Larissse un lâche Ravisseur
> Me vint-il enlever ou ma Femme, ou ma Soeur?
> Qu'ai-je a me plaindre? Ou sont les pertes que j'ai faites?
> Je n'y vais que pour vous, Barbare que vous êtes,
> Pour vous, à qui des Grecs moi seul je ne dois rien.
> . . . .
> Votre Fille me plut, je prétendis lui plaire.
> Elle est de mes serments seule Dépositaire.
> Content de son hymen, vaisseaux, armes, soldats,
> Ma foi lui promit tout, et rien à Ménélas.
>
> Have ever from Scamander's bans ships sailed
> That dared descend on fields of Thessaly?
> Has ever any dastard ravisher
> Kidnapped my wife or sister in Larissa?
> What's my complaint? What losses have I suffered?
> I'm going for you, barbarian as you are;
> You, whom I'm the one Greek owing nothing;
> . . . .
> Your daughter pleased me and I think I please her
> She is my vows' sole beneficiary.
> Happy to wed her, I pledged all to her;
> Ships, arms, soldiers, nothing to Menelaus.
>   (4.6.1376–96)

Achille proclaims his complete independence; he is a free agent who is motivated (he claims) only by love. Yet this love, as an unpolitical force, places him in direct conflict with the representative of the law, Agamemnon, who is also and at the same time the man who controls access to the object of Achille's desire. Once again, the Oedipal conflict between an elder male and a young powerful prince exacerbates to the point of rupture the fault lines in the political structure ("Ton insolent amour, qui croit m'épouvanter, / Vient de hâter le coup que tu veux arrêter" [This bumptious love of yours, dreaming to daunt me / Has only sped the blow you wished to stay]). It is here, in this *chassé-croisé* of politics and desire that the altar, the ambiguous symbol of sacrifice/marriage, takes on an ever growing significance as it comes to represent in a very concrete way the varying valences of sublimation and sexuality in the construction of any political community. It is significant that the rivalry of the two men for the young virgin heightens to the point of precipitating at the altar the tragic denouement of the play where Iphigénie/Eriphile at last can satisfy the demands of the gods, the bloodlust of the Greeks, and the refined dramatic criteria of Racine's more civilized spectators.

The role of the altar, that silent, ambivalent, and ominous presence in all of Racine's tragedies, takes on a particular prominence in *Iphigénie*. Since this is the only tragedy that specifically invokes a ritualized, propitiatory sacrifice as its central plot device, it is not surprising that the altar, while never actually present on stage, should nevertheless be a constant presence in the tragic dynamics of the play, drawing, like some malevolent magnet ("hérissé de dards, de javelots" [bristling with spears and javelins]), all the characters inexorably toward it. The word *autel* is perhaps the red thread that is woven throughout the text, from the first mention of it by Agamemnon quoting the oracle, which establishes his dilemma ("Vous armez contre Troie une puissance vaine, si dans un sacrifice auguste et solennel / Une fille du sang d'Hélène / De Diane en ces lieux n'ensanglante l'autel" [In vain you threaten Troy until the moment when / By a sacrifice that's solemn and austere / A daughter of the blood of Helen / Stains with her blood Diana's altar here]), to the last description in the play, which brings about the tragedy's resolution:

> À peine son sang coule et fait rougir la terre;
> Les dieux font sur l'autel entendre le tonnerre;
> Les vents agitent l'air d'heureux frémissements,

> Et la mer leur répond par ses mugissements;
> La rive au loin gémit, blanchissante d'écume;
> La flamme du bûcher d' elle-même s'allume;
> Le ciel brille d'éclairs...
>
> Her blood has hardly flowed, reddening the earth,
> When Heaven's thunder bursts upon the altar;
> The winds in happy shudders tear the air
> And the sea responds with all her mighty moaning,
> While groans the farther shore flecked white with foam;
> And of itself the pyre's flame sudden flares.
> The sky flashes with lightning...
>   (5, scène dernière, 1777–83)

At the same time this presence is marked as an enigma: is the altar there for a sacrifice or for a marriage? And finally why are these two terms, supposedly so opposite, so interchangeable?

It is because of the inherent ambivalence of the altar that Racine is able to advance his plot with all the tragic misprisions of his characters. Agamemnon uses the altar as marriage bait, luring his unsuspecting wife and daughter into the Greek camp. For them, as well as for Eriphile and Achille, the altar remains a symbol of the wedding they assume will take place, while at the same time, for Agamemnon, Ulysse, Calchas, the assembled Greeks, and the audience, the altar is there to receive the blood of the innocent young virgin. It is only once Agamemnon's deceit is revealed that the significance of the altar is radically altered from the scene of a marriage—

> Princesse, mon bonheur ne dépend que de vous.
> Votre père à l'autel vous destine un époux:
> Venez y recevoir un coeur qui vous adore.
>
> Princess, my happiness depends on you.
> Your father has ordained a husband for you:
> Accept at the altar my adoring heart.
>   (3.4.851–53)

to a site of immolation:

> Cependant aujourd'hui, sanguinaire, parjure,
> C'est peu de violer l'amitié, la nature,
> C'est peu que de vouloir, sous un couteau mortel,
> Me montrer votre coeur fumant sur un autel:
> D'un appareil d'hymen couvrant ce sacrifice,

Il veut que ce soit moi qui vous mène au supplice?
Que ma crédule main conduise le couteau?
Qu'au lieu de votre époux je sois votre bourreau?
Et quel était pour vous ce sanglant hyménée,
Si je fusse arrivé plus tard d'une journée?
Quoi donc? À leur fureur livrée en ce moment
Vous iriez à l'autel me chercher vainement;
Et d'un fer imprévu vous tomberiez frappée,
En accusant mon nom qui vous aurait trompée?

And yet today, bloodthirsty and forsworn,
He's not content to lay his murderous part
At the altar showing me your steaming heart:
But, covering his crime with a wedding wreath,
Propose I should lead you to your death?
With knife in hand, in my credulity,
Not husband but your butcher I should be?
How bloody would have been your nuptial fate
If I had come back only one day late!
What? Victim now of their conspiracy,
To the altar you would go and not find me.
And stricken, by an unexpected sword,
Would die accusing me for breaking word?
        (3.6.973–86)

There has been, we might say, a change of hearts (from "un coeur qui vous adore" [a heart that adores you] to "votre coeur fumant sur un autel" [your heart steaming on the altar]) in the rhetorical space that has opened up between the marriage altar and the sacrificial altar, and in this space lies the entire ambivalent horror of this familial/political tragedy. It is a tragic space that has been there all along but constantly playing hide-and-seek with all the participants in this drama, hiding and revealing itself under a rhetoric of narcissism, melancholia, and passion. On the one hand, the altar is always a locus of appropriation, either the bride by the groom or the victim by the executioner; only the rhetoric attached to the ceremony changes, infused for the first with a supposedly positive valence and by the second with a sacred one ("sacred" containing in itself the ambivalent meaning of both a taboo and a transgression). But it must be said that in a highly patriarchal culture such as the Greek society of the play, based as it is on the exchange of women and the sacrifice of sexuality, which established the homosocial community of brothers, marriage is also always an appropriation.

It is an appropriation underlined by Racine's playing on the ambivalent metaphor/metonymy of the learned word "hymen," which signals both a metaphor for marriage and a metonymy for the woman offered in marriage, the hymen that is so important to virginity's sacrifice, proving to the man who has deflowered her that his wife is now squarely placed within his family as the guarantor and perpetuator of his lineage. At the same time, as both Loraux and Detienne have written, the sacrifice can also be seen as a sexual act where the violence of the sacrificial act is analogous to a deflowering in that it changes the status of the young virgin offered up to the gods at the same time that it kills her.

It is here, therefore, in this ambiguous space, the space of violence and sexuality, that the play reaches its frenzied conclusion. In this open breach, Eriphile seizes the opportunity to destroy the marriage that exacerbates her jealousy and envy. It is here that the conflict between Achille and Agamemnon erupts into daylight, pitting the older father against an invulnerable, immortal rival. Finally, it is here that the entire tragic destiny of the Atreides becomes concentrated in the battle that opposes Clytemnestra to Agamemnon, a struggle between the prerogatives of the body, of blood and family, over and against the political sacrifices necessary for the survival of the community of brothers. Clytemnestra's and Agamemnon's clash here is but the beginning of a long, drawn-out, and horrific combat, the repercussions of which will echo through the years and that Racine felt obliged to coyly underline ("Vos yeux me reverront dans Oreste mon Frère. / Puisse-t-il être, hélas moins funeste à sa Mère!" [You'll see me in Oreste, my dear brother. / Ah! may he be less fatal to his mother!]). It is a combat that will pit mother against father, child against parent, and son against mother and will mark the ethical history of Western political institutions down to this day.

And it is here in this conflicted space of betrayed hearts that the doubling that Racine has created comes at last to bear its tragic fruits. Maddened at the idea that Iphigénie will escape her fate, Eriphile betrays her attempted flight to the Greeks. Trapped by the army and dragged to the altar, her mother imprisoned, and her lover vowing to disobey her wish to die, Iphigénie is brought before Calchas—the looming representative, in this play the double of Agamemnon, the ruthless primal father, surrounded by the frenzied Greek host:

Ce n'est plus un vain Peuple en désordre assemblé,
C'est d'un zèle fatal tout le Camp aveuglé.
Plus de pitié, Calchas seul règne, seul commande.
La Piété sévère exige son Offrande.

They are no more a meek, bewildered flock;
Blinded by deadly zeal the whole camp's run amok.
No pity more. Calchas alone commands;
Strict piety her sacrifice demands.
     (5.3.1619–26)

The knife is raised, readied for the immolation. At the very moment of highest tension, Achille and his men (we are told) burst onto the scene, disrupt the sacrifice, and threaten the unity of the Greeks and their mission. Into this melee, which comes as close to a state of political chaos as we ever get in Racine, the fear of a return to some elemental violence has erupted in the middle of the Greek community, threatening its destruction. At this moment of exacerbated tension, Calchas, at last possessed by the god(s), proclaims the truth of the oracle: it is not Iphigénie whom the gods desire but Iphigénie aka Eriphile—who, he says, has been led to the altar by "ses propres fureurs" (her own furies)— who is their intended victim. In other words, it is this Fury, the Racinian supplement, who must pay with her blood for the release of the Greek fleet. Revealing the secret of her origins, Calchas announces that she is the daughter of Theseus and Helen and thus of the same blood as Iphigénie. He finally gives her the answer to her obsessive question, Who am I? At the same time as was predicted, Calchas's revelation also signals her end:

On admire en secret sa naissance, et son sort.
Mais puisque Troie enfin est le prix de sa mort,
L'Armèée à haute voix se déclare contre elle,
Et prononce à Calchas sa sentence mortelle.

All marvel at her birth and at her fate.
But since Troy could be won but by her death,
The army raised their clamour, loud against her.
Pronouncing her death sentence to Calchas.
     (5, scène dernière, 1767–70)

The assembled community, true to the logic of the sacrifice, cries out for her blood, which Calchas, raising the sacrificial knife, is about to

spill. But before he can strike, Eriphile/Iphigénie, faithful to the isolation she has lived with all her life, pushes him aside, seizes the sacrificial blade, and plunges it into her breast. She has transformed the sacrifice
into a suicide, but a suicide that, while representing her independence
and alienation from any community, satisfies the wrath of the gods.
The effects are immediate; the earth heaves, the waves roar, the wind
picks up. In other words, the entire cosmos responds to the death of
this young woman.[46] The nefarious double becomes the perfect scapegoat of all the hypocrisy of the Greeks and their "first family." She has
removed herself from the scene of the world. Her suicide/sacrifice assures
the integrity of her sister/other, an integrity that was sorely jeopardized
throughout the play threatened both by the sacrifice of her life, on the
altar of the Greek polis, and the sacrifice of her virginity, on the altar of
her marriage to Achille, her "amant furieux." At the same time, however, what also has been sacrificed by Eriphile's desperate gesture is the
tragic, if not the tragedy. The entire ruse of introducing a double has
the effect of Racine's turning away from Euripides, his most tragic
model, of avoiding the tragic itself. For now, at the end of the play we
are left, despite the discomfort we feel at Eriphile's act (but are we not
secretly relieved by her death—she was, after all, so unsympathetic?),
with order restored, with the family reunited, and with the promise of a
happy ending, the marriage of the two young lovers. Iphigénie leaves
the play as she entered it, intact, neither married nor sacrificed. Her
marriage is left in abeyance. It will have to wait while Achille and his
fellow Greeks go off to punish and plunder Troy, to eliminate, that is,
their Oriental br/others, who represent all the seductive but destructive
appeal that the Greek miracle will have to suppress in order to establish its empire of reason and order in the France of Louis XIV.

6

Phèdre (et Hippolyte): Taboo, Transgression, and the Birth of Democracy?

Phèdre is generally considered Racine's greatest, most searing tragedy. Despite their different critical, theoretical, or ideological approaches, most modern commentators agree that *Phèdre* represents the apogee of French neoclassical tragedy; it stands as the culmination of Racine's oeuvre.[1] At the same time the play stands out as quite possibly the single most symbolic achievement in the annals of French literature. Few works can rival *Phèdre*'s place in the French canon, and few have the quasi mythical/mystical relation to French culture as this last profane tragedy of Racine. Racine himself, we are told in the biography penned by his son Louis, would agree with his critics in finding this his most perfect play, the one he was most proud of having written:

> Il a cependant été toujours convaincu, que s'il avait fait quelque chose de parfait, c'était *Phèdre*; et sa prédilection pour cette pièce était fondée sur des raisons très fortes. Car, quoique l'action d'*Athalie* soit bien plus grande, le caractère de Phèdre est comme celui d'Oedipe, ou de ces sujets rares qui ne sont pas l'ouvrage des poètes et qu'il faut que la fable ou l'histoire leur fournissent.[2]

> He was always convinced that if he had created one perfect thing it was *Phèdre*; and his predilection for this play was based on very important reasons. For, although the plot of *Athalie* is much grander, the character

197

of Phèdre is like Oedipus' or those uncommon subjects that are not the
creation of poets but rather must be supplied by either myth (legend)
or history.

While contemporary historians and biographers of Racine tend to dismiss Louis' narrative of his father's life and career as unreliable, he did
seem, as the citation shows, to have had at least one acute insight into
the fascination Phèdre has maintained over generations of audiences.
On one hand, he opines, Phèdre, like Oedipus, is an exceptional ("rare")
character insofar as neither can be said to be the invention of an individual (author) but rather both come to the poet out of the obscure
mists of mythology ("fable"), garbed in all the accretions across centuries of repeated legends and their subsequent reworkings by generations
of authors.[3] On the other hand, the comparison of Phèdre to Oedipus is
also, on Louis Racine's part, a stroke of genial intuition (probably a
unique instance for Louis), prefiguring as it does Freud's own attempt at
explaining the universal hold he attributes to Sophocle's Oedipus Tyrannos: "If Oedipus Rex moves a modern audience no less than it did the
contemporary Greek one, the explanation can only be that its effect
does not lie in the contrast between destiny and human will, but is to
be looked for in the particular nature of the material on which that
contrast is exemplified."[4] In other words, it is the matter of the tragedy,
passion, calumny, and murder committed in the tightly restricted confines of the family that continues to resonate across the centuries and
despite enormous social and political changes in the dark heart of contemporary audiences. Finally, the coupling of Phèdre with Oedipus in
Louis Racine's comments reveals, most probably unbeknownst to him,
an insight into a particular underlying dynamics of sexuality and politics that constitutes the tragic knot at the center of the play's drama
and whose hold on the audience, relayed by some of the most sensual
verse in French, exerts an affective pull that carries us into the same
whirlwind of passion and death that consumes and destroys the two
eponymous characters of this tragedy, Phèdre and Hippolyte.

Phèdre et Hippolyte, we should recall, was the original title of Racine's
tragedy, the two victims joined from the beginning by a grammatical
formula the very impossibility of which the entire play, its drama and its
tragedy, will seek to confirm. This impossible relation, impossible because
taboo, because incestuous, nevertheless was underlined by Racine in

the title he gave his play and by which it continued to be known during the first ten years of its existence. The tragedy became simply *Phèdre*
only in its second printed version of 1687. By changing the play's title
Racine effectively eclipses the role of Hippolyte and by the same token
signals that from then on Phèdre is to take her place alongside Andromaque, Bérénice, and Iphigénie in his feminocentric pantheon.[5] There,
with her suffering sisters, Phèdre becomes the absolute icon of feminine
passion, a victim of love and lust, a woman undone by forces she believes
to be beyond her control; she is a slave to a curse that has undone all
the women in her family and that now wreaks its greatest havoc on her.

Although we will probably never know what change of heart led
Racine to rebaptize his most famous tragedy, it does strike me as a curious and significant redirection of attention away from the young hero/
victim and onto the passion of this other, female victim with interesting consequences for the political and sexual dynamics of the Oedipal
scenario that we have been following, sometimes more, sometimes less
overtly, in the overarching ideological framework of Racine's theater.
Certainly the importance, even the centrality, of Hippolyte as a character has been insisted on by both Mauron and Barthes in their readings
of the play. Barthes reminds us, "So it is actually Hippolytus who is the
exemplary character in *Phèdre* (though not the principal one); he is truly
the propitiatory victim."[6] Mauron, for his part, claims that Hippolyte is
the pivotal character in the play: "In *Phèdre* it is Hippolyte who occupies
the center: loved by Phèdre, lover of Aricis, accused of incest by his father, he is situated at the intersection of the three principal dramatic
relations that structure the play, and, nevertheless, he appears weak—
he is the always endangered center threatened with dismemberment by
the fragmenting passions so characteristic of the Racinian universe."[7]
And it is Hippolyte, I might add, who in this play incarnates in perhaps
the most direct way both the political promise and the Oedipal threat
that the young prince must negotiate in order to be able to slay the
monster and take the father's place, that is, to become king. *Phèdre* develops in the most constricted and lethal of scenarios the defeat of this
quest and shows how not only the prince but an entire world order can
be undone by the untamed havoc of sexuality gone wild ("Ce n'est plus
une ardeur dans mes veines cachée. / C'est Venus toute entière à sa
proie attachée" [It's no mere passion tingling in my veins: / It's Venus

tense extended on her prey!]). It is here, in this complicated scenario of passion, politics, and sacrifice, that for the first and only time in Racine's dramatic career we are witness to the actual immolation of the child/son by the father, a father who too quickly believes and accepts accusations of violent incest and whose revenge has untold consequences for the future of Athenian (that is, Western) polity.

From the beginning of Racine's tragic career, from *Andromaque*, the question of the sacrifice of the child has been the single most powerful plot device for advancing the dramatic action of his tragedies. Of all the innocent victims in Racine (Astyanax, Britannicus, Xipharès, Iphigénie, Joas) Hippolyte is surely the most pathetic. While in *Andromaque* the danger represented by Astyanax is perceived by the Greeks to be a purely political threat (they fear his revenge for the sack and destruction of Troy), by *Phèdre* this same danger has become so internalized in the Oedipal conflict of the characters that politics and sexuality seamlessly coalesce. All the characters are entrapped in a reciprocity of desire in which each, by mirroring the desire of the others, becomes for those others a monster:[8]

> OENONE: Mais, ne me trompez point, vous est-il cher encore?
>   De quel oeil voyez-vous ce prince audacieux?
> PHÈDRE: Je le vois comme un monstre effroyable à mes yeux.

> OENONE: But tell me true, is he still dear to you?
>   How do you look upon this haughty prince?
> PHÈDRE: I look upon him like some monstrous fiend.
>   (3.3.88–84)

>   THÉSÉE TO HIPPOLYTE:
>   Perfide! Oses-tu te montrer devant moi?
>   Monstre, qu'à trop longtemps épargné le tonnerre,
>   Reste impur des brigands dont j'ai purgé la Terre.
>   Après que le transport d'un amour plein d'horreur
>   Jusqu'au lit de ton Père a porté la fureur
>   Tu m'oses présenter une tête ennemie!

>   What traitor! You dare show yourself before me?
>   Foul monster, whom too long Jove's thunder spares,
>   Fell brigand, who still soil the earth I cleansed.
>   After your fiendish passion spurred you wildly
>   To desecrate the bed of your own father,
>   You dare to show to me a face I hate!
>   (4.2.1044–49)

ARICIE TO THÉSÉE:
Prenez garde, seigneur: vos invicibles mains
Ont de monsters sans nombre affranchi les humains;
Mais tout n'est pas détruit, et vous en laissez vivre
Un...

Take care, my lord. Your ever-conquering hands
Have freed humanity of countless monsters;
But all are not destroyed and you let live
One...
      (5.3.1443–46)

At the end of Racine's career, politics and sexuality only reiterate, in ever more tightly constructed scenarios, the essential violence inherent in the Oedipal structure that was already present in his first tragedy. Sexuality, as Leo Bersani has written, in its most fundamental aspect is always incestuous and thus always inimical to society at large, to the family as produced by that society, and finally to the very subject formed at their conjuncture.[9] In other words, it is sexuality that is monstrous and that produces the monsters of which society must rid itself in order not to descend into chaos and fragmentation and in order not to live sullied (the idea of "souillure," to which I will return). This sexual monstrosity is the always present threat of the return of what society, in the person of the father and his law, has had to suppress in order to become civilized. But this suppression requires a constantly exercised violence in order to assure against its return. Society is united precisely because individual desire has in some way—in many different ways—been channeled into collective enterprise, into societal living. What this means is that the sacrifice of individual desire is relayed into a communality of mutually held ideals of which the father is the vehicle. At the very beginnings of community, in the first collective gesture, lies the renouncement of a portion of individual pleasure, a sacrifice of one's own desire. Sexuality is corralled into law and politics, as the distribution of power among contiguous individuals is born. At the same time, this containment is never totally successful; the repressed returns in those figures of otherness that patriarchy cannot entirely subdue—the haunting fear of female sexuality, the woman as passion, and the equally mistrusted image of the child, the potential rebel, who has not as yet been brought into line. And this, of course, is where in Phèdre the two main characters in opposition and in harmony enter into a very dangerous antagonism with the father, with Thésée, and all that he has come to represent. The theme of monstrosity will be relayed throughout this play as a metaphor for all that is uncivilized, all that threatens the polis, all, that is, that seems contrary to the rule of law put into place with so much difficulty by Thésée. At the same time, we cannot help but think, given the intuition of Louis Racine, of that other slayer of monsters, Oedipus, who also thought that he had driven chaos from his city and established a viable civil society by his slaying of the monstrous, sexually appetitive Sphinx. But as we have seen, the Sphinx seems to spring up with each new iteration of Oedipus and his legend to finally arrive, having migrated from the gates of Thebes, at Athens, or rather now more precisely at Trézène, where Phèdre, the latest incarnation of the Racinian Sphinx, pines away with lust for her stepson, the "superbe" Hippolyte.

It comes as no surprise that the Oedipus complex, even inverted, is quite obvious in the plot of *Phèdre*.[10] What perhaps is less obvious is the political dimension of the Oedipal scenario, which in this play is represented on several levels, most prominently by Theseus, who has had, at least in legend, the only direct contact with the incestuous, parricidal king of Thebes. Oedipus, exhausted from his wanderings and at the end of a life exemplary for its tragic misprisions, comes to the city of Athens. Rather than being met with opprobrium, he is greeted by the king of that city, Theseus, with hospitality, which restores to him the humanity of which he himself had declared himself unworthy. Welcomed by Theseus, Oedipus, in gratitude and just before disappearing forever into the grove of the Eumenides, bestows on him the "secret of kingship."[11] This secret becomes Theseus's own legacy, which he is to transmit to his own heir, forming a new genealogy of rulers. At the same time and concomitantly we cannot forget, as Didier Anzieu reminds us, of the other overlapping similarities that exist between the myths of Oedipus and Theseus—of, that is, the intermingling of politics and sexuality that forms, in different registers, the opposing valences of civilization and desire, of life and death, that cohabit in their ambivalent intermeshing demands, the parameters of human subjectivity. Anzieu tells us that the myth of Theseus is analogous to the Oedipus legend:

> Like Oedipus, Theseus goes looking for his father and kills him, but from the beginning he knows who his father is, and it is indirectly that he provokes his death. In the same way Theseus's incest is displaced from his mother to his sister-in-law while Phèdre's is displaced from her son

to her stepson. In Theseus's fate the Oedipus complex will be expressed by approximations.[12]

Anzieu calls Theseus "un Oedipe en demi-teinte" (a toned-down Oedipus). In other words, the two legends complete and complement each other.[13] The two heroes share in different, attenuated versions (for Theseus) a common subtext wherein sexuality and politics are inextricably interwoven in a narration that presents both the pleasures and, more important, the dangers of life in the polis, a life led supposedly under the light of reason. At the same time and by the same legends, we also learn that this reason, the rule of law, exists only in the bright light of day when the lurking forces of the id are restrained. Under the cover of darkness, real and metaphorical, civilization tends to fade away while the passions erupt in violence.[14]

It is this uncontrollable id, that is, her lust for Hippolyte, that Phèdre claims Venus has ignited in her blood to devastating effect:

> Je le vis, je rougis, je pâlis à sa vue.
> Un trouble s'éleva dans mon âme éperdue.
> Mes yeux ne voyaient plus, je ne pouvais parler,
> Je sentis tout mon corps et transir et brûler.
> Je reconnus Venus, et ses feux redoutables,
> D'un sang qu'elle poursuit tourments inévitables.[15]

> I saw, I blushed, I paled at the sight of him;
> A strange disquiet seized my stricken soul;
> My eyes could see no more, I could not speak;
> I felt my body burn and freeze in turn
> I recognized the fearful sting of Venus
> The destined torments of the blood she hunts.
>   (1.3.273–78)

The violence of her desire is met with the equal intensity of the law, which Phèdre, as a civilized being, has internalized; the restrictions of society, her position as wife and queen, and the demands of respectability are what she struggles to maintain, even as she acknowledges, litotically, how close she is by her heritage to the murkier, prehuman passions that constantly drag her family back away from culture and into nature:

> Ô haine de Vénus! Ô fatale colère!
> Dans quels égarements l'amour jeta ma Mère!

> O hate of Venus! Spite implacable!
> To what perversions love drove my mother!
>   (1.1.249–50)

Phèdre declines an entire female genealogy (her mother, Pasiphaë; her sister, Ariane; and herself) of woman undone by the pull of perverted desire. Venus, as we know, infuriated by being revealed by the Sun's indiscreet rays in flagrante delicto with her lover Mars, takes revenge on this trespass by condemning all the female members of the Sun's family to fatal, unnatural passion. Phèdre is the last in this accursed line. And, she claims, the most perverse:

> Puisque Vénus le veut, de ce sang déplorable
> Je péris la dernière, et la plus misérable.
>
> Since Venus wills it, of this wretched blood
> I die the last and most forlorn by far.
>   (1.1.257–58)

But Phèdre, although more passionately vocal about her uncontrollable desire, is not the only character on whom Venus has been casting her spell. Hippolyte, too, we learn from the beginning of the play, has fallen prey to Venus:

HIPPOLYTE: Hippolyte en partant fuit une autre Ennemie.
            Je fuis, je l'avouerai, cette jeune Aricie,
            Reste d'un sang fatal conjuré contre nous.
THERAMÈNE: Quoi vous-même, Seigneur, la persécutez-vous?
            Jamais l'aimable Soeur des cruels Pallantides
            Trempa-t-elle aux complots de ses Frères perfides?
            Et devez-vous haïr ses innocents appas
HIPPOLYTE: Si je la haïssais, je ne la fuirais pas.

HIPPOLYTE: It is another enemy I flee:
            I flee, I must confess, Aricia,
            Remnant of a doomed breed that schemed against us.
THERAMÈNE: What, my lord? Will you too persecute her?
            Did the harsh Pallantids' fair sister ever
            Take part in her perfidious brothers' plots?
            And must you hate her charming innocence?
HIPPOLYTE: Ah! If I hated her, I would not flee her.
            (1.1.49–56)

It is obvious, therefore, from the very beginning of the play that Racine has introduced us immediately into a world of violence and passion where each of the two main characters admits to a love that is marked as taboo. Despite their great differences, both of the title characters are smitten by a passion that is articulated as being outside the law of the father. Phèdre's passion for her stepson, Hippolyte, is clearly marked as incestuous.[16] Hippolyte, who has never before ventured into the thickets of love, does so now, against the explicit interdictions of his father ("Mon Père la réprouve, et par des lois sévères / Il défend de donner des Neveux à ses Frères" [My father frowns on her; and by strict laws / Bans issue from her to succeed her brothers]). Aricie, Hippolyte's newfound love, has been condemned by Theseus for political reasons to a sexless existence.

We know that Racine, fearing the ridicule of his contemporaries, decided not to follow Euripides' depiction of Hippolytus as averse to women (that is, homosexual) but instead chose to have his character, although decidedly more chaste than his father, fall in love with one special but unfortunately politically compromised woman. In *Phèdre*, the threat of the female, so present in all Racine as inherently "a-polis," is doubly articulated in its passive and aggressive variants by the two leading female protagonists, Phèdre and Aricie. Using the recent studies of the phantasmatic aspects of female sexuality by several French women analysts, Eugène Enriquez offers an explanation of why the place and status of female sexuality seems to pose a threat to masculine notions of political stability. Emphasizing the specter of the archaic mother as destabilizing for both men and women, Enriquez's (classically Freudian) point seems particularly suggestive for understanding the dynamics at work in the tragic vision presented by both Phèdre's and Hippolyte's transgressive choices. For Enriquez:

> The social order is founded on symbolization and repression. There can be no order without words that prohibit and words that represent, no order without taboos and safe havens. But woman (either mother or daughter) threatens the social when she enunciates the primacy of pleasure, of bodily relations, of the double relation, of reality over words, representations and mediated relations.
>
> Man can only be fascinated and terrorized by the threat that a precocious femininity poses to the realm of law and order. All the more so because it is never simply a question of "women left to themselves," the young man also . . . can fall victim to this impossibility of freeing himself from the archaic mother.[17]

In *Phèdre* this threat to the civilizing process is countered by Thésée.
Thésée represents for the play, for his wife, and for his son the ultimate
hero of Greek culture precisely because his prodigious feats have imposed
social order on the primeval chaos of mythological Greece. He has slain
countless monsters and brigands and seduced as many women met along
the way. The two sides of the heroic equation are made to coalesce to
the point that "woman" and "monster" become inseparable, especially
in Hippolyte's brooding over his father's exploits and his own inability
to imitate them. Theseus's feats have left an indelible impression on his
son, who can only repeat them to himself as a litany of what he has not
accomplished, of what he is not:

> Attaché près de moi par un zèle sincère
> Tu me contais alors l'histoire de mon Père.
> Tu sais combien mon âme attentive à ta voix
> S'échauffait au récit de ses nobles exploits;
> Quand tu me dépeignais ce Héros intrépide
> Consolant les Mortels de l'absence d'Alcide;
> Les Monstres étouffés, et les brigands punis,
> Procuste, Cercyon, et Scirron, et Sinnis,
> Et les os dispersés du Géant d'Epidaure,
> Et la Crète fumant du sang du Minotauro...
>
> In your sincere devotion to my welfare,
> You used to tell me then my father's story.
> You know how much my soul, all ears to you,
> Glowed at the tale of his resounding deeds,
> When you depicted my heroic sire
> Consoling mankind for Alcides' absence;
> So many monsters smothered, brigands smitten,
> Procrustes, Sceiron, Sinis, Cercyon,
> And Epidaurus' giant's bones, wide-scattered,
> And Crete with blood of Minotaur bespattered...
>   (1.1.73–79)

The slaying of monsters is, as we know, only half of the story. Unfortunately for him, Hippolyte, ashamed and embarrassed, refuses to listen
to the other half:

> Mais quand tu récitais des faits moins glorieux,
> Sa foi partout offerte, et reçue en cent lieux;
> Hélène à ses parents dans Sparte dérobée,
> Salamine témoin des pleurs de Péribée,

Tant d'autres, dont les noms lui sont même échappés,
Trop crédules esprits que sa flamme a trompés;
Ariane aux rochers contant ses injustices,
Phèdre enlevée enfin sous de meilleurs auspices;
Tu sais comme à regret écoutant ce discourse,
Je te pressais souvent d'en abréger le cours,
Heureux! Si j'avais pu ravir à la Mémoire
Cette indigne moitié d'une si belle Histoire.

But when you told of deeds less glorious,
His proffered heart a hundred times accepted;
In Sparta Helen stolen from her parents;
In Salamis pale Periboea in tears;
So many more, whose very names escape him,
Poor trusting creatures whom his passion snared:
Sad Ariadne wailing to the rocks,
And lastly, Phaedra, won with better grace.
You know how painful to me were your tales,
How often I would beg you cut them short.
Happy if I might blot out from my mind
This tarnished half of such a shining story.
     (1.1.83–94)

Hippolyte wants only half a father. He refuses to recognize his father's sexuality, going so far as to express (obliquely, it is true) an aggressive desire to "castrate" Thésée ("si j'avais pu ravir à la Mémoire / Cette indigne moitié" [Happy if I might blot out from my mind / This tarnished half of such a shining story]). Hippolyte has a resistance to the father's sexuality:

Cher Theramène, arrête, et respecte Thésée.
De ses jeunes erreurs désormais revenue
Par un indigne obstacle il n'est point retenu.

Pray, stop, Theramenes, respect my father.
Free now from al his youthful aberrations.
He is not in base dalliance detained.
     (1.1.22–24)

From the very beginning this resistance creates what appears to be Hippolyte's tragic double bind. On the one hand, he wants to be a hero like his father. On the other, refusing the sexual prowess that is an integral part of this heroism, he is trapped in his own asexual nature. He can never come into the place of the father because that place demands a sexuality that by Hippolyte's very bisexual inheritance is denied him. Hippolyte's dilemma is the quandary of all Racine's tragic characters who long for the absolute but are unable to attain an ideal that is out of their grasp because of an internal division that they ignore but that sunders their being, reminding them always that they are, in fact, not one, not absolute, but two.

Hippolyte is the tainted product of the cross between nature and culture, between the world of the father, of politics, of Athens, and the savage universe of Antiope, his Amazon mother. From Antiope, we are told, comes his aversion to sexuality. But with such an antecedent this aversion can only be interpreted as the refusal of the sexuality of the father, the refusal to assume a sexuality that is already inscribed in a patriarchal political network of absolute ideality. It is for this reason that Hippolyte is figured as always being on the point of leaving the scene of the tragedy to follow in his father's footsteps and yet forever remaining. The reasons for his remaining are not as strange as they might at first appear. Actually, given his conflicted ascendancy, Hippolyte has nowhere to go. He says he wants to leave to become like his father, to do what his father has done. Yet his bivalent nature never permits him to enter wholly into that world. Hippolyte always remains on the far side of the sexuality that defines Thésée's dominion over the world, always also within a sexuality that is other. When Hippolyte falls in love with Aricie this love only relays his bisexual nature; he falls in love outside paternal sexuality. His passion is transgressive because the only object it can find is out of bounds, outside his father's law.

Phèdre is, of course, in sexual reversal, the mirror image of Hippolyte. It may first strike us as odd, if not perverse, to see Phèdre and Hippolyte as but two differently gendered variations of the same, that is, a bisexual figuration, a two-headed monster of recalcitrant sexuality, but because of the very obvious differences in the plot of the tragedy these differences should not blind us to the structural similarities that ally them to each other as victims of the familial order that will destroy them both.[18] Both are condemned to the role of the victim by the internal, inalienable difference that they bear as children of a tainted, dual lineage. Phèdre's predisposition to victimization is double: daughter of Minos and Pasiphaë, she is torn between light and darkness, day and night; from her mother she descends directly from the Sun, and from her father's chthonian nature she inherits an affection for the shadowy realms of forests and dim interiors. From her mother she is heir to the curse Venus has placed on all the females in her lineage, and from her father, "juge aux Enfers" (judge in Hades), a conscience that hounds her. To all this must be added her position of outsider; she has been brought to Athens from Crete, Athens's traditional enemy whose exaction of a terrible tribute from the Athenians was finally ended by Theseus's slaying of her half-brother, the Minotaur.

It is a sign of Racine's particular genius that he was able to re-create an entire mythological tradition, inherited from archaic Greece, in a tragedy that is in essence so radically modern. Racine musters with the particularly acute erotic charge of his verse the compelling genealogies of his protagonists; he creates what is the mark of his (and our) modernity, a tragedy where his heroes struggle not so much with a dramatic situation that has been imposed from without (as do, for instance, the protagonists of Corneille's dramas) but rather with their own internal contradictions. The tragedy of *Phèdre* is the drama of the divided self, the tragedy of a being (of beings) whose existence is torn apart not by the impingements of the world but by the conflicting demands of unconscious desire and guilt, which we are given to understand by the constant references to mythological lineages that are allegorical representations of these contradictory forces.[19]

This is not to say that Racine's characters or his tragedies exist as asocial or asocietal creations in a fantasy universe with no relation to the real of the world in which they live. On the contrary, the suffering of his characters, their tragedy and tragic fate, is precisely a symptom of their society.[20] It is perhaps as symptom that Racinian tragedy as a form of representation is most intimately reflective of its social context, of the context not so much of a sociology of seventeenth-century France (or more precisely of the world of a rather limited but influential circle of theologians, artists, and economic and political figures circling the royal court) as of the dominant strains of an ideology that is as elusive as it is hegemonic. What is really at stake, I would argue, in the hermeneutics of the Racinian corpus is not so much determining the exact correspondences between his immediate social milieu(s) and his texts as understanding the ways in which his plays, and here most acutely *Phèdre*, express the desires of that or those milieu(s). The tragic "socius," to borrow a term from Pierre Bourdieu, whose outlines, desires, and fears Racine's dramaturgy traces, corresponds to certain political, economic, and libidinal strategies, delineating, perhaps unbeknownst to itself, a being subject and subjected to the centralizing tenets of evolving absolutism.

As I have argued in the introduction to this volume, absolutism, always an evolving, never actually achieved monarchal ideal, is a complex geopolitical strategy that is, in essence, patriarchal and that establishes an exclusionary model of the state, overarched by a theologically based metaphorical chain that equates God the Father to the king, father of his people, and to the father, head of each individual household.[21] In this model, the dominant figure of the father is exclusionary and unitary. Just as the emblem Louis XIV chose for himself, the sun, is a self-contained exclusive (one might say narcissistic) symbol of self-sufficiency, difference, in its diverse forms, must be suppressed in order not to destabilize the political edifice that is being so painstakingly put into place.

The dichotomizaton of subjectivity that we have been exploring in the main protagonists of *Phèdre*, Phèdre and Hippolyte, and in their internal contradictions, therefore places them irrevocably at odds with the ambient social structures that enfold and define them. Their internal split, their difference within, could be seen, on one level at least, as representing the battleground where an impossible desire for an integrity of being precisely forecloses its realization as anything other than a fantasy. The invisible Oedipal parameters informing subjectivity as an impossible plenitude of being fluctuate in Racine between two more archaic—one might call them pre-Oedipal—poles that are immediately gendered: on the one hand, the haunting guilt, an original debt to the father whose love can be won only by suffering and death (the sadistic spectacle of that suffering), and on the other, the alternative of a dispersion, either as the aphanisis of the subject in a suffocating embrace or in its violent sundering in a murderous attack of the mother (the masochistic, because passive, pole).[22] In either case, what we have is an archaic fantasy of a destructive, devouring, merciless parent—a father/mother—in whose gaze stands, or rather trembles, the child.[23]

The irony of this compelling fantasy of the absolute is that in order to attain the father, that is, to have him acknowledge the existence of his offspring, the child must first risk the passage through castration (sacrifice) and death. It is this desire that inheres in all the protagonists of Racine's world and that in *Phèdre* defines Hippolyte's dilemma, pushes them, in their drive for totality, against themselves. In a perverse fashion this is exactly what, because they desire it, proves itself to be forever beyond their grasp, forever an ideal that drives them on, that sunders them in their very being, and that, despite their own subservience to that desire/God, can do nothing other than produce the monsters that crush them.

While Racine's dramatic plots focus on the tragic predicament of his protagonists, torn apart as they are by their internal contradictions, this predicament is always brought to the foreground by a political crisis. All the tragedies are situated on the fault line separating the death of an old political regime and the birth of another, as yet unfocused, order. This crisis, internalized in the Racinian hero as a passionate, guilt-ridden rift in his/her own emotional world, is exacerbated by being presented against a background of impending political chaos. What we hear echoing across the Racinian world, and more precisely here in *Phèdre*, is that something in the order of that world has been irrevocably changed: "Cet heureux temps n'est plus. Tout a changé de face" (Those happy days are over. All has changed) declares Hippolyte at the beginning of *Phèdre*.

In a sense, following the model of Sophocles's *Oedipus Tyrannos*, Racine constructs his tragedy so that we are plunged from the start into a familial crisis that is also a political turning point threatening the entire world order of the play.[24] Quickly, however, Racine moves from the political instability of the outer world into the psychological turmoil of the play's protagonist. In an extremely subtle play of inversions, the tragic plot works itself out resolving the political crisis by and through the sacrifice of the tragic hero. In a sense, therefore, Racine moves from the larger political stage of an empire in crisis to the narrower, but analogous, ferment of the tragic hero who, becoming the victim of the world's crisis, is immolated to expiate the sins of society and, by so doing, restores order to it.

In *Phèdre* the political crisis is precipitated by Theseus's absence. His disappearance has profound emotional and political consequences for all the main characters. In the most elementary sense the king's decision to join Pirithoüs on a new adventure prompted the removal of Phèdre, Aricie, and the "court" from Athens to Troezen, shifting the erotic balance of power that had, unbeknownst to him, created a reasonable modus vivendi for his desirous wife. Phèdre, overcome by her passion for Hippolyte and fearing his presence, had schemed to have him leave the court, leave Athens, and remain in Troezen:

> Pour bannir l'Ennemi dont j'étais idolâtre,
> J'affectai les chagrins d'une injuste Marâtre,
> Je pressai son exil, et mes cris éternels
> L'arrachèrent du sein, et des bras paternels.
> Je respirais, Oenone. Et depuis son absence
> Mes jours moins agités coulaient dans l'innocence.
> Soumis à mon Epoux, et cachant mes ennuis,
> De son fatal hymen je cultivais les fruits.

> To exile him, the foe I idolized,
> I postured as a cruel stepmother;
> Despatched him from his fathers' warm embrace.
> I breathed once more, Oenone, in his absence,
> In innocence my calmer days flowed on.
> A faithful wife, I hid my secret grief,
> And raised the fruits of my unhappy marriage.
>   (1.3.293–300)

Their sojourn in Troezen changes all that, and not only for Phèdre. For Hippolyte, as well, Theseus's radical realignment of his family, their removal from Athens to Troezen, not only brings Phèdre into a promiscuous proximity to Hippolyte but also conveys the captive Aricie into his presence with the deleterious consequences Theramène has noticed:

> Avouez-le, tout change. Et depuis quelques jours
> On vous voit moins souvent, orgueilleux, et sauvage,
> Tantôt faire voler un char sur le rivage,
> Tantôt savant dans l'art par Neptune inventé,
> Rendre docile au frein un Coursier indompté.
> Les forêts de nos cris moins souvent retentissent.
> Chargés d'un feu secret vos yeux s'appesantissent.

> Admit the change in you; for some time now
> You are less often seen, proud and untamed,
> Driving a chariot furious on the shore,
> Or, expert in the art that Neptune fashioned,
> Breaking a champing, rearing charger in.
> Less often with our shouts the woods re-echo:
> Charged with a hidden fire, your eyes grow heavy.
>   (1.1.128–34)

In other words, the father's disappearance from the scene, which signals his vanishing from polity, immediately implies the eruption of desire. It is as if with the father gone, the hold of his law, the force of civilizing repression, loses its grip on the protagonists, allowing passion to burst forth, unleashing its monsters in the midst of this displaced family. But it is his announced death that effectively sends this world spinning out of control. In a strategically placed *coup de théâtre*, just after Phèdre has revealed her incestuous desire and guilt to Oenone, we are told that the long-vanished king, who until now has been presumed missing, is actually dead:

> La mort vous a ravi votre invincible Epoux,
> Et ce Malheur n'est plus ignoré que de vous.
>
> Death has deprived you of your dauntless consort,
> And only you are unaware of it.
> (1.4.319–20)

The immediate effect of the revelation of this death is a political crisis: who is to inherit the throne, who will govern Athens? In turn this political crisis only exacerbates desire by bringing all the protagonists into more direct contact. It is with the pretense of appealing for Hippolyte's protection of her still-underage son ("Mon Fils n'a plus de Père... Vous seul pouvez / ... embrasser sa défense" [My son is fatherless ... / ... You only can espouse his cause]) that Phèdre engages him in a conversation that quickly dissolves into her passionate declaration of love:

> Oui, Prince, je languis, je brûle pour Thésée.
> Je l'aime, non point tel que l'ont vu les Enfers,
> Volage adorateur de mille objets divers,
> Qui va du Dieu des Morts déshonorer la couche;
> Mais fidèle, mais fier, et même un peu farouche,
> Charmant, jeune, traînant tous les coeurs après soi,
> Tel qu'on dépeint nos Dieux, ou tel que je vous vois.
>
> Yes, prince, I languish and I burn for Theseus.
> I love him, not as he appeared in Hades,
> Most fickle lover of a thousand women,
> About to stain the bed of the god of Death;
> But faithful, proud, a little shy perhaps,
> Engaging, young, bewitching every heart,
> Just as they carve our gods, just as I see you.
> (2.5.634–40)

Undone by her irrepressible passion, what begins as a political plea ends with Phèdre's metaphorical descent into a labyrinth of desire where, lost in her erotic reveries, she has given herself the role of her sister Ariane, playing the accomplice of a Hippolyte who has replaced Thésée:

C'est moi, Prince, c'est moi dont l'utile secours
Vous eût du Labyrinthe, enseigné les détours.
Que de soins m'eût coûtés cette Tête charmante!
Un fil n'eût point assez rassuré votre Amante.
Compagne du péril qu'il vous fallait chercher,
Moi-même devant vous j'aurais voulu marcher,
Et Phèdre au Labyrinthe avec vous descendue,
Se serait avec vous retrouvée, ou perdue.

I, Prince, alone, my vital help alone
Would have taught you the Labyrinth's twists and turns.
How many cares your dear head would have cost me!
A thread would not have satisified your lover.
Companion in the risk you had to brave,
I would myself have run ahead of you;
And Phaedra, down with you in the Labyrinth,
Would have returned with you or with you perished.
        (2.5.655–62)

The confusion and startled rejection of this scenario by Hippolyte is interesting for more than one reason:

Dieux! Qu'est-ce j'entends? Madame, oubliez-vous
Que Thésée est mon Père, et qu'il est votre Epoux?

Gods, strike me deaf! Madam, do you forget
Theseus my father is, and is your husband?
        (2.5.663–64)

His panicked denial of what he has heard not only underlines his surprise at the highly erotic, barely disguised fantasy that Phèdre has seductively elaborated for him; with his emphasis on "father" and "husband" he also underlines both the incestuous nature of this fantasy and, perhaps more tellingly for him, its maternal, inhibiting subtext. Not only has Phèdre, in this fantasy, taken the place of Ariane, she has also taken the place of Thésée: it is she who, unable to let the lover become the hero he wishes to be by confronting and slaying the monster, reinforces the image of the possessive, devouring lover/mother whose passion does not allow any separation between herself and her lover/son, thus depriving him of any chance at being the man he so desperately wants to become. Phèdre's erotic reverie represents, for Hippolyte, her monstrous, Sphinx-like being. Instead of answering her riddle, Hippolyte flees and seeks solace with Aricie.

In a considerably less heated dialogue, Hippolyte also uses the contradictory political messages he has received on the death of his father as an excuse to see Aricie. In his initial conversation with her he not only frees her from the isolation into which she had been placed by Thésée but restores her to her rightful place on the Athenian throne:

> Je vous cède, ou plutôt je vous rends une place
> Un Sceptre, que jadis vos Aïeux ont reçu
> De ce fameux Mortel que la Terre a conçu.
> ....
> Athènes dans ses murs maintenant vous rappelle.

> I yield or rather give you back a place,
> A scepter handed to your ancestors
> By that heroic son whom Earth had borne.
> ....
> Athens now calls you back within her walls.
> (2.2.494–501)

No sooner, however, does Hippolyte speak of politics than politics reveals itself to be a poor substitute for speaking of love:[25]

> Moi, vous haïr, Madame?
> Avec quelques couleurs qu'on ait peint ma fierté,
> Croit-on que dans ses flancs un Monstre m'ait porté?
> Quelles sauvages moeurs, quelle haine endurcie
> Pourrait en vous voyant, n'être point adoucie?
> Ai-je pu résister au charme décevant...
> ....
> Je me suis engagé trop avant.
> Je vois que la raison cède à la violence.
> Puisque j'ai commencé de rompre le silence,
> Madame, il faut poursuivre. Il faut vous informer
> D'un secret, que mon coeur ne peut plus renfermer.

> I hate you, Lady?
> However boorish I might be depicted,
> You think a monster bore me in her womb?
> What barbarous manners, no, what hardened heart
> Would not soon melt away at sight of you?
> How could I combat the seductive spell...?
> ....
>   I fear I've gone too far.
> I see my passion sweeps aside my reason.
> Since I, my lady, now have broken silence,

> I must continue and confess to you
> A secret that is bursting from my heart.
>   (2.2.51–28)

What we see so masterfully orchestrated in the scenes where each protagonist in turn, Hippolyte and Phèdre, declare his/her love is the downward spiral of tragedy, the inextricable interweave where the political
releases from within itself the libidinal that has been repressed but not
suppressed, and which in turn exacerbates the decomposition of civil
society. Once this rift has been opened, once, that is, the monster of
sexuality reemerges, the world is thrown into disarray, and this confusion, a crisis of polity, calls out for the protective presence of a leader, a
hero who can destroy the monster and return order to a society where
chaos threatens.

The sexual/political crisis in *Phèdre*—but also, I would argue, in the
general dramatic plots of Racine's oeuvre—represents a generalized
malaise that lies beneath the polished surface structures not only of
Louis XIV's France, a nation never quite free from the memories and
fantasies of more than a century of political and religious upheaval, but
of contemporary world affairs, too. Across France, and indeed Europe,
the seventeenth century witnessed wars, plagues, and the terror and
scourge of witch hunts. There was hardly a space of more than four years
during this entire period when wars (local, national, or international)
were not ravaging some corner of the European continent.[26] In 1643,
for instance, the English preacher Jeremiah Whittaker tells the House
of Commons that "these are days of shaking and this shaking is universal: the Palatinate, Bohemia, Germania, Catalonia, Portugal, Ireland and
England."[27] Louis XIV, in his *Mémoires,* describes for the dauphin the
state in which he found France upon ascending the throne:

> But you must try to picture for yourself the prevailing conditions:
> formidable insurrections throughout the realm both before and after my
> majority; a foreign war where because of these internal troubles France
> had lost considerable advantages, a prince of my own blood and of an
> illustrious family leading my enemies; countless plots in the Realm; the
> *parlements* having acquired a taste for it, still hung on to a usurped
> authority; at my own court there was very little disinterested loyalty,
> and because of that those of my subjects who appeared the most
> submissive were as worrisome to me and as feared as the most rebellious.[28]

The fear of chaos, especially in societies whose past had precisely been grounded in rigid hierarchical structures, is obviously exacerbated in periods of great social change. Nevertheless, this fear, although inflamed by the experience of social unrest, reaches well beyond the actuality of a particular historical event and finds its terrifying power in the most archaic strata of the human psyche. Those political theorists influenced by the work of Freud have pointed to this fear of chaos as constitutive of the dialectical relation all civilizations maintain with their own internal contradictions:

> All civilization is a struggle against chaos. Not against chaos as it might or might not have actually existed in prehistoric times, but against the phantasms of a primordial chaos, of a primeval disorder, of an immixture, of the undifferentiated, against an ordinary violence. Culture turns back into its opposite, chaos... In any case, chaos always points to the same danger: a world without guideposts, without restraints, where anything could happen and where "the worst is always a certainty." Chaos is the constantly retreating horizon in front of which all social organization and institutions are constructed. It returns us to our ancestral fear. We embrace any and all protection against it.[29]

Beneath the premonitions of social chaos we can detect an ambivalent message, both a fear and a desire. Fear, of course, of total societal anarchy but also a desire to make themselves heard for a cessation of the whirling anarchy, for the imposition of order upon chaos, for a leader, a new imperator, who, subsuming disparity in his own body, the shining body royal, imposes unity on difference.[30] Beneath the horror and fascination with dispersion lurks an appeal to a stable unity: the monarch, in his own person and persona, is made to incarnate the contradictory hopes and desires of his people—the desire of and appeal to the absolute.[31]

That these two apparently opposite forces, centrifugal vectors of dispersion and centripetal pressures of cohesion, coexist and are represented in both comic and tragic representation should not surprise us: any cultural sphere is always a space of mediation, a space in which contradictory drive, forces of progress and forces of conservation, and vestiges of the past and indefinable aspirations of the future are constantly jockeying for control.[32] What is perhaps more difficult to understand is the enormous attraction absolutism had for the great masses of the European populace. "Absolutism," writes Roland Mousnier, "was ardently desired

by the masses who saw their only chance of salvation in the concentration of all power in the hands of a single man, the embodiment of the
kingdom, the living symbol of desired order and unity."[33] This new leader
becomes, in the words of Nannerl Keohane, "the ordering principle of all
social life, the ultimate source of authority and energy within the state."[34]

Thésée returns to play just such a role for the imploding society of
Phèdre. He returns as the hero/king, to assume the punishing role that,
as we've seen, has been his defining function from the start and that he
will now have to take on once again. Only this time the monsters he is
called on to vanquish are not hiding in the wastelands or waterways of
Greece but are present in the very heart of his own family. In times of
crisis, in times when the fear of social anarchy becomes an overriding
anxiety, the need for a sacrificial victim, for the appeasing blood of the
sacrifice, becomes overwhelming.[35] Hippolyte, by his innocence, by his
refusal to speak, to expose to his father's sight the adultery of his wife
("Ai-je dû mettre au jour l'opprobre de son lit?" [Was I to shout the
opprobrium of his bed?]), but also, and more tellingly, by his own transgressive love, has unknowingly become for his father the symbolic
monster that he must extirpate from society in order for that society to
regain a semblance of stability.

There is, however, something dramatically troubling by Thésée's
immediate and obstinate acceptance of Oenone's accusation of his son.
Returning from death, Thésée, instead of being greeted by the warm
embrace of his family, is met with embarrassed silence, half-uttered
excuses, and a family in flight from his presence. Distressed by this strange
homecoming, Thésée quickly acquiesces to Oenone's tale of attempted
rape. His response is instantaneous and unequivocal:

> Ah! Qu'est-ce que j'entends! Un Traître, un Téméraire
> Préparait cet outrage à l'honneur de son Père?
> Avec quelle rigueur, Destin, tu me poursuis!
> Je ne sais où je vais, je ne sais où je suis.
> O tendresse! O bonté trop mal recompensée!
> Projet audacieux! Détestable pensée.
> Pour parvenir au but de ses noirs amours
> L'insolent de la force empruntait le secours.
> J'ai reconnu le fer, instrument de sa rage;
> Ce fer dont je l'armai pour un plus noble usage.
> Tous les liens du sang n'ont pu le retenir?

What do I hear? Could such a wanton rogue
Attempt this outrage on his father's honour?
O fate, how mercilessly thou pursuest me!
I know not where I go, nor where I am.
O love, paternal goodness, ill rewarded!
Outrageous plan! Abominable thought!
To achieve his black and most lascivious end
The dastard even had recourse to force!
I recognized the sword, his fury's tool,
The sword I gave him for a nobler use.
Could all the ties of blood not hold him back?
(4.1.1002–11)

Thésée's outburst, his rage, and his subsequent desire for revenge are strikingly emblematic of a wounded narcissism that reveals more about his own self-centered view of the world than it does of any concern for either his son or his wife. Although Thésée is likely to strike a modern audience more as a bombastic fool than as a hero, I think that his reaction is symptomatic for what it reveals about the unconscious fears that lurk in the shadows of even the most brilliant sun/king in a patriarchal society, fears that cannot be so easily conquered when the object of those fears is not simply another female but his own son and heir.

As I mentioned earlier, Charles Mauron has defined *Phèdre* as an inverted Oedipus. By "inverted" he means that in this case it is the mother who lusts after the son and the father who kills him. This reading is perfectly justifiable within the terms of Mauron's (kleinian) frame, but it strikes me that it makes short shrift of what I see as the more perverse consequences of an Oedipal crisis that pits the father against the son (and vice versa) insofar as this antagonism is so often overlooked, or better yet, repressed, when the political dynamics of patriarchal absolutism go unexplored.

As recent ethnographers and psychoanalytically informed sociologists have remarked, the father-son relation in most societies is marked by ambivalently weighted feelings of love, antagonism, and aggression:

Every father in every society knows that he can be killed by his son and this is why he will attempt to foil this plot by prohibiting his son from becoming autonomous by sacrificing him. But at the same time every father knows that he is a father only by accepting that his son will one

day repudiate him as genitor and will instate him as a subject by an act
of his will.[36]

While Hippolyte has been spending his time preparing to become like
his father, his father has been off on yet another adventure that tests
his virility and confirms his heroic stature. That heroism, we learn, was
severely put to the test. His companion in this new adventure is fed to
the dog(s) and he himself imprisoned:

> Moi-même il m'enferma dans des Cavernes sombres,
> Lieux profonds, et voisins de l'Empire des Ombres.
> Les Dieux après six mois enfin m'ont regardé.
> J'ai su tromper les yeux par qui j'étais gardé.
> D'un perfide Ennemi j'ai purgé la Nature.
> A ses monstres lui-même a servi de pâture.

> And as for me, he entombed me in dark caverns,
> Deep regions, bordering on the realm of shades.
> After six months, the gods at last paid heed;
> I managed to elude my jailor's eyes:
> Cleansed Nature of a faithless enemy,
> And carved him up, himself, to feed his monsters.
>   (3.5.965–70)

His escape and return to hearth and home finds him confronted with a
charge and a change that would signal a generational revolution: the
(supposed) sexual attempt by the son to accede to the father's place. In
other words, what the accusation of incest really reveals is the insecu-
rity of male dominance, of the need to constantly defend one's hierarchical position, of the necessity of the primal father to reassert his unique
authority by castrating the young male (son) who attempts a sexual,
but also political, revolution. We should remember that Theseus solved
his own generational problem by eliminating (inadvertently!) his own
father Aegeus, king of Athens. While returning from his victory over
the Minotaur, Theseus forgot the agreed-on promise he had made to
his father to hoist, in the case of the successful accomplishment of his
mission, the white sail of triumph so that his father, seeing the sail from
afar, would be relieved by the news of his son's success. Theseus, however, in his excitement, fails to remember this promise and does not
display the white sail. Seeing the ship return without the agreed-on

signal, his father, in an excess of grief and disappointment, leaps into the sea to his death.

Just as Hippolyte refuses to acknowledge the sexuality of his father, Thésée projects a sexuality onto his son that is, one can speculate, a reflection of his own desire. In either case these misprisions prove deadly for both. Hippolyte wants to believe the father is not sexual, not a potent force to be recognized and reckoned with. In this Hippolyte can be seen as acceding, as he does in the rest of his behavior, to the virginal, asexual side of his nature inherited from Antiope. In the son's fantasy, Thésée's body, too powerful, too seductive, has been eliminated. Yet this fantasized castration of the father returns to haunt and eventually destroy the son. Thésée has gone through death—"il m'enferma dans des cavernes sombres / Lieux profonds et voisins de l'empire des ombres" (he entombed me in dark caverns / Deep regions, bordering on the realm of shades)—and reemerged on its far side, more threateningly potent as the incarnation of the law. He thus enters the universe of the play, a doubly guilty world, ready to punish, blindly and arbitrarily, any who are suspected of sinning against the father, of encroaching on his prerogatives, and of breaching his laws. Thésée returns to the world as the primal father incarnate—absolute, judgmental, and punishing. And Hippolyte, of course, is the most notable victim, the sacrificial victim who, despite all his protests to the contrary, is guilty. He is guilty of lusting after the (always prohibited) woman, be that woman Phèdre or Aricie. Hippolytes' fate in the masculine dynamics of kingship and sexuality is to be the sacred (guilty/innocent) victim of patriarchy. There is no other possible position available to him in the world of mythic devolution. The son, by acceding to the woman (the taboo object of paternal prerogative), threatens the rule of the father and must therefore either (as both Oedipus and Theseus have done before him) remove the father and take his place or die.

Hippolyte dies condemned by his father and his world. His death is a sacrifice of the child to the order of Oedipal patriarchy, and it is predestined from the very beginning by the law that presides over the world of absolutism. In a world that wants the rule of the integral, Hippolyte, like Phèdre, is an anomaly, a dual being, a cross between nature and culture in the world of the father, the world of politics, and the savage universe of his mother. As Lucien Goldmann has suggested, sovereignty in Racine is unable to tolerate any compromise.[37] Desire and its movements are absolute. It would nevertheless be an error, I feel, to see *Phèdre* as an unequivocal celebration of that absolutism. Although we know that on one level Racine's own career in society was based almost exclusively on his desire to be recognized by the monarchy, that he was most satisfied the closer he came to the monarch, his tragedies play out the ambivalence of this unifocal drive by uncovering precisely what in this monolithic ideology is occulted.[38]

The sacrifice that is central to Racine's entire opus turns on ridding the community of the monstrous within itself. Concomitantly this monstrous is represented by both the aggressivity of female sexuality and by the untamed duality of the child. In a world of sovereignty, the woman, but even more so the child, because always double, always the product of two, represents what is most inimical to an ideology that desires the absolute. Although the duality of being inheres in all children, in fact, in all of us, undermining any ideology of the One, this same ideology must ignore this contradiction. It must (unconsciously, of course) present the seamless image of an uncompromised, integral icon: the shining body of the leader/king as the symbol of the integrity of being, of the flight away from fragmentation and disunity that this uncorrupted, seamless (masculine) body represents. It is therefore a particularly aggressive counterattack by patriarchy on its descendants who threaten that image that Racine's theater plays out by offering them up in diversely perverted sacrifices. At the same time, however, this acting out reveals the hidden ambivalence of all sacrifice, for by attacking its children, patriarchy, in a very obvious (masochistic) sense, is shown to be obliged to always turn in and attack itself. Thésée's sacrifice of Hippolyte will prove to be also the sacrifice of Thésée, his tragedy. His jealous outrage will deprive him of the son whose existence confirms him in his role as father, that most powerfully overdetermined sociopolitical role in patriarchy: with Hippolyte dead, Thésée has no future as a father ("Ô mon Fils! Cher espoir que je me suis ravi! [O son, dear hope, that I myself have blasted!]"); his status of king is threatened and little hope remains for seeing his line perpetuated throughout eternity.[39]

After Thésée's prayers to Neptune are answered, after we have learned of Hippolyte's last act of courage, his slaying of the "bull from the sea" sent by Neptune, the monster he had always dreamt of defeating, and after he has been dragged by his own team of horses to his death, that other monster, Phèdre, appears on stage for the last time to inform Thésée of her guilt and to die. Cursed by Venus, misled by her "mother" Oenone, Phèdre can claim she was innocent, unable to fight against forces so much more powerful than a "faible mortelle." Innocent, that is, in her own eyes, until she was overcome by that other monster, the green monster of jealousy:

> Hippolyte est sensible, et ne sent rien pour moi!
> Aricie a son coeur! Aricie a sa foi!
> Ah Dieux! Lorsqu'à mes voeux l'Ingrat inexorable
> S'armait d'un oeil si fier, d'un front si redoubtable,
> Je pensais qu'à l'amour son coeur toujours fermé
> Fût contre tout mon sexe egalement armé.
> Une autre cependant a flechi son audace.
> Devant ses yeux cruels une autre a trouvé grâce.
>
> Hippolytus can feel, but not for me!
> Aricia wins him, heart and soul, Aricia!
> Ah gods! When the inexorable villain
> Against my longing stood so proudly proof,
> I thought his heart, still adamant to love
> Was likewise proof against my entire sex.
> And yet another's made his hard heart quiver;
> In his fierce eyes, another has found favour.
>   (4.5.1203–10)

At this point Phèdre, overcome by jealousy, becomes responsible. By not revealing, as she had first intended, her guilt to Thésée, Phèdre is now alone with her guilt. She can no longer blame the gods, Oenone, or her lineage. She alone is responsible for not speaking the truth, for allowing Oenone's calumny of Hippolyte to go unchallenged; and thus she becomes guilty for his death. Her entire existence (in this play) has been a slow descent into death interrupted only long enough for her incestuous passion to condemn an innocent victim and to create a political crisis that at the end of the play has left the state bereft of a future.

Phèdre kills herself by taking a poison, which, she announces, "Médée apporta dans Athènes" (was brought by Medea to Athens). Aligning herself in death with Medea, the infanticidal sorceress, only underlines Phèdre's monstrous nature with its close ties to a primitive, prehuman sexuality that defies the attempts of men to construct a restrictive but sustainable polis. The poison allows her just enough time to disculpate Hippolyte and, more important to her, to cleanse the world sullied by her presence in it:

> J'ai pris, j'ai fait couler dans mes brulantes veines
> Un poison que Médée apporta dans Athènes.
> Déjà jusqu'à mon coeur le venin parvenu
> Dans ce coeur expirant jette un froid inconnu,
> Déjà je ne vois plus qu'à travers un nuage
> Et le Ciel, et l'Epoux que ma présence outrage.
> Et la Mort à mes yeux derobant la clarté
> Rend au jour, qu'ils souillaient, toute sa pureté.

> I've taken, poured into my burning veins,
> A poison that Medea brought to Athens.
> The venom now has reached my very heart,
> Seizing this failing heart with a strange cold;
> I now can see no more, save through a haze,
> Heaven and my husband, whom my presence stains;
> And Death, snuffing the luster from my eyes
> Repurifies the sunlight they defiled.
>   (5, scène dernière, 1636–44)

Is there at the end of this most poignant of Racine's tragedies any future for Thésée, for Athens? Any future, that is, for Western society? The final verses of the play have always struck a strange chord in its critical reception. Should the play simply have ended with the "pureté" of the world restored by Phèdre's suicide/sacrifice? What is the interest, or the relevance, for Thésée's sudden decision to appease the shades of his son by adopting Aricie ("me tienne lieu de Fille" [shall my daughter be])? What are the political consequences of this act for a king who has lost his son and wife?[40]

Although the tragedy of *Phèdre (et Hippolyte)*, following Euripides, represented only a small slice of the legend of Theseus and his family, we know that Racine had read more widely. Particularly, he asserts, "J'ai même suivi l'histoire de Thésée telle qu'elle est dans Plutarque" (I've even followed the story of Theseus as it is recounted in Plutarch).[41] In that history, as we have seen, besides his heroic deeds Plutarch tells us that Theseus was responsible for establishing democracy in Athens, that is, for instituting the political system for which Athens was to become the ideal model in the West's imagination throughout the centuries.

This shift, according to Plutarch, was orchestrated by Theseus himself as he establishes a government in which he renounces his own kingship in favor of the first model democracy. Along with his legendary prowess in ridding the Greek world of the monsters and brigands that bedeviled it, Plutarch tells us, Theseus was also responsible for organizing Athens into a model polis.[42] In other words, Theseus's political trajectory takes him from being a hero (his legendary status as slayer of monsters and womanizer) who makes Greece safe, cleansing it of polluters, to king and finally to the first democrat of Athens. In a sense we could offer the hypothesis that the sacrifice of Hippolyte was the tragic but necessary immolation of not only the son but, as we've seen, an entire system of male devolution. By sacrificing his son, Thésée also radically alters his own investments in a system that both exults and destroys him. At the end of the play, Thésée, by adopting Aricie, revalidates the memory of the band of brothers (the Pallantides) he has slaughtered to become king. Thésée, through this reinsertion of Aricie's fraternal heritage, divests himself of the monarchy and from his place of primal father metamorphoses into but one member in a fraternal democracy. Thésée radically redirects the fate of Athens by allying himself to Aricie and to her brothers, becoming himself transformed from an absolute ruler to a modern subject, from a figure of mythology to the architect of democracy. By the sacrifice of the son and by the suicide of the incestuous, polluting wife, the entire history of Athens is transformed. A new world emerges, unsullied, from the corrupting mists of mythology. We might even say that the revolution that is *Phèdre*'s final promise moves us from the world of myth into the realm of history, into, that is, the world that we claim as our own.

7

Esther, Athalie:
Religion and Revolution in
Racine's Heavenly City

One of the great mysteries in Racine's career is his apparent decision, after *Phèdre*, to abandon the theater. Many explanations have been offered to justify this sudden silence. For some, his having finally attained a position at court for which he had employed his poetic genius and that now satisfied his careerist ambitions meant that he no longer had any reason to continue his theatrical vocation.[1] For others, a religious conversion or rather a reconversion to his Jansenist origins turned Racine definitively away from the theater, which was, as we know, fervently condemned by Port-Royal. Finally, for yet others, Racine grew tired of the constant public battles he was forced to wage in order to defend his dramatic creations. Too many "cabales," too many attacks and counterattacks, had finally gotten the better of him. Of course, we will never know which of these explanations, or more probably which combination of them, is the real reason for Racine's putting an end to his rather spectacular career as a dramatist. In any case, leaving his theatrical calling behind him, Racine marries, settles into the life of a busy courtier, and dedicates himself with his friend and accomplice Boileau to his new duties as royal historiographer.

Ten years pass before he is summoned once again, this time by Mme de Maintenon, Louis XIV's morganatic wife, to the theater. Mme de Main-

226

tenon, having decided to use her time, influence, and wealth to rescue the daughters of impoverished noble families, founds an educational institution at Saint-Cyr where these young ladies are taken in, given a proper Christian education, and sent away ready for the responsibilities of running a noble household. At Saint-Cyr they acquire the requisite social and domestic skills to become pious Christian wives. Mme de Maintenon, aided by her niece, Mme de Caylus, designed an educational curriculum where the young wards are given lessons in the social skills and the various arts so necessary for the formation of a well-rounded aristocrat. It is for these last finishing touches that Racine is called into service. Mme de Maintenon asks him to prepare for the young ladies of Saint-Cyr a play that would enhance their knowledge of diction, song, and recitation while at the same time offering them a lesson in piety.

> La célèbre Maison de Saint-Cyr ayant été principalement établie pour élever dans la piété un fort grand nombre de jeunes Demoiselles rassemblées de tous les endroits du Royaume, on n'y a rien oublié de tout ce qui pouvait contribuer à les rendre capables de servir Dieu dans les différents états où il lui plaira de les appeler. Mais en leur montrant les choses essentielles et nécessaires, on ne néglige pas de leur apprendre celles qui peuvent servir à leur polir l'esprit, et à leur former le jugement. On a imaginé pour cela plusieurs moyens, qui sans les détourner de leur travail et de leurs exercices ordinaires, les instruisent en les divertissant.[2]

> The famous institution of Saint-Cyr having been principally established to educate in piety a large number of young noble ladies gathered from all over the realm, nothing was omitted in an education that would make them able to serve God in the different circumstances in which it would please Him to employ them. But, while all the necessary and essential subjects were taught, those things that refine intelligence and fashion judgment were not neglected. Several methods were employed to these ends that, without distracting them from their normal lessons, instructed while amusing them.

It is thus in order to instruct while amusing her students that Mme de Maintenon asks Racine for "quelque sujet de piété et de morale une espèce de Poème, où le chant fût mêlé avec le récit; le tout lié par une action qui rendit la chose plus vive et moins capable d'ennuyer" (some piously moral subject, a type of Play, where singing would be mixed with the story, the whole thing held together by a story line that would make it lively and less likely to bore).[3] In other words, Mme de Maintenon wants a play from which is banished any profane material that would risk overly stimulating her charges but that would be exciting enough not to repel them. The result was *Esther*.

Racine's first biblical tragedy was given rather elaborate treatment. Lavish costumes were provided the young actresses, the musical accompaniment was composed and conducted by Jean-Baptiste Moreau, "maître de musique de la chambre du roi" (music master to the king's chamber), and the performances were honored by the presence of the king, the dauphin, the deposed king and queen of England, important courtiers, ecclesiastic dignitaries, and so on. The first performance of *Esther* was a great success. The initial triumph encouraged yet other performances with ever greater throngs of courtiers vying for the chance to attend. Finally, it seems, the success of Racine's contribution to the education of Saint-Cyr's young wards was judged too threatening by the very guardians of the young ladies' morality who commissioned the work but who now feared that, rather than learning a dour lesson in Christian principles, the young actors were actually being seduced by those worldly pleasures they were supposed to flee. The performances were summarily halted. The next time Mme de Maintenon importuned Racine for a play for her young ladies, that play, *Athalie*, the last he was to pen, would be staged without costumes, without music, and without the curious ladies and gentlemen of the court in attendance.

Racine's delving into Holy Scripture for his last dramatic works produced two very different tragedies. The first, *Esther*, recasts the biblical narrative of the Jewish orphan Esther, who is chosen by the Babylonian king Assuérus as his new queen. Angered by his first wife Vashti's refusal to dance before the members of his court, Assuérus summarily dismisses her and, after an empire-wide search for a new beauty, replaces her with Esther:[4]

> Peut-être on t'a conté la fameuse disgrâce
> De l'altière Vasthi, dont j'occupe la place,
> Lorsque le Roi contre elle enflammé de dépit
> La chassa de son trône, ainsi que de son lit...
>
> You have perhaps heard tell the loud disgrace
> Of haughty Vashti, who, I have succeeded,
> And how the king, against her hot with rage.
> Drove her both from his throne and from his bed.
>   (1.1.31–34)

One of Mme de Maintenon's instructions to Racine was that the play she envisioned for her young wards not contain a love interest. It was feared that such an interest would be too distracting and therefore would not be able to fulfill the role of pious instruction she hoped the drama would provide. Although prohibited from composing a drama where sexual desire causes the downfall of his characters, Racine nevertheless insists once again, at the very outset of this new tragedy, on the intricate interweave that joins the sexual to the political in the complicated plot of this didactic drama. The coupling of the throne room with the bedroom during the expository passage of this biblical drama underscores what will remain veiled throughout the play: the inherently passionate but repressed aspect of the political machinations of the imperial vizir Aman, as he sets about to destroy not only his archrival Mardochée but the entire Jewish people.

In *Esther*, Racine's typical heterosexual plot of frustrated love/lust is here transformed into a homosocial, if not homosexual plot, where the personal vendetta of and competition between two men, each representing the struggle for power of repressed minorities at the very center of the Babylonian empire, is exacerbated into racial hatred and genocide. In other words, Racine complicates his plot by replacing the heterosexual love interest by what can only be called an exacerbated homosocial rivalry whose intensity portends cataclysmic disaster for an entire nation, the Jews, who are held in captivity in Babylon. Unbeknownst to her husband and to his minister, Esther is a Jew and thus a potential victim of the genocidal fury of Aman. In *Esther* the sacrificial victim is no longer a lone child who trembles under the gaze of all those adults who wish him dead: here it is an entire people, all the children of Israel, who are to be immolated:

> Quel carnage de toutes parts!
> On égorge à la fois les enfants, les vieillards;
> Et la soeur, et le frère;
> Et la fille, et la mère;
> Le fils dans les bras de son père.
> Que de corps entassés! Que de members épars,
> Privés de sépulture!
>
> What slaughter all around!
> Old men and babes are murdered found,

> Sister and brother
> Daughter and mother,
> The son in the arms of his father!
> What battered corpses, limbs scattered and bound
> With no one to bury
> Them!
>   (1.5.316–21)

This scene, yet another of Racine's famous intercalated tableaux that, as in *Andromaque, Iphigénie, Mithridate,* and *Phèdre* and preceding the even more terrifying nightmares of *Athalie,* function as rhetorical intrusions, primal fantasies that, as hypotyposes, interrupt the narrative flow of the drama and plunge us into a more profoundly unbounded space of sexuality and violence.[5] The traumatic vision of the slaughter of the Hebrews reproduces, on yet another metaphysico-theological level, the annihilation of the body politic of Israel already dispersed in the first Diaspora. Here, however, it is rendered all the more pathetic by the intensely affective familial rhetoric that poignantly reduces the obliteration of an entire people to the destruction of a family ("mère, soeur, frère, père" [mother, sister, brother, father]), thereby introducing, I would argue, the familial, that is, Oedipal, dynamic that is obfuscated by the ostensibly passionless sweep of the dramatic plot.

I am not the first person to comment on how the rivalry between Mardochée and Aman simply repeats the fraternal competition and jealousy that has been an omnipresent, if not obsessive, plot device in all Racine's profane tragedies from his very first, *La Thébaïde.* Although here the two rivals are not brothers, they are reflections of each other in all other ways. In a sense, in *Esther* the fraternal jealousy is no longer directly targeted as a sexual, Oedipal rivalry; here the two rivals vie for the attention (love) of the hidden God.[6] For Aman, the king is his god, while for Mardochée, God is his king. In both cases, the king/God remains very much, in his awful, vengeful power, absent. In *Esther* the Babylonian sovereign enhances his terrible authority by making himself invisible to his subjects:

> Hélas! Ignorez-vous quelles sévères lois
> Aux timides mortels cachent ici les Rois?
> Au fond de leur Palais leur majesté terrible
> Affecte à leurs Sujets de se rendre invisible.
> Et la mort est le prix de tout Audacieux,
> Qui sans être appelé se présente à leurs yeux.

Alas! Do you not know the rigorous laws
That screen kings here from all their timorous subjects?
Their awful majesty delights to be
Invisible within their palace depths;
And death's the fate of all intruders who
Appear before them without being called.
    (1.3.191–96)

Death is the punishment for a subject who should present himself/ herself before the Godhead without being summoned. It is to this sacrifice that Esther is summoned by her zealous guardian, Mardochée, who has learned of Aman's plot to destroy the Jews. He knows his only hope is the seductive appeal of his niece and ward, Esther. He is willing to risk her life to save his people:

Quoi? Lorsque vous voyez périr votre Patrie,
Pour quelque chose, Esther, vous comptez votre vie!
Dieu parle, et d'un Mortel vous craignez le courroux!
Que dis-je? Votre vie, Esther, est-elle à vous?
. . . .
S'immoler pour son nom, et pour son héritage,
D'un enfant d'Israel voilà le vrai partage.

What? When you see your people perishing,
Esther, you hold your life of some account!
God speaks; and yet you fear the wrath of man!
What am I saying? Is your life your own?
. . . .
To perish for His name, His heritage,
Such is the true lot of a child of Israel.
    (1.5.205–18)

Finally, Esther's sacrifice is the immolation of her innocence. Daring to approach the hidden God ("Sans mon ordre on porte ici ses pas? / Quel Mortel insolent vient chercher le trépas?" [Who dare approach without my order! / What insolent foot comes here to seek out death?]), Esther faints with fear (desire?):

J'ai cru vous voir tout prêt à me reduire en poudre.
Hélas! Sans frissoner, quel coeur audacieux
Soutiendrait les éclairs qui partaient de vous yeux?
Ainsi du Dieu vivant la colère étincelle . . .

I thought I saw you from your lofty throne,
That thunder girts, reducing me to dust.

> Alas what brazen heart, without a shudder
> Can bear the lightning darting from your eyes?
> Thus burns like fire the wrath of the living God . . .
>   (2.7.650–53)

She is revived only by the extension of his scepter ("Le sceptre d'or, que vous tend cette main / Pour vous de ma clémence est un gage certain" [The golden scepter that my hand extends / To you is sure pledge of my clemency]), sign of his love (desire) for her. In this way, despite the injunction not to write a love story, Racine introduces passion, that is, the intervention of love, the king's desire for Esther and for her beauty, that revives her and allows her, by revealing who she is, a Jew, to save herself and her people from Aman's wrath. Racine rescripts Esther's sacrifice and redemption as a *chasse-croisé* of heterosexual love and homosocial jealousy. The love of the king, equated to the love of God for his chosen people, wins out over the unnatural forces of hatred and jealousy. At the same time, of course, hatred also gets its due: Aman (and in the Bible, all his children) suffer the fate he had planned for the Jews— they are all hanged on the gallows that he had prepared for Mardochée.

Esther is not, the truth be told, a riveting psychological drama. From the beginning it has functioned as a pious morality tale for schoolchildren, enhanced by costume, music, and the curiosity of a jaded public. Although his recent editor claims that it would be an error to think that the Racine who wrote *Esther* is not "vraiment Racine" (truly Racine), it would also be an error to believe that the passion and tragic shiver the audience experiences in his other plays has not been sacrificed here for other, albeit less worldly, goals.[7]

Such is not the case with Racine's next biblical tragedy and last great play, *Athalie*.[8] Here, despite the absence of a traditional love interest, Racinian passion reaches an incandescence that is almost unequaled in his previous works. *Athalie* is, as Roland Barthes has written, a "mythic battle of the sexes," a battle, I might add, between those two principles, maternal and paternal, that have vied for power and dominance in all Racine's preceding tragedies. It is a battle fought to the death. And at its center, once more, but this time fully present, is the child whom these two great forces struggle to control, even if this control means his immolation.

As we move through the great tragedies, that space that Leo Bersani has called the "clean blankness of being," that vast field of possibility that was left to Astyanax at the end of *Andromaque*, gradually and inexorably shrinks, turns in on itself.[9] Caught up in the ever more convoluted play of familial binding, it loses its purely immanent potential to become, finally, bound in and to the representation of the last, the only, child of Racinian tragedy: Eliacin/Joas of *Athalie*.[10] In a curious fashion this move from a child whose function in representation is purely phantasmatic—Astyanax is never seen on stage—to the final actual presence of the child (Eliacin) corresponds to an obverse dialectic on the part of the Racinian parent. As Mauron has shown, the father who is absent in the first series of tragedies returns in *Mithridate*, grows in stature and terror through *Phèdre*, and ends in *Athalie* as pure immanence: the father finally becomes one with God. Nevertheless, as the very titles of Racine's tragedies attest—*Andromaque, Iphigénie, Phèdre, Athalie*— this paternal apotheosis is necessarily accomplished through and across a dialectics of sexuality, of a mythic struggle for dominance of the opposed forces of masculinity and femininity. In contrast to this receding image of the father we have the ever more precise, more disquieting representation of the Racinian mother. In this battle for supremacy—a struggle that ends, as we know, with the ultimate destruction of the powerful, threatening mother (Athalie) and with the triumph of the father (let us not forget that the very last word Racine wrote for the theater was *père*)—it is the women, not the men, who are the center of the Racinian world. Certainly it is the passion of those heroines and their ultimate defeat that is at the heart of the most troubling of Racine's tragedies. It is this coupling of femininity with maternity and this maternity's indentured service to patriarchy that create the tragic dimension of Racine's greatest heroines.

In his preface to *Athalie*, among the other picturesque details about the ancient Hebrews, their religion, and the schism that forms the history of his new tragedy, Racine reminds us that the Temple, the scene of his tragedy, was situated exactly on the mountain where Abraham took his son Isaac to be sacrificed to his God:

> C'était une tradition assez constante que la montagne sur laquelle le temple fut bâti était la même montagne où Abraham avait autrefois offert en sacrifice son fils Isaac.

> It was a fairly constant tradition that the mount upon which the Temple was built was the same mountain where in former times Abraham had offered up his son Isaac in sacrifice.[11]

This same detail is repeated in the play itself:

> N'êtes-vous pas ici sur la montagne sainte
> Où le père des Juifs sur son fils innocent
> Leva sans murmurer un bras obéissant,
> Et mit sur un bûcher ce fruit de sa vieillesse,
> Laissant à Dieu le soin d'accomplir sa promesse,
> Et lui sacrifiant, avec ce fils aîné,
> Tout l'espoir de sa race en lui seul renfermé?

> Do you not stand here on the holy mount
> Where Abraham our father raised, unmurmuring,
> His obedient arm upon his guiltless son,
> Placed on a pyre this fruit of his old age,
> Leaving to God Fulfillment of His promise,
> And sacrificing with his son beloved,
> The whole hope of his race, contained in him?
>   (4.5.1438–44)

Racine's double insistence on recalling this other origin—monotheism's origin in the (aborted) sacrifice of the son by the father—only reinforces the love/hate ambivalence that we know to be the lot of all human children caught up in the conflicted desires of the Oedipal scenario. The father/God of the Old Testament, who demands unreflective obedience to his law and punishes all transgression with death, can be seen to correspond to the tyrannical, murderous, unreachable father of the primal horde who castrates his sons. In a curious fashion the myth of revenge, at least in those great religious myths that Racine also inscribes in his text, never actually represents the destruction of the father. That revenge is always occulted, always repressed, but nonetheless present, as fantasy and as theater. It is here, in Racine's reinscription in his theater of the founding myths of Western culture, in his conflation of the trajectory of individual desire and social idealization, that we can begin to understand the role and the fascination of infanticide/parricide in classicism's tragic universe. The Racinian stage functions as an altar on which is played out, through the fantasies of a particular playwright, an entire society's feelings of ambivalence toward those very structures, sexual and political, that define it to itself as culture.[12]

   Like Racine's other great tragedies, *Athalie* begins on a somber note: times have changed and chaos (or at least the menace of social upheaval) reigns: "Que les temps sont changés" (How changed the times are!), declares the Hebrew general Abner as he enters the Temple at the beginning of the play. On a day that should be reserved for rejoicing, there is only sadness. The very order of nature is perverted by a woman. Athalie has seized power by murdering her own descendants, the children of her son Ochosias. In addition she has betrayed the God of the Israelites and returned to the pagan god of her mother, Jézabel:

> L'audace d'une Femme arrêtant ce concours
> En des jour ténébreux a changé ces beaux jours.
> D'Adorateurs zélés à peine un petit nombre
> Ose des premiers temps nous retracer quelque ombre.
> Le reste pour son Dieu montre un oubli fatal,
> Ou même s'empressant aux autels de Baal,
> Se fait initier à ses honteux mystères,
> Et blashpème le nom qu'ont invoqué leurs pères.
>
> A womans's hardihood has halted that,
> And turned to funeral days those festive days.
> Today, of faithful worshippers, a few
> Alone dare trace some shadow of the past.
> The rest have fatally forgotten God,
> Or worse, have flocked to be initiated
> To shameful mysteries at Baal's altars,
> Blaspheming him, their fathers have invoked.
> (1.1.13–20)

While Phèdre claimed that by her suicide she had restored purity to a sullied world, the theme of female pollution returns, we might say, with a vengeance in *Athalie*. Athalie would seem to correspond to the innermost fears of patriarchy: a woman who unsexes herself, first as a new Medea slaying her own children and then in her quest for political sovereignty by refusing the social/religious limits placed on her sex. Athalie strides into the Temple, shocking the assembled worshippers by transgressing the sacred limits of sexual difference:

> Une Femme... Peut-on la nommer sans blasphème?
> Une Femme... C'était Athalie elle-même.
> . . . .
> Dans un des parvis aux hommes réservé
> Cette Femme superbe entre le front levé,
> Et se préparait même à passer les limites
> De l'enceinte sacrée ouverte aux seuls Lévites.
> Le peuple s'épouvante et fuit de toutes parts.

> A woman... Can I name her without sin?
> A woman... It was Athaliah.
> . . . .
> This haughty woman, with her head raised high,
> Intruded in a court reserved for men
> And was about to pass the very limits
> Of the enclosure meant alone for Levites.
> The affrighted people fled in all directions.
>   (2.2.395–401)

More so than in any of Racine's previous dramas, Athalie is persistently identified by her double, monstrous heritage; a descendant of both Ahab and Jezebel, she combines in her person the specter of Medea (the fear and the fascination of the "mère meurtrière"), the sexual debauchery associated with and inherited from Jezebel, and the questioning, devouring Sphinx.[13] In one of his most hallucinatory passages Racine fixes the indelible image of that most frightening of fantasies, the murderous mother amid the jumbled bodies of her slain offspring:

> Hélas! L'état horrible où le Ciel me l'offrit,
> Revient à tout moment effrayer mon esprit.
> De Princes égorgés la chamber était remplie.
> Un poignard à la main l'implacable Athalie
> Au carnage animait ses barbares Soldats
> Et poursuivait le cours de ses assassinats.
>
> Alas! The dreadful state Heaven gave him me
> Comes ever back to me to freeze my heart.
> The room was crowded out with murdered Princes.
> Armed with a dagger, ruthless Athaliah
> Spurred on her savage soldiers to the slaughter,
> And went on to the end, still murdering.
>   (1.2.241–45)

Racine's insistence on situating his plays—and here *Athalie* is only the most concentrated example—at the violent center of the sacred, at the locus where sacrifice and spectacle are conflated and form the single, densely contracted scene of tragedy, always responds to another scene, an even more primal scene of carnage, an originary memory for which the present sacrifice is the surrogate, the attempted propitiation. In *Athalie* the originary scene is double.[14] It is both the murder of the innocents, the children of Ochosias, and the "first" slaughter by Jéhu of Athalie's family, but most specifically of her mother:

C'était pendant l'horreur d'une profonde nuit;
Ma mère Jézabel devant moi s'est montrée,
Comme au jour de sa mort pompeusement parée,
Ses malheurs n'avait point abattu sa fierté...
....
Et moi je lui tendais les mains pour l'embrasser;
Mais je n'ai plus trouvé qu'un horrible mélange
D'os et de chairs meurtris et trainés dans la fange,
Des lambeaux pleins de sang, et des members affreux
Que des chiens dévorants se disputaient entre eux.

It was a brooding, horror breathing night.
My mother Jezebel appeared before me,
Arrayed in pomp, as on the day she died.
Her pride was quite untamed by her misfortunes;
....
And I, I stretched my hands out to embrace her.
Yet all I found was but a horrid mush
Of bones and mangled flesh, dragged in the slush,
Of bloody strips, and limbs all shameless scarred,
That bit by bit the wrangling dogs devoured.
           (2.5.490–93, 502–6)

Despite the fact that her reign has, in her terms, been a successful one ("Par moi Jérusalem goûte un calme profound" [Through me Jerusalem tastes lasting peace]), that she has shown herself to be both a canny diplomat and a reasonably tolerant ruler, she is indelibly marked as monstrous, an infanticidal mother, a blasphemer, a foreigner ("Vous de nos Rois et la femme et la mere / Etes-vous à ce point parmi nous etrangère?" [But you the wife and mother of our kings, / Are you so great a stranger to our ways?]). Athalie would seem to be the most complete incarnation of the fantasized phallic mother in all Racine. And it is as such that she is set up to do battle with the equally fierce, uncompromising representative of a vengeful (male) God, the high priest Joad. The violent struggle that will be waged by these two characters is not only over the possession of the child, Eliacin/Joas; it is an eschatological combat for the soul of an entire nation. The stakes of this struggle for sovereignty are enormous, for on the outcome of their battle depends not only the life of a child but the instauration of the new Jerusalem, the assurance of the promise of eternal salvation for all mankind through that child's descendant Jesus Christ. We might say that this battle is sexualized by having each of the two combatants symbolize the two extreme limits of the struggle:

Athalie, the murderous mother, the daughter of Jezebel, denotes the old decadent and sinful Jerusalem, perverted and pagan, while Joad (and by extension, Eliacin) represents the rebirth of a new, masculine order, the new Jerusalem of Joad's ecstatic prophecy:

> Quelle Jérusalem nouvelle
> Sort du fond du désert brillante de clartés,
> Et porte sur le front une marque immortelle?
> Peuples de la terre, chantez.
> Jérusalem renaît plus charmante, et plus belle.
>
> What new Jerusalem cometh forth,
> Radiant as a bride, from the wilderness,
> Upon her brow the crown of immortal worth?
> Jerusalem, reborn of loveliness.
> Sing, O ye peoples of the earth.
>   (3.7.1159–63)

On the outcome of this, Racine's final battle of the sexes, depends the future not only of the Hebrew monarchy in particular but of the Christian West in general. In order, however, for this new Jerusalem to emerge, the old one must die. It is in this transitional space separating and joining the old political order to the new, in the space of sacrifice, that the tragedy of *Athalie* reveals its universal importance.

The tragic heart of the play where the battle for sovereignty rages between the two ferocious combatants is a strangely confused space of sexual indeterminacy. On the one hand, Athalie represents, on more than one level, not only a projection forward, in the sense that her reign postmortem, that is, after the massacre of the innocents, has been both peaceful, tolerant, and productive, but, more frightening, a projection backward to the archaic figuration of the phallic mother, that fantasized combination of the sexes in which the valence of activity, power, and threat is still radically attached to the image of "the woman with a penis."

On the other hand, Joad, Athalie's rival and mate, who throughout the play, in his role of surrogate father and surrogate God, stands for all that is implacable and incorruptible in this world of decadence and disorder, comes to be seen not only as the father of his ward but, more strangely, as a maternal presence as well. Josabet, the timorous, loving, but ineffectual mother, too nervous in the presence of the prize she has snatched from the jaws of death, too unsure of her own role, abandons all care of the child to Joad:

> Du jour que j'arrachai cet enfant à la mort,
> Je remis en vos mains tout le soin de son sort;
> Même, de mon amour craignant la violence,
> Autant que je le puis j'évite sa présence
> De peur qu'en le voyant quelque trouble indiscret
> Ne fasse avec mes pleurs échapper mon secret.

> Right from the day I snatched this child from death,
> I placed his destiny within your hands.
> Fearing, indeed, the violence of my love.
> I try as much as able to avoid him,
> Lest seeing him, some telltale agitation
> Might let escape my secret with my tears.
>   (1.2.189–94)

Josabet's inability to assume the maternal function out of fear of destroying her ward thrusts Joad into the ambivalent role of father-mother. Only on an apparent level of dramatic necessity is the unicity of Joad's masculine identity ever so slightly fractured by this intrusion of a maternal function that makes of Joad both father and mother to the orphan; on a more profound archaic level, be it that of the psyche or of myth, this attribution only adds to Joad's role of representing some primal father, an image that corresponds, once again, to a fantasy of unlimited power, a power that defies the sundering (and thus the limitation) of gendering and allows him to correspond, in homologous fashion, to the hybridized terror that is Athalie.[15]

Unlike Racine's other young male protagonists, Eliacin/Joas, raised in the Temple, is from the beginning firmly situated in a world of men. The difficult separation from the mother and from the world of women that all Racine's other males must achieve (or die trying) has been *ab origine* done for him. Joas has no mother: he has been "sacrificed" by Athalie and resurrected into the life of an anchorite, living and serving in the sacred space of God. Perhaps it is for this reason, the fact that he has no emotional pull toward the maternal, that Eliacin/Joas, of all Racine's males, is most apt to confront the Sphinx and confound her.

Although there are pointed references in the play to the two most celebrated child sacrifices in the Bible, Abraham's (aborted) immolation of Isaac and Jephte's offering up of his daughter in expiation to a vow made to God, there is, it seems to me, clearly an underlying reference to the Oedipus legend: the young prince whose father, Laius, tried to kill him, who was raised by adoptive parents in ignorance of his own origins, and who had to confront both parental enmity and the monstrousness of female difference in order to accede to his rightful throne. Surely here, in Racine's last tragedy, the affective force of both the Greek myth and the biblical legend meet in this rescripted encounter of the innocent boy and the murderous (m)other who is made to bear (as was Jocasta in *La Thébaïde*) all the parental guilt: the father is always protected from the child's rage.[16]

The final duel between the young prince and the Sphinx takes place in the Temple that Athalie had defiled. Distressed by a recurring dream where she sees herself murdered by a mysterious child, Athalie invades the Temple, looking for its "hidden treasure." To her surprise she catches sight of a child who looks exactly like the boy she saw in her dream:

> J'entre. Le peuple fuit. Le sacrifice cesse.
> Le grand Prêtre vers moi s'avance avec fureur.
> Pendant qu'il me parlait, ô surprise! ô terreur!
> J'ai vu ce même Enfant dont je suis menacée,
> Tel qu'un songe effrayant l'a peint à ma pensée.
> Je l'ai vu. Son même air, son même habit de lin,
> Sa démarche, ses yeux, et tous ses traits enfin.
> C'était lui-même.

> I entered: all fled, sacrifices ceased;
> The High Priest made towards me, pale with fury.
> While he upbraided me. O fearful stroke!
> I saw the very child that menaced me,
> Just as my dreadful dreams presented him.
> I saw him; in the self-same mien and linen,
> His gait, his eyes, in fact his every feature.
> The same!
>   (2.5.532–39)

Torn between the contradictory advice of the renegade priest Mathan and the Hebrew general Abner, Athalie hesitates on what course to take: should she have the child killed or should she, following a more rational path, find out who he is? Her nightmare and the sudden coincidence of the child glimpsed in the Temple confound her. The typical resoluteness that has defined her seems shaken: the sight of this child has undone her unnatural (masculine) will to power, and returned her to the natural, biological weakness of her sex:

> Ce n'est plus cette Reine éclairée, intrépide,
> Elevée au-dessus de son sexe timide,
> Qui d'abord accablait ses ennemis surpris
> Et d'un instant perdu connaissait tout le prix.
> La peur d'un vain remords trouble cette grande âme,
> Elle flotte, elle hésite, en un mot elle est femme.
>
> She is no more that bold, clear-sighted Queen,
> Raised high above the weakness of her sex,
> Who shattered all at once her startled foes,
> And knew full well the price of moments lost.
> A vain remorse entangles her great soul:
> She flounders, hesitates, just like a woman.
>   (3.3.871–76)

At her insistence Eliacin is brought before her to answer a series of questions. Although the more timorous members of the Temple community fear the worst, Eliacin successfully responds to all of the queen's queries with typically elusive, almost allegorical, rejoinders. He was abandoned by his parents and found, he tells her, "among wolves ready to devour him." Brought to the Temple, he was there raised and protected by divine intervention. The questions and answers continue until, at last, Athalie asks the boy if he would like to come and live with her in her palace. She would, she tells him, "treat him as her own son." At this, the most intensely affective moment of their encounter, Eliacin, at the idea of being taken as her child, retreats into the protective male world he knows, exclaiming elliptically but with obvious repugnance that such a move would force him to leave the father he knows (and loves) for a mother such as he knows Athalie to be ("Quel père je quitterais! . . . / Pour quelle mère!" [What father I would abandon . . . / For what mother!]). It would seem that here, once again, as in the famous encounter between Oedipus and the Sphinx, the right answer to counter the threat posed by this female monster is "man." Eliacin affirms his commitment to the father and his world. He refuses the maternal and its lure, opting instead for a life within the male community in which he has been raised.

Athalie's undoing is brought on by the fascination this child holds over her. His childlike grace and the mellifluous voice with which he responds to her interrogation seduce her. She is, we are made to believe, responding both to the *voix du sang* (so prevalent in all seventeenth-century recognition drama) and to some renascent maternal instinct that she believed vanquished:

> Quel prodige nouveau me trouble et m'embarrasse?
> La douceur de sa voix, son enfance, sa grâce,
> Font insensiblement à mon inimitié
> Succéder... Je serais sensible à la pitié?

> What miracle dismays, distresses me?
> The sweetness of his voice, his childish grace,
> Make my antipathy insensibly...
> Can it be possible I pity him?
>   (2.2.651–54)

It is her attraction to this boy that re-sexes her, that is, causes her to let down her guard and be resituated in the traditional equation of woman equals mother, which she had so spectacularly defied. "Hesitant, unsure" Athalie, seduced by the child she had tried to kill, walks into the trap Joad (and divine intervention) set for her. Wanting the boy and the "treasure" she believes is hidden in the Temple, Athalie, "un poignard à la main" (a dagger in her hand: a description that, repeated twice in the play, reminds us of her infanticidal fury), brazenly rushes into the Temple unescorted. Thinking the Temple undefended and the Hebrews too cowardly to resist her army, Athalie is defeated by her hubris. Once she passes the Temple's threshold she is immediately isolated from her troops; the Temple doors swing shut, trapping her inside. Alone within the sacred walls she has defiled, Joad uncovers the treasure he has, in effect, been hiding in the sanctuary: he reveals Eliacin, the last of the children of Ochosias, the only descendant of David to escape Athalie's murderous wrath, now crowned king:

> Paraissez, cher Enfant, digne sang de nos Rois.
> Connais-tu l'héritier du plus saint des Monarques,
> Reine? De ton poignard connais du moins ces marques.
> Voilà ton Roi, ton Fils, le Fils d'Ochosias.
> Peuples, et vous Abner, reconnaissez Joas.

> Come forth, O child, dear scion of our kings.
> Do you recognize our saintliest monarch's heir,
> O Queen? Your dagger's marks at least acknowledge.

This is your King, your Ahaziah's son.
Ye nations, Abner, recognize Jehoash.
   (5.5.1718–22)

Ensnared, undone, defeated, Athalie is led away by the armed Levites and put to death outside the Temple walls. Eliacin/Joas's reign begins and with it the construction of the New Jerusalem the high priest had seen in his prophetic vision.

Having successfully triumphed over the last, most terrifying mother/monster in the Racinian canon, the reign of the prince/father begins in rejoicing. Seated on his throne, Joas would seem to embody in his still young person the fantasy that has underlain Racine's entire dramatic production. The Sphinx has been vanquished, and with her defeat the new heavenly city of seventeenth-century Christian absolutism can, at last, impose its vision of polity on the world.

If the entire tension of Racinian tragedy—its sexually and politically informed myths of incest, aggression, and sacrifice—is, as I believe, underpinned by an ideology of the absolute, of the one, an ideology whose ramifications inform all aspects of political life, then we can understand how this drive toward a unity of being must of necessity continually enter into conflict with all that it attempts to repress, deny, and evacuate in order to maintain its own hold on reality. This conflict is most obviously embodied in the opposition established in his plays between the fantasized but equally terrifying images of a retentive, devouring, sexually aggressive mother and an absent, judgmental, punishing father.[17] At stake in this conflict is the survival of the child, that enigmatic, dangerous (because still undecided) pawn, the chink in the armor of patriarchal power whose life is constantly threatened by the two parents who seek to possess him. It is the undecidable fate of this child that hangs in the balance. The child's survival, and thus any possible future for society as a whole, depends on the outcome of the primitive, fierce struggle between the two archaic parental fantasies.[18]

It would appear that *Athalie* finally resolves the conflict in favor of the father and his reign. With the evil queen's defeat, order is returned to the world: the rightful (male) heir is restored to the throne of his forefathers, the usurping queen and her pagan God(s) are banished, and holiness returns to the Temple and to the kingdom. With the defeat of Athalie/Baal, with the continuation of David's line, the coming of the savior and thus universal salvation are assured. It is a benevolent father who protects and, although he may work in strange ways, assures the triumph of righteousness. The play ends with the promise of salva-tion for those who walk in the path of the father:

> Par cette fin terrible, et due à ses forfaits,
> Apprenez, Roi des Juif, et n'oubliez jamais,
> Que les Rois dans le Ciel ont un Juge sévère,
> L'Innocence un Vengeur, et l'Orphelin un Père.

> To this disastrous end, due to her crime,
> King of the Jews, pay heed: remember, rather,
> That kings in Heaven have a Judge sublime,
> Avenger of the oppressed, of orphans Father.
>   (5.7.1813–16)

In a sense we might think, returning to the underlying myth of Racin-ian tragedy, the legend of Oedipus *tyrannos,* that what we have in *Athalie* is the final triumph of the politics of masculine hegemony: the young prince has confronted the Sphinx, triumphed over her, and come into his place as king. This would represent, on the level of dramatic narra-tion, the apotheosis of Racine's indentured allegiance to an ideal of monarchal authority that he pursued throughout his life.[19]

We know, however, that this triumphant ending, the final apothe-osis of the king/God of absolutism, is a sham. Unfortunately, the reign of the absolute is, because of the very realities of human nature, only ever an asymptotic promise, a goal that remains constantly out of reach be-cause human beings no more than the societies in which they live and which circumscribe them can be reduced to "one." They are never homo-geneous but contain a multitude of conflicting desires, aspirations, and hatreds that are, of course, the other side of Oedipus—the aggressive, sexual side that undermines any attempt at establishing a hieratic stasis.

Although Racine ends his play and his career with a ringing tribute to the paternal, the echoes of difference and of diversity continue to resound, muffled but nonetheless heard. Athalie, as she is led away to her death, defies one last time the fanatical rule of the father as she reaffirms what the father wishes to ignore—"one" is not possible, diver-sity rules, and this rule will undermine the new reign. Joas, this child, this king, her grandson, is condemned to transgression because he too is not pure but heterogeneous, a monster, as much the offspring of Athalie as of David:

Voici ce qu'en mourant lui souhaite sa Mère.
Que dis-je souhaiter? Je me flatte, j'espère,
Qu'indocile à ton joug, fatigué de ta Loi,
Fidèle au sang d'Achab, qu'il a reçu de moi,
Conforme à son Aïeul, à son Père semblable,
On verra de David l'héritier détestable
Abolir tes honneurs, profaner ton Autel,
Et venger Athalie, Achab, et Jézabel.

What say I, wish? Sure hope, it is, I cherish,
That chafing at Thy yoke, Thy tiresome law,
Staunch to the blood of Ahab I bestow,
In the ways of his sire and grandsire versed,
Men shall behold Thy David's heir accursed
Attack Thy worship, all Thy prophets slaughter,
Avenging Ahab, Jezebel, me, their daughter.
(5.6.1783–90)

And, of course, history will prove her right. The seemingly eternal cycle of Oedipal jealousy and fratricide will continue: Joas will murder Zacharie, resituating himself in the line of Cain and Abel, Etéocle and Polynice, Britannicus and Néron, and so on.

In a strange twist, can it be that what has continually been fought, resisted, and vilified as monstrous is actually a vivifying force of resistance that might be equated to life itself? What Racine worships, and what we, the theatergoing public, seem to revere with him, this hieratic, static father, is but an avatar of death. The stasis that the desire for the absolute tends toward is a narcissistic drive, a drive that ultimately ends in ruin. Yet, in the apparently never-ending ambivalence of all drives, death is held off precisely by what that very drive would suppress, which it labels "monstrous." Difference and heterogeneity are not something foreign, not something exotic and/or other but constitutive of the very internal split that makes us human. It is the great force of Racinian tragedy that although on one level it casts out this foreign, female, exotic other, at the same time it incorporates into the very seduction of plots the appeal that the repressed represents for the hegemonic, master discourse of Western culture. By so doing it shows us that this play of forces is never able to be resolved. The absolute is always seduced by its own monstrous creations, which forever tantalize it and by so doing undermine it. And this might finally help us understand the obsessive attraction those passionate Racinian Furies, those Sphinx-like creations of feminine difference, held over their creator and us. Of course they are terrifying; they embody all those male fears and fantasies of inexhaustible female sexuality, of the lure of the maternal and thus the horror of the destruction of individuality. But if we remember, as Stallybrass and White remind us, that "disgust always bears the impress of desire," we can see how they are dangerous precisely because they are desirable, and it is this desire that the Western world from the Greeks onward has striven to hold at bay.[20]

At the end of his creative life Racine appears to leave a message of piety and hope. Nevertheless, the echoes of his tragedy remind us that this hope is perhaps nothing more than wishful thinking *(un voeu pieux)*. The reality of psychic conflict trumps absolutism or, for that matter, any univocal system of power that attempts to repress heterogeneity, fueling a never-ending spiral of conflict. Across the centuries, at the end of another prodigious life that was equally fruitful in its explorations of the ways myths reveal and repeat the most archaic conflicts of sexuality and power, aggression, and love, Freud came, like Racine but in a very different register, to an equally tragic conclusion. Writing in 1930, with the threat of a new and more deadly totalitarianism hanging over him, his family, his life's work, and Western civilization, Freud could not, any more than Racine, foresee the triumph of what he called "eros," the life-enhancing, community-building forces that tend toward preserving society over those darker, destructive forces of hatred and aggression that undermined it and that once again took the form of a decidedly deadly infatuation with a primitive, destructive father/leader. Freud did, however, demonstrate how those forces are continually at play within us, splitting us into multiple, contradictory, and fractious beings. These forces, embodied in Racine's great protagonists, adumbrated (for the first time on the seventeenth-century stage) the outlines of our modernity by reflecting characters divided against themselves. They are playthings of the forces (the gods, God, history) that formed them and break them. Could we not say that Racine was one of the first artists to portray the conflicts that Freud would theorize three hundred years later? That those contradictory drives exist in us all, making each of us, like Racine's passionate protagonists, a battleground where we must constantly struggle in order not to succumb to the irresolvable dilemma posed by our condition as both desiring and political beings, conflicted and split, rent by our own unavowable desires. And Freud no more than

Racine could offer any hope that this conflict would be resolved in a unilateral fashion, no happy ending for the tragedy of human existence.

Perhaps Racine could, as is normal for a man of his time and of his upbringing, retreat into a practice of piety with the faith that salvation would be his. His tragic characters, however, do not seem to offer that hope nor to suffer from that illusion. On the contrary, more like Freud's somber pronouncements, Racine's plays seem to tell us that the struggle is eternal and that although we can never be sure of an eventual triumph, we can be certain that the tragic conflicts it produces will continue to haunt us.[21] It is perhaps this haunting—the constant return of the past, embodied in the myths that Racine so seductively projected into his tragic creations and those creations' spellbinding hold on us— that continues to inform the way we love and live a conflict that is as impossible for us as it was for that original tragic hero, Oedipus, left to wander destitute across the expanse of a mythic land we now call Greece. From ancient Greece to his transposition by Racine on the stage of seventeenth-century France, Oedipus and his myth continue to confound us: his tragic fate, its desire and fear, is ours as well.

Notes

Preface

1. Roland Barthes, *Sur Racine* (Paris: Seuil, 1963), trans. R. Howard, *On Racine* (New York: Hill and Wang, 1964), viii: "Hence it is ultimately his very transparence that makes Racine a veritable commonplace of our literature, the critical object at zero degree, a site empty but eternally open to signification.... Racine is doubtless the greatest French author... a sovereign art of accessibility, which permits him to remain eternally within the field of any critical language."

2. See, for example, the recent tricentenary volume *Les épreuves du labyrinthe: Essais de poétique et d'herméneutique raciniennes; Hommage tricentenaire*, ed. Richard-Laurent Barnett, special issue, *Dalhousie French Studies* 49 (Winter 1999); the biographical study of Racine by A. Viala, *Racine ou la vie du caméléon* (Paris: Seghers, 1990); the recent critical survey by R. Tobin, *Jean Racine, Revisited* (New York: Twayne, 1999); and G. Forestier's recent biography, *Jean Racine* (Paris: Gallimard, 2006).

3. For a good general discussion of the history of antitheatricalism, see J. Barish, *The Antitheatrcal Prejudice* (Berkeley: University of California Press, 1981); and more specifically for France, H. Phillips, *Church and Culture in Seventeenth-Century France* (Cambridge: Cambridge University Press, 1997).

4. Prince de Conti, *Traité de la comédie et des spectacles* (Paris, 1667). Quoting Tertulian, 37: "But spectacles are a type of *voluptas*"; and 15: "Poets are the masters of the passions they describe but not of those which they arouse."

5. I am referring here, as I will continue to do, to Foucault's idea of the "great enclosure," the symbolic movement he describes in *Histoire de la folie à*

l'âge classique (Paris: Gallimard, 1961) by which difference is imposed through a defensive gesture of othering. This gesture, translated into epistemic terms, is one way the early Foucault proposed to see the rupture between the world of the sixteenth century (of the Renaissance) and that of the eighteenth (classical representation). The seventeenth century straddling this divide participates unevenly in both.

6. For the history of the imposition of the three unities and the notion of *bienséances*, see J. Schérer, *La dramaturgie classique en France* (Paris: Niaet, 1959).

7. For an overview of the fear of both the body and the body's presence in/as theater, see J. Delumeau, *Le péché et la peur: La culpabilisation en Occident, xiii–xviii siècles* (Paris: Fayard, 1983).

8. *Mémoires du curé de Versailles*, quoted in Raymond Picard, *La carrière de Jean Racine* (Paris: Gallimard, 1956), 425.

9. See Picard's discussion of the production of *Athalie* at Saint-Cyr in *La carrière de Jean Racine*, 415–22.

10. Leo Bersani, *A Future for Astyanax: Character and Desire in Literature* (Boston: Little, Brown, 1976), 19.

11. Quoted in Picard, *La carrière de Jean Racine*, 176.

12. Preface to *Bérénice*, in *Jean Racine: Théâtre Poésie*, ed. G. Forestier (Paris: La Pléiade, 1999), 451.

13. Quoted in Ricard, *La carrière de Jean Racine*, 221. Picard tells us in reference to *Bérénice* that "Racine was right to be proud of the tears that had honored his tragedy: they were a sign of his audience's communion in tender feelings" (166). For an extended essay on tears in Racine, see C. Biet, "Racine et la passion des larmes," in *Racine* (Paris: Hachette, 1994).

14. Joyce McDougall, *The Many Faces of Eros* (New York: W. W. Norton, 1995), 157.

15. In both this Preface and the following Introduction I reprise themes that I previously developed on Racinian tragedy. See more specifically "Racine's Children," in *Subjectivity and Subjugation* (Cambridge: Cambridge University Press, 1992), and "Racine's Oedipus: Virtual Bodies, Originary Fantasies," in *Baroque Bodies* (Ithaca, N.Y.: Cornell University Press, 2001).

Introduction

1. For some of the classical studies of the development of French neoclassical doctrine, see H. Peyre, *Qu'est-ce que le classicisme?* (Paris: Nizet, 1965); R. Bray, *La formation de la doctrine classique en France* (Paris: Nizet, 1957); E. B. O. Borgerhoff, *The Freedom of French Classicism* (Princeton, N.J.: Princeton University Press, 1950); and J. Schérer, *La dramaturgie classique en France* (Paris: Nizet, 1950).

2. L. Bersani, *A Future for Astyanax: Character and Desire in Literature* (Boston: Little Brown, 1976), 56.

3. A. Ubersfeld, in *Lire le théâtre* (Paris: Editions Sociales 1982), 11: "But theater appears as a privileged art, of major importance, because it demonstrates

better than the other how the individual psyche becomes invested in a communal relation. The spectator is never alone: his gaze, at the same time that it embraces what is shown to him, embraces the other spectators, who in turn see him."

4. Jean-Pierre Vernant and Pierre Vidal-Naquet, *Mythe et tragédie en Grèce antique* (Paris: Maspero, 1973), 2:82.

5. Ubersfeld, *Le théâtre et la cité*, 10.

6. Vernant and Vidal Naquet, *Mythe et tragédie*, 2:24–25: "But tragedy appears, thus, more than any other literary genre, rooted in social reality, this does not mean that it is the reflection of it. Tragedy does not reflect this reality, it questions it. By presenting it torn, divided against itself, tragedy renders reality entirely problematic."

7. Ibid., 2:17.

8. Mullaney, *The Place of the Stage: License, Play, and Power in Renaissance England* (Chicago: University of Chicago Press, 1988), introduction, passim.

9. Ibid., 130.

10. Ralph Giesey, *Cérémonie et puissance souveraine* (Paris: A. Colin, 1987), 10.

11. Ibid., 10.

12. Ibid., 77.

13. Ibid.

14. Hélène Merlin-Kajman, *Public et littérature en France au XVIIe siècle* (Paris: Belles Lettres, 1994), 335: "The theater of Racine has often been compared to a ceremony; the term seems to me to be particularly inappropriate. Racinian representation, which certainly corresponds to the epoch of court society, conveys it into the archaic order of sacrifice."

15. For another view of the sacrificial aspect of Racinian tragedy, see A. Ambroze, *Racine: Poète du sacrifice* (Paris: A. G. Nizet, 1970).

16. The work of René Girard has been important and influential for the comprehension of the role of sacrifice in Western representation and, according to him, the constitution of Western society. *La violence et le sacré* (Paris: Grasset, 1972), *Le bouc émissaire* (Paris: Grasset, 1982), and *La route antique des hommes pervers* (Paris: Grasset, 1985) have made a forceful if controversial case for the role of sacrifice in society. His considerable work on the importance of violence and sacrifice as constituting the originary communal crime instituting and perpetuating societal cohesion has been influential in elaborating a seductive (and reductive) theory of the imaginary of social organization. Although I cannot do justice here to Girard's many perceptive insights, I would not like to fall into what is an essentially theological (Christological) explanation of a political myth. For this reason I prefer the more properly psychoanalytic interpretation of the sacrificial ceremony offered, as will be seen, by Guy Rosolato, among others.

17. "Every sacrificial act . . . should be a point of departure, an origin," writes Rosolato (*Le sacrifice: Repères psychanalytiques* (Paris: PUF, 1987), 117. In the following discussion on sacrifice/theater I will be borrowing from my discussion in *Baroque Bodies: Psychoanalysis and the Culture of French Absolutism* (Ithaca, N.Y.: Cornell University Press, 2001), esp. chap. 5, "Racine's Oedipus."

18. Rosolato, *Le sacrifice*, 87. Rosolato states that "the sacrificial victim marks the boundary between outside and inside.... The sacrifice has value only on the inside of the tribe."

19. Ibid., 68: "There is, therefore, a symbolic birth or rebirth of the group the symbol of which, insofar as its origin is real, historical and mythic becomes fixed on the sacrifice."

20. See, for an elaboration of this analogy, M. Greenberg, *Corneille, Classicism, and the Ruses of Symmetry* (Cambridge: Cambridge University Press, 1986), introduction.

21. The primordial role of theater as a social mediator by which the individual is inserted in the collective is underscored by Ubersfeld (*Lire le théâtre*, 39). For a discussion of the translation of the scene of sacrifice in the seventeenth century from the executioner's block to the religious practices of Catholicism, see J. M. Apostolidès, *Le prince sacrifié: Théâtre et politique au temps de Louis XIV* (Paris, Minuit, 1985).

22. Loraux, *Façons tragiques de tuer une femme* (Paris: Hachette, 1985), trans. A. Forster, *Tragic Ways of Killing a Woman* (Cambridge, Mass.: Harvard University Press, 1987), 33.

23. Freud, "Psychopathic Characters on Stage," *Standard Edition of the Complete Pyschological Works of Sigmund Freud*, trans. James Strachey (London: Hogarth Press, 1953–74), 7:307: "Suffering of every kind is thus the subject matter of drama, and from this suffering it promises to give the audience pleasure. Thus we arrive at a first precondition of this form of art: that it should not cause suffering to the audience, that it should know how to compensate, by means of the possible satisfactions involved, for the sympathetic suffering which is aroused."

24. For a renewed overview of theatrical production of the first half of the seventeenth-century, see Christian Biet, ed., with Charlotte Bouteille-Meister et al., *Théâtre de la cruauté et récits sanglants en France (XVIe–XVIIe siécle)* (Paris: R. Laffont, 2006).

25. M. Foucault, introduction to *Les mots et les choses* (Paris: Gallimard, 1965).

26. M. Foucault, *Histoire de la folie à l'age classique* (Paris: Gallimard, 1961).

27. For a more elaborate discussion of these shifts in familial demographics, see M. Greenberg, introduction to *Subjectivity and Subjugation in Seventeenth-Century Drama and Prose: The Family Romance of French Classicism* (Cambridge: Cambridge University Press, 1986).

28. *Sur Racine* (Paris: Seuil, 1963); trans. R. Howard, *On Racine* (New York: Hill and Wang, 1964).

29. J. Rose, *Sexuality in the Field of Vision* (London: Verso, 1996), 166: "But sexuality—the crucial ways it determines and structures our lives—cannot be understood without acknowledging the importance of fantasy, and fantasy in turn reveals aspects of subjectivity which crush the splendour of our (conscious) dreams."

30. See, for instance, J. Laplanche, *Entre séduction et inspiration: L'homme* (Paris: PUF, 1999), 287: "Myth proposes a schema for a new conveyance for

facing 'existential' anxiety, caused by enigmatic elements that appears as anomaly, contradiction or scandal."

31. Lévi-Strauss, *Le cru et le cuit* (Paris: Plon, 1964); trans. J. and D. Weightman, *The Raw and the Cooked* (New York: Harper and Row, 1969), 18: "Myths are anonymous: from the moment they are seen as myths, and whatever their real origin, they exist only as elements embodied in a tradition. When the myth is repeated, the individual listeners are receiving a message that, properly speaking, is coming from nowhere; this is why it is credited with a supernatural origin" and in another vein. Jean-Paul Valabrega, *Phantasme, mythe, corps, sens* (Paris: Gallimard, 1969), 92: "Every myth deals with origins. Every question about origins always opens onto a myth."

32. Lévi-Strauss, *Structural Anthropology*, trans. C. Jacobson and B. Grundfest Schoepf (New York: Basic Books, 1963), 213: "We define the myth as consisting of all its versions; or to put it otherwise, a myth remains the same as long as it is felt as such." Valabrega, *Phantasme, mythe, corps, sens*, 150: "Since a myth always refers to another myth, it is never anything but a variant along an uninterrupted chain. Created to explain the origin and to give an explanation of it, the myth itself has no assignable origin."

33. Valabrega, *Phantasme, mythe, corps, sens*, 118: "Myth, truthfully speaking … is neither one nor the other, neither individual nor collective, but precisely both at once."

34. The connection between mythology and seventeenth-century theater is a subject of much scholarship. See in particular C. Delmas, "Du mythe au xvii siecle," in *Mythe et histoire dans le théâtre classique* (Toulouse: SLC, 2002), 81: "There were constant exchanges between history and mythology throughout the seventeenth century, historical material, often only slightly dramatised, was mythologically structured while the dry arguments of ancient tragedy were elaborated around political and amorous themes in order to make them more human in the eyes of a modern audience." J. M. Apostolidès, in his *Le prince sacrifie*, prefers the term "mythistoire" to speak about this interconnection.

35. Lewis, "Sacrifice and Suicide: Some Afterthoughts on the Career of J. Racine," *Biblio 17, Actes de Baton Rouge* (1986): 58–59.

36. Jacqueline de Romilly, in her overview of Greek tragedy *La tragédie grecque* (Paris: PUF, 1970), makes a curiously similar point (from an entirely different critical perspective) when she writes: "It is clear that there existed in different countries historical tragedies. But, in these tragedies, history is treated a bit like myths, history serves as an example, only the human meaning is maintained. It is modified according to one's desire. Also, it must be said, inversely, that the Greek myths were, originally, supposed to retrace a history, distant and heroic, but in essence, true. So, in a sense, the difference between the two is not really a radical difference" (19).

37. Pierre Kaufmann, *L'inconscient du politique* (Paris: PUF, 1979), 41: "The normative State hides its own origins from us."

38. M. Detienne, *L'invention de la mythologie* (Paris: Gallimarad, 1981), 9. See also Freud, "Writers and Daydreaming," in *Standard Edition*, 9:152: "It is

extremely probable that myths, for instance, are distorted vestiges of the wishful phantasies of whole nations, the secular dreams of youthful humanity." See also K. Abraham, "Dreams and Myths: A Study in Folk Psychology," *Clinical Papers and Essays on Psychoanalysis* (New York: Basic Books, 1955), 54: "It is in legends and fairy-tales that the phantasy of a nation is revealed."

39. See N. Lukacher, *Primal Scenes: Literature, Philosophy, Psychoanalysis* (Ithaca, N.Y.: Cornell University Press, 1986); and J. Laplanche and J-B. Pontalis, *Fantasme originaire: Fantasmes des origines, origines du fantasme* (Paris: Hachette, 1985).

40. Rosolato, *La portée du désir ou la psychanalyse même* (Paris: PUF, 1996), 91.

41. Green, *The Tragic Effect: The Oedipus Complex in Tragedy*, trans. A. Sheridan (New York: Cambridge University Press, 1979), 27: "The encounter between myth and tragedy is obviously not fortuitous. First, because every history, whether it is individual or collective, is based on a myth. In the case of the individual, this myth is known as phantasy."

42. Rosolato, "Trois générations d'hommes," in *Essais sur le symbolique* (Paris: Gallimard, 1967), 98.

43. E. Enriquez, *De la horde à l'Etat: Essai de psychanalyse du lien social* (Paris: Gallimard, 1986), 66: "Individual psychology is also and at the same time a social psychology." Or Rosolato, *Le sacrifice*, 180: "Individual psychology is constructed according to social references, communal ideals."

44. Cornelius Castoriades, *World in Fragments: Writings on Politics, Society, Psychoanalysis, and the Imagination*, ed. and trans. David Ames Curtis (Stanford, Calif.: Stanford University Press, 1997), 133: "Individuals become what they are by absorbing and internalizing institutions; in a sense they are the main concrete embodiment of these institutions."

45. Enriquez, *De la horde*.

46. N. O. Keohane, in her *Philosophy and the State in France* (Princeton, N.J.: Princeton University Press, 1980), describes the almost visceral feeling of security the king inspired in his subjects: "It would be hard to exaggerate the importance the concept of the French King as representative of the common interest, the source and embodiment of the good of all. . . . There was a sense of security when the monarch was personally in charge of things, a trust in the benevolence of his will, which can only be explained by the belief that he apprehended and spoke for the good of the entire society in a way no other human being could approach" (59). Enriquez offers a more psychoanalytic explanation of the fascination the leader exercises over his people: "What is at stake in fascination is the possibility for men to lose and to find themselves in a being . . . This fascinating being represents, theatrically and directly, what he, little man that he is, could become. He makes him live vicariously the heroism that is buried in him. He gives him over to his deepest desire to be recognized, identified, loved. He is capable of making him able to transform and to transcend himself" (*De la horde*, 355).

47. See Louis' own description of himself as such in *Mémoires*, ed. J. Longnon

(Paris: Tallandier, 1978), 111, where he describes himself as "a true father of his family who provides for his household and divies out, equally to all his children, their rations."

48. See D. Bell, *The Cult of the Nation in France: Inventing Nationalism, 1680–1800* (Cambridge, Mass.: Harvard University Press, 2001), where, although dealing mostly with the eighteenth and nineteenth centuries, he does fix the origins of a modern sense of nation in France during the reign of Louis XIV.

49. Enriquez, *De la horde*, 144: "without the great man there is no 'people,' without the murder of the great man, still no possibility of a 'people.'"

50. Freud, *The Interpretation of Dreams*, in *Standard Edition*, 4:262.

51. For a discussion of the different versions and interpretations of the Oedipus legend throughout history, and of the particular use Freud makes of Oedipus, see S. Rudnytsky, *Freud and Oedipus* (New York: Columbia University Press, 1987).

52. M. Delcourt, *Oedipe ou la légende du conquérant* (Paris: Faculté de philosohie et lettres, 1944), 108.

53. M. Gauchet, *Le désenchantement du monde, une histoire politique de la religion* (Paris: Gallimard, 1985).

54. J. Rose, *Sexuality in the Field of Vision*, 166: "But sexuality—the crucial ways it determines and structures our lives—cannot be understood without acknowledging the importance of fantasy, and fantasy in turn reveals aspects of subjectivity which crush the splendour of our (conscious) dreams."

55. D. Anzieu, reminds us in his exploration of the construction and ramifications of the oedipal legend, "Oedipe avant le complexe ou de l'interprétation psychanalytique des mythes," *Les Temps Modernes* 245 (October 1966): 675–715: "Oedipus, king of Thebes, is a descendant of Harmony, the only daughter of the illicit loves of Ares and Aphrodite: in Oedipus incest and parricide will find their most unadorned expression, just as Ares and Aphrodite are the chief representatives of aggressivity and sexuality" (682).

56. Green, *The Tragic Effect*, 7–8: "To ask oneself whether kinship relations constitute the tragic or whether the tragic elucidates these kinship relations may be meaningless, formulated in that way. Let us say rather that they reveal something essential about the subjectivity that is inseparable from the tragic, by uncovering the relation of the subject to his progenitors, that the study of these relations may be fully conceived only in the context of the tragic, so revealing its role as constituent of subjectivity."

57. A. Ubersfeld, *Lire le théâtre*, 15, 265.

58. Green, *The Tragic Effect*, 23

59. Victor Turner, *The Anthropology of Performance* (New York: PAJ Publications, 1986), 102.

60. Enriquez, *De la horde*, 258: "In a group with a tendency towards union . . . individual desire and group desire tend, almost, to coincide."

61. Green, *The Tragic Effect*, 233: "The whole tragedy unfolds like a ritual exclusion. The whole ritual of the tragedy is linked here with the rite from

which the tragedy sprang. . . . The ritual of initiation is, in tragedy, reduced to participation in the spectacle. . . . This spectacle narrates the exclusion of a man who transgressed the prohibitions, but it also cements the unity of the members of the city through their common participation in a ceremony."

1. La Thébaïde

1. R. C. Knight, *Racine et la Grèce* (Paris: Bovin, 1950). G. Forestier, in the notes to his edition of *Racine: Théâtre, Poésie*, tells us, "*La Thébaïde* was not a success" and that it "went almost unnoticed" (1230). As for Racine's possible interest in writing his own version of *Oedipus Tyrannos*, see François Fénélon: "M. Racine, qui avait fort étudié les grands modèles de l'antiquité, avait formé le plan d'une tragédie française d'*Oedipe*, suivant le goût de Sophocle" (M. Racine, who had a deep knowledge of the great models of antiquity, had planned a French version of *Oedipus*, in the manner of Sophocles). *Lettre à l'Académie*, chap. 6, quoted in G. May, *Tragédie cornélienne, tragédie racinienne: Étude sur les sources de l'intérêt dramatique* (Urbana: University of Illinois Press, 1948), 194.

2. Racine, preface to *La Thébaïde*, in Forestier, *Racine: Théâtre, Poésie*, 119.

3. Vernant and Vidal-Naquet, *Mythe et Tragedie*, 2:27.

4. J. M. Apostolidès, *Le prince sacrifié* (Paris: Minuit, 1983), 178.

5. One could look here to a particularly "perverse" attitude—of Racine, of his Jansenist upbringing—that would bear the particularly Christian imprint E. Enriquez tells us marks a turning point in the West's relation to the body and sexuality. That is, in Enriquez's terms applied here to Racine, we would see that Christianity in its very message recognizes the libidinal pull that is at the very heart of human desire—sexuality—only to immediately condemn and turn away from it. The relation between desire and guilt so essential to Racinian tragedy would thus find its cultural anchoring in the Christian tradition Racine was raised in, turns away from, and than turns back to. Enriquez, *De la horde*, 291: "Thus Christianity places sexuality (with its procession of drives, modes of attachment and seduction) at the origin of man. . . . It claims that man is the fruit not of the *word* and of the *law* of God as in Judaism, but the fruit of *libido*. It thus recognized the central place of libido and it immediately attempts to deny it."

6. M. Delcourt, *Oedipe ou la légende du conquérant* (Paris: Faculté de philosophie et de lettres, 1944), vii: "The legend of Oedipus is certainly the most complete of all the political myths."

7. The following list of works is meant to be merely a subjective sampling of the recent work that combines, in powerful ways, psychoanalysis, anthropology, psychiatry, sociology, political theory. It is far from exhaustive. G. Devereux's now classic works *Essais d'ethnopsychiatrie générale* (Paris: Gallimard, 1970) and *Ethnopyschanalyse complémentariste* (Paris: Flammarion, 1985) (both works translated from the English): Tobie Nathan, *Psychanalyse païenne* (Paris: O. Jacob, 1995); J. Walthan, *Du commerce avec les diables* (Paris: Les empecheurs de penser

en rond, 2004); P.-L. Assosun and M. Zafiropoulos, *L'anthropologie psychanalytique* (Paris: Economica, 2002); P. Kaufmann, *Psychanalyse et théorie de la culture* (Paris: Denoël, 1974); G. Rosolato, *Essais sur le symbolique* (Paris: Gallimard, 1967); A. Green, *La déliaison: Psychanalyse, anthropologie, littérature* (Paris: Les Belles Lettres, 1992); E. Enriquez, *De la horde*.

8. I am referring to the three-volume collection of essays *Le mythe: Pratiques, récit, theories*, ed. C. Bergé, M. Boccara, and M. Zafiropoulos (Paris: Anthropos, 2004).

9. Enriquez, *De la horde*, 110.

10. C. Mauron, talking about passions in Racine, describes the same phenomenon: "Racine is the painter of the passions; but any strongly marked passion becomes regressive and any regression evokes oedipal or pre-oedipal situations" (*L'inconscient dans l'oeuvre et la vie de Racine*, 29). The importance of the primal fantasy or scene for Racine has been discussed in M. Greenberg, *Baroque Bodies: Psychoanalysis and the Culture of French Absolutism* (Ithaca, N.Y.: Cornell University Press, 2001), esp. chap. 5, "Racine's Oedipus."

11. G. Rosolato *La portée du désir* (Paris: PUF, 1996), 66: "We can affirm that any quest for the origin is intrinsic to the functions of phantasm."

12. See Enriquez, "Deuxième partie: Le lien social, domination et pouvoir," in *De la horde*.

13. L. Althusser, "Idéologie, et appareils idéologiques d'Etat," in *Positions* (Paris: Editions Sociales, 1976), 101.

14. For an especially compelling reading of the role of the represented sacrifice of young virgins in Greek tragedy, see Loraux, *Façons tragiques de tuer une femme*.

15. Enriquez, *De la horde*, 224: "The social bond only exists in the splendor of day, the passions only awaken once night has fallen when reason trembles and culture undoes itself."

16. Jean-Pierre Vernant, *Les ruses de l'intelligence: La Métis des Grecs* (Paris: Flammarion, 1993); Vernant and Pierre Vidal-Naquet, *Mythe et tragédie* (Paris: Maspero, 1972); Jean-Pierre Vernant, *Entre mythe et politique* (Paris: Seuil, 1996); *Mythe et pensée chez les Grecs* (Paris: Maspéro, 1966). P. Slater, *The Glory of Hera: Greek Mythology and the Greek Family* (Princeton, N.J.: Princeton University Press, 1968); M. Delcourt, *Oreste et Alcméon: Étude sur la projection légendaire du matricide en Grèce* (Paris: Les Belles Lettres, 1959).

17. For a more detailed analysis of the role of the king as an apotropaic symbol of national unity, see M. Greenberg, *Baroque Bodies: Psychoanalysis and the Culture of French Absolutism* (Ithaca, N.Y.: Cornell University Press, 2001).

18. Rosolato, *Le sacrifice*, 180: "Sacrifical activity becomes exceptionally active during periods of crisis, when conflict endangers power, the power of the leader, when a new ideology begins to make itself known and still belongs to a minority who has not yet the means to accomplish its objectives or still yet when it is a question of overthrowing a tyrant or, on the contrary, reenforcing his menaced hold on power."

19. The many books of Vernant and of Vernant and Pierre Vidal-Naquet have explored the political emergence of theater in classical Greece. See, for instance, Vernant, *Mythe et religion en Grèce ancienne* (Paris: Le Seuil, 1990), and *La mort dans les yeux* (Paris: Hachette, 1985); Vernant and Vidal-Naquet, *Oedipe et ses mythes* (Brussels: Edition Complexe, 1985), *La Grèce ancienne*, 2 vols. (Paris: Seuil, 1990), and *Mythe et tragédie en Grèce ancienne* (Paris: Maspéro, 1972).

20. The translation I am using omits the last four verses: "This same blood that gave them to heavenly light / Gave them a fatal penchant for crime / And their hearts infected by this mortal poison / Opened up to hatred before opening to reason" (my translation).

21. See O. Seyffert, *Dictionary of Classical Antiquities* (New York: Meridian Library, 1956), and P. Grimal, *Dictionnaire de la mythologie grecque et romaine* (Paris: PUF, 1958).

22. *Sang* appears sixty-seven times in the text, followed by *trône* (thirty-nine) and *roi* (thirty-seven).

23. R. Barthes, *On Racine*, trans. R. Howard (New York: Hill and Wang, 1964), 64–65.

24. Aristote, *Politique*, trans. J. Aubonnet (Paris: Gallimard, 993), 57: "Moreover, the disorder of women is harmful to the spirit of the law and to the happiness of the state."

25. E. Enriquez has glossed Freud's discussions on the dialectic nature/culture as it is ideologically sexualized in the following terms (*De la horde*, 214): "Social order is based on symbolization and repression. There is no order without words that prohibit and without words of reference, no order without taboos and without permissible areas. But woman (mother or daughter) threatens the social order when she articulates the primacy of 'jouissance,' of a relation of body to body, of the dual relation, of reality over words, representations, over the mediated relation."

26. The Antigone bibliography is immense. From Hegel through the recent analyses of Irigaray and Lacan, the ethical role of Antigone has been a source of endlessly rich debate. J. Butler's *Antigone's Claim: Kinship between Life and Death* (New York: Columbia University Press, 2000) is one of the most recent rereadings of the Antigone tradition. For an interesting introduction to the ethical debate around the character/role of Antigone, see E. Kaufman, "Why the Family Is Beautiful (Lacan against Badiou)," *Diacritics* 32 (Fall–Winter 2002): 135–51.

27. For a reading of the fraternal relation in *La Thébaïde* and its relation to the problems of primogeniture, see R. Goodkin, *Birthmarks: The Tragedy of Primogeniture in P. Corneille, T. Corneille, and J. Racine* (Philadelphia: University of Pennsylvania Press, 2000).

28. We must remember, as Georges Forestier reminds us in his edition of Racine, that although Racine found the rivalry of the brothers in Euripides, it was his idea to make them twins and to add to their rivalry a visceral hatred (*Racine: Théâtre, poésie*, 1247).

29. See M. H. Huet, *Monstrous Imagination* (Cambridge, Mass.: Harvard University Press, 1993), for a discussion of the history of twinship and monstrosity.

30. The idea of the double in psychoanalytic theory is linked to narcissistic identification, which itself is always a vehicle for agressivity. See Rosolato, *Le sacrifice:* "l'identification narcissique" (narcissitic identification), which is always "porteuse d'agressivite" (bearer of aggressivity) (24). The narcissist wants us to be like him but prohibits it (24). See also his remarks on "doubling": "Doubling erases differences, suppresses the Other and therefore loses the foil for unicity" (30). For Freud's initial analysis of the deadly aggression the double represents, see "The Uncanny," in *Standard Edition*, vol. 17.

31. It is interesting that on several occasions in the play we see the use of the word *chimère* to describe an aberrant idea or attitude—"Nature, for him, is but a chimera" (591); "I don't indulge in such chimerical thoughts" (271)—an echo of yet another female monster destroyer of young men in the Greek canon.

32. See T. Reiss, "Le Thébaïde ou la souveraineté à la question," in *L'Age du théâtre en France* (The Age of the Theater in France), ed. D. Trott and N. Bovisier (Edmonton: Academic Publishing, 1988). He traces all the references in the play's debate between the brothers about the role of the king to several contemporary, political theorists, Bodin, Cardin Le Bret, Naudier, etc.

33. For two recent readings of the interconnection between political philosophy and literature in the seventeenth century, see C. Jouhaud, *Les pouvoirs de la littérature* (Paris: Gallimard, 2000); and H. Merlin-Kajman, *L'absolutisre dans les lettres et la théorie des deux corps: Passions et politique* (Paris: Champion, 2000).

34. It would seem that for the Greeks the most basic definition of "tyrannos" and the words related to it "have in common the idea of leading some organized formation of people" (s.v. "Tyrant," in Oskar Seyffert, *Dictionary of Classical Antiquities* [New York: Meridian, 1956]).

35. See E. Canetti, *Crowds and Power*, trans. Carol Stewart (New York: Viking Press, 1963).

36. P. Corneille, "Discours de l'utilité et des parties du poème dramatique," in *Corneille: Théâtre complet*, ed. Pierre Lievre (Paris: Gallimard, 1950), 13.

37. My translation.

38. Barthes, *On Racine*, 13.

39. I am not ignoring the desperate suicide of Ménécée, but it would be an error to confuse his act with a ritual sacrifice.

2. Andromaque

1. I will not be dealing with *Alexandre* in my discussion. Although I recognize its thematic significance, its overall importance for the Racinian tragic does not strike me as compelling.

2. See the notes in Forestier, who lays out in great detail the lineage of the Romanesque "héros galant" (*Racine: Théâtre, poésie*, 1318–26 passim).

3. For a more detailed discussion of the organization of the Greek army, see the chapter on *Iphigénie*.

4. Barthes, *On Racine*, 48.

5. "It is a universal fact that the bond of reciprocity that founds marriage is not established between men and women but between men by means of women who are the principal occasion for this exchange." Lévi-Strauss, *Les structures élémentaires de la parenté; The Elementary Structures of Kinship*, trans. James Harle Bell, John Richard von Sturmer, and Rodney Needham (Boston: Beacon Press 1969), 149. See also Enriquez, *De la horde*, 279.

6. L. Bersani, in his chapter on *Andromaque* in *A Future for Astyanax* (Boston: Little, Brown, 1976), and L. Horowitz in her article "Second Time Around," *L'Esprit Créateur* 38, no. 2 (1998): 23–33, point to the repetition and yet the sense of diminishment in the children of these heroes.

7. I am of course referring to the now-classic study *Saturn and Melancholy: Studies in the History of Natural Philosophy, Religion and Art* by Raymond Klibansky, Erwin Panofsky, and Fritz Saxl (Nendeln, Liechtenstein: Kraus Reprint, 1979).

8. Most classical scholars see no difference between Greeks and Trojans. Some, however, have argued for a distinction based on the sheer number of Priam's wives. See, for example, Stephen Scully, *Homer and the Sacred City* (Ithaca, N.Y.: Cornell University Press, 1990). R. Girard argues for a radical difference between Troy and the Greek camp, but his argument is based entirely on an idealization of the specifically Greek polis. Edith Hall in *Inventing the Barbarian* (Oxford: Oxford University Press, 1989) does argue that while there is no difference in Homer, in tragedy, which of course comes after the massive war with Persia, there are distinctions drawn between Greeks and Trojans. I am indebted to P. Rose for these references.

9. Forestier, in his "notice" to *Andromaque* in his *Racine*, 1339–42, outlines the different metamorphoses undergone by the character Oreste as it is adapted from the Greeks, through Seneca and Horace to Racine.

10. G. May, *Tragédie cornélienne, tragédie racinienne: Étude sur les sources de l'intérêt dramatique* (Urbana: University of Illinois Press, 1948), 160.

11. A. Green, *The Tragic Effect*, 37: "The *Odipodeia* and the *Oresteia* constitute essential, fundamental models in which the problematic of all tragedy—and perhaps of all human endeavour—is situated."

12. *Funeste* echoes fourteen times in the play, seven in the mouth of Oreste.

13. Freud, *Mourning and Melancholia, Standard Edition*, 14:244.

14. For a reading of the contradictions of Andromaque's fixation on the past/present, see R. Goodkin, "A Choice of Andromache's," *Yale French Studies* 67 (1984): 225–47. See also H. Stone, "Beyond the Promise: Racine's Andromaque," *Symposium: A Quarterly Journal in Modern Literatures* 43, no. 4 (Winter 1989–90): 284–303.

15. Rosolato, *Le sacrifice*, 180.

16. Freud, *Standard Edition*, 14:245: "The patient is aware of the loss which

has given rise to his melancholy but only in the sense that he knows whom he has lost but not what he has lost in him."

17. Ibid., 250.

18. L. Marin, *La parole mangée* (Paris: Klinckieck, 1986), 215: "And we must never lose sight of the fact that the desire for absolute power is but one aspect of the death drive." See also A. Green, *N.R.P.*, no. 13 (1976): 37–80: "The desire for power is in its essence narcissistic, it is a desire for the One, a unitary utopa, an ideal totalisation."

19. As Freud reminds us in "On Narcissism, An Introduction," in *Standard Edition*, 14:88: "It seems very evident that another person's narcissism (that is their enclosed self-involvement) has a great attraction."

20. Barthes, *On Racine*, 22: "In Racine there is what we might call a fetishism of the eyes."

21. C. Buci-Glucksmann, *La folie du voir* (Paris: Galilee, 1986), 48: "The generalized scopic drive hides a real work of cultural mourning, an implementation of the death drive that undermines and fragments any signifying intentionality." Jacqueline Rose, in her reading of the instability of identity—sexual and political—also attaches that fragility to the psychic import of vision: "Freud often relates the question of sexuality to visual representation . . . moments when perception founders . . . or in which the pleasure of looking tips over into the register of excess. The sexuality lies less in the context of what is seen than in the subjectivity of the viewer (in the relationship between what is looked at and the developing sexual knowledge of the child). The relationship between viewer and scene is always one of fracture, partial identification, pleasure and distrust" (*Sexuality in the Field of Vision* [London: Verso, 1996], 227).

22. Mauron, *L'inconscient dans l'oeuvre et la vie de Racine*, 238–39: "*Andromaque* is situated exactly where the Trojan War is transformed into a familial drama, and it is here that the real Racine begins, because the conflict becomes interiorized." There are more than 115 references in the play to vision: "eye," "eyes," "looking," "seeing," "spectacle," and so on.

23. For a view of Andromaque as not the eternal model of maternal solicitude, see Ronald W. Tobin, "Andromaque's Choice," *Orbis Litterarum: International Review of Literary Studies* 58, no. 5 (2003): 317–34.

24. Derrida, *Voyous: Deux essays sur la raison* (Paris: Galilée, 2003), 148; trans. Michael Naas and Pascale-Anne Brault, *Rogues: Two Essays on Reason* (Stanford, Calif.: Stanford University Press, 2005), 104.

25. Barthes, *On Racine*, 79: "To dismiss Hermione is precisely to shift from a collective constraint to an individual order. . . . It is this repetition that Pyrrhus wants to prevent."

26. For a more detailed discussion of the evocative powers of Racinian verse and of the incantatory power of the voice, see my "Racine's Oedipus: Virtual Bodies, Originary Fantasies," in Greenberg, *Baroque Bodies: Psychoanalysis and the Culture of French Absolutism* (Ithaca, N.Y.: Cornell University Press, 2001), 209–68.

27. See Rosolato, *Essais sur le symbolique* (Paris: Gallimard, 1969), 63.

28. For the complex discussion of this convoluted scenario, see Rosolato, "Trois générations d'homme," in his *Essais sur le symbolique*.

29. Enriquez, *De la horde*, 257: "We must thus recognize the possibility for the group of collectively living unconscious fears, of inventing solutions to answer these challenges, and to admit that this collective lived experience cannot be substantially distinguished from an individual experience."

30. Which is precisely why, according to Goldmann, she is tragic. See *Le dieu caché: Étude sur la vision tragique dans les "Pensées" de Pascal et dans le théâtre de Racine* (Paris: Gallimard, 1955).

31. Enriquez, on mother/son incest, *De la horde*, 191: "The prohibition seeks first to distance and separate definitively the son from the mother. Because the mother does not want to give her son, whom she experiences as a part of her, up. The son must constantly fight against the phantasm of maternal wholeness: The mother may be devouring, possessive, castrating, or simply loving, she nevertheless exerts through her love a form of violence on the child's body."

32. A. Green, *The Tragic Effect*, 177: "As Marie Delcourt reminds us, infanticide was the least serious of familial crimes. Parricide alone was inexpiable." M. Delcourt, *Oedipe ou la légende*, 60: "No crime to the Greek mind was more terrible than parricide."

33. In his reading of the play, T. Reiss sees its importance as aiding in establishing the legality and the genealogy of the French monarchy in the persona of Andromaque. See Reiss, "Andromaque and the Search for Unique Sovereignty," in *The Shape of Change*, ed. A. Briberick and Russell Ganim (Amsterdam: Rodopi, 2002), 23–51.

34. Rosolato, *Le sacrifice*, 83–123.

35. See A. Green, *The Tragic Effect*, 210.

36. Rosolato, *Le sacrifice*, 74: "As for the murder of the father I would propose that in the myth of monotheism it never appears directly. Each example has, in fact, as its goal to avoid its happening. We must, therefore, admit that this murder constitutes the secret and fundamental kernel, in relation to which the substitutes for the sacrifice are organised and by which the alliance is realized."

37. Rosolato, *La relation d'inconnu* (Paris: Gallimard, 1987), 87: "Nevertheless, since Freud, psychoanalysts have uncovered a latent impulse in this schema, all the more disguised as the patriarchal system is all the more powerful. Under the cover of the murder of the son, the death wishes towards the father insinuate themselves. The ritual, replacement victim, supports, symbolizes the father."

38. Barthes, *On Racine*, 39: "The catastrophic alternative of the Racinian theatre; either the son kills the Father, or the Father destroys the son: in Racine, infanticides are as numerous as parricides."

3. *Britannicus*

1. Its corollary as the ideal Republic is obviously also a source of emulation from the Renaissance to the Revolution.

2. See J. M. Apostolidès, *Le roi machine: Spectacle et politique au temps de Louis XIV* (Paris: Minuit, 1981), and *Le prince sacrifié* (Paris: Minuit, 1985).

3. Racine, preface to *Britannics*, in Forestier, *Racine*, 373: "But, they say, this Prince was barely fifteen when he died. He and Narcisse are made to live two years more than they live. I would not have mentioned this objection if it hadn't been made, heatedly, by a man who allowed himself to lengthen the reign of an Emperor to twenty years who only reigned eight" (the reference is to Corneille).

4. He counters with another Junia—Junia Calvina—whom he nevertheless must defend against the charges of incest (ibid.): "She tenderly loved her Brother and their enemies, according to Tacitus, accused them both of incest, although they were only guilty of being a bit indiscreet."

5. Green, *The Tragic Effect*, 7: "The family, then, is the tragic space *par excellence*, no doubt because in the family the knots of love—and therefore of hate—are not only the earliest, but also the most important ones."

6. Foucault, *The History of Sexuality*, trans. Robert Hurley, vol. 1 (New York: Pantheon, 1978), 108.

7. C. Mauron, *L'inconscient dans l'oeuvre et la vie de Racine*, 70–73.

8. Both Mauron and Barthes underline the repetitive scenario of the "son trying to free himself from the castrating presence of the domineering mother" in all of Racine. In a certain sense we might invoke Charles Peguy, in this context, who said of Racine: "He always wrote the same tragedy... but he did so by constantly varying the givens." *Victor Marie, comte Hugo* (Paris: Gallimard, 1934), 168.

9. It is interesting to note in this regard, especially in the narration of Rome's burning, that Suetonius reports that during that conflagration, Néron, who prided himself on his talents as a musician, sang an "epic song of the destruction of Troy." Just one more interestingly perverse connection between the Néron legend and the mythological universe of Racine's previous tragedy.

10. H. Merlin-Kajman, *Public et littérature en France au xvii siècle* (Paris: Les Belles Lettres, 1994).

11. Forestier, *Racine*, 444.

12. We are reminded here of Barthes's pertinent observation that in Racine, it is power that determines the sexuality of Racine's characters: masculinity and femininity, he reminds us, reside not in the biological sex of the protagonist but in his/her relation to power.

13. Jean Laplanche and Jean-Baptiste Pontalis, *Vocabulaire de la psychanalyse* (Paris: PUF, 1967), trans. D. Nicholson-Smith, *The Language of Psychoanalysis* (New York: W. W. Norton, 1973), 307: "One could pursue this line of reasoning further still and define human sexuality itself as essentially 'perverse' inasmuch as it never fully detaches itself from its origins, where satisfaction was sought not in a specific activity but in the 'pleasure gain' associated with functions or activities depending on other instincts."

14. Freud, *Three Essays on the Theory of Sexuality*, *Standard Edition*, vol. 7.

15. Laplanche and Pontalis, *Vocabulaire de la psychanalyse*, 307: "In Psychoanalysis, the word 'perversion' is used exclusively in relation to sexuality. Where

Freud recognizes the existence of instincts other than sexual ones, he does not evoke perversion in connection with them."

16. J. Clavreul, "Le couple pervers," in *Le Désir et la perversion* (Paris: Seuil, 1967), 109: "We thus understand the importance that the mother's look can have. Certainly because she is the spectator of the young pervert at that historic, decisive moment of discovery. It is in this sense that this look participates in the creation of the illusory field."

17. Ibid., 108.

18. Ibid., 112: "It is clear that it is as the purveyor of the look that the Other will be the partner, that is to say, above all the accomplice of the perverse act."

19. Ibid., 110.

20. Ibid., 105: "Thus the desire to see and to know is not, structurally, different from sexual desire."

21. Green, *The Tragic Effect*, 18.

22. S. Doubrovsky, "L'arrivée sur scène de Junie," *Littérature* 32 (December 1978): 27–54.

23. Both Mauron, *L'inconscient dans l'oeuvre et la vie de Racine*, and Doubrovsky, *Corneille et la dialectique du héros* (Paris: Gallimard, 1963), insist on the ambivalence of Néron's conflicted relation to his mother.

24. See M. Godelier and J. Hassoun, *Meurtre du père, sacrifice de la sexualité* (Strasbourg: Arcanes, 1996). These two terms that the anthropologist Godelier coins correspond, it seems to me, to the difference psychoanalysis draws between "biological sexuality" and "psycho-sexuality." "Sexuality-desire is the savage part of the human being, a permanent source of intentions and actions of each individual vis-à-vis others which must be domesticated" (32).

25. Ibid., 44.

26. Ibid., 46: "Through the reproduction of relations and kinship groups, other relations are at the same time reproduced: political, religious, economic, even esthetic."

27. Ibid., 47: "It is, by the way, because in all societies sexuality is used in the functioning of multiple realities, realities that have nothing to do directly with the sexes and with reproduction that not only does sexuality fantasize about society, but also society fantasizes about sexuality."

28. The warning given to Mlle de Chartres by her mother in *La Princesse de Clèves*.

29. See M. Delcourt, *Oedipe ou la légende du conquérant* (Paris: Droz, 1944). See also J. J. Goux, *Oedipe philosophe* (Paris: Aubier Montaigne, 1992), trans. C. Porter, *Oedipus, Philosopher* (Stanford, Calif.: Stanford University Press, 1993), and "Le mythe d'Oedipe comme initiation esquivée," in Godelier and Hassoun, *Meurtre du père*, 67–78.

30. Delcourt (*Oedipe ou la légende du conquérant*, 110) reminds us that the Sphinx and the Keres etc. were creatures of the "Night," and that they were avid for "sperm and blood." J. J. Goux, in *Oedipe philosophe*, and S. Heath, in "Difference" (*Screen*, November–December 1978) both discuss the importance

of Oedipus's "intellectual" defeat of the Sphinx for the history of Western philosophy. See chapter 4 of this volume.

31. Racine very clearly subscribes to this definition of "hero," which is given its clearest elaboration in Thésée (to which I will return in my discussion of *Phèdre*.) It is also interesting to note the difference between the Greek idea of a hero and Freud's. For Freud, as we know, a hero is the man who dares to confront and overthrow the gods (the father).

32. I am obviously playing a bit loose here, but not too loose. The expression, untranslatable to English, *nouer l'aiguilette*, which means "to render impotent," was an accusation often used against old women accused of witchcraft. It is connected to a whole series of fertility calamities for which they were held responsible, for example, crop failures, barren (nonreproductive) domestic animals, male impotence, etc.

33. G. Balandier, *Pouvoirs sur scène* (Paris: Balland, 1980), 19.

34. Foucault, in *Les mots et les choses* and *Histoire de la folie à l'age classique* (Paris: Gallimard, 1966).

35. F. Moretti, "A Huge Eclipse," *Genre* 15 (1982): 29. See also S. Mullaney, *The Place of the Stage: Play and Power in Renaissance England* (Chicago: University of Chicago Press, 1988), 130: "Hegemonic culture is . . . a historical dynamic, an ongoing, diachronic negotiation between the old and the new. The dominant culture in any given period cannot hope to include or even account for all human aspirations and energies; present culture is continually limited, challenged or modified by culture past and culture yet to come."

36. Barthes, *On Racine*, 13: "It is their situation in the relation of force that orchestrates some characters as virile and others as feminine without concern for their biological sex."

37. Doubrovsky, *Corneille*.

38. See J. Lacan, "La signification du phallus," in *Ecrits* (Paris: Seuil, 1966).

39. See J. Starobinski, *L'oeil vivant* (Paris: Gallimard, 1961), 73: "In Racine, behind what one sees, is what one barely perceives, and further still, something, the reality of which one feels, without seeing anything at all."

40. This analogy of Agrippine to the gorgon Medusa simply reinforces the association to the Sphinx, the underlying symbol of feminine monstrosity for Racine, the Spinx and the Gorgons being related creatures of the night in Greek mythology.

41. In her study *Sexuality in the Field of Vision*, Jacqueline Rose reminds us of the instability of any sexual identity, especially when the subject is overwhelmed by the visual: "Freud often relates the question of sexuality to visual representation . . . moments when perception founders . . . or in which the pleasure of looking tips over into the register of excess. . . . The sexuality lies less in the context of what is seen than in the subjectivity of the viewer (in the relationship between what is looked at and the developing sexual knowledge of the child). The relationship between viewer and scene is always one of fracture, partial identification, pleasure and distrust" (227).

42. Enriquez, *De la horde*, 191: "The prohibition aims at distancing and then definitively separating the sons from their mother. The son must struggle against the maternal fantasy of union: that the mother be devouring, possessive, castrating or simply loving, she, by her love, exerts violence on the child's body." Also his rather peremptory assertion: "The law of human life, the possibility of civilization is, 'do not return to the mother'" (193).

43. Barthes, *On Racine*, 34: "The Racinian world, as a matter of fact, has an effect of judgment: it observes the hero and ceaselessly threatens to censure, so that this hero lives in the panic of what will be said? *(qu'en dira-t-on).*"

44. Doubrovsky, *Corneille*, insists on the play of "imaginary" and "images" in the tragedy.

4. *Bérénice, Bajazet, Mithridate*

1. See J. J. Goux, *Oedipus, Philospher*, trans. C. Porter (Stanford, Calif.: Stanford University Press, 1993), 185–86.

2. S. Heath, "The Ethics of Sexual Difference," *Discourse* 17 (Spring–Summer 1990): 128.

3. D. Anzieu speaks about the similarities of the Oedipus and Theseus legends. See "Oedipe avant le complexe ou de l'interprétation psychanalytique des mythes," *Les Temps Modernes* 245 (October 1966): 675–715. See also Vernant and Vidal-Naquet, *Mythe et tragédie en Grèce antique*, 181: "Oedipus—is from now on *apolis*—he incarnates the figure of the exclude—at the same time that he is sullied he is sacred and saintly, *hieros et eusebes.*"

4. G. Deleuze and F. Guattari, in *L'anti-Oedipe* (Paris: Minuit, 1975), trans. R. Hurley, M. Seem, and H. Lane, *Anti-Oedipus* (New York: Viking Press, 1977), write of the colonizing potential of the Oedipal: "Oedipus is always colonization pursued by other means... where we Europeans are concerned it is our intimate colonial education" (170).

5. For a detailed study of the elaborations of the term "despotic" and the image of the despotic Oriental, see L. Valensi, *Venise et la sublime porte: La naissance du despote* (Paris: Hachette, 1987). I am indebted to Valensi for much of the information that makes up these paragraphs.

6. Valensi, *Venise et la sublime porte*, 99: "From 1634 onward the word [despotic] appears; as an adjective it will be regularly used and associated with 'government,' 'dominion,' and 'authority.'"

7. Ibid., 81 (quoting Bodin).

8. J. Chardin *Voyage en Perse* (Amsterdam, 1711), 235; quoted in Grosrichard, *Structure du Sérail* (Paris: Seuil, 1979): "Since they are raised in harems with women and eunuchs, Muslim sovereigns are so little able to rule that it is better for the general welfare of the people and for the safety of the state that a subaltern govern in their stead... and since these Oriental kings usually only think of satisfying their senses, it is all the more necessary that there be someone who thinks about the preservation and glory of the empire."

9. See R. E. Giesey, "Medieval Jurisprudence in Bodin's Concept of Sovereignty," in *Jean Bodin*, Verhandlungen der internationalen Bodin Tagun in München (Munich: Verlag C. H. Beck, 1973), 181.

10. Villars, *La critique de Bérénice* (quoted in Forestier, *Racine*, 516). Voltaire, preface to his *Oedipe*, 1730: "But *Bérénice* is blameworthy only because it is an elegy rather than a simple tragedy."

11. Racine, preface to *Bérénice*, in Forestier, *Racine*, 450.

12. Ibid., 451. This highly charged emotional affect seems to be the leitmotif of critics throughout the ages—Voltaire, Frederick of Prussia, Balzac, Claudel, among others.

13. Ibid. 450: "Truly, we have nothing more touching in all the Poets than the separation of Dido and Aeneas in Virgil."

14. Ibid.

15. This locus of the voice—this voice becomes one with the dead father—can be compared to that "atopical voice" that Derrida attributes to Socrates as the founding moment in the Western tradition of metaphysics of presence. In this way, Racine's gesture of inscribing Titus's image of himself—his masculine self-image—repeats the founding gesture that situates its origin (the origin of his "I") in the space of the dead (Oedipal) father. As N. Lukacher writes in *Primal Scenes: Literature, Philosophy, Psychoanalysis* (Ithaca, N.Y.: Cornell University Press, 1986), 46: "The voice of the Logos is the echo within the self of an earlier incarnation. Through the Logos, the origin of the self, the absolute earliest incarnation of the self, remains present to the self." This "incarnation" of Vespasian/father/emperor calls to Titus with a seduction more powerful than Bérénice's.

16. Freud, "A Neurosis of Demoniacal Possession in the Seventeenth Century," *Standard Edition*, vol. 19.

17. See the discussion of blood in Foucault, "Le dispositif de sexualité," *La volonté de savoir* (Paris: Gallimard, 1976), 99–175.

18. C. Mauron has, of course, offered the most detailed analysis this double valency of Racine's female characters.

19. Freud, *Standard Edition*, 11:70.

20. Enriquez, *De la horde*, 191. See also Mauron, *L'inconscient dans l'oeuvre et la vie de Racine*, 84: "The voluntary rupture of the hero, pushing away a possessive woman, or at least, thought to be so. Bérénice assumes the figure of a too tender mother who wants to keep her son, who is going into the world of men, with her."

21. The preceding discussion of *Bérénice* follows closely the extended analysis in "Racine's *Bérénice* and the Allegory of Absolutism," in M. Greenberg, *Canonical States, Canonical Stages: Oedipus, Othering, and Seventeenth-Century Drama* (Minneapolis: University of Minnesota Press, 1994).

22. G. Couton, in his edition *Corneille* (Paris: Gallimard, 1980), 1608, reminds us of the connections made by his contemporaries of Louis XIV and Titus: "His contemporaries saw in the image of Titus, Louis XIV as military conqueror... his contemporaries also saw in Titus Louis XIV as lover."

23. Louis XIV, *Mémoires*, ed. J. Longnon (Paris: Tallandier, 1978), 259.

24. For a more extended analysis of *Bérénice*, see Greenberg, *Canonical States, Canonical Stages*, chap. 5.

25. See Freud's "Medusa's Head, *Standard Edition*, vol. 19, and the classic if now much debated article by L. Mulvey, "Visual Pleasure and Narrative Cinema," in *Visual and Other Pleasures* (Bloomington: Indiana University Press, 1989).

26. J. Starobinski, *L'oeil vivant, essai* (Paris: Gallimard, 1961), 73.

27. For an extended analysis of the fantasmatic function of the seraglio in the Western imaginary, see Alain Grosrichard, *La Structure du sérial: La fiction du despotisme asiatique dans l'Occident classique* (Paris: Seuil, 1979). G. Forestier, in his commentary to the play, likewise notes "a culture whose mysteries evoked fantasies almost as much as Greek myths and the most dramatic episodes of Roman history" (*Racine*, 1491).

28. Forestier in his notes to *Bajazet* writes: "The seraglio was thought, historically... as the privileged space where love and power entered into conflict" (1504), and Barthes has also insisted on the "space" of the seraglio as the space of tragedy: "In *Bajazet*, the site is intentionally closed, as if the entire fable were merely the form of a space; the Seraglio" (*Racine*, 97).

29. *The Complete Plays of Jean Racine*, trans. Samuel Solomon (New York: Random House, 1967), 2:3: "It is an occurrence that took place in the seraglio not more than thirty years ago. The Comte de Cézy was then ambassador at Constantinople. He was apprised of all the details concerning the death of Bajazet; and there are numerous persons at Court who remember having heard him relate them when he had returned to France.... The Chevalier of Nantouillet is one of this number. And it is to him that I owe this story and even the project that I undertook of composing a tragedy out of it."

30. Racine, preface to *Bajazet*, in Forestier, *Racine*, 625.

31. Mauron, in fact, advises students of Racine to simply forget about the debate on the actual origins of the play and to concentrate on analyzing its own inner coherence: "The plot itself had no historical reality," he writes, and after mentioning Segrais and Heliodorus, he goes on to say, "In short, it is better to read the tragedy without concern for its sources." *L'inconscient dans l'oeuvre et la vie de Racine*, 94.

32. Once again we are reminded of Louis XIV's advice to the dauphin never to let women or the desire they inspire play any role in politics.

33. My (literal) translation.

34. See M. Greenberg, *Corneille, Classicism, and the Ruses of Symmetry* (Cambridge: Cambridge University Press, 1986). For a discussion of the sacrificial aspect of marriage, see Freud, "The Taboo of Virginity," *Standard Edition*, vol. 11.

35. Jacqueline Rose reminds us of what is at stake (psychically) in such an insistence on the clear division of the world into two well-defined, separate, sexes: "The lines of that division (i.e., sexual difference) are fragile in exact proportion to the rigid insistence with which our culture lays them down: they constantly converge and threaten to coalesce"(*Sexuality in the Field of Vision* [London: Verso, 1986], 226).

36. Barthes, *On Racine*, 13.

37. Ibid., 99–100: "Bajazet is a male confined in a female milieu where he is the only man. He is a drone who is fed and fattened by Roxanne for his genital power... Bajazet is imprisoned in the shadows, set apart, ripened for the pleasure of the Sultana."

38. See for this very "primitive" fantasy—where the two sexualized, destructive parental presences are interchangeable—S. Leclaire's essay *On tue un enfant* (Paris: Seuil, 1975), 18: "Slowly the 'archaic' logic of the unconscious is imposed: just as the mother, in a position of power, appears endowed with a penis, the father, in the position of protector can appear heavy with child."

39. In other words, as Marie Delcourt tells us, they represent two contrasting but complementary roles: "Sister of Ephialates, she is a destructive demon; sister of the Sirènes, she is a lost soul." *Oedipe ou la légende du conquérant* (Paris: Druz, 1944), 109.

40. It would be interesting to compare the fate of Bajazet, sequestered in the world of women so that he cannot be a threat to the power of his brother, to the rumors that circulated in the seventeenth century regarding Philippe d'Orléans, Louis XIV's younger brother. According to these rumors, related by the Abbé de Choisy in *Mémoires de l'abbé de Choisy habillé en femme*, ed. G. Mongrédien (Paris: Mercure de France, 1966), Philippe was purposely kept in the company of women: "All that was done on the orders of Cardinal Mazarin who wanted to effeminize him so that he would not cause the King any harm, as had Gaston caused to Louis XIII" (219). The fact that this theory has been debunked by all serious historians does not invalidate the way contemporaries fantasized the roles of masculinity and femininity in relation to the complex issues of royal devolution.

41. Barthes writes, "Acomat is not explicitly, in Racine, a eunuch (as he was in Segrais' tale), but he has the attribute of asexuality, old age, which he himself presents as a state of nonparticipation" (*On Racine*, 98).

42. Louis XIV, *Mémoires*, 260.

43. Enriquez, *De la horde*, 243: "If without the father there cannot be children (in the social sense of the term) without children, that is, individuals able to recognize the law of the father and to identify with the ideals of which this law is the vehicle, there cannot therefore be such a thing as a father."

44. It strikes me as odd that Forestier, in his notes to *Mithridate*, claims that "*Mithridate* is a roman tragedy" (1525), despite the fact that the play is situated in the Orient, all the characters are orientals, and the Romans exist only as a constant source of anxiety and threat. Rome may be the raison d'être of Mithridate's military/political life, but given the ideological thrust of the play, it exists as that which defeats the Orient, concluding, to my mind at least, Racine's series of political reflections on the East.

45. Mauron, *L'inconscient dans l'oeuvre et la vie de Racine*, 121: "The incest is barely disguised. Mithridate and Monime consider themselves morally married, even though the marriage has been put off because of the war. The sons believe themselves and are seen as incestuous although decency is maintained. As for

parricide, the second part of the Oedipus complex, Pharnace in bearing arms against his father is guilty of it. Xipharès, on the contrary, retreats in front of this extreme step."

46. As Rosolato succinctly puts it in "Du père," in *Essais sur le symbolique* (Paris: Gallimard, 1969), 59: "Killing the father becomes confused with the fantasy of destroying the Law."

47. Barthes, *On Racine*, 48: "All of Racine lies in that paradoxical moment when the child discovers that his father is wicked, yet wants to remain his child."

48. As Enriquez states in his psychosociological analysis of social formations, *De la horde*, 246: "The son is and always remains he who wishes the father's death in order to accede in turn to the role of subject and father.... The son (in so far bearer of a law) exists only through the father by this same father has his power snuffed out...The father is always he who forbids and an object of identification, the son always the creator and destroyer of his father."

49. What I am referring to here is the difference Rosolato establishes (following Lacan): "By calling him *Idealized Father* we are referring to this 'father' of prehistoric times, ferocious, jealous all powerful whose dominion over others and over his sons is limitless, protector in exchange for a total submission to him....For this father we apply but one principle, all or nothing, victory or defeat. This image is opposed to the...*Dead Father*, the symbolic foundation of the dissolution of the oedipal dynamic, of the instauration of patrilinearity." "Trois générations d'hommes dans le mythe religieux et la généalogie," in *Essais sur le symbolique*, 63.

50. See Enriquez, *De la horde*, 89: "Love is a bond, but a restrictive bond and it is the only tie that is truly restrictive."

51. See Rosolato, in particular "Du père" and "Trois générations d'hommes dans le mythe religieux et la généalogie" in *Essais sur le symbolique*, as well as his *Le sacrifice: Repères psychanalytiques*.

52. Rosolato, "Trois générations d'hommes dans le mythe religieux et la généalogie," in *Essais sur le symbolique*, 61: "But first we must establish what unites all sacrifice to the murder of the Father: sacrifice cannot be understood without its propitiatory effect; it always supposes that guilt is felt in respect to the divinity: and as Freud has strongly underlined it, this human guilt must be connected, without question to the relation to the Father, or more exactly as a consequence of the oedipal wishes for his death. But we must go even farther and consider that every sacrifice is first an execution (in mythic time) of and at the same time of the Father, through every victim."

53. Enriquez underlines the logical political aporia of the role of the father and thus the necessity of myth. Analyzing *Totem and Taboo*, he writes: "The father as such only exists once he is put to death actually or symbolically: the father only exists as a *mythic being*. When he is real and incarnate, if he provokes fear and anxiety he becomes the leader, the one who is greater than the others....But the father in his mythic function, inspires reverence, fear and love, all at once, the father smothers, castrates and is he who must be killed or

at least, gone beyond, he is also the bearer and guardian of prohibitions. Thus his murder is accompanied by guilt and veneration. There is no such thing as a 'real' father. The father is always a dead father, the dead father a mythic father" (*De la horde*, 44).

54. Forestier explains in great detail both why *Mithridate* is and is not the most Corneillean of Racine's tragedies. See his "Notice," in *Racine: Théâtre, poésie*, 1525–32.

55. The lines of Emilie: "Puisse le grand moteur des belles destinées, / Pour prolonger vos jours, retrancher nos années" (Let the driving force of great destinies, prolong your days by shortening ours).

56. "Should we be surprised that *Mithridate* . . . is considered in our time— with the exception of *Alexandre*—as the least Racinian of Racine's tragedies, and thus of his plays the one that is the least often performed?" writes Forestier in his "Notice," 1527.

57. Quoted in ibid., 1526.

58. Ibid., 1527: "On 5 November, 1684, we read, in effect in the *Journal* of Dangeau, that scrupulous chronicler of all the comings and goings of the king of France: This evening there was a 'French' play; the King came, and the play that was chosen was *Mithridate*, because it is this play that he likes the best."

59. Louis describes his role as father thus: "I thus appeared to all my subjects like a true father, head of his household who provides for all his family and shares equitably all his provisions with his children" (*Mémoires*, 111). He tells the dauphin that a king should be "the father to all, he must be careful to help them all, in whatever be their state, to achieve the perfection which is appropriate (to their station)" (221).

5. Iphigénie

1. Racine, preface to *Iphigénie*, in Forestier, *Racine*, 697.

2. Louis Racine, *Vie de Racine* (quoted in Forestier, *Racine*, 1561).

3. Forestier tells us that "*Iphigénie* was one of the century's greatest 'tear-inducing' plays" (*Racine*, 1574).

4. We might speculate, as Mauron has rather convincingly done, that the theme or even more specifically the image of Iphigenia's sacrifice had a particularly strong unconscious resonance in Racine. Mauron (*L'inconscient dans l'oeuvre et la vie de Racine*, 219) quotes this scene from Louis Racine's biography (*Vie de Racine*, 131): "This tender father attended the 'sacrifice' [equals her taking of the veil] of his daughter and would still cry when he wrote its details in a letter. . . . It is not surprising that a victim from his own flock should cost him so many tears since he never would attend such a ceremony without crying, even if the victim was indifferent to him." Mauron comments: "Here we see, at once, Racine living his tragic scenario and his childhood identification. He is both victim and officiating priest. Or rather, he is a spectator taking part in this double identification, and crying."

5. By which I mean a sacrifice as an organized religious/political ceremony complete with victim, sacrificing priest, and sacrificial altar, carried out according to a defined rite, in the presence of a community of witnesses/participants.

6. Racine, preface to *Iphigénie*, in Forestier, *Racine*, 698: "How could I possibly sully the stage with the horrible murder of a person as virtuous and lovable as Iphigenia had to be? And how, on the other hand, could I possibly end my tragedy with a *deus ex machine* and a metamorphosis which might have been believed to some extent at the time of Euripides, but which would be too absurd and too incredible to us?"

7. Green, *The Tragic Effect*, 37: "Simply that the ... l'Oedipodeia and the Oresteia constitute essential, fundamental models in which the problematic of all tragedy—and perhaps of all human endeavour—is situated."

8. Perhaps one of their main points of juncture is to be first found in the story of Pelops, father of Atreus and thus grandfather of Agamemnon and Menelaos. It was as a guest at his home that Oedipus's father Laius raped Pelops's son, Chrysipus, the crime that was at the "origin" of the gods' curse of his own family. See Green, "Thésée et Oedipe," 156: "Even if we take the myth of Oedipus as our reference point, no myth by itself can represent all the aspects of the Oedipus complex."

9. Barthes, *On Racine*, 114: "In no other play has Racine presented a family so solidly constituted, provided with a complete nucleus (father, mother, daughter) with collaterals ... and in imminent alliance."

10. Green, *The Tragic Effect*, 18.

11. Mauron, *L'inconscient dans l'oeuvre et la vie de Racine*, 29: "Racine is the painter of passions; but any strong passion becomes regressive and all regressions evoke oedipal or pre-oedipal situations."

12. Loraux, *Façons tragiques de tuer une femme*, trans. A. Forster, *Tragic Ways of Killing a Woman* (Cambridge, Mass.: Harvard University Press, 1991), 10: "Hanging was a woman's death. As practiced by women it could lead to endless variations, because women and young girls contrived to substitute for the customary rope those adornments with which they decked themselves and which were also the emblems of their sex. ... Veils, belts, headbands—all these instruments of seduction were death traps for those who wore them." Or again, 23: "It is by men that women meet their death, and it is for men, usually, that they kill themselves. ... So the death of women confirms or reestablishes their connection with marriage and maternity."

13. Ibid., 57: "There must have been an ambiguous thrill to the *katharsis* when, during a tragic performance, male citizens watched with emotion the suffering of these heroic women, represented on stage by other male citizens dressed in women's clothes." The composition of the audience in ancient Athens is a matter of some dispute. Loraux seems to imply (in agreement with many scholars) that the audience was exclusively male. Others contend that the audience was mixed, made up of Athenian (male) citizens, some women,

and "metics." Consider, for instance, this recent commentary: "Attendance at the theater was not only considered a right and privilege of Athenian citizenship... but the sources give ample evidence for the participation of all Athenian residents, whether metics or slaves, as well as large numbers of foreigners. From 1796 to the present day, several classical scholars have argued for the exclusion of women and children from the festival. In our opinion, the testimony of ancient authors shows clearly that women (and boys) were present in the audience." Eric Csapo and William J. Slater, *The Context of Ancient Drama* (Ann Arbor: University of Michigan Press, 1994), 286.

14. I am thinking of classical studies by Frazer and Robertson Smith that were important to Freud in his study of totemism, and more particularly of the contributions of the French sociologists, Durkheim, Mauss, and Hubert, for example, down to W. Burket's more recent *Homo Necans*. Here, too, the recent and voluminous work of R. Girard has been influential, particularly in literary studies.

15. Enriquez, *De la horde*, 63: "In order for guilt to appear, it is enough to *dream* of murder."

16. See, for instance, Freud's essay "The Dissolution of the Oedipus Complex," *Standard Edition*, vol. 19.

17. See Rosolato, *Le sacrifice repères psychanalytiques*, 36: "Finally, it is imaginary guilt which has the most nefarious effects because it can induce violence."

18. Ibid., 139: "By underlining the fantasies and the obsessional mechanism centered on the death of the father, Freud allows us to understand their social role, that is both the common consent and the social contract which are built on a guilt that is shared based on identical fantasies."

19. Both Rosolato and Enriquez insist on the absolute primacy of the leader as he who represents, by idealization, the enormous libidinal investment of his subjects, as well as these same subjects' potential for the violent overthrow of the same leader should he fail to realize their unconscious desires. See Enriquez, *De la horde*, especially chaps. 2 and 5, and Rosolato, *Le sacrifice repères psychanalytiques*, passim.

20. Rosolato, *Le sacrifice repères psychanalytiques*, 41: "To destroy together, to kill together, always remains on the horizon of man, often as an exalting aspiration."

21. As I earlier pointed out in my discussion of *Andromaque*, this other is a purely political invention: Trojans and Greeks are virtually identical in religion, customs, etc. It is, of course, the narcissism of small differences that turns brother into other.

22. As Enriquez puts it in *De la horde*, 50: "Civilization is born by and through repression. There can be no social body (of institutions, organization) *without the establishment of a system of collective repression*."

23. Rosolato, *Le sacrifice repères psychanalytiques*, 71: "This peace inside the community, established by a solidarity imposed by the sacrifice, redirects violence, not only from the inside, but also away from the leader, who, because of his privileged position, could be the object of envy and resentment."

24. Ibid., 180: "Sacrificial activity takes on an especially ample aspect during periods of crisis, when conflicts endanger the power of the leader." Loraux makes a similar point but underlining the "masculinist" ideology that sacrifice would uphold, in *Façons tragiques*, 64: "When the danger is most acute their blood flows in order that the community of *andres* live."

25. Rosolato, *Le sacrifice repères psychanalytiques*, 7: "Sacrifice is eminently interesting for the psychoanalyst because it established a bridge between individual psychology and social structures. . . . The sacrifice upholds sublimation, that is, the transposition of socialized libidinal satisfactions. It uses and controls guilt and in this way, it serves to maintain their subjective fixation, the doubling back on the self by renunciation where the instincts are channeled, by the limitation and the accepted abandonment of reason, by constructing of belief and by a voluntary and active adhesion to death. Besides this, sacrifice has an effect of therapeutic catharsis by exploiting morbid tendencies, mainly hysterical, obsessional and paranoid ones, for both the individual and the community."

26. Ibid., 75: "Let us think of the characteristics of the scapegoat: its innocence, its humanity, especially its weakness which are the negative of the Idealised Father, all powerful, brutal and hated by collective envy, guilty of all his arbitrary violence."

27. Loraux, *Façons tragiques*, 68: "When the victim is a virgin, the sacrifice is tragically ironic in that it resembles, all too closely, marriage"; and then again, 39, "Should we find meaning . . . that in a sacrifice a virgin loses her virginity." And finally, 40: "One comes to the strange conclusion that a sacrificed virgin loses her *partheneia* (virginity) without winning a spouse." Marcel Detienne makes the same claim: "Of course we have slaughtered virgins—but by a man's hand so that to lay one's hands on the (pure) throat of a virgin is, in fact, a deflowering of her." M. Detienne, review of Loraux's *Façons tragiques de tuer une femme*, *Archives des sciences sociales des religions* 68 (1989): 265.

28. Rosolato, "Trois générations d'homme," in *Essais sur le symbolique*, 67: "As for the ram, trapped in the tangles of reality, its horns in the bush, it is obviously a seminal beast. . . . Everything happens therefore as if the Eternal, silent during the operation, has come in the person of the Angle, through the consecration of the ram, to ensure a fecundating power."

29. Forestier, *Racine*, 1575: "But Agamemnon ceaselessly tries to avoid the divine order and therefore cannot be compared, even vaguely to Abraham."

30. I am here using the concept of doubling in a way that is congruent with but not identical to the use Mauron makes of the same term; cf. *L'inconscient dans l'oeuvre*, 109–20.

31. Ibid., 30: "*To resemble* will absolutely end up in a lethal confrontation, and *not to resemble* justifies a mortal combat against evil, objectified absolutely and crystallized. . . . The narcissist wants us to be like him but forbids it, he rejects, in order to show that there is no community possible, violence erupts in these reversals that form a vicious circle."

32. Rosolato, "Le narcissisme," 8: "Death is the ultimate reference point,

always present. Narcissus would be gazing at himself even in the waters of the Styx."

33. For an extended discussion of this phenomenon, see M. Greenberg, introduction to *Subjectivity and Subjugation in Seventeenth-Century Drama and Prose* (Cambridge: Cambridge University Press, 1994).

34. A. Green, *Narcissisme de vie, narcissisme de mort* (Paris: Minuit, 1983), 55.

35. Ibid., 51.

36. All the theorists of narcissism beginning with Freud have shown the dyadic coupling of narcissism and melancholia. In *Mourning and Melancholia* Freud writes: "The disposition to succumb to melancholia . . . lies in the narcissistic type of object choice" (*Standard Edition*, 14:250). See also J. Kristeva, *Soleil noir, dépression et mélancolie* (Paris: Gallimard, 1987); B. Grunberger, *Le narcissisme: Essais de psychanalyse* (Paris: Payot, 1975); and Green, *Narcissisme de vie*. Louis Marin, in *La parole mangée* (Paris: Klincksieck, 1986), 215, insists on the relation between narcissism, absolutism, and death: "And we should never lose sight of the fact that the desire of absolute power is one of the manifestations of the death drive."

37. M. Borch-Jacobsen, *Le sujet freudien* (Paris: Aubier Flammarion, 1982), 120.

38. An image perhaps only matched in its "Kreaturlichkeit" by the "récit de Théramène" in *Phèdre* with the description of Hippolyte's savaged body.

39. For Enriquez, following his analysis of Freud's social theories, this would be the definition of "women" in a male world. *De la horde*, 92: "Woman is therefore what questions man about his desire, recognizes him in his power, or obliges him to recognize his impotence and his limits, it is always Diotima who comes to the banquet to which she has not been invited in order to speak the truth about beings and things. Collective formations seek certainty and not truth. Woman, as an incarnation of the unknown, the untamed, represents the danger, the abyss where virile certainties can be shattered."

40. Ibid., 223: "Social functioning is a passional functioning (and not rational) where phenomena of belief and mechanisms of illusion are at work and that no one, for however intelligent in his individual life can escape. . . . Societies are, by nature, refractory to any effort to establish the truth. Societies are founded on a desperate effort of all their members to elude each other, because they can only exist by believing that they are in the possession of certainties, by situating themselves in the site of truth."

41. *Standard Edition*, 18:80.

42. Once again, Rosolato gives us a clinical frame for understanding how melancholia can lead to self-destruction: "We should remark that all depressions have a narcissistic axis and a *suicidal raptus* we would think has no antecedent that would allow us to predict it, reveals its *melancholic center*, whose elements are composed, as we know, of narcissistic identification, fantasmatic oral incorporation, ambivalence in regards to the object and the prevalence of a liberated death drive" (*Le sacrifice*, 46).

43. I am referring, of course, to the categories Mauron sets up in *L'inconscient dans l'oeuvre et la vie de Racine*.

44. It is interesting to recall, of course, that Nike and the Furies were closely related in Greek mythology. Nike was the guarantor of a just victory, just as the Furies were the guarantors of just punishment.

45. The rivalry between Agamemnon and Achille that Racine introduces into this play is, of course, a reflection of a similar conflict (over Briseis) that causes so much damage to the Greek cause at the beginning of the *Iliad*.

46. See J. M. Apostolidès' reading of the "cosmic orgasmic" response to Eriphile's suicide, in *Le prince sacrifié*.

6. Phèdre (et Hippolyte)

1. G. Forestier, *Racine*, 1615: "With *Phèdre* French tragedy seems to have finished in a brilliant way its slow mutation from a tragedy of plot to a tragedy of character"; Barthes, *On Racine*, 116: "The profoundest of Racine's tragedies"; Mauron, *L'inconscient dans l'oeuvre et la vie de Racine*, 145: "*Phèdre* sums up Racine's theater." And again, Mauron, in *Phèdre* (Paris: Corti, 1988, 39): "The very structure of *Phèdre* reproduces Racine's entire oeuvre."

2. L. Racine, *Vie de Racine* (Paris: Les Belles Lettres, 1999), 137.

3. I am translating *caractère* as "character" following the definition given of it in the 1694 edition (the first) of the *Dictionnaire de l'Académie française*: "It is also taken in the sense of that which distinguishes one person from others in respect to their ways of being or their intelligence." I would think what L. Racine is expressing here is the idea that rather than being creations of an individual author, he thinks of Phèdre and Oedipus as being archetypical figures whose particular characteristics (legends, myths, historical accomplishments) lend themselves to reinvention by succeeding generations of artists.

4. Freud, *The Interpretation of Dreams, Standard Edition*, 4:262.

5. Need I remind us that Euripides' play, on which Racine bases his own version, bears the title *Hippolytus* and that there is, therefore, a strange slippage from the original Greek version to *Phèdre et Hippolyte* and then further to just *Phèdre*?

6. Barthes, *On Racine*, 115.

7. *Phèdre*, 14.

8. Barthes, *On Racine*, 122: "At first, the monstrous threatens all the characters; they are all monsters to each other, and all monster-seekers as well."

9. Bersani, *A Future for Asytanax* (Boston: Little Brown, 1976), 42. I should recall, at this point, the work of F. Orlando, in particular *Lettura freudiana della Phèdre* (*Toward a Freudian Theory of Literature: With an Analysis of Racine's "Phèdre*," trans. Charmaine Lee [Baltimore: Johns Hopkins University Press, 1978]), who along with Mauron was one of the first scholars to offer a psychoanalytically informed reading of *Phèdre*.

10. Mauron, *L'inconscient dans l'oeuvre*, 146: "For the theme of *Phèdre* is a

reversed oedipus where the son will be declared completely innocent, the mother incestuous despite herself, and the father murderous by mistake."

11. See J. J. Goux, *Oedipus, Philosopher*, trans. Catherine Porter (Stanford, Calif.: Stanford University Press, 1993), 186: "The most rejected, the most excluded of men—this age and polluted body of a criminal—becomes the miraculous source of blessings for Athens. Oedipus is transformed from an untouchable human wreck into a perpetual and inexhaustible treasure."

12. D. Anzieu, "Oedipe avant le complexe," in *Les temps modernes*, 686.

13. See A. Green's discussion of the overlap of the two legends, "Thésée et Oedipe: Une interprétation psychanalytique de la Théséide," in *Psychoanalyse et culture grecque* (Paris: Les Belles Lettres, 1980), 109–58.

14. Enriquez, *De la horde*, 224: "The social bond only exists in the splendor of the day, the passions only awake at night when reason totters and culture is undone."

15. J. DeJean sees these lines as Racine's rewriting of Sappho's famous description of "love at first sight" (in the poem that begins "To me he seems like a God…") in her *Fictions of Sappho* (Chicago: University of Chicago Press, 1989).

16. Forestier underlines, in his notes to *Phèdre*, that Racine is in clear opposition to his seventeenth-century predecessors and stresses the incestuous nature of Phèdre's desire for Hippolyte (*Racine*, 1614): "Racine was careful not to follow his seventeenth-century French precursors who had softened the givens of the story of *Phèdre et Hippolyte* by presenting the heroine not as the wife but as the fiancée of Thésée—thus depriving the subject of one of its essential dimensions, the double temptation of adultery and incest."

17. Enriquez, *De la horde*, 214, and "*L'ordre des sexes*," 279–317.

18. The structural, rhetorical, and transgressive doubling of Phèdre/Hippolyte has been commented on by almost all recent critics of the play, Mauron, Barthes, Forestier, Goldmann, etc.

19. J. P. Valabrega, *Phantasme, mythe, corps et sens* (Paris: Payot, 1980), 115: "Myth precisely constitues the being subject."

20. Enriquez, *De la horde*, 66: "Individual psychology is also and simultaneously a social psychology," and 19: "Every symptom is the indelible mark of the social itself."

21. For an extended discussion of the imbrication of absolutism and patriarchal monarchy, see M. Greenberg, *Subjectivity and Subjugation in Seventeenth-Century Drama and Prose: The Family Romance of French Classicism* (Cambridge: Cambridge University Press, 1994).

22. The fantasy of the archaic or phallic mother, a concept Melanie Klein and her followers borrowed from Freud, can be defined, for our purposes, as "the image of the archaic mother is one of an omnipotent mother, having the right of life and death and not allowing the child to detach from her body to lead an independent life. This mother is represented, at worst, as devouring, enveloping the other, and at best, as an intruder… in all cases as simultaneously a persecutor and symbol of lost paradise" (Enriquez, *De la horde*, 282).

This would seem to be a reasonably accurate description of the maternal role Oenone plays for Phèdre. The fantasy of the archaic mother often has her endowed with a penis. This very archaic fantasy is allied to the equally archaic image of the primal father, often pictured pregnant. Both images reveal the unconscious indistinction, in fantasy, of a unisexed and terrifying parent.

23. See Mauron, *L'inconscient dans l'oeuvre*, 132 and 169. For other, more sociological or literary-historical attempts to situate the tragedies of Racine within the cultural and religious context of the seventeenth century, see P. Bénichou, *Morales du grand siècle*; L. Goldmann, *Le dieu caché*; J. Orcibal, *La genèse d'Esther et d'Athalie* (Paris: Vrin, 1950); R. Picard, *La carrière de Jean Racine* (Paris: Gallimard, 1956); and E. Zimmerman, *La liberté et le destin dans le théâtre de Jean Racine* (Saratoga: Anma Libri, 1982).

24. As Mauron has pointed out in his reading of Racine, in the tragedies leading up to *Mithridate* the political crisis is precipitated because the place of the father is vacant, creating turmoil in the universe of the drama. From *Mithridate* on, the father returns, only to find his place usurped or in danger of being usurped (*L'inconscient dans l'oeuvre*, 26–31).

25. Forestier has underlined the interrelation of politics and love in *Phèdre* in the following way (*Racine*, 1633): "And it is because of the dynastic problem that the supposed death of Theseus creates that Hippolyte must meet with Aricie and Phèdre must see Hippolyte: the confrontation of three political legitimacies in two encounters both of which rapidly degenerate into declarations of love."

26. For the "crisis of the seventeenth century," see G. Parker, *Europe in Crisis, 1598–1648* (Ithaca, N.Y.: Cornell University Press, 1979); T. Rabb, *The Struggle for Stability in Early Modern Europe* (Oxford: Oxford University Press, 1975); and R. Mandrou, *Sorciers et magistrats en France au XVII* (Paris: Seuil, 1980).

27. Quoted in G. Parker and L. Smith, introduction to *The General Crisis of the Seventeenth Century* (London: Routledge and Kegan Paul, 1978), 3.

28. Louis XIV, *Mémoires*, 33 (my translation).

29. Enriquez, *De la horde*, 101.

30. See Enriquez, who, elaborating on Freud (particularly on Freud's discussion of the role of the primal father in *Totem and Taboo*), writes: "Freud does not deny that individuals can live alongside each other, he simply believes that they cannot exist as a group, as a 'people' without reference to a 'unique' [subject]; the 'people' is thus formed by individuals who are joined together by libidinal force, and this libido cannot traverse the social sphere unless it emanates from an individual who can conjure it up, or, like the father of the primal horde, reject it" (*De la horde*, 144).

31. See. E. Hobsbawm, "The Crisis of the Seventeenth Century," in *Crisis in Europe, 1560–1660*, ed. T. Aston, 12: "Only in one respect did the seventeenth century as a whole overcome rather than experience difficulties.... Most of Europe found an efficient and stable form of government in absolutism on the French model."

32. See, for example, R. Williams, *The Country and the City* (New York:

Oxford University Press, 1973), and *Problems in Materialism and Culture: Selected Essays* (London: NLB, 1980).

33. R. Mousnier, *Les XVI et XVII siècles* (Paris: PUF, 1953), 249.

34. Keohane, *Philosophy and the State in France* (Princeton, N.J.: Princeton University Press, 1980), 17.

35. G. Rosolato, *Le sacrifice*, 180.

36. Enriquez, *De la horde*, 196–197, and again, 319: "The relations 'father-son' are marked by *ambivalence* and at times by *savagery*."

37. Goldmann, *Le dieu cache*, 47.

38. Mauron, *L'inconscient dans l'oeuvre*, 258: "Since Alexandre, since Titus, we know with what delectation Racine had not stopped wanting to identify himself to the king. This assimilation, for quite a while, was equated by him as a symbol of salvation. Any participation in royal majesty inebriated him." For other, more recent accounts of Racine's relation to the monarchy, see A. Viala, *Racine: La stratégie du caméléon* (Paris: Seghers, 1990), and G. Forestier, *Jean Racine* (Paris: Gallimard, 2006).

39. Enriquez, *De la horde*, 319: "If without a father there can be no children (in the sociological meaning of the word), without children, that is individuals able to recognize the law of the father and identify with the ideals for which it is a vehicle, there can be no father either."

40. The fate of Phèdre's children seems of little interest to the participants in this drama. Are they still alive? The reference to Medea is ominous.

41. Racine, preface to *Phèdre*, in Forestier, *Racine*, 818.

42. Plutarch, *Life of Theseus*, 53: "He gathered together all the inhabitants of Attica into one town, and made them one people of one city, whereas before they lived dispersed, and were not easy to assemble upon any affair for the common interest. Nay, differences and even wars often occurred between them, which he by his persuasions appeased, going from township to township, and from tribe to tribe. And those of a more private and mean condition readily embracing such good advice, to those of greater power he promised a commonwealth without monarchy, a democracy, or people's government, in which he should only be continued as their commander in war and the protector of their laws, all things else being equally distributed among them; and by this means brought a part of them over to his proposal. The rest, fearing his power, which was already grown very formidable, and knowing his courage and resolution, chose rather to be persuaded than forced into a compliance. He then dissolved all the distinct statehouses, council halls, and magistracies, and built one common state-house and council hall on the site of the present upper town, and gave the name of Athens to the whole state, ordaining a common feast and sacrifice, which he called Panathenaea, or the sacrifice of all the united Athenians. He instituted also another sacrifice called Metoecia, or Feast of Migration, which is yet celebrated on the sixteenth day of Hecatombaeon. Then, as he had promised, he laid down his regal power and proceeded to order a commonwealth."

7. Esther, Athalie

1. This seems to be the opinion of A. Viala. See his *Racine: La stratégie du caméléon*.

2. Racine, preface to *Esther*, in Forestier, *Racine*, 945.

3. Ibid., 946.

4. "Dance" is one of the possible interpretations of the biblical passage. Others include "display her beauty," i.e., show herself naked, or "dance naked" before the assembled guests. See *The Oxford Bible Commentary*, ed. John Barton and John Muddiman (New York: Oxford University Press, 2001), 326–27. For an approach to Jewish femininity in Racine, see S. Maslan, "La fémininité juive et le problème de la représentation dramatique" *Papers on Seventeenth-Century French Literature Biblio* 17 (1999): 305–13.

5. See Greenberg, *Baroque Bodies: Psychoanalysis and the Culture of French Absolutism* (Ithaca, N.Y.: Cornell University Press, 2001), esp. 262–67.

6. Mauron (*L'inconscient dans l'oeuvre et la vie de Racine*, 289) does remind us that in the Bible there is a reference to the supposed attempted "rape" of Esther by Aman, underlying the sexually predatory nature of the minister and his attack on the "Father's wife."

7. Forestier, "Notice," 1675: There are a "number of readers who, although admiring the poetry of the work, but deploring what they see in it of blandness and compunction regret that in *Esther* Racine is not Racine. . . . Racine is as much Racine in *Esther* as he was in *Phèdre*."

8. For an interesting dual reading of both biblical tragedies, see F. Jaouën, "Esther/Athalie: Histoire sacrée, histoire exemplaire," *Seventeenth-Century French Studies* 21 (1999): 123–31

9. Bersani, *A Future for Astyanax*, 50.

10. One of the few articles to concentrate on the presence of the child on the seventeenth- (and eighteenth-)century French stage is D. F. Connon, "The Child on the Tragic Stage in Seventeenth- and Eighteenth-Century France: Racine, La Motte, Saurin, *Romance Studies* 27 (Spring 1996): 15–29.

11. Racine, preface to *Athalie*, in Forestier, *Racine*, 1010.

12. In the above paragraphs I am reprising an argument I have made in greater detail in *Subjectivity and Subjugation in Seventeenth-Century Drama and Prose*, esp. chap. 6, "Racine's Children."

13. See S. Guénoun, "*Athalie*, un point entre littérature et psychanalyse," *Cahiers du Dix-septieme: An Interdisciplinary Journal* 1, no. 1 (Spring 1987): 179–93, for a more Lacanian reading of the play.

14. For another reading of Athalie's dream, see F. Dumoura, "Le Songe d'Athalie ou le retour du même," *Information Littéraire* 55, no. 4 (October–December 2003): 18–25.

15. See S. Leclaire, *On tue un enfant* (Paris: Seuil, 1975), 18: "Slowly, the archaic logic of the unconscious is imposed: so that in the same way that the mother in a position of power appears endowed with a penis, the father in a position of protection appears heavy with child."

16. Barthes, *On Racine*, 54.

17. For another reading of the father in *Athalie*, see H. Stone, "The Seduction of the Father in *Phèdre* and *Athalie*," in *Actes de Baton Rouge: Papers on French Seventeenth-Century Literature*, ed. Selma A. Zebouni (Paris, 1986), 153–64.

18. H. McDermott, "Matricide and Filicide in Racine's *Athalie*," *Symposium: A Quarterly Journal in Modern Literatures* 38, no. 1 (Spring 1984): 56–69, talks, in another register, of the importance of the ambivalence of the killing of the mother and/or the child in *Athalie*.

19. Mauron, *L'inconscient dans l'oeuvre et la vie de Racine*, 285. A. Viala, in his *Racine, ou la politique du caméléon* (Paris: Seghers, 1990) also insists on Racine's fascination with making his way at court.

20. Peter Stallybrass and Allon White, *The Politics and Poetics of Transgression* (Ithaca, N.Y.: Cornell University Press, 1984), 105.

21. Freud, *Civilization and Its Discontents, Standard Edition*, 21:145: "The fateful question for the human species seems to me to be whether and to what extent their cultural development will succeed in mastering the disturbance of their communal life by the human instinct of aggression and self destruction. . . . And now it is to be expected that the other of the two 'Heavenly Powers' eternal Eros, will make an effort to assert himself in the struggle with his equally immortal adversary. But who can foresee with what success and with what result?"

Index

Mitchell Greenberg is Goldwin Smith Professor of Romance Studies at Cornell University. His books include *Canonical States, Canonical Stages: Oedipus, Othering, and Seventeenth-Century Drama* (Minnesota, 1994) and *Baroque Bodies: Psychoanalysis and the Culture of French Absolutism.*